Benjamin Elijah Mays,
Schoolmaster of the Movement

RANDAL MAURICE JELKS

Benjamin Elijah Mays,
Schoolmaster of the Movement
A Biography

The University of North Carolina Press Chapel Hill

Set in Minion Pro by codeMantra

The paper in this book meets the guidelines for permanence and
durability of the Committee on Production Guidelines for Book
Longevity of the Council on Library Resources.

The University of North Carolina Press has been a member
of the Green Press Initiative since 2003.

Library of Congress Cataloging-in-Publication Data
Jelks, Randal Maurice, 1956–
Benjamin Elijah Mays, schoolmaster of the movement :
a biography /
Randal Maurice Jelks.
p. cm.
Includes bibliographical references and index.
ISBN 978-0-8078-3536-4 (cloth : alk. paper)
ISBN 978-1-4696-1391-8 (pbk.: alk. paper)
1. Mays, Benjamin E. (Benjamin Elijah), 1894–1984. 2. Morehouse
College (Atlanta, Ga.)—Presidents—Biography. 3. African American
educators—Biography. 4. African Americans—Civil rights. I. Title.
LC2851.M72J45 2012
378.0092—dc23
[B]
2011045258

cloth 16 15 14 13 12   5 4 3 2 1
paper 17 16 15 14 13   5 4 3 2 1
THIS BOOK WAS DIGITALLY PRINTED.

For Mari Beth Johnson-Jelks,
whose love, sacrifice, generosity, and friendship
have been ours to share
for more than three decades

Contents

Illustrations

Acknowledgments

In the fall of 1994 this book began as a paper I presented at the centennial celebration of Benjamin Elijah Mays at Bates College in Lewiston, Maine. That paper, thanks to Dr. Lawrence Carter, dean of the Martin Luther King, Jr., International Chapel at Morehouse College, was subsequently presented at Morehouse and then published in his edited volume titled *Walking Integrity: Benjamin Elijah Mays, Mentor to Generations*. At that time, I did not know that it would take me nearly seventeen years to complete this book. In the meantime, I published *African Americans in the Furniture City: The Struggle for Civil Rights Grand Rapids*. A part of my research for that book led me to explore the neo-abolitionist community of Grand Rapids, Michigan, after the Civil War, which brought my attention to Reverend Samuel Graves, who in 1885, after leaving the pastorate of a highly esteemed congregation, the Fountain Street Baptist Church in Grand Rapids, became the second president of Atlanta Baptist Seminary for Men (today Morehouse College). As a result of Graves's ties and leadership, Morehouse received financial support from Baptist churches in Grand Rapids. Under his leadership (1885–90), the college settled in its present location, a Civil War battle site on the west side of Atlanta. In 1889, out of respect for Graves's work in resettling the college and seeing to its smooth operation, Graves Hall, the oldest building on Morehouse's campus, was dedicated. From there, the work of teaching young black men has continued for one hundred and forty-four years. No one could have predicted that a book on Grand Rapids, Michigan, would be linked to an intellectual biography of Benjamin Elijah Mays, Morehouse's sixth and perhaps most illustrious president, but the stars aligned and my research connected me to Mays with the help of so many along the way.

This book would not have come into being without collaboration from archivists, deans, colleagues, editors, friends, family, institutes, librarians, and students. My work would not have been possible without the wise counsel and generosity of Dr. Orville Vernon Burton of Clemson University (formerly of the University of Illinois). It was providential meeting this great soul and scholar from Ninety-Six, South Carolina, near the hamlet of Epworth, where Mays was born. Vernon has been a mentor, a friend, and guide throughout the development of this project. He shared with me his research on Mays and

South Carolina that he had filed away after writing the introduction to the reissue of Mays's autobiography *Born to Rebel*. Burton and his wife, Georgia Ann, opened their home to me both in Illinois and in South Carolina on numerous occasions. Dr. Darlene Clark Hine of Northwestern University, my graduate school mentor and friend, also deserves special recognition. I cannot thank her enough for the letters of support and her generosity toward me. I hope in some small measure this book is a return on her investment. Dr. Dennis Dickerson of Vanderbilt University, whose scholarship and friendship aided and abetted me in both of my book projects, has offered constant support as friend, mentor, and thorough critic. I could not have written this or my first book without his aid and generosity.

The manuscript was vetted by a host of scholarly friends whose criticism made this a better a book: the anonymous readers for UNC Press; Wallace Best, Princeton University; Jane Dailey, University of Chicago; Allison Dorsey, Swarthmore College; my lifelong friend Walter Fluker, Boston University; Glenda Gilmore, Yale University; Maryemma Graham, University of Kansas; Willie J. Jennings, Duke University Divinity School; Ralph Luker, historian, blogger, and independent scholar; Barbara Savage, University of Pennsylvania; Beth Barton Schweiger, University of Arkansas; and R. Drew Smith, Morehouse College.

Other scholars freely shared their research with me: Yolanda Smith of Yale Divinity School, Winston Grady-Willis, formerly of Syracuse University and now at Skidmore College, and Bobby Donaldson of the University of South Carolina.

My former employer, Calvin College, from the first day I stepped on its campus in 1992 supported this book. I am grateful for the totality of the college's support: the Alumni Board, the history department, the dean of Scholarship and Research, the provost's office, the office of development, and the Calvin Library and Information Technology staffs.

I have also benefited from the largesse of a Louisville Institute summer stipend that allowed me time off to travel to Washington, D.C.; New Haven, Connecticut; Madison, New Jersey; Terrytown, New York; and Atlanta, Georgia, to research this book during the summer of 2001. This book also benefited from the scholarly community of the National Endowment for the Humanities Summer Seminar 2006 held at Harvard's W. E. B. DuBois Institute for African and African American Research, led by Patricia Sullivan and Waldo Martin. My colleagues in this group thoroughly enhanced my understanding of the wider implication of the civil rights movement from a global perspective. This book was magisterially enhanced during a wonderful year of scholarly engagement and dialogue during the academic year 2006–2007 at the National Humanities Center (NHC), in Research Triangle Park, North Carolina, where I was a Rockefeller Foundation Fellow. My gratitude goes out to the entire NHC staff, who supported me and my fellow scholars. Also during my year as a NHC fellow, my life was enlivened by the graciousness of the Jennings household—Willie, Joanne, Njeri, and Safiya. Church, Sunday dinners, and jazz concerts were a delight. I am grateful as well to my dear friend Dr. Rhonda Jones, a fine scholar and an outstanding public historian who teaches at North Carolina Central University's history department, who introduced me to the scholarly and cultural amenities of Durham and Chapel Hill. Tuesday evenings over drinks in repartee with Rhonda, Bayo Holsey of Duke University, and other friends in Durham made me a more civilized human being.

Additionally, I must acknowledge my present scholarly home, the University of Kansas. I am forever grateful to KU for inviting me to be the Langston Hughes Visiting Professor of American Studies in the spring of 2007 and then persuading me to hang around. My KU colleagues who have heard about or discussed this project with me in some form or fashion have been most encouraging. They include Shawn Alexander, Tony Bolden, Derrick Darby, Deborah Dandridge, Dennis Domer, Jacob Dorman, Tanya Golash-Boza, William J. Harris, Tanya Hart, Nicole Persley Hodges, David Katzman, Cheryl Lester, John Edgar Tidewell, Sherrie Tucker, Bill Tuttle, and Peter Ukpokodu. I would also like to acknowledge the support staff at KU who have assisted me. Kay Isbell, Terri Rockhold, and Lisa Brown patiently aided me as I took the first steps in making this book a reality. Rock-chalk-Jayhawks!

I would be remiss as a teacher if I did not acknowledge my undergraduate and graduate students both at Calvin College and the University of Kansas. Their critical reflections, questions, and extreme competence have made me a better scholar. Special thanks go to my former undergraduate student assistants, including Raquel Gonzalez, Ashley Hutchison, Junior (Kingsley) Kanu, Marla Love, Thea Van Halsema, Christina Lux, Kyliah Clark Villa, Anna Canino Vasquez, and David Porter. I would also like to thank Dr. Elizabeth Hoffman Ransford, who as a Ph.D. student at Loyola University in Chicago did research for me at the Chicago Historical Society, and Hugh Murphy, my KU student assistant when I served as the Langston Hughes Visiting Professor of American Studies. Hugh did yeoman's work reading Mays's voluminous columns in the *Pittsburgh Courier* and the *Chicago Defender* and discussing them with me weekly.

I am tremendously grateful to the staff at the Howard University Moorland-Spingarn Research Center, especially Ms. Jo Ellen El Bashir. The Moorland-Spingarn staff's professionalism and warmth was comforting during my long days and years of research. I also want to acknowledge Karen Jefferson, archivist at the Clark Atlanta University Woodruff Library. Karen has assisted me with this project since I first began my research back in 1991. Additionally, I want to acknowledge Dr. Walter Fluker, who, as the head of the Howard Thurman Papers Project at Morehouse College, was an invaluable resource for this book. Thanks also go to Herman "Skip" Mason, archivist of Morehouse College, for his assistance with photographs. I am also deeply appreciative of the helpful staffs at the Edmund Muskie Archives at Bates College; the Clark Atlanta University Archives; the Columbia University Oral History Collection; the Drew University Archives, Madison, New Jersey; the Library of Congress, the Newberry Library, Chicago; the University of Chicago Regenstein Special Collections; the Yale University Divinity School Archives; the Rockefeller Foundation Archives; and the Virginia Union Archive, Richmond.

Editors are invaluable, and I am indebted to them. Sarah Van Timmermen, one of my former undergraduate students at Calvin College who has become a skilled copy editor, patiently read and reread many versions of this manuscript carefully, querying me and forcing me to be more stylistically consistent and less verbose. This book would not have been possible without David Perry, senior editor at the University of North Carolina Press. David challenged me to be thorough and to write this biography in an engaging and highly readable way. I am grateful to him for advancing me a contract and sticking with me when I felt exhausted by the book.

My only heartache in publishing this book has been the loss of a dear friend, the late Reverend Doctor Kwame Bediako of the Akrofi-Christaller Institute of Theology, Mission and Culture in Akropong, Ghana. It pains me that he did not see this book come to fruition in his earthly lifetime. We discussed my work and my thoughts on American Protestantism and the experiences of African Americans countless times in Ghana and in the United States. Though saddened, I sense that he, now a Christian ancestor, is delighted to know the book's time has come.

I could not have written this book without the support of my brothers outside the academy: Fred Davie, H. William Dungey, David Hatch, Frank Howell Jr., Robert Johnson, Keith Myles, and Tyrone Perry Sr. They have kept me sane and helped me keep my work in perspective.

I am also indebted to my extended family for their support. When my own mother departed this earth, my mother-in-law, Jeanne Johnson, stepped in. She traveled as far as Ghana to listen to me lecture about this project at the Institute for African Studies at the University of Ghana, Legon, West Africa. Thanks to my brother Kevin Jelks for daily conversations with me about life, love, sports, and politics. Kevin asked questions about my research and provided careful directions to various archives in New York City and New Jersey and drove me to New Haven. My sister Frances Jelks Brown, who over the course of my researching and writing this book had three sons, and my sister Jacqueline Camara, who shares our aunt's looks, provided bright smiles, warmth, laughs, and some good rum. Last, but not least, I want to thank my father, Osibee Julian Jelks, and my stepmother, Ann Jelks, for their prayers and encouragement.

Thanks especially to my immediate family—my wife, Mari Beth Johnson-Jelks, for her constant love, and my three children, Johannah, Jonathan, and Joshua, who are what Bennie Mays dreamed of for African American children.

Finally, I want to thank Bennie Mays himself for his rich legacy. Back in 1994, at Bates, I received one of the Mayses' Morehouse Centennial posters, which I had framed and hung in my office. Every time I looked at that poster, Mays appeared to stare back at me with the same relentless determination that he demanded of students at Howard University and Morehouse College. While writing this book, I reminded myself daily of one his oft-repeated sayings: "Not failure, but low aim is a sin." I can only hope that he would have been proud of this book.

Benjamin Elijah Mays,
Schoolmaster of the Movement

Martin Luther King Jr.'s funeral at Morehouse College, April 9, 1968. © Flip Schulke.

I Have Been a Baptist All My Life

On April 9, 1968, Benjamin Elijah Mays had the burdensome honor of delivering a eulogy for Martin Luther King Jr. on the campus of Morehouse College. *Time* magazine photographer Flip Schulke captured the somber moment: the retired college president faced a crowd that stretched as far as the eye could see. They were looking to Mays for words of comfort and inspiration as they tried to comprehend the civil rights leader's assassination and to summon the courage to continue the struggle. Of all that Mays accomplished in his life, he would be remembered primarily as King's mentor.[1] Yet Mays had a long career as a distinguished educator, liberal theologian, and unwavering advocate of civil and human rights. Through most of his life, he had worked in the South, led black institutions, and advocated a commitment to social justice among American Protestants. Mays stood out among the black leaders who sustained the struggle against segregation for decades before African Americans' drive for full citizenship burst into the national spotlight. His teachings and example inspired generations of African American students and clergy to develop their intellectual talents and calibrate their ethical compass in order to challenge injustice.

Looking at Schulke's photograph more than forty years later, we realize that Mays was eulogizing not only his spiritual son but also the civil rights mass protest that had emerged in the South during the postwar years and sparked a massive political rebellion on city streets across the nation. Mays's own life took him from the nadir of Jim Crow in the Deep South, to the long march of civil rights agitation and education, to the culmination of the Black Freedom struggle in the late 1960s. Long before King began his ministry in Montgomery, Mays had advocated that black churches become centers of civil rights activism, and he was delighted when they nurtured a democratic movement that brought down the walls of racial segregation in the United States. He had seen his dreams fulfilled by King's rise to national prominence from the ranks of Morehouse graduates and black Protestant clergy. The irony of that funerary occasion was not lost on him: Jim Crow had finally been vanquished, but King, along with many other leaders and activists, had been struck down. Mays stood not in triumph but in grief before a crowd as large as the one present in the last days of the 1965 march from Selma to the state capitol of Alabama. Soon a new generation of elected politicians and civic activists would take responsibility for the issues of citizenship, economic justice, and peace that remained unresolved. On that day, though, Mays was the man of the hour, drawing on his hard-won wisdom, long-term perspective, and unshaken faith in order to explain what King's life meant to the nation and the world, then and in the future. His funeral oration emphasized the theological foundations and ethical dimensions of this democratic movement for social change.

Mays's long career serves as a window on African American life in the first three-quarters of the twentieth century. Born in 1894 in rural Epworth, South Carolina, to parents who were ex-slaves and who toiled as sharecroppers and tenant farmers, he experienced firsthand the degradation and terror of the Jim Crow South. He grew up in the Afro-Baptist tradition that had melded the Atlantic world's revivalist movement with the folk theology and spiritual practices of African-inspired slave religion. For Mays, this form of Christianity emphasized the "otherworldly" dimension of faith. Its teachings were highly moralistic, and clergy with little formal education led it. Mays saw the Afro-Baptist faith tradition as a survival mechanism that enabled blacks to endure social evils rather than as a way to change them. In his young adulthood, Mays recognized that southern racism itself was rooted in biblical literalism and Christian fundamentalism. He believed that both white and black religious ignorance contributed to the maintenance of the antidemocratic spirit that underpinned social injustice.

Having grown up in this milieu, Mays felt both a calling to the ministry and a passion for higher education. His determined quest led him through networks of white and black Baptist institutions from black schools in South Carolina to Bates College in Lewiston, Maine. At Bates Mays first encountered modern biblical scholarship and began to espouse the Social Gospel as expressed in the writings of Walter Rauschenbusch. Central to his ministerial calling was a desire to gain a thorough knowledge of the Bible and other intellectual resources in order to preach and teach in a way that replaced prejudice with reasoned opinion, and blind adherence to custom with work for social progress. As the religious historian William Hutchinson would put it, Mays had a modernist impulse. Mays, like many mainline American Protestants, deemphasized doctrine and emphasized the ethical dimensions of religious thought in order to remedy what he saw as deficiencies in black religious life and to reinvigorate a faith that would be capable of confronting contemporary conditions. His theological liberalism matured at the University of Chicago, where he studied with Shirley Jackson Case, Henry Wieman, and Edwin Aubrey. Mays received his M.A. in

New Testament studies in 1925 and his Ph.D. in theology in 1935. His scholarly work centered on the critical investigation of black religiosity and institutional history. In *The Negro's Church*, coauthored by Joseph Nichols (1933), and *The Negro's God* (1938), he added his voice to a tradition of black Social Gospel thought that began in the late nineteenth century.

Mays then tackled the enormous task of expanding black clergymen's access to professional training and instilling his liberal theology into African American religious life. He served as dean of the Howard University School of Religion (now Howard University Divinity School) from 1934 until 1940, seeking accreditation for the school and training a cadre of students to serve the spiritual and political needs of black churchgoers. In this effort he joined forces with Mordecai Johnson, a proponent of the Social Gospel and the first black president of Howard, and the eminent preacher and theologian Howard Thurman. With Johnson, Thurman, and newly recruited faculty members, including James Farmer Sr., Mays attempted to fashion the School of Theology into a leading center of black theological modernism, as well as an institutional hub for thinking about nonviolent resistance to injustice that drew inspiration from Mohandas Gandhi's campaign against British imperialism in India. In 1940, when Mays was selected as president of Morehouse College in Atlanta, Georgia, he reframed his educational vision to prepare black youth for a wider range of professions and community service.

The intellectual historian Bruce Kuklick has shown that churchmen were dominant intellectual figures throughout the nineteenth century, but then the academy began to incline toward nonsectarian, agnostic approaches to research and scholarship. Mays's religious intellectualism and engaged approach to education, like that of his colleagues at other leading black colleges, points to an omission in Kuklick's analysis. Black religious intellectuals continued to function as vital public thinkers and educational leaders well into the mid-twentieth century. African Americans did not abandon this tradition with the emergence of the pragmatic philosophy of John Dewey and the rigorous methods of the social sciences, as Kuklick suggests most intellectuals did. Rather, many learned clergymen led academic institutions.[2] Lerone Bennett, one of Mays's students and King's classmates at Morehouse who became senior editor of *Ebony* magazine, captured Mays's significance when he called him "the last great school master."[3] Mays's roles as college president and churchman were synergistic. His stature in the Protestant church reinforced his prestigious position as college president. Morehouse had strong ties to both white northern Baptists and black Baptists across the United States, and Mays was central to the college's connections with the black faithful and the Protestant establishment.

Ordained by the Baptists in 1921, Mays served only three years as a church pastor. As his career shifted toward academic leadership, Mays continued to be active in the denomination, and he represented the National Baptist Convention in international ecumenical forums such as the World Council of Churches and meetings of the international YMCA. In 1944, Mays was elected vice-president of the Federal Council of Churches (today the National Council of Churches of Christ), becoming the first black American to hold that office in any ecumenical body. He preached to many of the largest black Baptist and liberal white Protestant church congregations in the United States. Equally important, Mays developed sustained connections with ordinary black Christians. He promoted African Americans' educational aspirations and helped to define the theological dimensions of the civil rights movement in ways that few other black intellectuals were able to do. The pulpit enabled him to reach those without formal education as well as the learned, and he used it as a tool for inspiring and encouraging the next generation.

This biography explores important questions regarding the origins, development, and influence of Mays's ideas. He was deeply rooted in what the cultural critic Cornel West calls "Prophetic Christianity," a term gleaned from theologian Paul Tillich and applied to West's critical analysis of black churches.[4] According to Tillich, "The most important contribution of Protestantism to the world in past, present, and future is the principle of prophetic protest against every power which claims divine character for itself—whether it be the church or state, party or leader."[5] Tillich's description of the global influence of Protestantism begs the question: how did African American Christians draw on this tradition to advance an agenda of civil rights and full equality? This book examines the ideological foundations of the civil rights movement in Protestant theology by tracing Mays's intellectual trajectory. For Mays, religious faith extended far beyond the institutional church; he translated prophetic religion into ethical practice.[6]

In this exploration of Mays's thought in relation to civil rights, other questions about this democratic movement must be considered. What role did secularization play in the ideological, cultural, and political changes that enabled African Americans to mount a direct challenge to Jim Crow? While Mays was a believer, albeit a liberal one, many of his contemporaries, such as E. Franklin Frazier, drew on sociology and Marxist theory to address the issue of inequality. Frazier and other progressive black intellectuals were highly critical of black Christianity and black clergymen, viewing them as an obstruction to black activism. Although Mays shared many of these critics' concerns about social deficits in black churches, he continued to think that churches could serve their communities if they had educated, ethical, and vitally engaged leadership. In Mays's view, this kind of dynamic leadership served the entire black community and should not be confined to the clergy.

Mays gave a great deal of consideration to questions of ethical leadership in a movement for social change. He believed that leaders had to be honest and transparent in their dealings with whites as well as blacks. His concern with leadership raises important questions about the relationship between morality rooted in religion and pragmatic ideologies based on self-interest and analyses of power. While the moral dimensions of civil rights leadership helped to turn American public opinion against racial discrimination, what were the blind spots in this ideological framework? How effectively did this perspective guide the civil rights movement in addressing the socioeconomic inequalities that constrained African Americans' lives? Could religious leaders, while sustaining the morale of black churchgoers in the face of the humiliations meted out to them in daily life, also address the economic marginalization and chronic poverty that they suffered? Finally, following Mays's career requires us to reflect on the gendered character of African American religious life. As president of a men's college and an ordained minister in a denomination where men predominated in the clergy, in what ways did Mays support and/or diverge from the prevailing notions about masculinity and femininity held by black men in religious and civil society?

The theology Mays advanced aimed to undermine white supremacy in order to extend democracy, as well as to preserve faith. Many historians have overlooked the fact that the civil rights movement was as much a theological struggle as it was a secular social democratic movement. As historian David Chappell points out, "Ostensibly religious movements have political dimensions" and "political movements have religious dimensions."[7] Mays knew, as historian Joseph Crespino has recently argued, that "the civil rights movement was an attack not simply on segregated institutions but on the set of ideologies that supported those institutions and, by extension, on white southerners' theological worldviews. The religious nature of the southern civil rights struggle forced white southerners to explain anew the relationship between their Christian faith and their segregationist practice."[8]

Mays's antiracist theology, as expressed in his sermons and writings, arose out of and responded to the communal institutions that had shaped him: the Jim Crow South, the Christian church in its manifestation among African Americans, and black-led educational institutions. Because Mays worked almost entirely in black churches and church-related institutions, historians have neglected him and a whole cohort of black intellectuals whose written corpus was directed primarily to black Protestant audiences. Books on black intellectual and cultural life in the twentieth century have generally focused on great literary figures and the giant of African American and Pan-African thought, W. E. B. Du Bois. The perspectives of religious intellectuals have not been accorded the scholarly examination that their significance deserves. Mays and his counterparts believed they were reshaping the spiritual aspirations of black communities away from passive acceptance of racial injustices as God's will. The theological challenge as he saw it was to build upon a black slave religion by grounding it in modern historical understanding. He firmly believed that the rich inheritance of black Protestant faith had to be constantly adjusting to an ever-changing society. In fact, as a liberal theologian, Mays was in a position of institutional leadership, which gave him greater influence than nonreligious intellectuals over the lives of ordinary black people. More significantly, unlike many writers, scholars, and public intellectuals of his generation who distanced themselves from black religious and educational institutions, Mays chose to be a critical but committed member of a black Baptist communion and the leader of a black college. The National Baptist Convention Inc. was one of the largest black organizations in the United States, claiming to have more than two million members. At its national gatherings, Mays was able to reach thousands of people from across the country and influence women's organizations and clergymen.

Borrowing a term from Antonio Gramsci, the Italian Marxist theorist, Mays was an "organic intellectual." Gramsci explained that in order for dominant political classes to exercise power, they must do so with the consent of weaker political classes "by connecting the perceived interests of these groups with their own." When the dominant political class cannot achieve power through consent of its political inferiors, they often turn to coercion. From a Gramscian point of view, "intellectuals play a crucial part in the process by helping to create and perpetuate appropriate worldviews." Intellectuals emerge from their respective social classes and are crucial in shaping the views of the subservient social classes. "Class domination," in Gramsci's view, "is thus an intellectual and moral victory as it is an economic fact." According to Gramsci it was necessary for the subservient classes to be educated—"revolutionary struggles ultimately is a matter of education." In order for those who are oppressed to counter their oppression, they must generate their own "organic intellectuals" who help to shatter the prevailing conventional wisdom of those in power. While Mays was certainly not a revolutionary Marxist—in fact, most of Mays's attitudes were quite bourgeois in taste and sentiments—he nevertheless was an organic intellectual as a churchman and educator.[9]

As an organic intellectual, Mays was able to publish widely in church-affiliated periodicals and black-oriented newspapers in which he was critical of both black and white Protestant churches for their equivocations in challenging racism. Mays's genius was his ability to dwell at the epicenter of black life as a clergyman, educator, and proponent of civil rights in addition to being a bridge to white Protestants. He was an active leader in both the national and international ecumenical movements that significantly reshaped American Protestantism. He did this by primarily remaining rooted in southern regional culture.

Mays's voice and perspective were distinctly southern. For a long time, so much emphasis has been placed on the intellectual work and cultural production centered in the Northeast in the 1920s through the 1960s that regional variation in black intellectual traditions and cultural attitudes has been ignored until recently. As Mays wrote in the *Christian Science Monitor*, "I am a Southerner. With the exception of eight years of college and graduate study in New England and the Middle West, I have elected to live in the South." He stayed in the South because he was convinced that his best work could be done there. For Mays, being a southerner meant staying in touch with his roots in rural culture and affirming the communal ties of family and religion that were the legacy of the slave community. He understood that only a mass movement of southern blacks could jolt the region out of its racism and impoverishment and precipitate a nationwide transformation. Mays's southern roots gave him greater authority as he exhorted black and white Christians to take up social action based upon their faith commitments. This he believed was in keeping with the best of the Baptist social teaching.[10]

In 1964, Mays published an article titled "I Have Been a Baptist All My Life" that emphasized freedom as the core value of Baptist faith and practice. The freedom of thought and speech enjoyed by Baptist clergy due to the democratic structure of the denomination was, he felt, vital to enabling them to address contemporary controversial issues from the pulpit and in public. "This freedom has sometimes been abused," he acknowledged, "but for a Baptist preacher it is a good and sure feeling to have the right to say what he thinks and believes without interference from some bishop or anybody else higher up." With conviction he commented, "There is something in the beliefs of the Baptist—freedom of conscience, the dignity and worth of every man, each man's individual right of direct access to God—that has given the Negro preacher the power he has, the conviction and the ability to preach and move people." In Mays's mind, the freedom of conscience found in Baptist doctrine was the key to unleashing blacks' indignation to fight for their civic freedoms. At the center of the Baptist heritage, dating as far back as seventeenth-century New England's Roger Williams, was a deeply democratic faith, a faith that racial oppression violated. For Mays, a Baptist, the demands for civil rights were a theological necessity.

This was the rich intellectual tradition that nourished Martin Luther King Jr. as he worked to mobilize blacks in the Deep South and their diasporas throughout the North during the era of mass protest. In King's mind, no one understood this Baptist heritage, from which King's social thought derived, better than Mays, his mentor. It was at King's request, then, that Mays eulogized him. When Mays spoke to those who walked to Morehouse College that hot April afternoon, he was not only mourning King's loss but also expressing his democratic faith. That afternoon, he preached that the freedom to dissent and the right social actions were foundational to the ongoing struggle to build a more just American society that King envisioned. What the nation heard that afternoon was what King and other black college students had been indoctrinated with during Mays's years as president of Morehouse.

Benjamin Elijah Mays had lived through the most trying times of the twentieth century. He had developed an approach to theology and education that brought the resources of mind and spirit to bear upon vital social issues that could sustain a democratic faith. This faith inspired generations of black Christians to persevere in the struggle for liberation and the transformation of American society. Mays stands as a towering figure at the crossroads of black intellectual life, religious institutional life, and civil rights activism.[11] Examining his life and ideas sheds a powerful light on the decades of systematic work that laid the foundation for the religiously based, theologically informed, and ethically guided movement for justice that reshaped the United States in the mid-twentieth century.[12]

This book is a chronological narrative of Mays's life and writings up until the publication of his autobiography, *Born to Rebel*, in 1971. The autobiography is an overview of Mays's lifelong thoughts about religion and race in America, but it does not fully address all aspects of his life. In writing this intellectual portrait, I consulted Mays's voluminous papers and correspondence in order to provide a fuller picture of his life. Mays's autobiography, though important, omits a great deal and was a meditation on the events of the late 1960s and early 1970s. In fact, after he published the autobiography, he continued to be a vigorous social commentator and public servant until his death in 1984.

— 1 —
My Earliest Memory Was a Mob

Not even an omnipotent God can blot out the deeds of history.
—MAYS, *Quotable Quotes of Benjamin E. Mays*

"I remember a crowd of white men who rode up on horseback with rifles on their shoulders. I was with my father when they rode up, and I remember starting to cry. They cursed my father, drew their guns and made him salute, made him take off his hat and bow down to them several times. Then they rode away. I was not yet five years old, but I have never forgotten them."[1] So began Benjamin Mays's description of his coming of age in an era of fear and terror. Mays was born in 1894 as the curtain of Jim Crow fell over the American South, violently segregating worlds into black and white.[2]

The mob terror that had so thoroughly shaped Mays's earliest memory and imagination stemmed from the Phoenix riot of 1898, a politically calculated mob action by the supporters of South Carolina governor Benjamin Tillman to eliminate the last vestiges of black political activity.[3] What was worrisome to Tillman and his acolytes was the possibility that their rivals within the Republican Party might use black votes to realign the party against their political initiatives.[4] Ostensibly, the justification for the riot existed because of the Republican political activism of the Tolbert family. The Tolberts were a well-off, formerly slaveholding family that had lived in Greenwood County since the Revolutionary War era. Although they had opposed secession, four Tolbert brothers fought on the side of the Confederacy, but then they endorsed Republican candidate Ulysses S. Grant in the 1868 presidential election. During Reconstruction, the Tolbert family, allied with blacks in Greenwood County, controlled the black vote and exercised substantial control over the Republican Party. By 1894, the Tolberts's alliance was strong enough that they decided to run Red Tolbert as the Republican candidate for Congress. The alliance encouraged black males to vote at the polls in the rural town of Phoenix, South Carolina.[5] The Tolberts, it was alleged, hoped to use their votes to challenge Tillman's proposed changes to the South Carolina State Constitution in 1895, which fueled the potential of reactionary violence by the Democrats. By 1898, the local Democratic Committee chair assured a violent response if black men came out to vote.[6] As Election Day neared, vigilantes terrorized black residents of Edgefield, Abbeville, and Greenwood counties. Twelve black men were shot dead ("two or three" of them were Mays's father's close friends), and one rural church in Greenwood County was set on fire. The terror was so extensive that Mays later remembered his father saying, "Negroes were hiding out like rabbits."[7] On the afternoon the vigilantes road into Epworth, the then four-year-old Mays had scurried under a nearby white neighbor's porch and tearfully viewed his father being terrorized. Mays's father was lucky to have survived the attack. The marauding offenders, many of whom were known in the region, were never held responsible for their actions.

In response, many local black residents either moved to other regions within the state or deferred to local white political rule.[8] The tragic irony of this "riot" was that the Republican Party had not been a significant political threat in South Carolina since 1882, the year when the Democrats (under Tillman's leadership in the state House) wrested control of the South Carolina legislature from the Republican majority. Upon completing their takeover of the legislature, the Democratic lawmakers moved to change all the laws governing voter registration and balloting to curtail black political participation.[9] Outbreaks of violence like the one that took place in Phoenix were aimed at eliminating the black vote.

Violent political maneuvers such as the Phoenix riot were justified by a civil religiosity known as the Lost Cause.[10] The propaganda of the Lost Cause created an effective narrative that redefined white southern life and historical reality. Its proponents alleged that the real victims of terror were white planters and yeomen who had been unfairly victimized by the rapacious North during the Civil War. Advocates of this theory argued that the war was fought over states' rights rather than the entrenched interests of slave owners. The premise of this theory was that white southerners were actually the heroes of the war for defending states' rights and believed that southern heroism needed to be enshrined. Monuments and statues of Confederate figures were constructed across the states of the old Confederacy—from Richmond to Edgefield to New Orleans. This characterization of white southerners as victims and heroes eventually unleashed a ritualized barbarism against the formerly enslaved and their descendants. Lynchings and execution-style murders were strategic and very effective. The advocates of the Lost Cause successfully disguised their undemocratic usurpation of political power by creatively inventing a civil religion that was congruous with the deeply felt religious pieties of the white South. As a result, mob political violence flourished.[11]

By Mays's fourth birthday, the sectional tensions between the North and South resulting from the Civil War had begun to ease.[12] Mays, though not fully aware of all the ramifications at the time, was an eyewitness to the congealing of white supremacy in the American South, which blatantly insured that the citizenship rights of blacks, Chinese, and Native Americans would be diminished throughout all parts of the United States. Further, Americans would naively assuage the national collective conscience and unite through militarism in the global south in the Spanish American wars in Cuba and the Philippines. Mays's localized experience of racial terror in the South was concurrent with the political transformations occurring throughout Asia and Africa.[13]

Mays's memory of political terrorism shaped his Christian intellectual imagination during his lifelong fight for social justice and democratic freedoms. Throughout his adult life he would constantly strive to create an antiracist theological framework to eradicate Jim Crow's affects on black people. He dedicated himself to studying, preaching, and teaching to counter the humiliating scars that segregation inflicted on black Americans. He strived to do this by laboring tirelessly to acquire a formal education and by advancing theological education among black students. Mays's quest for education was grounded in notions of middle-class respectability and what it meant to be a middle-class man, but he also believed that theology could serve black people as they pursued their citizenship claims. Central to his intellectual pursuits was the black Baptist Church, one of the paramount institutions in the day-to-day lives of black people.

Throughout his life Mays was anchored in the black Baptist Church. Mount Zion was the first church to provide Mays a reaffirming space for his humanity. It was a place that reinforced the idea that, as his mother, Louvenia Mays, put it, "you are as good as anybody!" "This assurance," Mays recalled, "was helpful to me even though the white world did not accept my mother's philosophy."[14] One need only scrutinize his childhood remembrances to realize that at the center of his South Carolina upbringing was a complex network of families anchored by local Baptist churches.

In the aftermath of the Civil War, small black Baptist churches sprang up like wild flowers throughout the rural South.[15] Black people survived slavery and the violent politics of Jim Crow by virtue of both familial and religious networks. Historian Steven Hahn has thoughtfully observed that, following the Civil War, the anchors of black political life were black congregations.[16] Rural churches, he explains, "were bound unmistakably to local lattices of kinship, work, and obligations." Rural congregations in the South were "community centers, assuming the range of vital functions. Almost invariably they established Sunday schools and welcomed other educational activities, disseminated important community news and information, helped resolve disputes among members, defined collective norms, and brought sanctions against their transgressors."[17] For blacks living in South Carolina, family, religion, and education were a holy triumvirate. Baptist churches were indeed the center of life for black and white families alike.[18] For Mays, being a Baptist was akin to being born with black skin. "The truth of the matter is," he wrote, "I was born and brought up in a Baptist community with no other denominations close around, and the Baptist Church was the center of things."[19] In fact, black membership in the Baptist church exceeded that of any other denomination in South Carolina.[20] As one state historian has noted, by 1906, 55 percent of black South Carolina residents were Baptist.[21] "Negroes," Mays explained, "had nowhere to go but to church. They went there to worship, to hear the choir sing, to listen to the preacher, and to hear and see people shout. The young people went to socialize around and talk. It was a place of worship and a social center as well."[22]

Small rural congregations such as Mount Zion had a long and complex history serving black southerners.[23] However, the most important thing they did was to provide space where black Baptist congregants received religious instruction that taught them about freedom and equality before God. This kind of education was always a counterbalance to terror. As religious historian Albert Raboteau explains, "At the core of this [Baptist] piety was the Reformation insight that salvation was based not on external observance and personal merit, nor on the intercession of church and clergy, but on the relationship of the individual sovereign will of God. With this view of the religious life the person inevitably turned inward and searched his or own heart to discern the workings of God's Spirit there." This type of theological understanding "encouraged individual autonomy in matters of religious conscience, an autonomy difficult to control, as the fissiparous tendencies of Protestantism have frequently shown." Even in slavery, black Baptists, especially, "institutionalized the spirit of Gospel freedom by insisting on the autonomy of each congregation." It was precisely this emphasis on "independent church polity" that "offered more opportunity than any other denomination for black members to exercise a measure of control over their church life."[24] If this were true under the condition of slavery, it was all the more true under the harshness of violent political repression and segregation. This Baptist theological emphasis deeply influenced Mays's outlook on the meaning of community and freedom.

Mays's devotion to these concepts was nurtured by two people, his mother, Louvenia Carter Mays, and his pastor at Mount Zion Baptist Church, the Reverend James F. Marshall. He cited his mother innumerable times in his writings as teaching him piety—especially prayer. "My belief in God," Mays recalled, "reaches back to my early childhood. As early as I can remember my mother called the children to prayer each night just before we retired for bed. God was very real to my mother. So, I caught her spirit and relied heavily on God and prayer."[25]

But there was more to his mother's "spirit" than Mays gave credit. He was reared in a community with rich cultural practices tied to West Africa, which influenced the cultural flavor of the entire state of South Carolina. In colonial America, slaves of African descent outnumbered British descendants. And following the Civil War, roughly 50 percent of the population of the state was black.[26] Although Mays grew up in a heavily black populated region of South Carolina, he was too young and too ignorant to understand his own connections to any African ancestors or to be aware of the rich cultural legacy of West and West Central Africa present all over South Carolina. He admitted he knew "virtually nothing" about "his ancestors." His mother's deep religious piety, however, was a by-product of the Atlantic world's new religiosity.

Louvenia Mays's pious teachings were rooted in a rich past that she was unlikely aware of either. It was a past full of the "cut and paste" and the mixing of cultures of Africans and Europeans who arrived in the lower southeastern part of the colonial United States.[27] There were the circle dances—or the ring shout, as it was called; there were bodily convulsions and catatonic stiffness found in ceremonial spirit possession rites; and there was exuberant flaying of hands and ecstatic screeches of joy and sorrow—the shout—all combined with the folkways of English and West African worlds as Protestant revivalism crisscrossed the Atlantic Ocean.[28] Historian Mechal Sobel has suggested that enslaved Africans adapted and reshaped West African belief systems and the English Baptist version of Christianity to serve their particular needs.[29] She notes that it was common for "slave children to experience religion in the family circle." And even more, children "saw their mothers, fathers, grandparents, aunts, and uncles die and be reborn. They heard shouts and 'moans' as a routine part of their family lives. They were prayed over as children and they 'knew' their own religious commitment would play a central role in shaping their" lives. Baptism, Sobel has observed, was the "ticket" for black family members to be joined together beyond death.[30] Although Mays was born nearly thirty years after the end of slavery, the cultural pattern described here resonated in his home.[31]

Mays's religious experience fit well into the cultural pattern of evangelical conversion found among his slave forebears. He would recall in later years, with a rather subdued tone,

> One Sunday morning when I was thirteen I was sitting in the church listening to the sermon and the morning began to be different from any other. I can't tell about it or describe it, because I don't know what happened. . . . When the appeal came, I got up and went down front and gave the minister my hand. I cried a little and I felt lifted up and it was a new kind of feeling. I was a boy and did not understand what had happened, but there was something within me that I had never known before and I felt a little excited and happy and very safe.

"This was back in 1908," he continued. "That same week I was baptized, but baptism did not produce any special feeling in me. I had already had my experience, and baptism was just something that came after."[32] It may be that Baptism was no big deal to Mays as an adolescent, but in his mother's eyes, Mays, whom she affectionately called "Bubba," had done what was right in the eyes of God and his community.[33]

Mays never quite understood the emotive behavior of Mount Zion congregants and in rural black southern religion. He attributed his mother's "outbursts" as solely tied to his father's alcohol abuse and his family's impoverishment. Indeed, her church served as an emotional outlet for her in coping with domestic trials, but it was also part of her culture, a culture that that she shared with other women.[34] And it was out of this culture that she exerted the strongest influence on Mays's earliest theological formation. Blinded by patriarchy and other bourgeois ideas about what was acceptable religious behavior, he failed to recognize the depth of black women's culture at Mount Zion. Louvenia Mays was part of a network of black women who made up the majority of the church's constituents. While men were the leaders in these congregations, holding the formal roles as preachers and deacons, the women were the spiritual guides, caregivers, and primary fund-raisers that helped keep the Mount Zions of the rural South alive.[35]

Although later in life Mays was suspect of the emotive aspects of black religion, he was not totally dismissive of the expressive culture of Mount Zion in his youth. Indeed, it was the emotive preaching that led him to his Christian conversion. The preaching style of Mount Zion ministers and the expectation of congregants fit right into the pattern of antebellum slave culture, too.[36] Mays said of his boyhood minister, James Marshall, "He could moan, and did. Almost invariably he made some people shout. If he did not moan a bit and make the people shout, his congregation felt he had not preached well." He added, "Although Marshall taught the people to be honest and upright . . . he preached primarily an opiate to enable them to endure and survive the oppressive conditions in which they lived at the hands of white people in the community."[37]

Marshall, as Mays's reminiscences makes clear, was no radical preacher. Nonetheless, even poorly educated ministers like Marshall were considered dangerous to the segregationist order. Uneducated black ministers, after all, had played prominent roles in antebellum slave rebellions and political organizing during the Civil War and Reconstruction.[38] Navigating the terrain of violent repression and familial economic needs was difficult, and it forced Marshall, and many others like him, to craft their messages to acquiesce to white expectations and to protect their families and congregants. Mays recalled that Marshall "relied on [a local] white minister to help him keep his church."[39] In fact, Marshall was a first-rate ecclesial politician—and he needed to be, for, according to Mays, he "had ten children or more; and from his four churches he received a total of only $800 a year."[40] "Pastor Marshall," Mays wrote, "stayed *in* with the local white Methodist preacher, although Marshall believed that all who were not Baptists were hellward bound. When certain elements in the church wanted to get rid of Marshall, he invited the Reverend Pierce Kinard, a white Methodist, to come to Zion and advise the Negroes to keep Marshall, which of course effectively ended the incipient move to have Preacher Marshall removed."[41]

Marshall's actions were not reprehensible if viewed in light of the fact that, as Mays described it, "most black churches were too small and financially dependent to take a public stand. The average [rural] congregation numbered about eighty members and worshiped in modest structures, often built with financial assistance from local white planters."[42] Mount Zion was one of these countless rural congregations scattered across upcountry South Carolina. According to Mays, it was "six miles from the town of Ninety Six and four miles from our house." Worship was held "every second Sunday" because Marshall had to divide his time between several other rural congregations. Mays certainly may have resented his minister's social posture as he became a young adult and more educated, but youthful resentments and adult social realities are two different things entirely.[43] In a manner similar to slave preachers, who at times dissimulated and used the master class for their own ends, Marshall played church politics.[44]

Marshall's influence on Mays's early life was second in importance only to that of his mother's. It was Marshall's preaching that challenged him to accept Christ as his Savior. It was under Marshall's pastoral guidance that the entire Mays family was baptized as repentant believers. And it was from Marshall's example that Mays learned about the freedom of the Baptist minister to speak truths to his congregation. Mays would later describe this freedom as the genius of black Baptist preachers. "There is something in the beliefs of the Baptist—freedom of conscience, the dignity and worth of every man, each man's individual right of direct access to God—that has given the Negro preacher the power that he has, the conviction and the ability to preach and to move people," he wrote. "From the ecclesiastical point of view he is free because there is no hierarchy to dominate him." Drawing on theological ideas regarding conscience that went as far back as seventeenth-century England, Mays learned that the minister has the freedom to say, "what he believes and [to] preach his faith."[45]

The sense of freedom and independence that Marshall demonstrated provided Mays a rich example of male leadership. Later in life, Mays would look to Marshall's model of ministry not for the theology he preached but for his integrity. For all of Marshall's lack of political militancy, he remained a religious dissenter believing that a minister was accountable to God. Failure to tell the truth to God's people was an unpardonable sin. For Mays, Marshall's only real sin was his unwillingness to confront southern racism.

Mays differed from his childhood minister in two important and interrelated ways. First, Mays desired education and status for himself. His heroes, he related, were Frederick Douglass, Booker T. Washington, and the black South Carolina Reconstruction politicians.[46] Marshall's status was limited to the respect he received from his congregants and the communities he served. For Marshall, the central affirmation in his ministry was the moral life of his members before God. As Mays remembered, "Marshall preached funerals according to the life the deceased lived." Marshall was so great that his word was taken as prophetic, and no one around Greenwood County wanted him "to *put bad mouth* on them."[47] Marshall believed that Baptist ministers needed little, if any, formalized theological education. He was of the ministerial tradition in which a preacher was inspired by God and not by human conventions.[48] According to Mays, Marshall "set a good example for his people," and many of his congregants believe that he "had special power with God."[49]

The second difference between Marshall and Mays was theological, which was made loud and clear when Mays declined to have his childhood minister ordain him. According to Mays, Marshall "never forgave me for not seeking ordination at Zion." Mays's rationale for not seeking Mount Zion's approval and licensing of his calling probably centered on his anxiety about his social status. At the time of his ordination, Mays had transitioned from a child of agrarian impoverishment to a man with an elite education. "[M]y training at Bates and the University of Chicago," Mays maintained, "had given me a point of view about religion and theology which differed widely from that of my fifth grade educated pastor at Zion."[50] For example, Mays "never heard him utter one word against lynching," and he recalled Reverend Marshall intervening when a visiting preacher at their church "attempted to condemn white people."[51]

Marshall was not the only person at Mount Zion to make an impression on Mays. The people who traversed the back ways and country roads to attend the church also fueled Mays's ambition and religious imagination. He remembered:

> Each Sunday in June, we had what we called "Children's Day." I do not remember exactly how old I was—possibly nine—when I participated, having committed to memory a portion of the Sermon on the Mount. After my recitation, the house went wild: old women waved their handkerchiefs, old men stamped their feet, and the people generally applauded long and loud. It was a terrific ovation, let alone tremendous experience, for a nine-year-old boy. There were predictions that I would "go places" in life. The minister said I would preach; and from that moment on the Reverend Marshall manifested a special interest in me. . . . The people in the church did not contribute one dime to help me with my education. But they gave me something far more valuable. They gave me encouragement, the thing I most needed. They expressed such confidence in me that I always felt that I could never betray their trust, never let them down.[52]

The encouragement and communal life at Mount Zion affirmed Mays's self-esteem and nurtured his childhood ambition.

The people of Mount Zion also nurtured Mays's intellect. Bible readings and reading the Bible aloud at Mount Zion were communal activities both in Sunday school and during the worship service. Biblical passages and imagery helped frame his earliest imagination and understanding of the world. According to Mays, the Bible as he learned it in his home and in Baptist Sunday school lessons was unquestionably an influence on him. "There were only a few books in the Mays' house and no magazines," Mays recalled. "We had the Bible, a dictionary, picture books about Booker T. Washington, Frederick Douglass, and Paul Laurence Dunbar, and Sunday school books."[53] Sunday schools were pedagogically significant for black southerners. Black-led Sunday schools, like their white counterparts throughout the South "focused on the Bible and used uniform lesson plans, as well as supplemental texts and newspapers. Yet while the outlines were the same for blacks as they were for whites, black teachers emphasized issues of importance to their race."[54] In Sunday school, memorizing Bible passages and reciting them were key ingredients in Mays's budding consciousness.

If the young Mays rebelled against segregation, his rebellion came directly out the ancient apocalyptic and eschatological notions of justice found in the beatitudes and the exuberant call and response of Mount Zion's members. Religion in Mays's community may never have been the proactive political ideology he wished it to be, but it was a spiritual tradition that kept hope and individual dignity alive to sustain rural blacks to fight another day.[55] And the young Mays certainly needed faith, because his family faced stark social realities as poor farmers. The livelihood of his family, who worked their fields tirelessly, was intimately tied to the ebbs and flows of the cotton economy, which deeply affected their own interpersonal dynamics.

Mays's parents, Hezekiah and Louvenia, were born into slavery in 1856 and 1862, respectively. They were a part of the last generation of black Americans to be born under chattel slavery. Together they experienced the high hopes and the failed promises of the Reconstruction era as young adults. By the time Benjamin was born, Hezekiah and Louvenia had been thoroughly conditioned to the political brutalities and uneven cycles of an agricultural economy. Hezekiah Mays made his living first as a sharecropper and later as a tenant farmer. "As far back as I can remember," Mays said, "I think we owned our mules. Any man who owned his mules or horses, buggy, wagon, or other farm equipment occupied a little higher status than the one who worked for wages or was a sharecropper." The tenant farmer worked on an annual contract, whereas the wage hand received pay monthly. "The sharecropper," Mays explained, "worked on the 'halve.'" He "had his house, mules, and other farm implements provided for him. The owner of the land received half of all the sharecroppers made."[56]

The Mayses were industrious. According to Mays, his father believed in the biblical notion that "a man should earn his living by the sweat of his brow." For Hezekiah that "meant working on the farm in the blazing hot sun."[57] Hezekiah's work ethic, however, infrequently paid off. Mays wrote, "Father usually rented forty acres of land for a two-mule farm or sixty acres if we had three mules. . . . Father got only the money that came from selling cottonseeds. . . . To make sixteen bales of cotton on a two-mule farm was considered excellent farming." But, Mays continued, "after four bales were used to pay rent, we would have two bales left. The price of cotton fluctuated. If we received

Benjamin Mays's home in the vicinity of Epworth, South Carolina. Courtesy of
the South Carolina Department of Archives and History, National Register
of Historic Places.

ten cents a pound, we would have somewhere between five and six hundred
dollars." The Mayses' toil did not net them sufficient cash to support two
adults and eight children. Nor was it enough money to carry them into the
next planting season.[58] In their household every member of the family "worked
hard six days a week."[59] Yet their father still "had to pay back, with interest."[60]
When all the farm obligations were accounted for, the Mayses were still cash
strapped and poor.

Upcountry South Carolina farmers like Hezekiah Mays were extremely
productive. However, the amount of cash they received for their productivity
never created surplus capital, which meant that black farmers' productivity
went virtually unrewarded. The availability of credit was practically nil, causing
yeoman farmers to depend more heavily on crop liens to gain enough capital to
plant. Only merchants located in expanding railroad towns were accumulating
capital and wealth.[61] The shift of economic resources from farmers to urban
commercial merchants left all farmers disadvantaged. Belatedly, farmers began
organizing farmers' cooperatives and labor alliances, but at the same time, the
South Carolina legislature began passing laws that limited the amount of organizing that farmers could do. Contract law was designed such that the large
planters and rising commercial merchants of the New South, rather than the
small farmers, had the economic advantages. The laws were crafted to prevent
both white and black farm alliances from getting higher prices for their cotton.

Both groups would die on the vine. And when legislative manipulation was not enough to secure commercial merchant and large planter dominance in the New South, then terror was another means.[62]

Before Mays was born, his parents had been thoroughly circumscribed economically and silenced politically. As a farm family, they lived under constant paramilitary threats dating back to 1876, when the massacre in Hamburg, South Carolina, took place. Hezekiah Mays was twenty years old at the time. In the town of Hamburg, black militias were lined up to celebrate the Fourth of July when two white farmers allegedly ran their buggies through their procession. An argument broke out between the farmers and the militiamen, and then the farmers move on. A couple of days later, the farmers took the militia to court for allegedly obstructing the road. The militiamen were then told to turn over their arms to a former Confederate general. When they refused, a full-scale battle took place between the black militiamen and a group of white farmers. One white farmer was killed. Later, at least four of the black militiamen were captured and executed. This marked the beginning of the "Democratic Redemption" in South Carolina led by General Wade Hampton, who would be elected South Carolina's governor. The point of the massacre was to disarm black men so that they would not be a political threat. It happened not far from where Hezekiah and Louvenia farmed. We will never know for sure all the effects it had on them, but we do know that personal humiliation combined with political powerlessness left Hezekiah as a sometimes frustrated and angry man.[63] Men in his day were expected to exercise power; he had none civically or economically. By late-nineteenth-century standards, his manhood was threatened, left him with only one option, reestablishing his manhood by domineering his family.

Mays described his home life as not being "pleasant." He wrote, "Quarreling, wrangling and sometimes fighting went on in our house." Mays attributed much of this to his father's drinking: "All too many times we children had to hold him from hurting Mother. He would take out his knife and threaten to cut her." But Mays's mother was anything but passive. "Mother had to talk back," he wrote, which he believed fueled his father's rage even more. Hezekiah Mays even drank at church, which embarrassed the young Mays. In fact, Mays "made a pledge at twelve years of age not to drink liquor." Over time, Mays softened his views on his father's alcohol abuse: "My father was not a heavy drinker. He simply could not hold his liquor." The greater truth was that drinking turned this "kindly man" into an obnoxious and violent person who made the young Mays "shiver in his presence" and run for safety. Mays acknowledged, "I was afraid of my father until I was past eighteen."[64] Although he moderated his views about his father's alcoholism later on life, the reality was his father's drinking harmed their bond as father and son.[65]

Hezekiah Mays was not alone in his alcoholic rages. Men in his era drank heavily whether in the factory, the fields, or the office.[66] Alcohol abuse simply added more burdens to a poor man's already burdensome life. Mays's older sister, Susie Glenn, recalled that their father's abuse of alcohol began in 1891, when she was twelve. If her memory was correct, Hezekiah Mays's affinity for strong drink coincided with the economic spirals, family hardships—by this time the Mayses had lost a son to typhoid—and the political violence that suffocated his hopes. Glenn's reminiscences of their father also portrayed a man of frustrated ambition. As a slave, Hezekiah learned "his alphabet" from "a white boy." "Father could read printing fairly well and could figure a bit," she added.[67] Hezekiah Mays was obviously no alcoholic slouch, since he had been ambitious enough to accumulate resources that were required to be a tenant farmer, but the vicissitudes of life and circumstances beyond his control drove him to bouts of drinking.

In addition to his alcohol abuse and violent behavior Hezekiah's frustrations were also evident in the demands he placed upon his sons.[68] Sons were field hands and the only free labor that a sharecropper or a tenant farmer had to command. The culture supported by law was patriarchal, and sons, until they reached the age of majority, could be commanded by their fathers to labor for them.[69] The difficult and often thankless work of farming often turned fathers and sons into dire enemies,[70] and this was the situation for Mays and his brothers, John, the eldest, who was born around 1890, and Hezekiah (H. H.), who was born in 1892. When they could, all of Hezekiah's sons quit farming and escaped the cyclical impoverishment associated with cotton production. At one time, the family wanted Hezekiah to purchase land and become an independent farmer. This was a fanciful wish, Mays acknowledged in retrospect, since he and his brothers eventually left South Carolina knowing that they would never profit from farming.

John Mays initially took up farming but eventually moved to Cleveland.[71] H. H. left the farm "after an altercation" with Hezekiah. As Mays put it, H. H. "pulled his sack off and left the cotton field and his home, never to return except on visits to the family." He "was the only one of [Mays's] siblings to finish high school." H. H. made his way to New York City seeking better opportunities.[72] Eventually, Hezekiah turned his ire and frustration on Mays.

Mays, however, claimed that he enjoyed farm life. "I did not leave the farm and am proud to proclaim that I was a *good* farmhand—much better than the average." He eventually left the farm, just as his two older brothers had done, to advance himself in the world through education—a world Mays's father could hardly have understood, having lived his entire adult life within the confines of Aiken, Greenwood, and Edgefield counties.[73]

The world that blacks and whites shared in South Carolina was harsh and violent, especially among men. Patriarchal families and codes of honor dictated that personal injury or insult would be met with violence. These codes of honor defined rural black communities just as much as their white counterparts' social ethos.[74] Even boyhood fights could turn ugly, as Mays experienced: "I recall one fight when I was cut by one of the two boys with whom I was fighting. I was cut on the hand, the arm, and the head. When I got home, I was bloody." His father angrily chastised him for fighting, never letting him explain how the fight began, "that the two boys had *laid* for me when I passed their house returning from the store. They had jumped me." Mays reasoned that he had "two choices: run or fight." He "chose to fight."[75]

Fights often got out of hand because of guns. Mays never owned a pistol, but his "brothers did, and most of the boys in the county carried pistols," and too often they were too often used in rural clashes.[76] Mays explained, "Negroes lived under constant pressures and tensions all the time in my community. . . . They knew that if attacked they dare not strike back—if they wanted to live." However, they did strike back. "I believe to this day," Mays observed, "that Negroes in my county fought among themselves because they were taking out on other Negroes what they really wanted but feared to take out on whites." He continued, "It was difficult, virtually impossible, to combine manhood and blackness under one skin in the days of my youth. To exercise manhood, as white men displayed it, was to invite disaster."[77] The violence and the anger that existed tore at the bonds of kinship and affection.

Mays's family experienced this kind of violence first hand: An envious brother-in-law murdered Mays's oldest brother, James, as he plowed. According to Mays, James's wife inherited property from her parents, which they farmed. When James's wife died, he inherited her property. When James decided to marry again, his former brother-in-law could not stand the thought of James and his new wife owning what was once his family's property, so one day he followed James as he went out to tend the fields and murdered him. As Mays painfully acknowledged, after James's murder, "since nothing in the racial situation in my county was conducive to encouraging sensitive Negroes to remain, my brother John soon left, ending up in Cleveland, and H. H. made his home in New York."[78] Violence external and internal to the black community ate away at community. Those who could escape the South ran as fast as they could.

In reality, however, an escape from the violence of Jim Crow was virtually impossible. Every southern-born black man had inscribed into his physical posture what the writer Richard Wright vividly described in his famous essay, "The Ethics of Living Jim Crow." Mob violence was instructive; its lesson was subordination. As Mays described it, "In the perilous world, if a black boy wanted to live a halfway normal life and die a natural death he had to learn early the art of how to get along with white folks." White violence made black parents ever fearful and watchful over their children. "When my parents admonished their children, *be careful and stay out of trouble*," Mays continued, "they had only one thing in mind: *Stay out of trouble with white people*." "I am not wise enough to say categorically what this system did to Negroes in Greenwood County," Mays wrote.

> They were poor, inadequately trained, and dependent on the white man
> for work. Few dared to stand up to a white man. When one did, he got
> the worst of it. . . . It was not unusual to hear that a certain Negro had
> been run out of town, or, fearing he would be, had left the county before
> *they* could get him. Most Negroes grinned, cringed, and kowtowed in
> the presence of white people. Those who could not take such subservi-
> ence left for the city as soon as they could—with or without their father's
> permission.[79]

The other aspect of Jim Crow's ethics was sexual. The rules required that black men avoid contact with white women. Mays recalled his mother "admonish[ing] my brothers and me to stay clear of white women." She told her sons that "white women were dangerous and would surely get us into trouble." Lynchings and mob violence were often tied to black males' supposed sexual desire for white women. As Mays observed, however, "while white men used physical force to protect white women or to avenge alleged attacks on white women by black men, Negro parents had to contrive other methods to protect their daughters, often without success." His "parents did what they could to prevent exposure of my sisters to white men." Jim Crow's gendered rules were rarely broken or challenged.[80]

Additionally, black men were always seen as a physical and martial threat to white men, especially after the Civil War. White men based their understanding of racial supremacy on a largely unexamined set of ideas regarding manhood.[81] This masculine ideological framework justified dispossession of what supremacist believed to be lesser men's, that is, nonwhites', citizenship rights. Jim Crow's violence against black men had a much longer history, as historian Gail Bederman observes. The violent culture that developed in the rural South was a legacy of slavery. "Slavery showed all Southerners the significance of physical force in human relations," she argues. "The opportunities for cruelty and the need for readiness in the case of slave violence affected the consciousness of all Southern whites, and the most extreme forms of violence in the postbellum period—lynching, night riding, and Klan violence—were directed almost exclusively against blacks." This was the hidden tension among blacks and whites in the South, and white men especially projected their tensions and fears by subordinating black men.[82] This was perfectly illustrated when Hezekiah Mays was made to kowtow before the mob in his front yard. Kowtowing was a daily ritual. Being a black male was a threat, and, no matter what the circumstance, white males had to slap down any sign of pride and self-respect. In his early adulthood, Mays would learn this stinging lesson when a young white male physician, Dr. Wallace Payne, walked past him at the local post office and slapped him on the face for no apparent reason, telling him, "Get out of my way, you black rascal, you're trying to look too good anyway." Mays summed it up well: "I was black and a black man had no rights, which he, Wallace Payne, was bound to admit, let alone respect. My life meant no more to him than that of a rabbit. I was black and he was white; accordingly, with or without provocation, he could—with impunity—do to me what he wished."[83]

It was against the headwinds of racial oppression and economic subordination that Mays's worldview was formed. For Mays, the denigration that had been meted out to him and his father required no other kind of response, at least from his Christian point of view, but a resistance that was spiritual as well as muscular and combative. Mays's religious idealism had to involve resistance in order for him to fight the countless indignities heaped upon black people in the South. Nationally, white Protestant men feared their Christianity being weakened and feminized in late-nineteenth-century America as Christian instruction became primarily the domain of women. Feminized Christianity, it was believed, weakened support for the more brutal methods of colonization that were sweeping across northern Europe and the United States and around the globe. However, black men in opposition to physical and psychic assault, as a part of the oppressed colored people of the world, to paraphrased W. E. B. DuBois, adhered to a masculine version of Protestant Christianity to maintain their sense of communal pride and their political struggle.[84] Viscerally, and without much reflection, Mays viewed his faith through a masculine lens.[85]

What is amazing is that Mays held fast to religion at all. Living in the South provided enough spiritual travails for him. The hardship and racism he faced led him "to the conclusion that the Southern white was my enemy—not only my enemy but the enemy of all Negroes. Everything I had seen, and most of what I heard, should have convinced me that the white man was superior and the Negro inferior." For whatever reason, he "was not convinced" that being an inferior was his fate. "I was bothered," he penned, "I was haunted night and day. I once startled my saintly mother by telling her that if I thought God had deliberately made me inferior I would pray no more. I did not really believe that God had done this to me."[86]

To be sure, there were plenty of comforting psychological reasons for Mays to hold on to a religious worldview based on his family and cultural ties. However, not all black Americans who faced the same difficulties had faith in the notion of a just God or any god at all. In later years, Mays would learn of the atheism of those around him, a point of view he honestly acknowledged but rejected. He recalled a conversation with his wife's grandfather: "Grandfather Blount died at the age of ninety-two. He never joined the church because he did not believe that God exists. When I tried to get him to see that it was the justice of God that enabled him to escape slavery, he reminded me that many slaves, better men than he died in the system, and some slaves were killed." Blount pointedly told Mays, "If there is a God, He is not just!"[87]

Mays felt alienated, too, but, unlike Grandfather Blount, whose religious alienation stemmed from the slave experience, Mays's came from racial segregation. "I never felt completely at home in my native county," Mays wrote. "The experiences I had in my most impressionable years, hearing and seeing the mob, observing the way my people were treated, noting the way in which they responded to this treatment, never having developed any white friends in the county, and living all my years in a rented house—all this left me with a feeling of alienation from the county of my birth."[88]

Also unlike Grandfather Blount's experience, Mays's life was positively framed around a Christian point of view and the idea of a just God. He remained rooted in a faith tradition that some might have reasonably argued he should have abandoned since that same faith was being trounced by night-riding political terrorists in his own community. Nevertheless, he held fast to the faith his mother instilled.

Mays's formative years coincided with a highly transitory time for the nation and black Americans. "The sacred ideologies of the former slaves were being transformed by mobility, education, and 'Yankee' condescension," historian Lawrence Levine observes. "This transition in black life, in addition to the racial polarization occurring throughout the United States, opened up new values, with different ways of thinking that had not been available to the mass of slaves. These shifting sensibilities can be seen as black American folk religiosity moving away from a religiously focused agenda to one concerned about the material world."[89]

As Mays thought back to his parents' lives, notwithstanding their domestic struggles, he described them both as industrious and God-fearing people. To him, "the rugged honesty of [his] parents" was exemplary. "I am intolerant of dishonesty, particularly intellectual dishonesty," he wrote. "Wherein men ignore or distort the truth and plot to take advantage of others for their indulgence. My parents did little or no ethical philosophizing, but they *lived* their ideals of industry and honesty." They were his "living example" of integrity.[90] And it was in their weather-beaten home that he formed a deep inner consciousness that led him to wrestle with the social conditions that he faced.

Mays, like so many other rural black southerners, fled the South, at least temporarily in his case, to be free of the social debasement that the South's established economic and cultural order imposed upon his life. Yet with vividness he recalled the "thoroughfare connecting Greenwood and Saluda and other small towns" that ran past his childhood home as being both frightening and idyllic. It was on that road where trouble arose, such as the Phoenix riot. He recollected hearing the vicious whispers and drunken conversations of angry white men. "I trembled in my bed at night as white men passed by making the night hideous with their wild behavior," he penned. But the road was also warm and welcoming, a place along which black and white people stopped to "get fresh, cool water," even though white racial supremacy was maintained in the simplest act of drinking water. Little did he know then that this road, which held both joyful memories of swinging and playing on a large oak tree adjacent to his home and mournful ones of terrors in the night, would be the same one that would take him beyond South Carolina's riotous mobs, beyond the hangman's noose, and, most of all, beyond his childhood fear of dying at an early age.[91]

— 2 —

I Set Out to Learn How the Sixty-Six
Books of the Bible Were Produced

He who starts behind in the great race of
life must forever remain behind or run faster than the man in front.
—MAYS, *Quotable Quotes of Benjamin E. Mays*

"Beginning with my mother, my oldest sister, and my brothers and my other brothers and sisters who were sympathetic with my desire to learn and get an education, I have felt my indebtedness to people," Mays recollected at the age of eighty-seven. "Mother never went to school a day in her life," he penned, "but she prayed that God would help me in my ambition to go to school." He recalled that his oldest sister, Susie, fourteen years his senior, taught him to read and count and that his academic abilities quickly became a matter of familial pride. "The members of my family were proud of my learning ability and never expected me to use incorrect English, although I heard it in our home. I always felt that I had to do well for the family's sake." And though "the members of my family had not distinguished themselves in any art, profession, trade, or technology, and had accumulated no wealth," he reminisced, "I was proud of my family as if they had achieved some degree of fame or greatness."[1]

Mays spent his adolescent and young adult years struggling to attain formal education. He, like his slave forebears, linked education to political and personal freedom. For him, formal education was his sword in cutting through the web of social oppression that made his life's chances slim. He was unaware in his youth that his quest to be educated was a part of a much larger black intellectual tradition originating in the religion of slaves. Whether or not Mays was thinking about it at the time, he seemed to grasp that "literacy was more than a path to individual freedom." As historian Janet Duitsman Cornelius explains, "It was a communal act, a political demonstration of resistance to oppression and of self-determination for the black community." His view of education, which was conceived in the pews of Mount Zion, facilitated "a liberating consciousness." The first literacy goal in Mays's family was for him to be able to read the Bible. In the evangelical Christian tradition, of which Baptist beliefs

Benjamin and Susie Mays Glenn, ca. 1967. Courtesy of
the Moorland-Spingarn Research Center, Howard University.

are one derivation, all saved people were required to be conversant in the Bible.
But learning to read the Bible was not an end in itself. "The ability to read
the Bible," one scholar explains, "gave the reader the special mastery and control over this 'sacred text' essential to leadership in the black church. African-
Americans who could read were designated preachers by their own people as
religious authorities because they held the key to the Bible without having to
depend on whites to interpret Scriptures for them."[2] In pursuing an education,
Mays pursued authority and power to interpret the world around him free of
white bias. He was unaware in his youth that his quest to be educated was a part
of a much larger black intellectual tradition, a "Bible politics of literacy," found
in the rebelliousness of slave religion.[3]

The historian Carter G. Woodson, an older contemporary of Mays, also observed that the Negro church's "emphasis on the Bible unconsciously stimulated the efforts toward self-education." "Whether a Negro attended Sunday
school or not," Woodson explained,

he heard the minister read to him from the Bible two or three times
a week dramatic history, philosophical essays, charming poetry, and
beautiful oratory. Hearing these repeated again and again and under
circumstances securing undivided attention, he had many of these
precious passages sink into his heart like seed planted in fertile ground

to bring forth fruit fourfold. . . . Under the continuous instruction of the Negro preacher, who in expounding the Bible drew such striking figures and portrayed life, death, and the beyond in a dramatic fashion, the youth not only experienced the emotion so characteristic of the Negro communicant but his intellectual appetite was whetted with the desire to seek after the mysteries.[4]

The intellectual curiosity that the Bible stimulated when presented in this way had a profound impact on black cultural life. Woodson's passage above could serve well as an introduction to a description of Mays's formative years as a student. Mays's desire to seek an education beyond just a rudimentary one was also rooted in his communitarian understanding of religious uplift. All Protestants believed it was their religious responsibility to serve as moral exemplars and leaders on behalf of the disfranchised and the less fortunate and in community affairs. Gaining formal education, however, was just the first step in his own proverbial Exodus story.[5]

By 1902, at the age of eight, the year Mays became "marked" to preach, his promising intellect was already apparent. Each Sunday, he would walk the four miles to his church to attend Sunday school lessons. "Though preaching was one Sunday a month," Mays explained, "there was Sunday school every Sunday." In Sunday school there were no lessons planned by age groups, so he sat with adults, listening and commenting on the Bible lessons. He was also "marked" as a student by the time he began attending the Brickhouse School, a one-room schoolhouse that was "named after a large brick house, owned by a white man" who lived nearest to the school.[6] He recalled that in 1900 it "was a happy day for me when I entered the Brickhouse School at the age of six." His sister's tutoring at home gave him an academic advantage. Mays recalled his head start: "Since I was the only one in the beginners' class who could [recite my alphabet and count], I was praised and highly complimented by the surprised teacher." His teacher, Miss Ellen Waller, "*bragged*" about his abilities at Mount Zion. "The next church Sunday, the second Sunday in November," Mays recollected, "my teacher sought my parents and told them, with other people standing around, *Bennie is smart*." This confirmation of his intelligence was a boost. "From that moment on, I was the star of that one-room school. The experience made a tremendous impression on me, so much so that I felt that I had to live up to my teacher's expectation."[7]

Being affirmed intellectually at the Brickhouse School was exactly the intent of former slaves who founded it and schools like it across the South. "Former slaves conceived of the school, donated their churches to house it or built new cabins from scratch, provided fuel and paid tuition. Sometimes a freeperson even taught in the school until a better trained northerner arrived."[8] Though simple in construction and often designed with crude and rustic interiors, schools like Brickhouse were built by freepersons of color with hopes and expectations to nurture the intelligence and abilities of their own children. To the recently freed slave generation, the one-room schoolhouse was the gateway to a brighter future.[9]

Ellen Waller, the daughter of a well-off black farmer and Mays's first teacher, was not unique in her role. Black women eagerly served in these schools with a sense of missionary zeal to undo the ignorance that was a legacy of chattel slavery. Teachers like Waller were paid meager wages and subjected to the harshest scrutiny by the county government. Those who controlled the bureaucratic levers to enforce segregation attempted to starve the oxygen from the brains of black children, but these teachers persevered. For them, "teaching amounted to a political act."[10] When a black woman schoolteacher affirmed and encouraged a child's innate gifts, she was defying the powers of state-enforced subjugation.

Though the people of Mount Zion prophesied Mays's success and the Brickhouse School experience affirmed his innate intellectual talents, it was not readily apparent to Mays at the time that he would enjoy the kind of success that his community had predicted. The cotton field and the plow and the laws of inequality were ever before him. And it was those laws that had for many years determined the fate of the educational system and informed many rural black southerners' view of education. Hezekiah Mays was a case in point. "My greatest opposition to going away to school was my father," Mays explained. "When I knew that I had learned everything I could in the one-room Brickhouse School and realized how little that was, my father felt that this was sufficient—that it was all I needed." The senior Mays believed there was "only two honest occupations for Negro men—preaching and farming. My father must have repeated this dictum a thousand times. What did schooling have to do with farming? Would reading all the books in the world teach a man how to plant cotton and corn, gather the grain, and harvest the crop? Since my father saw no future for his sons except farming, education was not necessary." And what about young Mays being marked to preach? Education in his father's mind "was equally superfluous for the ministry. God *called* men to preach; and when He called them, He would tell them what to say!"[11]

Hezekiah Mays associated formal education with egotistical and dishonest behavior. "One of my cousins," Mays explained, "a bright sixth or seventh grade scholar who taught at one of the county schools for the miserably paid Negro teachers during that period, forged a note on a bank, skipped town, and was never caught." His father would always associate this cousin's dishonesty with his education. "Whenever I pressed my father about further schooling," Mays penned, "he would always remind me of what my cousin had done." According to Hezekiah Mays, "The more education, the bigger the fool and crook!"[12]

Mays had very little tolerance for his father's attitude toward education. The nearest educational institution to Epworth was the Brewer Normal, Industrial, and Agricultural School, which was modeled after Hampton and Tuskegee Institutes and supported by the American Missionary Association. Mays recollected that the majority of black students dropped out of Brewer.[13] However, it was nothing more than an elementary school with a grandiose name. The institution had a very limited effect on the black community of Greenwood County. Well-off, and perhaps well-educated, white farmers might have held fast to Jeffersonian ideals about the gentleman farmer, but those ideals were not a tenant farmer's reality, black or white. To Mays's father, eking out an existence by the sweat of one's brow was the only thing a man needed to know besides the Bible. Whatever rationale Hezekiah Mays held for his distrust of formal education, it was an indisputable wedge between him and his son.[14] When Mays looked back on those years, he remained steadfast in his sentiments that his father was "the chief obstruction" to his aspirations.

It was Mays's illiterate mother who intuitively understood and appreciated her son's driving ambition to educate himself beyond the confines of the Brickhouse School, even though she initially wanted him to stop his education at the eighth grade and become the teacher there.[15] She gave him two things: "her love and her prayers." The piety he learned from his mother continued to resonate with him in his teen years and fed his hopes. His recounting of his quest for education evokes the spirituality that infuses many slave narratives. "I prayed frequently as I worked in the field and many nights in the moonlight," he wrote. "I often plowed to the end of the row, hitched the mule to a tree, and went down into the woods to pray. On moonlight nights, I would leave the house and go into the fields to pray." His "prayers were all variations of the same theme: a petition to God to enable [him] to get away to school." Education was "a goal that drove and prodded [him], day and night. His prayers were filled with youthful exuberance. Often while praying, he mimicked "the older people" of his church asking God to remove "every *hindrance and cause*" that blocked his access to education. Looking back, Mays wryly conceded that if God had answered his prayers, his father would have been removed from his life.[16] Prayer had power when combined with action. For Mays, prayer gave him willpower and purposefulness.[17]

Ultimately, the Reverend James Marshall intervened on Mays's behalf and persuaded Mays's father to allow him to continue school. Marshall held a strong sway over the senior Mays. In 1886, after an earthquake, perhaps fearing divine retribution, one hundred men, including Hezekiah Mays, decided to be baptized by Marshall. This mass baptism extended Marshall's influence throughout the community and was helpful when he broached the subject about the young Mays's wish to leave home to attend another school.[18]

In 1909, when Mays was fifteen, his father allowed him to "go to a small Baptist Association School in McCormick, South Carolina."[19] The operation of the school was constrained by the agricultural cycle, which meant that he, like all black children growing up in a cotton region, could attend school only four months a year, from October to March, rather than the standard nine months. Similar to the Brickhouse School, the McCormick School was really ill-equipped to advance Mays's academic development and burgeoning intellect. Earning an eighth-grade education would have been sufficient for most people, whether black or white, in settling down into the cyclical routines of southern agrarian life, but Mays wanted more.[20] In fact, after attending the McCormick School for only two years, Mays was qualified to be a student teacher. He, however, wanted more for his life.

His desire for more education brought him into open disagreement with Reverend Marshall, whose hope for Mays was to teach at the McCormick School. Mays's refusal to return to McCormick severed the relationship between him and his childhood pastor. Marshall must have interpreted Mays's defiance as ingratitude because, after all, it was he who persuaded Mays's father to allow him to travel twenty-four miles from home to attend the school. Reverend Marshall did not understand Mays's inner ambition and drive. He almost certainly did not comprehend the yearning of a young man who plowed in the fields and prayed that God would remove *every cause and hindrance* before him, even if that meant defying his religious benefactor. It is certainly not uncommon for a young person to rebel against authority figures. What set Mays apart from other young, rebellious rural southern men during this time is that rather than defying his elders via drinking, sexual carousing, and fighting, he did so by pursuing a formal education. In the toiling agrarian environment of the rural South at that time, with its prohibitions against black social mobility, Mays's desire was both insubordinate and dangerous. And, in his father's parochial world, his son's desire seemed impractical since, in his view, a man in Mays's position should marry and plug away on the land until God called him home. For Mays, however, his devotion to education was tied to his path to both personal and civic freedom.[21]

He knew that the cycle of farm life—harnessing the mule-plow, planting, hoeing, and picking—dominated the lives of black people and interfered with his ambition to attain more education. To him, cotton continued to be the "mother of all poverty," and attending only four months of school annually was not sufficient to escape the cotton field. Therefore, Mays resisted his father's ignorance and his own self-doubts in order to continue his pursuits. As he explained, "When Father saw that I was determined to go to a better school and knew that I had to have money in order to do so, he angrily threw a ten-dollar bill at me. So I made my way to Orangeburg without Father's blessing but with my mother's prayers."[22] Perhaps Louvenia, acted on her prayers in ways Mays never knew. Maybe she determinedly goaded Hezekiah into begrudgingly giving her youngest child the ten dollars he needed to attend school.

Mays left his home in Epworth in the fall of 1911 and traveled to Orangeburg, South Carolina, to attend South Carolina State College. By the time Mays arrived, the college had been through several transitions. In 1872, during Reconstruction, the college was established by the state as part of Claflin University. It was to be known as the College of Agriculture and Mechanics' Institute for Colored Students. This small and fragile college was quickly thrown into the fray of South Carolina's post-Reconstruction politics in 1876 when Governor Wade Hampton replaced the college's politically appointed trustees for new ones. By 1895, Governor Benjamin Tillman had officially severed the school from Claflin University and renamed it the Colored Normal Industrial Mechanical College. This last incarnation of the college was made possible through a legislative appropriation of $5,000 a year for five years to erect buildings using convict laborers. What an irony: state-funded black higher education in South Carolina was founded on the backs of enforced labor of imprisoned black men. According to a historian of South Carolina, the Colored Normal Industrial Mechanical College, or State College, opened in the fall of 1896 "with faculty [that were] graduates of Howard, Harvard, Colgate, Oberlin and Lincoln Universities, West Point, Drew Theological Seminary, and Benedict College." Its course and departmental offerings were "college, normal, preparatory, model school, music, art, industrial mechanical and agricultural."[23] It is truly amazing that the college survived on the miserly yearly sum that the South Carolina legislators had budgeted for it.[24]

When Mays arrived on State College's campus, he found it to be a warm and affirming environment. It did his "soul good" to attend a school with "an all-Negro faculty and a Negro president." For Mays, this all-black faculty was an antidote to his political subjugation and feelings of inferiority. The college

Young Benjamin Mays and an unidentified friend, ca. 1912.
Courtesy of the Moorland-Spingarn Research Center, Howard University.

was a place for the restoration of pride and dignity for black people in a world where they were forced to be lowly, humble, and deferential. Like the teacher at the Brickhouse School, State's faculty encouraged Mays's aspirations and fueled his self-confidence. "The inspiration which I received at State College was and is of incalculable value," he wrote.[25] It affirmed his belief that black people, when given the opportunity, could be leaders in every kind of endeavor. He would remain forever loyal to his alma mater.[26]

During his first two years at State College, Mays reluctantly returned home at the end of February to assist his father with the planting, and his father begrudgingly aided him with his school fees. While Mays welcomed his father's financial aid, he felt that the long break he had to take to work on the farm interfered with studies. "I was vividly aware that time has swift wings," he wrote, and he had been unable "to remain in school more than four months in any year." So, in 1913, at age nineteen, when his father sent word for him to return home he "determined that—at whatever cost—[he] would remain at State for the full term." Initially, he sought help from his mathematics teacher, who wrote Hezekiah Mays asking him to let Benjamin finish the school year. Hezekiah refused, so Mays took matters upon himself: "I wrote Father explaining that I could never get anywhere if I continued to go to school only four months a year. I told him too, that I could not come home until school closed in May. So the break with my father came and it was final. I disobeyed him without regret and with no pangs of conscience." He added, "It was crystal clear to me that I must take my education into my own hands and that I could not and must not permit my father to dictate or determine my future." Hezekiah threatened Benjamin, informing him that he would send the sheriff to get him, "but fortunately he did not carry out his threat. Had he done so, [Mays] would have been compelled to go home."[27] He was on his own.

The fee to attend State College for a full nine months was $54, or $6 dollars a month. In order to secure his room and board, Mays borrowed $3 a month, for two months, from his brother John. To make the additional money he needed to earn during his first year, he worked cleaning campus outhouses at night. It was his good fortune during the following academic year that the Pullman Company came to State College recruiting porters. It was the Pullman Company that aided his exit strategy from the farm. When the Pullman Company offered him a job, he needed money to buy his uniform. Though it was a bit of a struggle, he eventually secured an $18 loan from his mathematics instructor, Professor Levister.[28] The $27.50 per month, plus tips, that he made over the summer was more than enough to cover his school fees and to buy clothes. The job changed his life.

While State College provided him a high school education, his job with the Pullman Company provided him with a different kind of education—worldly exposure. While it may be true that porters made themselves subservient in order to earn tips from white passengers, the Pullman Company, no matter how bad it was in hindsight, was one of the few avenues for young men like Mays to escape the drudgery of rural life.[29] The job, with all of its flaws and abuses, allowed him to earn enough money during the summers to continue his education. As a Pullman porter, he learned that racial discrimination had a northern version. In a layover in Detroit, he bought a drink in a restaurant; when he finished drinking from the glass, "the white waiter smashed it."[30] On these summer trips around the country, he watched, learned, and took stock of the things going on all around him.

In school, Mays once again demonstrated that he was the brightest in his class. He pursued his studies with ferocity and received the encouragement

Young Benjamin Mays dressed in a new suit and hat, ca. 1915.
Courtesy of the Moorland-Spingarn Research Center, Howard University.

of the faculty, especially from Professor Nelson C. Nix, one of Mays's most important teachers at State College. As he made clear, "I studied hard and long in high school, not because I had to in order to keep up with my classmates but because I really wanted to learn. I was aiming for something; I did not know what. Vaguely, yet ardently, I longed to *know*, for I sensed that knowledge could set me free."[31] Mays recalled that his drive and ambition was unique among his classmates. He described them as being academically slothful, but one can detect a bit of smart-kid jealousy in his intolerance of typical high school behavior. "The boys," he wrote, "had their minds on the girls; the girls had their minds on the boys. The boys would sit on campus looking at their girlfriends for hours at a time; and for hours at a time the girls would parade the campus, the better to be looked at." With some disdain he observed, "Study or no study, however, most of them passed their work." He also recalled that the few students who did apply themselves were considered "*bookworms*."[32]

The truth of the matter was, State was financially starved by the state legislature and dependent on tuition and fees, so the administrators and teachers were economically tied into a system that did not give them the luxury to turn away students who could afford to pay. Students like Mays, therefore, were a delight for the State College faculty to teach.

The flaws of its student body notwithstanding, the college provided Mays a more expansive social life and contacts. At school he met some equally ambitious, talented men and women who became a part of a lifelong social network.[33] And more importantly, he met his first love, a fellow student named Ellen Harvin. Tenderly he wrote, "Ellen was the kind of girl who could understand a boy like me—lured by a dream, driven to try to accomplish something worthwhile in life." By the time they graduated from State, they were engaged. The couple married four years later, because Mays was resolute that he did not want to get married before he completed college, and Harvin agreed.[34]

In 1916, just a few months shy of turning twenty-two and with his mother there to see him, Mays graduated from State College, once again at the top of his class as its valedictorian. In the unsophisticated world of the black South, Mrs. Mays's presence at her son's graduation was no small feat. With pride Mays mused over that day: "It was a great thing for me to have my mother at my high school graduation. Orangeburg was 125 miles away from Ninety Six, and this was the farthest she had ever traveled up to that time. She saw in my graduation an answer to her prayers." She beamed with pride as he gave the valedictory address, "Watch the Leaks." His father did not attend graduation, and this would turn out to be the only graduation of his that his mother would attend.[35] But God had answered her and her boy's prayers.

That fall, Mays entered Virginia Union University in Richmond. Virginia Union had been founded in 1899, after being reorganized with other Baptist-affiliated institutions for black women and men.[36] He settled on Virginia Union after failing to be admitted to a boarding school so that he could attend an Ivy League college. One of his State College instructors, F. Marcellus Staley, a Morehouse graduate, persuaded Mays that Virginia Union would be a good choice. Virginia Union, under the leadership of George Rice Hovey, had grown steadily. Despite pressures by philanthropic foundations to change to a more "practical curriculum," it kept true to a classical liberal arts curriculum.[37] Mays "took college mathematics, English, German, and Latin" there. Although the school was considered good for a Negro college, in Mays's mind it was not good enough. "I enjoyed my year at Virginia Union," he wrote, "and left only because I was determined to go to a New England College."[38] He wanted to compete with the best students, which he believed were at the New England colleges.

Mays enrolled at Bates College in Lewiston, Maine, in 1917. "My mathematics teacher, Ronald A. [Wakefield] and Charles E. Hadley, the YMCA faculty adviser, learning of my desire to study in New England, they wrote to President George Colby Chase of Bates in my behalf. As a result, I was accepted as a sophomore on probation, with the understanding that if I did passing work in the first six weeks' I would be a full-fledged sophomore. I passed my tests successfully."[39] Since we do not have Wakefield's or Hadley's letters, we do not know why the two men decided to assist him, but it is likely that Mays shared his dream with them and pressed them to come to his aid.[40] In the 1966 Bates College bulletin, Mays wrote that his status anxiety and sense of inferiority were behind his desire to go to New England: "After graduating from high school as valedictorian of my class . . . I thought I would go north for college where I could compete with whites. Then, I had the erroneous belief that the 'Yankee' was superior to the southern white man. So, I said to myself, I will go to New England and compete with the 'Yankee.' If I do well there that would be convincing proof that Negroes are not inferior to white men."[41]

As were many New England colleges, Bates was initially founded to prepare men for the clergy.[42] By the First World War, the college had become coed, training Christian men and women.[43] The college continued to hold on to its Baptist heritage through regular chapel services, YMCA, YWCA, and a strong religion department. By the time Mays entered the college in 1917, it was a four-year liberal arts college that instructed students in classical languages (Greek and Latin) and spoken European languages. Other courses taught ancient and European history, rhetoric, literature, religion, philosophy, mathematics, and the physical sciences. While classical liberal arts dominated the college curriculum, the social sciences became increasingly important areas of study.[44] Although Christianity played a vital role in campus life at Bates, the college had begun a gradual shift toward becoming a nonsectarian institution of higher education.[45]

Mays arrived at Bates contemplating a career as a Baptist clergyman, a profession that he felt a calling to and one he believed would give him the status to become a leader in the black community. Although he seriously contemplated other professional academic careers—in philosophy and mathematics—he chose the ministry, with the encouragement of his fiancé, Ellen Harvin.[46] It would be Mays's good fortune that Bates College had a progressive and abolitionist history and willingly opened its doors to black students.[47]

When Mays arrived at Bates, he desperately needed money to pay for his education. He recalled arriving at Bates with "$90—about $300 less than I needed to make it through the year."[48] In order to both earn scholarship money and establish a good reputation on campus, Mays entered the sophomore declamation contest. When he walked onto the Bates campus, his oral communication skills and experience were extensive. He had previously won two speaking prizes at State College and was a member of the debate team at Virginia Union. Over the summer he became enamored with Daniel Webster's "The Supposed Speech of John Adams." All summer long he had "rehearsed [the speech] before the mirror of a Pullman car on the New York Central Railroad." When he arrived in Lewiston, Mays asked for help preparing for the contest from Mrs. Fred Pomeroy, the wife of the chair of the biology department, who instructed students in speech and drama. With her assistance, he rehearsed his speech to perfection, and his hard work paid dividends. He defeated his five white competitors. His victory helped him to establish himself as a formidable and respected student on campus.[49]

"The Supposed Speech of John Adams," which Mays said "mightily impressed" him, was an oration taken from *McGuffey's Fifth Eclectic Reader*,[50] a textbook with which many school-aged children of the era would have been familiar.[51] In the postemancipation world that Mays was born into, as cultural historian Richard Mosier explains, "young black children were inducted in the mysteries of *McGuffey's Eclectic Readers* and similar textbooks." The readers promoted the idea of a society in which "no one had to be poor, in which there was no need to fail, in which all could be successful. . . . [Students] were taught by teachers who agreed with Ralph Waldo Emerson that 'The reason why this man or that man is fortunate . . . lies in the man,' and who constantly reaffirmed the central political symbols of individualism and the triumph of Will."[52]

According to the *McGuffey's Reader*, Daniel Webster originally gave the speech as he imagined John Adams giving it in defense of the Declaration of Independence and the American Revolution. It begins: "Sink or swim, live or die, survive or perish, I give my hand and my heart to this vote. It is true, indeed, that, in the beginning, we aimed not at independence. But *there's a divinity that shapes our ends*." This final quote from Shakespeare's *Hamlet*, act 5, scene 2, is the apogee of the speech. It gives notice that the break from England is decisive. The metaphysical force that drives the revolutionaries to break from the mother country cannot be resisted, even if it means risking death. In the age of Jim Crow, Mays's dramatic rendition of the speech was an act of defiance. Imagine Mays reciting this passage in particular:

> Sir, I know the uncertainty of human affairs, but I see—I see clearly through this day's business. You and I, indeed, may rue it. We may not live to see the time this declaration shall be made good. We may die; die colonists; die slaves; die, it may be, ignominiously and on the scaffold. Be it so: be it so. If it be the pleasure of Heaven that my country shall require the poor offering of my life, the victim shall be ready at the appointed hour of sacrifice, come when that hour may. But while I do live, let me have a country, or at least the *hope* of a country, and that a FREE *country*.[53]

He must have been captivating. The speech rings with the powerful assertion of liberty above all else. Delivered by a twenty-three-year-old black southerner in front of an all-white New England audience, the speech was an affirmation of Mays's own right to live in the world free of American tyranny. "Sir," Mays continued, "before God I believe the hour is come. My judgment approves the measure, and my whole heart is in it. All that I have, and all that I am, and all that I hope in this life, I am now ready here to stake upon it; and I leave off as I began, that, live or die, survive or perish, I am for the Declaration. It is my living sentiment, and, by the blessing of God, it shall by my dying sentiment; independence *now* and INDEPENDENCE FOREVER."[54] In making this speech, Mays confirmed himself as an intellectual partisan in the American revolutionary tradition; a tradition he believed arose out of the decisive actions of heroic individuals. In later years, the actions of heroic individuals would hold a significant place in his thinking.[55] Themes echoing from this speech would become familiar tropes throughout his years of public speaking.

Winning the declamation contest established Mays as one of the brightest students on campus and also provided him an opportunity to join the Bates debate team.[56] "My victory in the declamation contest . . . attracted the attention of A. Craig Baird, professor of English and Debating Coach," Mays recalled. "The same afternoon I won first prize in the contest, Professor Baird visited my room to urge me to try out for the debate team."[57] According to scholar Robert Branham, Professor Baird began teaching at Bates in 1913, after he completed "his divinity studies at Union Theological Seminary, where his instructors in speaking included Henry Sloane Coffin and the great preacher Harry Emerson Fosdick." In preparing his students, writes Branham, "Baird insisted that debate was the art of *selling ideas* and propagating the *social gospel* to make truth prevail." In his sophomore year, Mays was in Baird's English class, where he was instructed in argumentation and debate. Bates professor Trufant Foster had established this course in argumentation in 1901. "Mays read Foster's landmark textbook, *Argumentations and Debate*, in English III," Branham notes, "supplemented by materials written or provided by Baird. He also read Baird's *Outline of Argumentation and Debate Prepared for Students in Bates College.*" Baird's *Outline* was particularly significant for Mays in its treatment of racial topics. For example, "all Bates sophomores were required to read and discuss Moorfield Storey's [one of the white founders of the NAACP] essay on the 'The Negro Problem.'" In addition, students in the class had to "analyze Lincoln's refutation of the Dred Scott decision and [Frederick] Douglass' claim that the Declaration of Independence [did] not include black Americans." In Baird's outline "the appeal of prejudice" was considered a "fallacious method of *ignoratio elenchi*, or 'ignoring the question.'" What must have been most heartening for Mays was "Baird's illustration of the 'chain of reasoning' [that began] with the premise that 'All Negroes are men.'" English III was a required course for Bates students, and Baird's lessons taught students "to question generalizations, to demand and scrutinize evidence, to seek common ground, and to equip themselves for moral suasion."[58] Mays took these lessons to heart, and they served him well in his career as a preacher and teacher.

For Mays, being a Baptist at Bates was a shade different than being one in the South. In South Carolina, Mays was taught to interpret the Bible literally and that it was unfaithful to question any part of it.[59] It is important to understand that the Bible was ubiquitous in American life. Biblical references were used in public speeches and sermons, drawn upon for popular books, and inscribed on public buildings and monuments.[60] Many white religious leaders based their view of the inferiority of black people on the Curse of Ham, the story in the book of Genesis.[61] For black Americans, the Bible provided both liberationist motifs and a justification to submit to the prevailing social order. For Mays, the

Bible had to be intellectually reckoned with if the faith of his mother was going to be meaningful to him.

At Bates, Mays became exposed to a critical and historical examination of the Bible and Christian doctrine. One of the first books that Mays read as a philosophy major was James Stalker's *The Life of Christ*.[62] Stalker's pithy volume was the primary text used in Mays's Christian ethics course. The work complemented his instruction in his English III class, with its emphasis on moral reasoning and Christian thinking. What is interesting about this volume is that it portrays the life of Jesus as heroic. This introductory volume raised all the important issues germane to the debate surrounding the historical and cultural context of Jesus's life. It was written from the perspective of the Protestant Reformation, deemphasizing the central Roman Catholic doctrines on the saints and the mysteries of the mass.[63]

Stalker portrays Jesus as a powerfully sincere country boy from the backwaters of Galilee who emerged from obscurity to become a radical rabbinical preacher.[64] Stalker's Jesus is the assured debater and logician who confronted Roman power through its surrogates among Jerusalem's elite.[65] These parties carried out Jesus's execution through a conspiracy. The execution of Jesus was not the end of his life, and, according to Stalker, the resurrection of Jesus as proclaimed by Christians, though central to the faith, was more symbolic than real. The disciples claimed that Jesus's resurrection was debatable as a fact, but what was incontestable to Stalker was "the fact that suddenly they had become courageous, hopeful, believing, wise, possessed with noble and reasonable views of the world's future, and equipped with resources sufficient to found the Church, convert the world, and establish Christianity in its purity among men."[66] According to him what made Jesus the Christ, is this:

> But the most important evidence of what He was is to be found neither in the general history of modern civilization nor in the public history of the visible Church, but in the experiences of the succession of genuine believers who with linked hands stretch back to touch Him through the Christian generations. The experience of myriads of souls, redeemed by Him from themselves and from the world, proves that history was cut in twain by the appearance of a Regenerator, who was not a mere link in the chain of common men, but One whom the race could not from its own resources have produced—the perfect Type, the Man of men. . . . The experience of myriads of minds, rendered blessed by the vision of a God who to the eye purified by the Word of

Christ is so completely Light that in Him there is no darkness at all, proves that the final revelation of the Eternal to the world has been made by One who knew Him so well that he could not Himself have been less than Divine.[67]

These ideas would find their way into Mays's preaching in later years.

Mays received even more critical insight in courses he took in the Department of Biblical Literature and Religion, headed by Professor Herbert Purinton.[68] Purinton was a professor at Bates for thirty-eight years, and his field of study was biblical literature, a subject on which he authored three books, *The Achievement of the Master* (co-authored with Sadie Brackett Costello, 1926), *The Achievement of Israel* (1927), and *Literature of the Old Testament* (1930).[69] Purinton's department offered courses in the literary interpretation of the Bible, comparative history of ancient religions, and textual biblical criticism, all of which put Bates in the mainstream of academic Protestant liberalism.[70]

Here began Mays's introduction to the sociohistorical biblical studies of Shirley Jackson Case. Case—who later supervised Mays's master's thesis at the University of Chicago—had been Purinton's colleague at the Cobb Divinity School at Bates College in 1907–8, and the two had a lasting friendship throughout their professional careers.[71] Case's New Testament scholarship promoted a critical examination of the environmental factors that helped shape Christianity and influenced Christian writings. Of particular interest to Case, as well as other scholars of this generation, was locating the authentic historical context of Jesus.

The critical academic methodology was helpful to Mays as he attempted to make sense of Christianity as a faith in the modern world. Protestant liberals of this period diverged into two camps in terms of how they related "biblical faith to modern culture"—one evangelical and the other modernist. According to Kenneth Cauthen, evangelical liberals "were searching for a theology which could be believed by intelligent moderns."[72] Evangelical liberals considered themselves to be in continuity with historical faith in placing emphasis on the person and work of Jesus as the Christ, whereas the modernists were in less continuity with the historic faith. Nevertheless, Cauthen adds, they both "believed that there were elements in the Christian tradition which ought to be retained. However, the standard by which the abiding values of Christianity of the past were to be measured was derived from the presuppositions of modern science, philosophy, psychology and social thought. Nothing was to be believed simply because it was to be found in the Bible or Christian tradition."[73] The Religion Department at Bates was evangelically liberal.

Bates also introduced Mays to the Social Gospel movement, which had two main features. First, it was an influential movement within American Protestant churches whose impetus came through home mission societies beginning in the Reconstruction South.[74] This movement, guided by Christian beliefs, tried to positively socialize rural and industrial America by creating historically black colleges in the South—such as Virginia Union College—and, later, by developing settlement houses in northern industrial cities. Social gospel leaders included Jane Adams in Chicago and Booker T. Washington in Tuskegee. And it was promoted by religious organizations such as the worldwide YMCA and the YWCA.

Second, the Social Gospel movement espoused a specific set of theological notions that were formally elaborated upon in colleges, universities, and seminaries by a variety of scholars. One of the central thinkers to this movement was Walter Rauschenbusch, a Baptist clergyman and theologian.[75] Rauschenbusch believed that Christians could not be passive agents in the social order but should promote the teachings of Jesus.[76] He believed that the essential teachings of Jesus were not simply for the good of individual piety but for the good of society as a whole. The hellish conditions in which the urban poor dwelt were the result not of individual sinfulness but of the sins of society.

This kind of formally explicated religious perspective was quite liberating for an individual who came of age during Jim Crow's cruelest days. In the first instance, Rauschenbusch's approach to theology gave words to Mays's own disagreement with the conforming theology of his rural church, which he believed accommodated itself to the evil brutalities of segregated society of rural South Carolina. Secondly, the ethics of the Social Gospel held some affinities with the nonracial ethics of the Afro-Baptist tradition that he had learned both at church and at home. Mays's formative religious ethics held that everyone was equal in the eyes of God. This had been underscored by his mother's teachings. Mays always held on to his mother's belief about the equality of persons before God as counter to the racist image he received in the wider society. This principle of nonracialism grew out of the tradition of the black Christian's adherence to the "biblical doctrine of the parenthood of God and the kinship of all peoples."[77] In the context of racial oppression, this principle served as a point of criticism for a racially skewed interpretation of Christian doctrine. Thirdly, Rauschenbusch's theology offered a corrective to the singular emphasis in Baptist theology of individualistic piety and conversion as the most important act of Christian life. Rauschenbusch's emphasis on the Christian responsibility to society as whole was significant in Mays's thinking. If there is an irony in Mays's affinity for Rauschenbusch, it is that Rauschenbusch, the pastor to largely European immigrants, had very little to say about the sins of racial exclusion in the United States. Nevertheless, Rauschenbusch's ideas had given him at least a partial framework for theological thinking about Christianity and challenging racial exclusion.

Mays was also attracted to the Social Gospel movement's ideas of masculinity and manhood. The Social Gospel movement was theologically representative of larger cultural shifts surrounding manhood and power in an age of imperialism. Being Christian was the opposite of being feminine, which was gentle and soft; religion was brawny and muscular. "The Jesus of the Social Gospel was a reformer whose service, sacrifice, and love did not dissuade him from manly assertion," observes religious historian Susan Curtis. "Jesus affirmed the social ideal and freed men from the unrealistic psychological burden of individual success and salvation, but he was not effeminate."[78] For Mays, the idea of a manly and principled Jesus countered the image of his father being forced to kowtow to angry white men and seeded his theological imagination. His Jesus would help him fight back against the kind of emasculation that his father had experienced.

Finally, the Social Gospel allowed Mays to consider "the just society." It was in this period that Eugene Debs's rhetoric on socialist and Christian ideas had a significant impact on his thinking. He was committed to Debs's idea that "as long as there is a lower class, I'm in it. As long as there is a man in jail, I am not free."[79]

By the time Mays graduated from Bates, he had been enmeshed in theological liberalism. He did not view this as a form of heterodoxy and unfaithfulness.[80] Liberal theology provided him an intellectual and ethical framework for his Christian thinking and activism. Years later, as the president of Morehouse College, Mays would demonstrate his continued links to the Social Gospel by editing the first anthology of Rauschenbusch's writings.[81] By this time, Mays had also begun to solidify his intellectual understanding of the social character of Christianity and had historicized the Bible. At Bates he not only proved himself equal to his white peers, but he also began to craft a formal theological critique of racism.

Though the course work was inspiring for Mays, Bates College was not a place free of racism. For example, he was excluded from some debate team meets, and on one occasion a fellow student called him nigger without redress. Physical threats against black students became a distinct possibility when the motion picture *Birth of a Nation*, which portrayed the Ku Klux Klan as American heroes against rapacious blacks in the Reconstruction South, was shown in Lewiston. All of these events pained him. Bates College could not shield its few black students from the demoralization that blatant racism caused. He endured—by developing a fortress-like mentality and by inwardly steeling himself to cope with the never-ending disgraces heaped upon him. The legal and cultural apartheid that existed in the United States came in varying degrees, depending on the locale, but no place was free of it entirely. Lewiston was better than Epworth, but there was no real refuge for a black student to escape the constancy of racial animus and bigotry. Nevertheless, in this small college affiliated with the Northern Baptist Church and rooted in a New England abolitionist heritage, there was still enough room for a young man like Mays to grow intellectually and gain confidence.[82] "Bates College did not 'emancipate' me," Mays wrote. "It did the far greater service of making it possible for me to emancipate myself, to accept with dignity my own worth as a free man."[83] At the end of his time at Bates College, he once again graduated in the top tier of his class and was later inducted into the Phi Beta Kappa Society.

Although Mays's experience at Bates College was personally liberating, it was also formative in his social class sensibility. His success at Bates reshaped his social outlook. He was no longer the country boy; he was an educated and socialized middle-class man. His bourgeois outlook and Christian convictions ran seamlessly together for him. His responsibility as a college-educated man, inspired by religious conviction, was to uplift his people.[84] He remained rooted in a black communitarian tradition. Mays owed a debt to his family members and the community to which he felt intimately tied by circumstances of birth and ongoing struggle.

When Mays left Bates, he wrestled with the question of how to make his burgeoning ideas relevant to black people. He would have to figure out how to fuse theological modernism with his formative theological experience rooted in the rich traditions and folk culture of slave religion. Reading, debating, speaking, and studying classical texts in Greek and Latin at Bates had given him vital insights into the complexity of the world he inhabited. Bates was at a turning point in his life. From his college experience he took with him a belief that Christianity was not merely an opiate but socially relevant. He also left the college believing that the Christian experience was intelligible to the modern mind. Especially important was his recognition that the Bible could be studied, reflected upon, and explained historically. This new way of understanding the Bible was critical to him. The Bible, which served as one of the central texts in black American culture, needed to be understood and explained in a way that was meaningful and gave power to the black struggle. Behind his quest for a formal education was the knowledge that his ability to understand the context in which people lived during biblical times would help him counter the gross

Benjamin Mays (third row, second from right) pictured with honor students,
Bates College class of 1920. Courtesy of the Moorland-Spingarn
Research Center, Howard University.

distortions and manipulations of biblical texts regarding human dignity and freedom. In this regard, Mays agreed with James Stalker's insight that

[t]here is no power whose attraction is more unfailing than that of the eloquent word. Barbarians listening to their bards and story-tellers, Greeks, listening to the restrained passion of their orators, and matter-of-fact nations like the Romans have alike acknowledged its power to be irresistible. The Jews prized it above almost every other attraction, and among the figures of their mighty dead revered none more highly than the prophets—those eloquent utterers of the truth, whom Heaven had sent them from age to age. . . . Jesus also was recognized as a prophet, and accordingly, His preaching created widespread excitement.[85]

Mays realized that to preach liberation there needed to be a new biblical interpretation that could mobilize black communities to take action against Jim Crow's enforced apathy.

It was during his senior year at Bates that his desire to be ordained as a Baptist clergyman was confirmed. In order to fulfill his sense of calling, he decided to pursue graduate studies in religion. After having been refused admittance to Newton Theological Seminary because he was black, he was admitted to the University of Chicago Divinity School with the help of its dean, Shailer Mathews, and Professor Purinton.[86]

Having acquired the base of a formal intellectual framework in which to understand his Christian faith, he was more convinced than ever that Christianity was a faith that affirmed the individual's dignity and supported the idea of a just democratic social order. This explains why he claimed he never was shocked at the liberal theology of the University of Chicago.[87] "I never set out to be an educator," Mays said in a 1982 interview. "I went to the University of Chicago, not because I was going to learn how to preach. I went to the University of Chicago because I like their philosophy, that if you can interpret anything in the Bible[,] you need to know the political, social and economic conditions in which it was written." "Even coming from an orthodox faith," he concluded. "I set out to, I mean at Chicago, to learn how to understand how each of the 66 books in the [B]ible were produced."[88]

Bates had prepared Mays well for graduate study in theology, and Chicago was the next step in his intellectual journey. For Mays, the Bible would never again be a tool to justify the oppression of black people or make them docile. Racist biblical interpretations of the Bible would no longer hold credence.[89] His academic achievement would rebuff and defy the great "social sin" of racial exclusion. His insight into the ways of engaging the evils of racism were years away from being fully matured, but at this point, he had attained a sense of self-assuredness and self-confidence that enabled him to stand up for what he believed in. His arduous educational journey up to this point had also validated his youthful intuition and inchoate theological conviction that personal and political freedom and formal education were inextricably bound together.

In Search of a Call

To be able to stand the troubles of life, one must have a sense of
mission and the belief that God sent him or her into the world for a purpose,
to do something unique and distinctive; and that if he does not do it,
life will be worse off because it was not done.
—MAYS, *Quotable Quotes of Benjamin E. Mays*

An interviewer once posed a question to Mays concerning his choice to become an "educator" rather than be a full-time clergyman. Mays responded, "As a rule . . . I don't think there are many people who chart their course precisely."[1] This was certainly true for him. His career began inauspiciously after graduating from Bates. From 1920 until 1930 he lived a picaresque life in the sense that he moved through various jobs trying to gain status and prominence and a position to exercise his ministry.

Mays's decision to accept his calling as a Baptist clergyman was not simple. Ever ambitious, he did not want to be an ordinary black clergyman. Among many evangelical Protestants it was not necessary to have studied at a Bible college or seminary or to have earned a degree, let alone an advanced degree. If a congregation accepted an individual's calling to the ministry, their acceptance was sufficient acknowledgment that the call was legitimate. A larger association or denominational body endorsed calls in most instances following a local congregation's approval. However, not all calls were endorsed, and many times charismatic religious leaders formed their own congregations and denominations. This made Protestant ministry, especially among independent Baptists, highly competitive and required that ministers be skillful organizers and political tacticians. It also gave black Protestant congregants a means of choosing their own leadership outside the standards of what white or black middle-class deemed respectable. A minister's status in the black Baptist churches was more likely to be determined by skillful oration, showmanship, and a mass following. This is not to say that black Baptists were not concerned about issues of church doctrine; they were. Although these ministers guided their churches under Baptist rules and tenets, they were nevertheless often wily, shrewd, and sometimes Machiavellian, a point that Mays never forgot about his childhood minister, Reverend Marshall.

Mays faced two impediments to his ministerial aspirations. The first was his social status within his denomination. As a rural southerner, even one with a college degree, he had no standing in the growing number of churches in the cities to which black people migrated in large numbers. It might have been possible for him to have apprenticed in a large city church, provided a pastor was willing to nurture the ambitions of a potential rival. Black Baptist ministers who secured large economically stable congregations in cities jealously guarded their pulpits from young upstarts, who, with the right amount of charisma, might siphon off a significant number of congregants to form a rival congregation. Second, leadership within black Baptist congregations was often a family affair, that is, apprentice positions were open most often only to the sons (or sons-in-law) of ministers who were routinely groomed to succeed their fathers.[2] In addition, if Mays was fortunate enough to secure such a position, it would have been part-time, which would not have given him enough money to attend school. His best option after graduating from Bates, then, was going directly to graduate school.[3]

When Mays graduated from college, his plate was full; he needed to earn money to marry and support his fiancé, Ellen Harvin, start graduate school at the University of Chicago, and financially assist his parents. In August of 1920, Mays married Harvin in Newport News, Virginia, and then returned to South Carolina to visit his parents after a three-year absence. His vocational plans, with the encouragement of Ellen, were progressing along steadily. After he and his new bride visited his parents in the first weeks of September, he planned to work until the end of December. He intended to save his tips and wages to help pay his University of Chicago tuition. He would not anticipate the employment difficulties he would encounter.

Mays's employment record as a Pullman porter in the fall of 1920 was a living testimony to why the Brotherhood of Sleeping Car Porters (BSCP), the product of the successful unionization effort led by A. Philip Randolph and Milton P. Webster, was needed.[4] In November 1920, he and his fellow porters became fed up with the arbitrary employment rules of the Pullman Company and demanded pay equity. For example, as Mays explained, "It was customary not to pay a porter when he was being held for service in his home district."[5] That is, although the home porters were on call, they were not being paid. However, if a porter whose home station was New York was laid over in Boston, he would receive pay. Porters like Mays, who were "not regularly in the employ of the Pullman Company[,] resented this partiality." Pullman officials took economic advantage of these workers "by detaining their own men for special service while giving [regular] assignments to porters from other districts." In the case of the Boston layovers, the porters whose home base was Boston, Mays

Benjamin Mays and Ellen Harvin Mays, ca. 1921.
Courtesy of the Moorland-Spingarn Research Center, Howard University.

included, were held to guarantee that there would be enough porters to service the returning train passengers attending the Yale-Harvard football game in mid-November.

The Boston porters protested this inequity. Acting in concert, Mays explained, "a group of us decided to make our own time slips and sent a letter to the Pullman superintendent in Chicago explaining the situation and requesting pay for the week." The Chicago headquarters of the Pullman Company authorized the payment, but since Mays was the only college-educated porter to be a signatory of the letter to Chicago, he was suspected of organizing "the appeal" and then watched closely by the Boston office.[6] No one was fired, though, because the porters acted collectively and stuck together. With this tension in the air, it was only a matter of time before a clash would occur between Mays and his immediate supervisor. In December, he had a run in with a Pullman conductor over what appeared on the surface to be a simple miscommunication. Yet in a world orbiting on an axis of white male supremacy any misunderstanding between a black subordinate and a white superior was called insubordination. In Mays's case, the issue at hand was his initiative. He had efficiently cleaned up his sleeping car, and when his passenger departed he allowed another passenger to have the berth. When he consulted his conductor about the matter, the conductor told Mays that he had no room for another passenger. When Mays explained the situation and diagramed it for the conductor, the situation turned ugly. Taken aback by Mays's nondeferential attitude, the conductor began using profane language, and Mays in turn used "hot words." Mays had violated Jim Crow etiquette, and he was immediately dismissed.[7] His Pullman employment card read that he was "defiant and used profane language."[8]

This loss of employment put him in a quandary. He needed to save his money in order to visit his new wife over the Christmas holiday, but he also needed to the money to secure his start at Chicago. Mays's solution was to use his knowledge of the Pullman system and the assistance of his fellow porters to stowaway on various trains across the country from Boston to reach Chicago. He arrived just in time for registration.[9] This daring journey—the kind one is likely to read about in a slave narrative—demonstrated not only the collective savvy of the Pullman porters but also Mays's indefatigable determination. Arriving in Chicago with just $43 in his pocket, he registered for his classes and immediately got a job washing dishes.

Swift Hall, the famed building that houses Chicago's Divinity School, had not been built when Mays arrived on campus. What was firmly in place in Chicago, however, were Jim Crow's cultural customs. The University of Chicago was never known for its racial inclusiveness, but it did provide opportunity for exceptional black talent. The first time Mays ventured to the city was in 1919, shortly after the catastrophic race riot.[10] After visiting the university's campus, he wrote to a friend telling her that he would be a student there one day. His dream of attending the university, which had been instilled in him by his teacher Nelson Nix at State, had finally become a reality.[11] The university, he found, was welcoming in terms of being a student in a classroom, but everything else about the Southside campus, from housing to socialization, was racially segregated. "I found more prejudice at the University of Chicago and in the city of Chicago than I found at Bates and in the city of Lewiston,"

Mays later wrote. Wherever white southern students gathered north of the Mason-Dixon Line, racial demarcations had to be assiduously adhered to. "Most Southern students, and some Northern students, would not eat at the same table with Negroes." Since the university had cafeteria-style service in the Commons on a first-come, first-served basis, this caused many students, who were fearful of contacts with black students, a degree of consternation. "[We] took great pleasure in plaguing [them] by deliberately seating ourselves at a table where some white person had fled to escape eating with Negroes," Mays wrote. "I recall one man who moved three times to avoid the Negro students, who we followed from table to table, and finally, with ill-concealed disgust, he left without finishing his meal."[12] Although racial discrimination in Chicago was not as horrid as in South Carolina, being black was nevertheless troublesome. Even his professors had to be confronted publicly in order to acknowledge black students outside the classroom.

Mays lived on campus during his first three quarters at the Divinity School. During the summer quarter, he and Ellen were able to live off campus together as a married couple and as fellow students. Ellen was enrolled at the university as a special student.[13] Living with Ellen must have been a joy for him since she had remained in South Carolina teaching during their engagement.[14]

In the spring of 1921, the president of Morehouse College, John Hope, visited Chicago on a faculty recruitment trip. His visit came at the right time for Mays.[15] Hope had kept track of him since Mays had been at State and had followed his accomplishments at Bates. Hope spent a great deal of his time on the road fund-raising and personally recruiting qualified black faculty for Morehouse. Mays was flattered to have such a prominent black leader seek him out personally.[16] Hope recruited him to teach mathematics for the sum of $1,200 on an eight-month contract. Even though Mays's specialization was New Testament and theological studies, Hope needed the best-qualified college graduates to teach a variety of subjects.[17]

Mays was initially hesitant to leave Chicago before completing his master's degree, but, since he was married, the salary offer loomed large in his mind. His initial wariness about going to Atlanta waned, as he and Ellen desired more time together. The more they thought about it, the more Hope's offer appealed to them. She would return to her position teaching at Morris College, and they could visit each other by train more easily on the weekends. Mays made one more calculation in regard to taking the job at Morehouse. He knew that Hope was well connected, which would be helpful to him as he advanced his career. A letter from Hope could open doors for him.

Even though Mays had secured a job, financial worries continued to plague him. He needed money to get to Atlanta to buy necessities and a wedding ring for his wife.[18] He did not want to compromise his independence by borrowing money from his new employer. Using the network of black migrants from South Carolina in Chicago, he found a local lawyer from whom he could secure a loan so that he could purchase a train ticket to Atlanta, buy some clothes, and purchase a wedding ring for Ellen. At the close of the summer quarter of 1921, Mays and Ellen returned to the South, he to Atlanta and she to Sumter. When he arrived in Atlanta, he had no clue that he would stay there for three years. His intent was to teach at Morehouse for only one year and earn enough money to return to his graduate studies.

In Atlanta, as elsewhere in the South, segregation appeared as though it would never be breached.[19] Yet behind the shroud of segregation, there was a vibrant black world. By the turn of the twentieth century, Atlanta had a sizable black population that supported thriving black businesses, churches, fraternal organizations, and benevolent societies.[20] Black Atlanta boomed throughout the 1920s; as young rural dwellers migrated into the city with hopes of a better life, they found an already tight housing market even more constricted by their rising numbers.[21] Harsh work conditions and poverty were ever present, but there was also a richness that blacks infused into their everyday living, full of drama, laughter, entertainment, and tragedy.[22] Mays, however, never wrote of the joys of Atlanta in the 1920s. For him, Atlanta was the urban counterpart to rural South Carolina; "Going to Atlanta meant entering a new world in Negro-white relations. . . . It was in Atlanta that I was to find that the cruel tentacles of race prejudice reached out to invade and distort every aspect of Southern life." Segregation laws ruled all public interactions between blacks and whites, and it was brutally reinforced by the threat of the extralegal violence of mob rule.[23] The Ku Klux Klan—headquartered near Atlanta in Stone Mountain, Georgia— grew more ominous and significantly influenced the Georgia legislature. In Mays's mind, Atlanta was not the New South city full of economic possibilities but a city where black residents were domineered and made servile.[24] Segregation did not distinguish among the social classes. "The experience of one black man," wrote Mays, "was the experience of every black man whether he was a college professor, doctor, minister, janitor, or maid."[25]

There was very little organized opposition to the terror the Klan visited on the black community. One group that made an attempt to counter the Klan's activities was the Commission on Interracial Cooperation (cic), lead by a Methodist minister, Will Alexander.[26] However, given Atlanta's southern context, the cic was viewed as "liberal," that is, it simply wanted to begin a dialogue about better "race relations." In fact, the CIC began as a strategically tepid organization, which was unable to effectively fight the irrational hatred that sprang up immediately after World War I.[27] The fact was that many white southerners considered expressing opposition to lynching too radical.[28] Under this climate, it was politically pragmatic for local black leaders to ally with the CIC, even if it was a tepid organization. "In Atlanta, in 1921," Mays eloquently observed, "as I soon found to be the case throughout the South, segregation was god—the absolute—and worshiped not only in secular life but in the *House of God*. On His altars were sacrificed the bodies, minds, and very souls of Negro men and women and little children."[29]

Morehouse stood as an oasis for black men amid the harsh segregated conditions of Atlanta. The college was founded as Augusta Institute in 1867 to train teachers, ministers, and missionaries by an alliance of northern Baptists and black missionary Baptists in Augusta, Georgia. Within a couple of years, the alliance decided that the institute should be relocated to Atlanta and be renamed Atlanta Baptist Seminary. In 1885, under the leadership of its second president, Samuel Graves, the Atlanta Baptist Seminary was moved to Atlanta's West Side.[30] Ironically, this site had been a Civil War battlefield and the skeletons of Confederate soldiers were uncovered as campus buildings were constructed. In 1897, the school was renamed Atlanta Baptist College by its board of trustees.

Under the auspices of the American Baptist Home Missionary Society, the college remained devoted to classical and theological education, miraculously surviving the many calls for it to provide an industrial education.[31] Atlanta Baptist College endured even as the republic gave tacit approval to racial separation.[32] "Forgiveness" of the South for the Civil War by white northern religious leaders helped tighten the noose of racial segregation around the necks of all black people. But somehow the leadership of the college kept its doors open, and with it the possibility of black achievement to overturn the inviolable laws of segregation.

In the late spring of 1906, John Hope was named Atlanta Baptist College's first Negro president. He provided stable leadership in the face of the heinous attacks on Atlanta's black community. In September 1906, just as his first semester as president began, the infamous Atlanta race riot commenced. The systematic attack by white mobs on black Atlantans lasted for three days. The riot was the denouement of a process that had begun with steady police harassment of black neighborhoods and the convict-leasing system, which placed poor black men who had been convicted of petty crimes such as vagrancy into years of long labor. The "riot" was justified through racial propaganda, which convinced resentful poor whites that blacks were taking over and needed to be held down for their own good. The Atlanta riot, like its counterpart in Phoenix in 1898, was once again a battle for political control in the state of Georgia. The best way to for whites to accomplish this goal was the removal of potential political rivals. "Old tensions concerning the link between black immorality, black voting rights, and political corruption were revived and highlighted as part of the racially charged 1906 gubernatorial race," historian Allison Dorsey explains. "*Atlanta Constitution* editor Clark Howell and career politician Hoke Smith waged campaigns that utilized hatred and fear of the political, social, and economic presence of blacks. Both candidates asserted their desire to curb the 'nigger threat' to southern (i.e., white) society, which was manifest in black access to the political process and black 'pretensions' to social equality."[33] On September 22, a riot ensued in response to the bogus newspaper story that a black man had raped a white woman and the court had not fully meted out justice. The white rioters directed their attack not against residents of the poor black section of town, where the supposed rapists lived, but against innocent bystanders and the black middle-class business establishments. The pogrom achieved its desired effect.

Despite the intense violence against black Atlantans and the fear it created, John Hope not only raised money for the school, but he also constantly inspired Morehouse students.[34] He guided the college through a crucial ten-year period of steady growth, during which time it was renamed Morehouse College, in honor of one of the school's chief benefactors, Reverend Henry Morehouse of the American Baptist Home Missions. The name change kept the college intimately linked to its Baptist tradition. Under Hope's presidency, the school maintained its ties to Baptist denominations and vigorously promoted the activities of the YMCA to further enhance the religious virtues and physical stamina of Morehouse men.[35] Hope worked tirelessly to make this small Baptist College a safe harbor of intellectual and social freedom for black men in the midst of riotous terror.[36] In 1921, when Hope recruited Mays as an instructor, he had been Morehouse's president for fifteen years and the student body totaled 136.

Morehouse was not the powerhouse it is today in Atlanta. "There seemed little anyone [at Morehouse] could do to change the system [of segregation]," Mays explained. But the college never taught students to accept segregation, "let alone gloss over, the environment they found." The faculty of the college never "taught submission; neither did anyone encourage Morehouse students to attempt by force to overthrow or change the system." It was "by precept and example" that Morehouse students were shown "never to accept the system [of segregation] in their own minds as being inescapable or right." In retrospect, Mays thought Morehouse might have done more to advance the cause of civil rights. But "even in 1921," Mays wrote, "Morehouse did not encourage voluntary patronage of segregated facilities, nor follow the custom of providing special seats for white visitors."[37] Though this was a small gesture, in making it, the college preserved the dignity of both its faculty and students.

In order to protect the college, Hope became increasingly more conservative and accommodating to white southern power.[38] Mays, on the other hand, was a "New Negro" politically.[39] His politics had been transformed by the pull, the push, the allure, and the economic benefits of both southern and northern migration to cities. His political views were also changed by World War I, which had put issues of race and citizenship front and center in the larger world context. The politics that Mays espoused sought to transform the American "sacred order."[40] As a result, a political split became evident between Mays and Hope.

Mays brought academic rigor to Morehouse. In the courses he taught—mathematics, psychology, and religious education—students were expected to work hard for the grades they earned. The first confrontation between Hope and Mays occurred over cheating in Mays's psychology class. Mays became suspicious when a number of students who had failed previous tests passed the final exam. "Of the sixty or more students in the class, sixteen had failed the four monthly tests," Mays explained. "I concluded that if these sixteen passed the finals, something was 'dead up the creek.'"[41] In fact, unidentified students had stolen a copy of the exam. He explained to his students that he had no choice but to give a second examination. When students protested to Hope, the president ordered Mays not to give a second exam "on the ground that it was unfair to the innocent." Mays objected, saying that the president "had no right to interfere with [his] academic freedom."[42] Mays refused to grade the examinations, and a standoff between the two ensued until Mays finally relented. "I capitulated to avoid the charge of insubordination," he wrote. "I did not wish to resign my position, as otherwise I should have had to do. I graded the papers."[43]

This incident over grading was not merely a strong-willed young instructor being corralled by his college president. The tension that developed between Mays and Hope was indicative of a changing attitude and style. Mays, like Hope, had attended college in New England; however, Mays believed, even more so than Hope, that Morehouse students could not only meet but excel beyond the academic challenges placed before them. His own struggle to attain a college education made him all the more determined to instill rigorous study habits in his students. He believed that black college administrators must have high academic expectations of its students. Considering the harsh and brutal times, one might ask, what benefit was there for black American academic achievement? Who cared if young black men excelled? As a New Negro, Mays was thoroughly meritocratic. If black Americans could not meet the greatest intellectual challenges in the safety of colleges such as Morehouse, he reasoned, how could they win the struggle for human dignity and racial discrimination outside of academia? For him, it was his students' duty to study and achieve academically. This was at the heart of the battle against Jim Crow.

The other issue on which Mays differed with Hope dealt with "spying on students." Hope charged faculty members who oversaw student behavior to pry into students privacy. If the faculty member found something objection-able, he was to report it to the president, and the student would be sent home. Mays thought this was not the role of a faculty member and did not comply with Hope's mandate. Though Mays disagreed with Hope's paternalistic way of running the campus, he respected the president and the difficult work he did to keep the black college alive under the tyranny of segregation. In the end, Hope would write superb recommendations for Mays when Mays left Morehouse.

While teaching at Morehouse, Mays began envisioning the kind of ministry that best suited him. Whether he was aware of it or not, his enthusiasm for shaping the lives of future black leaders was growing. It was during his three-year stint at Morehouse that he encountered a remarkable group of students, including longtime friends Howard Thurman and Samuel Narbit. Mays served as their debate coach and encouraged their intellectual development.[44] Thurman fondly remembered that Mays awakened in him "a keen interest in philosophy."[45] Mays recalled that he and Thurman formed a friendship after he taught Thurman in a psychology class. Thurman "was so interesting and stimulating," Mays recollected, that he "associated with him at Morehouse more than [he] did many of the professors."[46] Narbit would be the first black American to receive a Ph.D. from Brown University in the field of biology, in 1932.[47] These three men would become lifelong institution builders, educators, colleagues, and interlocutors. It was working at Morehouse that gave Mays an inkling of his future.

It was not until Mays was asked to be the pastor of Shiloh Baptist Church, a small congregation near Morehouse, that an opportunity for ordination be-came available. Like many male Morehouse faculty members before him, Mays accepted Shiloh's offer and arranged to be ordained, and in January 1922, he became the pastor of Shiloh. The congregation was small, and their expecta-tions were limited. He was expected to preach Sunday sermons and oversee weddings and funerals. The people who attended Shiloh, according to Mays, "were unschooled—common laborers and domestic workers." "Oddly enough," he observed, "I had no difficulty preaching to these people who, though untrained, were highly intelligent. Needless to say, I felt no compulsion to preach to them about the historical methods prevalent in the Divinity School of the University of Chicago! I attempted to speak to their needs and they responded warmly and well." Shiloh's members "accepted me wholeheartedly, despite my inexperience, and some of them rebuked me kindly when they thought I needed it."[48]

Mays had a unique relationship with the people at Shiloh. His personal sojourn was a part of the congregation's collective sojourn. Under his leadership, Shiloh became a meeting ground for the college population and its working-class and poor neighbors.[49] Through his hands-on experience as pastor of Shiloh Baptist Church, Mays reached a deeper understanding of the religious needs of black Americans. In his role as pastor, Mays worked hard to become more adept at public speaking, seeking to effectively communicate with his congregants and to address their needs.

While Mays loved the people of Shiloh, he was bothered by their worship style that was rooted in rural folk culture, a style akin to that he experienced as a child at Mount Zion. As pastor, he quickly shortened the length of the worship service from two to three hours to an hour and fifteen minutes. He preached carefully outlined sermons with limited extemporaneous digressions, which Shiloh members had been accustomed to hearing. He emphasized that the members were to be well instructed in the Baptist polity and its mission. With such focus on discipline in worship and instruction, Mays was able to attract frequent visitors from the area colleges and other congregations. His ministry was oriented to the burgeoning urban middle class in Atlanta.[50] He also "created a stir" among his congregation when he violated the Baptists' rule against dancing. Mays explained, "[I] went to an Omega [Mays's fraternity] picnic one Saturday and danced with the young woman I had escorted there. I heard rumors shortly afterward that the church would dismiss me for this sin. Another rumor was that I would be called before the officers and reprimanded. I was not dismissed nor was I reprimanded." Though there were disagreements about what constituted acceptable behavior during worship services and in public places, the uniquely democratic Baptist polity allowed for an ongoing dialogue between Mays and his congregants.[51]

Those three years were golden. He had steady money from his teaching job, he was a pastor at a beloved church, and he was married. Nothing could have prepared Mays for the death of Ellen Harvin Mays, his wife of just two years. The grief that he experienced from her death is a topic he does not dwell on in his autobiography. "Ellen, my first wife," he wrote "while still teaching in South Carolina, died early in 1923 after an operation."[52] He was shaken by this loss. Ellen was the woman who had supported his ministerial ambition. She was his first love. She was the one who had accepted the bookish and striving country boy at South Carolina State College.[53] It was Ellen who had stayed faithful to him while he traveled to Maine to attend Bates College. He did not mention his great love for her in any of his autobiographical musings. However, his complete silence on the subject of her death speaks volumes. The grief, the heartbreak, the regrets, and the profound sorrow he must have felt on the sudden death of a faithful companion was a matter so excruciating that he took her loss to his grave without further comment.

Determinedly, despite his great personal tragedy, Mays continued on with his plans to return to Chicago to complete his master's degree. Even the death of his wife did not shake his faith in what he felt called to do. One can only imagine that such a loss might have shaken his religious foundation; however, there is no indication, at least in his writings, that this ever happened to him. In the fall of 1924, he returned to Chicago to do what he started in 1921, when Ellen Harvin Mays was still at his side.

"Things had not changed much at the University of Chicago during my three years' absence," Mays wrote. "Dormitories were still closed to Negro women; only one or two were open to Negro men. Many white students were still running when Negroes sat at the table with them in the Commons." Discrimination against black people was so pervasive that even international students, especially those from the subcontinent of India, avoided blacks. "Negro students were convinced that Indian students wore their turbans to make sure they would not be mistaken for Negroes. In those days, a Negro wearing a turban could ride through the South unsegregated and unmolested. All foreign colored peoples (except black Africans) fared better in travel."[54] Both black and white southerners moved to Chicago alongside of white ethnics and competed for affordable housing and jobs. This migration strained the affordable housing market and made wages even lower. The housing conditions and economic competition, which had made Chicago explosive in 1919, had grown worse by 1924. The pace of Afro-southern migrants fleeing from the rural hamlets of Arkansas and Mississippi quickened. The sheer number of southern black folk pushing up against the northern border of the Hyde Park neighborhood, where the university is located, caused the then heavily white populated neighborhood to be squeamish and hostile to its black Southside neighbors.[55]

Mays returned to Chicago determined not to be sequestered. He, along with some fellow students, "organized a forum for discussing the race problem at the university—in Chicago and in the nation." He chaired the forum, which became "the only place at the university where problems of race were frankly and openly faced." It was through this forum that Mays had the occasion to form his "first real friendship with a Southern white man."[56] He remembered this moment vividly: he believed that "southern whites were the Negroes' worst enemies" until "a graduate student in sociology, a Texan by the name of W. O. Brown, addressed the forum." Brown analyzed "segregation and discrimination as related to Negroes. He said in essence that segregation and discrimination against Negroes were based upon (1) the false conviction of white people that the Negro was biologically and inherently inferior to the white man, and (2) their assumption that they were therefore free to treat—or mistreat—any Negro as they saw fit. Segregation was a badge that the white man forced the Negro to wear so that he could be disregarded and exploited." Mays was astounded. "As I listened," he wrote, "I felt that I, who knew too well what segregation meant, was in the presence of a miracle: a Southern white man who was aware that the doctrine upon which segregation rested was false and who believed it was wrong." Brown and Mays became fast friends. The friendship allowed Mays to loosen fears about white southerners and to build friendships with other white southern men.[57] He had changed considerably in three years.

Mays had both experienced the personal alienation of the deaths of his brother James and his wife Ellen and tasted the success of academic achievement, all of which seem to compel him to speak out forthrightly about his political concerns without fear of dying. He had grown tired of hearing speeches that espoused the acceptance of the racial status quo as though it was foreordained. At one point, upon returning to South Carolina, he grew exasperated while listening to Mrs. Jesse Daniel Ames, a white member of the CIC.[58] It "sickened" him to hear her say to an audience in South Carolina "that the only way to advance the Negro child one step was to advance the white child two steps." He would no longer be a willing participant in the white South's denial of the brutality of racism. "I was becoming increasingly aware that in the interracial meetings Negroes and whites did not communicate. In the careful effort not to hurt each other's feeling . . . Negroes and whites often sat on different sides of the table, and as often lied to each other."[59]

Mays's first opportunity to publicly voice his new insights and convictions was in a speech he gave at the Negro Older Boys' Conference held at Benedict College in Columbia, South Carolina, in 1926. The invitation to give the speech came from Ralph Bullock, who was the boys' work secretary of the National YMCA. This invitation came as a result of a chance encounter at the train station in Atlanta.[60] "Bullock," Mays recollected, "heard me request a Pullman berth to

Orangeburg. Of course, I received the usual answer: 'All space has been sold.'" Upon hearing Mays's boldness, "Bullock introduced himself, saying, 'I want to meet a Negro who has the nerve to ask for a berth in Atlanta, Georgia.'"[61]

He crafted his talk carefully because he "knew that Negro high school students from all over South Carolina would be there." "These Negro boys needed inspiration," he wrote, just as he had needed it as a teen. In retrospect, Mays considered the speech, titled "The New Negro Challenges the Old Order," "moderate." At the time, however, it was an incendiary. In the speech he defined for the young men what it meant to be a "New Negro." He told them, "It must be admitted that the number of Negroes developing a new race psychology with respect to inter-racial affairs is very small. The New Negro is still a 'rara avis.' He who reads the leading Negro publications finds it easy to conclude that we have an enormous number of New Negroes; but the most casual observations, as we come in contact with leading Negroes in various communities, will prove this is not the case." Candidly he stated,

> To the average Negro, schooled and unschooled, young and old, the white man is still a little god—to be honored, revered, and idolized; or to be feared and obeyed. Ignorance and age do not adequately account for it. It does not necessarily follow that the young college Negro is *new* nor the aged and untrained Negro is backward and nonprogressive— *old*. These attitudes just described defy localization. They hold not only in sections where opportunities are few and conditions less favorable, but in communities where discrimination and inequalities are less pronounced. Therefore, it can only be said that increasing numbers of Negroes are beginning to be 'new' and are reacting to their environment in a way that distinguishes them from the Negro of tradition.[62]

He challenged these young men not to accept white southern religious premises. "Finally, as never before," Mays continued, "the New Negro is questioning the white man's Christianity. There was a time, not very long ago, when most Negroes accepted the white man's Christianity in good faith in spite of discrimination and other injustices that they received at the white man's hands." He thundered, "That day is rapidly passing. It is not the eloquence of his speech; nor his brilliant talks about the 'Jesus way.' The New Negro is watching the white man's activities." Mays hammered, "He is watching the inability of America to stop lynching; the unjust distribution of school funds; the robbery on the railroad in accepting the same fare from Negroes as from whites and according the Negro inferior accommodation; the discrimination in the courts; and the injustices in the social and economic worlds—these are the things that concern the Negro and he includes them in religion."[63]

He encouraged the young men not to impose limits on themselves: "As it is, Americans though we be, I must speak to you not as an American to Americans but as Negro to Negroes." Plaintively and with anger," he continued, "It is this regrettable fact that makes it difficult for me to define.... Young men, you must strive to be an agriculturist, not a Negro agriculturist—just an agriculturist! Strive to be a doctor, not a Negro doctor—just a doctor! Seek to serve your state, not as a Negro, but as a man. Aspire to be great—not among Negroes, but among men."[64] The speech was uplifting. The eight hundred young black men in the audience gave him a prolonged standing ovation.

In the spring of 1925, Mays completed his master's degree. He had initially wanted to stay to pursue his Ph.D., but once again he needed money. So he took a position at his old high school, South Carolina State, instead. Although he needed money, which was a constant in his early career, there were other reasons for him to return south. He could go back and grieve the loss of his first wife by being closer to where she was buried in Sumter County, South Carolina. He could also more easily see his parents. But, most important, he had met another woman that he was interested in marrying. He was well aware of the conditions at State; not much had changed since he departed, for the college was still poorly supported by the South Carolina legislature. "Nine years since I had been graduated from high school at South Carolina State," he wrote candidly, "the college department enlarged, but there was little if any improvement in the level of academic interest and achievement."[65]

Mays nevertheless felt an abiding loyalty toward South Carolina State College. It was the school that gave him, an economically deprived youth from the South Carolina countryside, a chance to get a high school education.[66] But it was also where he found the second of two loving companions. In September of 1925, he met Sadie Gray, a sociology instructor at State College and, like Ellen, a fellow black southerner. Gray also shared similar educational ambitions to those of Mays. She had graduated from the University of Chicago with a bachelor of arts degree and was pursuing a master's degree and professional certification as a social worker at Chicago as well.[67] Additionally, Gray held strong Christian convictions; she was a devout Methodist and belonged to the Colored Methodist Episcopal Church (today the Christian Methodist Episcopal Church), a denomination that had split with the Methodist Episcopal Church South in 1870.[68] In the summer of 1926, while both of them were taking graduate courses at the University of Chicago, they decided to get married.[69]

Sadie Gray Mays. Courtesy of the Department of Special Collections and University Archives, W. E. B. Du Bois Library, University of Massachusetts Amherst.

Their marriage immediately put them into an economic crisis. Gray's elderly father was going through foreclosure on a $2,000 mortgage. Gray and her sister had assumed their father's debt, which required that she have an income. Land was something every black family wanted, so Sadie and her sister were trying to save their family homestead when economic downturns resulting from the boll weevil infestation ate right through the cotton economy. However, as a married woman, Sadie Gray Mays was required by state law to resign her position. It was simple, though it was a grave injustice; the law established that a married woman's place was to be in the home not in the professional world; men were the breadwinners. Although they tried to persuade President Robert Wilkinson to grant an exception, this requirement was beyond his jurisdiction. As a desperate measure, the Mayses even wrote to South Carolina governor Thomas Gordon McLeod and argued that an exception should be made given the extenuating circumstances. McLeod never responded to their request. As Mays remembered, the "decision left us no choice but to seek a place where both of us could work." The crisis was averted in August 1926, when Jesse O. Thomas, the field secretary of the National Urban League (NUL), offered both of them jobs in Tampa, Florida, working for the Tampa Urban League (TUL).[70] Mays was reluctant to consider the position because he felt "morally obligated" to return to State College.[71] However, in light of the administrative rules at the college and their economic needs, the Mayses headed for Tampa. They arrived in Tampa in mid-September of 1926. Mays recalled that although "Tampa was not the 'city of our dreams,' we went there because we had to have jobs."[72]

Tampa was a southern city, but its pattern of settlement was far more complex than that of the piedmont southern cities in which the Mayses had lived. Tampa had been a military outpost during the removal and resettlement of Florida's Indian nations. It was during this period that the cattle trade with Cuba facilitated the growth of the city.[73] From the beginning of its history, Tampa had a culturally mixed population similar to that of other American Gulf Coast cities. Tampa's long history of trade with its Caribbean neighbors proved to be a boon when Cuban cigar manufacturers moved some of their operations to the city in 1880. "The cigar industry transformed Tampa from 'a sleepy, shabby Southern town' into a vibrant manufacturing center with a large immigrant population."[74] It also brought with it a large number of white and black Cubans to work in the cigar factories. The racially exclusive laws, which the Florida legislature adopted,[75] put the Spanish-speaking Afro-Cubans between a proverbial rock and a hard place regarding racial and cultural identity.[76]

The NUL was a Progressive Era organization founded by black women and clergy to provide social services for indigent southern blacks moving from the rural countryside to the cities. The local NUL affiliates were to provide employment services, housing assistance, and classes on social etiquette for newcomers. After the terrible race riots that occurred between 1917 and 1919 in East St. Louis and Chicago, the NUL began to offer to conduct surveys and studies of black communities in various cities. NUL officials believed that if empirical data were collected it would help the general public understand the situation in which black Americans found themselves unfairly trapped. They hoped that local data would help to create a tipping point for social change in city after city. The planning and executing of these surveys resulted in the recruitment of some of brightest black intellectuals of the era.[77] Although the NUL was a Progressive Era organization, it was still seen by some in the black community to be tied to a Washingtonian-style politics of racial accommodation. The Tampa Urban League (TUL), which formed and became affiliated with the National Urban League (NUL) in 1922, certainly accommodated segregation.[78]

Blanche Armwood Beatty, who served as the TUL's first executive secretary, was a case in point. She took the stance that blacks in Tampa should do their best to cooperate with the segregated city establishment.[79] Beatty had a four-year tenure with the TUL before she was pressured by the local black leadership to resign after the suspicious death of her husband by an "alleged chauffeur."[80] According to the NUL's national field director, Jesse O. Thomas, Beatty's "situation created an administrative environment which so impaired her usefulness that her services had to be terminated forthwith."[81] (She was subsequently hired as the supervisor of Negro schools.[82]) It took Jesse O. Thomas nearly two years to find the right person to replace her, and, lucky for him, he found the right couple.

The Mayses were officially welcomed to the TUL on October 4, 1926.[83] Benjamin was hired as the executive secretary, and Sadie was hired as a caseworker. Almost immediately Mays was thrown into the fire of local politics and was expected to quickly "grip" the intricacies of relations between "the white and colored people" in the city.[84] "I was expected to be both chief spokesman on Negro affairs and the liaison man between the black and white worlds: an impossible job," Mays recalled. "There was no paucity of problems, no dearth of needs: juvenile delinquency; a lack of recreational facilities; underpaid jobs and unemployment; police brutality; poor housing; inferior educational facilities for Negroes. . . . Hercules himself might well have been daunted in the face of his Augean stable!"[85] Immediately, however, he set out a work plan.

He began planning fund-raising efforts with the local Community Chest and made "industrial contact with employers." He also began preparing a formal survey of the local community. For this task he was assigned a white partner. He wrote to inform Jesse O. Thomas of the research partner assigned to him by the TUL's board: "The man who is coming to assist us in the survey is Arthur [Raper]." Since Raper was not someone Mays had chosen, he asked Thomas to "get all the data you can about this man and let me know about him at your first convenience." The only thing that Mays knew about Raper was that he worked for Will Alexander, the head of the CIC out of Atlanta. The survey was vital to the future plans of the TUL. He explained, "We want to go the limit in this survey in order to get it across so that some of our findings and recommendations may be acted upon for the welfare of our group." And in order to have some impact on Tampa, Mays realized that the survey needed to have "the backing of a strong white committee."[86]

In December 1925, Raper and Mays met to discuss the survey. Mays confirmed what his field director already knew, that Raper "did not have much experience in survey work." He observed, "I do not believe he has any advantage over me, unless it is the advantage of having the access to the study that the Inter-racial Commission has made in the various cities of the United States." And Mays was absolutely correct; Raper was quite inexperienced. Nevertheless, the CIC indicated to TUL board chair, Mrs. Ruth Atkinson, that it wanted

Raper to lead the survey. Mays objected, telling Atkinson that the "Interracial Commission was planning to monopolize the study and that [he], feeling that [he] had the backing of the National Urban League, was laboring under the impression that the study was to be a joint study." Mays told her he felt that way "out of respect for [himself]" and "in defense of the National Urban League, and because of the "the contribution" he could make to the study."[87]

To further complicate matters, Atkinson thought that Arthur Raper was "colored" and that the TUL would be able to "save expense" by housing him among the "colored people." When Mays informed Atkinson that Raper was white, "she was trebly [sic] surprised." Raper's whiteness made Mays's point clearer. Atkinson promised him that "she would see to it that the study would be a joint study." Mays had to compromise in order to accept Raper as a leader of the Tampa survey. He initially wanted a black person with NUL ties to assist him, but, resigned to the fact, he reluctantly acknowledged to Thomas, "I believe that it will be an advantage for me to make this study with a white man. . . . I will have access to more material working with a white man than if I worked with a colored man."[88]

In February 1927, Mays and Raper, along with J. H. McGrew, a national official of the YMCA, began conducting the social survey of Tampa.[89] The investigation was conducted in a similar manner as NUL urban studies had been all over the United States.[90] They spent a month gathering material and using volunteers from the NUL fact-finding committees to gather statistical details and to interview business, educational, health, and civic leaders. The study also included photographs of the various housing conditions in which blacks lived. The Tampa study placed its priorities on securing housing and employment for blacks, which not so subtly pointed to racial discrimination. The conviction of the NUL at that time was "that social reform must be grounded on 'the factual interpretation of authenticated data rather than emotional and sentimental appeal.'"[91] Directly confronting racism, it was believed, could be interpreted by powerful whites as angry and emotional; racial discrimination had to be approached coolly and practically.

The Tampa study was risky because it had to acknowledge the depth of segregation in the city. The report was unflinching in its assessment: "Interracial contacts between white and colored elements in Tampa, as elsewhere in the South, are for the most part limited to those of a business nature. The Negroes have separate schools, churches and lodges. Unlike most southern cities, the Negroes do not attend any of the downtown theaters, no provision being made for Negroes." The candor in the report was unwavering: "The common custom of using the back of the streetcar for colored is adhered to:

Benjamin Mays surveying a Tampa neighborhood. Courtesy of the Southern
Historical Collection, Louis Round Wilson Special Collections Library,
University of North Carolina at Chapel Hill.

the same practice is followed by intra-urban motor lines. Some of the inter-urban motor lines carry Negroes while in other instances separate busses are operated. A separate waiting room is provided at the railroad station. In the main, orthodox Southern traditions as to race relations prevail in Tampa."[92] The city of Tampa, though orthodox in its segregation, the report indicated was "unlike the typical Southern city in that it is cosmopolitan in type." For Mays, Tampa was more diverse in its black population than other southern cities. There were Jamaicans, Barbadians, Bahamians, and black Cubans all thrown into the mix of Tampa's black community. He wrote, "Of the State's Negroes, more than a third have migrated to Tampa from states other than Florida, while there is a considerable element of British subjects in addition to a large number of Cubans."[93]

The investigators had uncovered valuable data. For example, the survey demonstrated just how deeply racialized the social class structure was for black people in Tampa. The study documented the migration of blacks "from Georgia, Alabama, the Carolinas and other states, and those from foreign countries."[94] Poor housing conditions, poor sanitation, subpar schooling, and the economic disparity in wages as described in the study were prevalent in neighborhoods populated by the black working poor. The study pointed to a small percentage of black professionals who made a decent living from the patronage of Tampa blacks. However, what it did not describe was that these professionals had to fight for black patrons' loyalty because they feared that black people in Tampa viewed white professionals as being superior to their black counterparts. Black professionals, like the working poor they served, were also hamstrung by the rampant societal bigotry and racist protocols.[95]

Of special interest to Mays in the study was the role of churches in the black community. "Aside from the home," the study reported, "the Church is the most important factor in the life of the Negro." He emphasized that the power of the church in the community is that it "touches the lives of more people than any other institution, and for the majority of Negroes the minister is still the most outstanding leader. Any study of Negro life that excluded the Negro church, would be a vital omission." The report noted that there were a total of forty-two churches representing "ten denominations, with a total membership of 9,171," of which 4,903 were active members, and an "average [Sunday] attendance of 6,377."[96] The statistical data was revealing and, for Mays, deeply troubling. The study reported several things that troubled Mays. The first was that "of the total number of church members, practically 50%, or to be exact, 47% are inactive—forty-seven out of every one hundred enrolled in the churches of Tampa, are making no contribution to the life of the church." He was also alarmed by the gender and youth imbalance in the Tampa churches: "The church members under fifteen, and that is the future church, constitute only 21% of the total church membership—13% girls and 8% boys." And "women outnumber the men practically two to one—62% and 38% respectively." And finally: "Negroes in Tampa have twice as many churches as the Whites" given their population size.[97] The statistics that he reported meant that local black congregations were not having the influence on the lives of young people in the community. The report divulged that "13 of the forty ministers are Seminary trained: 27 have no Seminary training: 4 of the 40 are College graduates."[98] This brief sketch of Tampa's black churches barely scratched the surface on many issues, but it was revelatory enough.

One positive outcome of the study was Mays relationship with Raper. Though he was initially leery of working with Raper, their intense work together in Tampa developed into a lifelong camaraderie. Mays believed that Raper acquired a deeper understanding of the capriciousness of black southern life and that doing the study with two black investigators challenged Raper's views about race and racial discrimination. For example, Raper refused the Mayses first dinner invitation; when pressed, however, he joined the Mayses and other community leaders. At the end of dinner, Raper stated to Mays that he did not "feel funny" and admitted that it was his first time dining with black people. The other incident to have pricked Raper's conscience was when he drove Mays in a rental car while they surveyed the city and an angry police officer stopped them, "incensed that a white man should be acting as chauffer for a Negro."[99] The last thing that Raper would learn was the extent to which the white racial hierarchy would go to maintain its dominant status. When the investigation was completed, it had to be presented before the survey's primary sponsors, Tampa's Welfare League and YWCA. They insisted that Raper make the presentation. Mays recalled, "It was appropriate that I, as executive director of the Tampa Urban League, give the report and Mr. Raper insisted that I do so." The officials relented, but when Mays hurried to see the local newspaper coverage of the report the next morning, he learned "that the (white) press had given Mr. Raper alone credit for having made the report."[100]

He and Sadie Mays continued to be steadfast in handling their overwhelming workload. They negotiated with the juvenile court to get a black case-worker assigned to work there. They also managed to keep up with the Tampa city government's charter changes, they secured some safe recreational space for black children and families, and they kept "the Tubercular Sanatorium for Negroes open."

During this time, Tampa's black community became embroiled in a nasty intra-ethnic dispute about the Hillsboro County black schools when Blanche Armwood Beatty was appointed as the supervisor over Negro schools.[101] The local black leadership continued to be disenchanted with her readiness to compromise with the segregated city establishment. In a letter to NUL field secretary Jesse O. Thomas, Mays wrote, "During her tenure at the TUL, donations generated from the black community were virtually nil—or, $29 to be exact. It is not too harsh to state that some viewed Armwood Beatty as the white people's Negro."[102] He believed that she compromised too much and simply gave the white leadership of Tampa what they wanted without resistance.[103]

As the Negro school supervisor, Beatty angered black community leaders when she summarily fired the principal of the all-black high school, Mr. Shootes. "Mrs. Beatty has not only succeeded in getting herself reappointed but has succeeded in ousting Shootes," Mays wrote to Thomas. "The colored people are passing resolutions in behalf of Mr. Shootes. The following organizations have passed resolutions asking for his retention . . . The Ministerial Alliance, The Women's Auxiliary to the Tampa Urban League, The Service Club, The Negro Business League, The Parent-Teacher Association, etc." However, he continued, "Mr. Carmichael, the Superintendent of the City Schools, has telephoned Mr. Shootes, Father Culmer, and Rev. Jones, pastor of Beulah Baptist

Church, and asked them to stop this agitation. You see paternalism is at work. Though politely said, it is a threat and is said in so many words, *You Negroes be good.*" The superintendent's "calls have not curtailed the activities of the Negroes more determined to make themselves heard," Mays added. "Leading Negroes are tired of one Negro dictating to the Board of Education for the Negroes in Tampa. You can clearly see what the issue is. It is not so much a fight for Shootes as it is a fight against Mrs. Beatty. The Negroes feel that this is their last chance to protest and that if she wins in this, the dictatorship for the Negro will be secured."[104]

What troubled Mays about Armwood Beatty's leadership was that she represented the interests of black Tampa as though she were the only voice of leadership. Mays saw the rejection of Beatty's leadership as a positive force that demonstrated to "the white people" that "the day of one-man leadership where the Negro is concerned is a thing of the past, and that Negroes are beginning to be 'new' and will not stand for everything."[105] In his mind, disingenuous leadership could no longer be sustained.[106] For much of the Mayses' time in Tampa, the overall feeling of the black population was one of powerlessness.[107] As a result, community leaders were bickering with one another rather than focusing on the larger issues of ending racism and alleviating poverty.[108] Community leaders who behaved like Beatty, he concluded, did nothing to improve the plight of the community.

What made Tampa so unbelievably tiresome for the Mayses was the incessant assault on their personal dignity. Given the deplorable conditions in which the vast majority of blacks lived, and the Herculean efforts required to address them, one might have hoped that the Mayses would spend most of their energy gathering community forces to improve blacks' situation.[109] But their work was undermined daily by indignities they suffered. Any display of dignity in their work, from fund-raisers to community programs, was viewed as subversive to the city's hierarchy. The fact that the Mayses used courtesy titles when they introduced each other or referred to one another in a public setting in the presence of white people put their jobs in jeopardy, as did Sadie Mays's habit of referring to her black clients with courtesy titles when she introduced them to white board members. However, such acts violated the racial protocols of Tampa.[110]

The Mayses, nonetheless, persevered. When Mays reflected on his experience in Tampa he did so in religious terms. Jim Crow's "spiritual assaults of this kind make an indelible impression." "[Learning] how to live in a segregated society without accepting that society," Mays wrote, "[was] a constant battle, a battle that [was] won only by steadfast and continuous refusal to admit as inevitable or right that which [was] ugly and mean, stupid and cruel."[111] Both he and Sadie decided to face the problem of Jim Crow with dignified acts of resistance. When asked to compromise on appropriate titles for adults, such as Mr. or Mrs., they simply refused, even if it meant losing their jobs.

The proverbial straw that broke the camel's back was a pageant, titled "From Darkness to Light," that the students of Booker T. Washington High School staged at the Tampa Bay Casino. According to Mays, "The pageant was designed to portray the progress made by Negroes from slavery up to 1928," but the African Americans in attendance, who made up a majority of the audience, were forced to use the balcony. "When the balcony was filled, and Negroes were forced to stand," Mays explained, "it took an absurd amount of time and persuasion to obtain permission for them to sit in the empty dress circle seats to say nothing of the seats on the main floor, also largely unoccupied." As he noted, the pageant's title, reminiscent of a scene from Ralph Ellison's novel *Invisible Man*, in which black boys are put into a ring to fight each other before the cruel gaze of white onlookers. Mays thought that the pageant should have been called "Let Darkness Reign Forever."[112] After consulting with Sadie and the Ministers' Alliance, Mays decided that he had to speak out about the absurdity of that moment. He received full endorsement from the Ministers' Alliance (of which he was a member) after they read the draft of an article that he titled "It Cost Too Much."[113]

Not only did the editor of the *Tampa Bulletin*, a locally owned black newspaper, agree to publish the article, but he also endorsed it with an editorial. Explaining the nonsensicality of the event, Mays ended his article stating that such treatment "cost too much. It cannot be justified by law; cannot be justified by tradition. Neither justice nor money can justify it. . . . It sets a bad example before the ambitious youths of our city, does not help the Negro in developing group self-respect, and does not increase the white man's respect for him."[114] The article marked him as a radical among the white establishment in Tampa.[115] Within days of its publication, TUL's board of directors asked Jesse O. Thomas to come to Tampa.

To add fuel to the fire, a few weeks before the board meeting with Thomas, Mays pulled into a filling station where the attendant "inquired, 'What can I do for you boy?'"[116] Mays immediately pulled off the premises and later wrote a letter to "the proprietor of the station in which he described the treatment accorded him by the attendant and registered formal protest." The proprietor was outraged by Mays's letter and wrote the board expressing his displeasure at what "was adjudged the unorthodox behavior of the Executive Secretary of the Tampa Urban League."[117] The TUL board wanted to rid itself of the Mayses.

Their simple demands for respect were seen as a threat to the stability of the local social order. The board made plans to dismiss the two of them, but, having astutely seen the writing on the wall, the Mays preempted the board's decision by resigning.

On August 24, 1928, Mays presented his second and last executive secretary's report in Tampa's city hall. His eleven-page report foreshadowed the Great Depression. Already, black residents of Tampa were feeling the contraction in the American economy. Mays stated,

> Notwithstanding the fact that the past eleven months have been fraught with many difficulties; in spite of the fact that this has been an exceedingly lean year, financially; that the acute employment situation has increased the problem of social agencies and made it more complicated than at normal times, it is my honest assessment that the Tampa Urban League has accomplished more and has served the public in a larger and more effective manner during the past year than it did during the first twelve months of my administration. . . . The greatest problem facing the organization is our inability to find work for scores of men and women who make frequent visits to the League every week.[118]

Not only was finding work difficult; wages for those who were employed barely kept up with the cost of living. Added to this difficult employment situation was the inhospitable racial climate. "No part of the work is dearer to our heart than that of interracial relation," Mays continued. "In all our dealing with white people, we have been ever mindful of the possibility of an entire group being appraised thru [sic] us." Forced to speak on behalf of all black people, he stated, "We have endeavored to have the respect for the Negro raised rather than lowered. We have struggled to have him judged in the light of his possibility, his opportunity and the depths from whence he comes rather than the light of finality. We have striven to pursue a policy that differs widely from that of the average Negro who chances to come in frequent contact with white people." He urged candor in talking about race: "We believe any Negro who has one message for white people and another message for Negroes is a hypocrite, dangerous to both groups and retards the growth in interracial good-will and understanding. We believe that honesty is the best policy in interracial affairs as in all others; and that interracial foundation built on anything other than honesty and fair play is destined to crumble. To this end, we have tried to be fair to our white friends; we have been careful not to sell the Negro in an unfavorable light."[119]

The Mayses had been dedicated professionals in their work with the TUL. Mays had written fifty newspaper articles, and Sadie had hosted the eminent historian Dr. Carter G. Woodson as the first black person to give a presentation to the Florida State Conference of Social Work and had hosted a meeting of the Tampa Welfare League that was "the first interracial meeting of Negro and white women of Tampa."[120] In spite of never having wanted to live in Tampa, the Mayses showed extraordinary commitment to Tampa's black community.

The problems they faced and handled in their limited time at the TUL, an inadequately funded and staffed organization, would have burned out anyone. Mays's departing words before the Tampa Urban League were politically deft, and surely more gracious than the organization deserved:. "We are richer for having come to Tampa—richer in experience, and richer in friends."[121] Happily, by the time the Mayses left Tampa and moved back to Atlanta they had earned enough money to pay down the debt on Sadie's father's farm, but their experience in the city left them weary.[122]

Atlanta was just as provincial city as Tampa in its Jim Crow orthodoxies, but it had a larger black middle-class and gave the Mayses an opportunity to socially network and fulfill their career ambitions. Sadie initially took a job on the with the Georgia Study of Negro Child Welfare. Once Mays secured work in Atlanta, Sadie eventually returned to the University of Chicago to complete her master's degree in Social Work and began to teach at the Atlanta University School of Social Work.[123] Meanwhile, Mays took employment on the National YMCA staff working as a student secretary to black colleges. Channing Tobias, the senior secretary of the YMCA's Department of Interracial Services in the Colored Work Department, had tapped him for the appointment. The job not only focused his religious calling on educating black students but also allowed him to be a visible moral leader to black college students throughout the South.[124]

Mays's involvement with the YMCA began at South Carolina State College, continued at Bates and Morehouse, and lasted throughout his career. The YMCA began as a movement in England in 1844 when George Williams saw the need to establish a spiritually nourishing outlet for young men who were in business at the height of the Industrial Revolution. The organization spread rapidly and was adopted in the United States in 1852. However lofty the YMCA's religious goals were, it excluded black Americans prior to the Civil War.[125] It was the black-led organizational efforts during Reconstruction, especially in South Carolina, that attracted young black men.[126] The YMCA program was not only a constructive religious movement to nurture men; it also became a religious and political networking organization for black men.[127] The network gave them invaluable knowledge and contact with men and women from Asia, Africa, and Europe.

Mays had stayed connected to the YMCA even in Tampa when he had strategically recruited John H. McGrew, also on the national staff of the YMCA in the Colored Work Department, to be an investigator on the Tampa survey. Even before the decision to leave Tampa was complete, Mays was heavily involved in the National YMCA's program and an effort to address "Negro students[']" lack of rights "within the [YMCA's] National Student Division." He was a part of a group known as the "Committee of Eleven."[128] The Committee of Eleven was comprised of Mays and ten educational leaders representing African American schools and colleges. The committee worked to devise a commission, which would consist "of three members from the Negro Student Councils, three members from the Home Division, [and] three members from the Colored Work Department," to adjudicate the issues the committee presented.[129]

Within the Committee of Eleven, however, there was an intergenerational debate as to how best to challenge segregation inside the YMCA nationally. High-profile black college presidents, like R. R. Morton of the Tuskegee Institute and John Hope of Morehouse College, had advised the Colored Student Division to accepted segregation within the Y movement for the sake of having a positive outlet of spiritual and physical recreation on their respective campuses for black men. What was at dispute was how could a spiritually uplifting ministry to black men be effective if segregation was not directly challenged within the Y. At the commission meeting on May 24, 1928, which was held to reconcile the tensions that were brewing among the committee members, the younger generation reached a compromise with the older members. They noted: "We are impressed with the truth of Dr. Mordecai W. Johnson's statement: 'Negroes must do a contradictory thing; they must work with all their might against segregation, and at the same time strengthen their so-called segregated institutions as if they expected them to last forever. They must insist that the doors of Harvard and Yale be kept open to Negroes and at the same time build up Howard and Lincoln as if there were no Harvard or Yale.'"[130]

More important to Mays was the fact that the YMCA, by its very definition, had a mandate to serve all of humanity. As Mays and the black leaders of the National YMCA wrestled with the question of whether the Colored Work Department should be dissolved into the Student Division, they were between a rock and a hard place. If the department disbanded, they would lose positions and a degree of autonomy at the national level within the Student Division of the YMCA. But Mays believed that they had to risk losing power to do away with "a segregated movement." The only way to do this was to integrate and "conserve whatever values [from the Colored Works Department] we have that are worth saving." They could not reach a consensus on that issue. However, they did reach the consensus that the leadership work that had begun with young people was essential.[131]

Mays's participation on the Committee of Eleven, his considerable administrative skills at the Tampa Urban League, and his oratorical skills made him perfectly suited to join the national YMCA staff. "Many memories of associations with the YMCA in high school and college," Mays recalled years later, "impelled me to choose the offer of the National Board. I knew that the Negro leaders in the YMCA, such as James Moreland, Channing Tobias, J. H. McGrew, William Craver, and Ralph W. Bullock, were able and admirable men, each demonstrating manhood and dignity in a highly segregated organization." While this was certainly true, the YMCA also gave him room to carry out his calling. His ministry was to challenge students religiously. As a national YMCA leader, Mays was able to convey to hundreds of black college students his message that it was their God-given duty and responsibility to seek societal change. "In those days," he explained, "the Negro student secretary was highly respected on Negro college campuses. Negro students then, as now, needed to be encouraged and inspired to aim high and to reach for *unattainable goals*. . . . Any speech or informal discussion brought terrific response when it broadened their horizons, assured them that they were *somebody* and held out hope for the future. . . . The YMCA conferences brought Negro students something special, something deeper and more spiritual than the colleges could provide."[132] He gave countless talks to students across the South, including "The Goal and What Right I Have to Live," at Bethune-Cookman College; "The Unconscious Loss of Power," at Talladega College; "Youth Is the Time to Do Great Things," at Stanton High School; "In the Morning Sow Thy Seed," at Florida Memorial; "This Is a Hard World and You Must Have Something to Make You Carry On," "Earmarks of an Educated Man," and "Too Easily Satisfied," at the Stillman Institute. But Mays did more than just talk; he also supported students' action against segregation within the YMCA itself.

In 1912, the national YMCA had established an annual meeting of black students at Lincoln Academy in the city of Kings Mountain, North Carolina. As Mays explained, "For seventeen years now Kings Mountain has played a significant role in the deepening of the spiritual life of Negro students. Definite decisions relative to Christian work have been made resulting in life long dedications to the Jesus' Way of Life." Black students from the Southeast gathered together for "ten days given to intelligent, liberal study of the part religion should and can play in the life of undergraduates and in the complex social and economic world which the undergraduates will soon enter." The Kings Mountain conferences provided black southern men leadership training that they might not receive elsewhere. Students, Mays observed, "found identity" in the program at Kings Mountain. It "was an oasis in a desert of segregation and discrimination."[133]

Concurrent with the black students' conference, white students gathered in Blue Ridge, North Carolina. When white students visited Kings Mountain, they were included in all events and activities—though Kings Mountain was "segregated," it was never "segregating." Blue Ridge, on the other hand, was strictly a "closed society." In addition, the conferences held at Kings Mountain and Blue Ridge were to annually exchange delegates and build fraternal relationships between the two conferences. "However, Negroes who went to Blue Ridge could not go as fraternal delegates," Mays explained. "The reasoning behind this absurdity was that if Negroes were accepted as 'fraternal' delegates[,] the inference might be that they were regarded as equals." Black students were called "program participants," not fraternal delegates. Since the Kings Mountain conference was open to white members, organizers expected mutuality. Mays and Frank T. Wilson of the national YMCA office made the decision to stop sending black students from Kings Mountain to Blue Ridge. They felt they could not allow the Kings Mountain students to be injured by the insult of racial exclusion.

For Mays and his cohorts, the YMCA was a civil rights movement "halfway house."[134] Through the YMCA, Mays had an opportunity to pass on to black male students "a battery of social change resources."[135] In 1928, Mays invited his colleague Frank Wilson to the Kings Mountain conference to discuss his trip to India. Wilson and Juliette Derricotte were two black "members of a six-member delegation from the United States who attended the General Committee of the World's Student Christian Conference at Mysore, India."[136] Wilson's trip to India was significant in that it was a firsthand account of the nonviolent struggle being led by Mohandas Gandhi against the British. Providing this kind of candid information made provincial black southern students a part of the worldwide Christian student movement and knowledgeable about movements against colonialism.

To demonstrate their commitment to antiracism, Mays and other conference planners decided to invite white students to their meeting at Kings Mountain. They networked with white allies, most notably Howard Kester of the Fellowship of Reconciliation,[137] to arrange for "twelve [white] young men" to visit Kings Mountain on conditions that they were to participate in a nonsegregated student training. The event went off without incident and opened the door to other white participants, including women, to visit Kings Mountain. Not only did this kind of meeting enhance white students' knowledge about black people, it also dramatically altered the viewpoints of black students who felt racially inferior. As he had done at the University of Chicago, Mays facilitated interaction among students to confront their racist assumptions and feelings.

After this conference, Mays printed two comments from a letter by Joe Moore, a white student at North Carolina State College who had visited Kings Mountain, in the *Intercollegian*, a newsletter for student YMCA workers in Negro schools and colleges. "The first thing that impressed itself upon my very soul on entering the grounds of Lincoln Academy was the warm friendly welcome that greeted me," Moore wrote. "From the very first moment on I felt like I had known those Negro men all my life and it was like old friends meeting again." Moore was impressed by "the spirit of the men with whom I came in contact. It was the enthusiasm and eagerness for a greater way of life."[138] The YMCA was an institutional meeting ground for students to gain understanding, learn skills that could be employed in social activism, and envision a "future society."[139] Mays understood his role as a facilitator in building a social movement through the various opportunities to network with the YMCA.

In the same issue of the *Intercollegian*, Mays wrote an article titled "College Students and Religion" voicing his concern about black college students' dismissal of religion. "There is no denying the fact that among college students of the present day there seems to be a growing lack of appreciation for religion," he penned.

> Formerly students knew just what to do and just what to believe in order to be saved. . . . The modern scientific method has made untenable many of the former practices which to our parents and grandparents were very vital and real. Today religion is not so clearly defined. . . . There is a revolt against creeds, dogmas, rituals, and orthodoxy in Biblical interpretation, whereas in earlier days these were accepted without question. To me this is a hopeful situation. These things do not disturb me except when I find existing among students a profound superficiality and sophistication which cannot be based upon sound reason.[140]

He contended that religion should not be so quickly dismissed since it had occupied such a great place in the history of human thought. "To deny the validity of religion," he asserted, "is to give into the lie to all that the prophets taught and even of Jesus himself for his life was a life of religion."[141]

Mays urged students to seek a balance of ideas about faith and reason: "He, who lives in this modern age, enjoys the fruits of science and at the same time attempts to set aside as invalid all scientific truth is a fool. On the other hand, he who disclaims religion, sets aside this vast field of knowledge and human experience in an endeavor to discredit its validity, to say the least, such person is profoundly stupid." For Mays, religion was unavoidable. "It is an attempt to deny the inevitable for whether we think it or not we are completely religious though it may be the wrong kind. True religion is more than creeds and more than dogmas; it is neither form nor rituals; it is more than the Bible itself, for religious experience created all these; before they were, religion was—destroy them and the meaning and place of religion in human history will remain unchanged."[142]

There are no records of how students reacted to Mays's article. However, what is known is that he continued to be one of the most requested speakers at YMCA functions on black college campuses. Students related to his intellectual views on Christianity, religious faith, and his informed ethical stance.

During these picaresque years, Mays became a well-known national figure. He was now a role model for ethical leadership and an open dissenter against racial segregation. He simply refused to internalize the rules of segregation. At the University of Chicago, the TUL, and the YMCA he began to organize a movement to challenge the spiritual degradation that segregation imposed on all black people.

During these years Mays also acquired invaluable skills. He served as a pastor of Shiloh Baptist Church and began to understand the dynamics of pastoral leadership from direct experience. He taught at two different kinds of historically black colleges and came to recognize their administrative strengths and their political limitations. At the TUL, he learned the skills necessary to be a community leader and an effective organizer. The difficulties he encountered at the TUL were also good preparation for his future as an institutional leader. The social survey that he carried out and coauthored in Tampa would serve as the template for his larger survey of black churches. And his service to the YMCA and his devotion to students became the foundation of his lifelong ministry. Reflecting on his "zigzag" journey from Lewiston to Chicago to Atlanta to Orangeburg to Tampa and back to Atlanta, Mays concluded, "Conditions and circumstances at the moment will largely determine . . . what a man does."[143]

— 4 —
The Negro's God

What is it that man will live for, fight for, and die for?
What is it to which man gives his ultimate allegiance and ultimate
loyalty? Whatever that thing is, that's his God.
—MAYS, *Quotable Quotes of Benjamin E. Mays*

Black churches were weekly topics of conversations in black communities. Black periodicals regularly covered the building of new churches, denominational conventions, famous preachers, and church scandals.[1] And black churches were everywhere—on busy streets in storefronts, on quiet corners in buildings with impeccable masonry, and on rural roads in structures built with rustic clapboards. As northern migration advanced, black religiosity transformed the American urban landscape. For Mays, black Protestant churches were the central institutions in the everyday lives of countless black Americans and therefore needed to be understood historically and sociologically and modernized theologically. And that is exactly what he set out to do throughout the 1930s.

In 1930, Mays and Joseph W. Nicholson were the recipients of an Institute of Social and Religious Research (ISRR) grant to carry out a study on black churches. The ISRR, which was founded in 1921, was an independent institute funded by John D. Rockefeller Jr., who, over a thirteen-year period, contributed $3,000,000. "In its thirteen years of work, the Institute carried on research covering a wide range of topics including church organization, foreign missions, religious education, and race relations."[2] The ISRR had previously funded a study titled *The Education of Negro Ministers*, authored by William Andrew Daniels in 1925, and *Negro Problems in the Cities*, by T. J. Woofter Jr. in 1928. In 1927, the Association for the Study of Negro Life and History (ASNLH), whose chief executive was the historian Carter G. Woodson, had been awarded a grant by the ISRR to study Negro churches. The Howard University historian Charles Wesley, an African Methodist Episcopal clergyman, and his colleague Lorenzo Greene directed the field research.[3] Woodson rejected a draft of the study, calling it "worthless." Woodson did not believe that Wesley possessed sufficient objectivity because of his religious convictions. Dissatisfied with Wesley's study Woodson then sought out the sociologist E. Franklin Frazier to take it over. When Frazier refused, Woodson was forced to return the grant to the ISRR.[4]

Three years later, the ISRR approved Mays's proposal for a new study of the Negro's church. John R. Mott, the president of the ISRR board, and Trevor Arnett, its treasurer and a Rockefeller Foundation official, wrote to John D. Rockefeller Jr. informing him that the "study of the Negro Church is notable in that it marks the first attempt to study the most influential factor in Negro Life." In the ISRR's pre-publication literature, the study was called "A Study of Representative Negro Churches: A pioneer study, covering a sample of urban and rural churches in both South and North, by B. E. Mays and J. W. Nicholson." Mays had come to the attention of John Mott through his work in the YMCA. Channing Tobias, senior secretary of Interracial Services of the YMCA aided Mays in securing the position as the lead researcher on this project.[5] Nicholson, like Mays, had attended seminary and was a Ph.D. student at Northwestern University in Chicago researching black clergymen. Mott and Arnett considered the potential survey by Mays and Nicholson to be a vitally important contribution to the work of the ISRR.[6] The institute was pleased because "noted Negro churchmen and educators" had given their stamp of approval.[7] Mays and Nicholson received the funding just as the Great Depression began. Mays recalled that the two-year study "if not sent [from heaven], must surely [have been] heaven-bent."[8]

By the summer of 1930, the study by Mays and Nicholson was under way. In a letter to Jesse O. Thomas of the National Urban League (NUL), Mays outlined the study's intent: "The plan is to study the Negro Church as it actually exists, to appraise it on the basis of factional data, to discover causes for significant factors obviously at work in the Church and religious life to the extent to which the Church is a dominant factor in Negro life, and to indicate, if possible, the trend of the Negro's religious life as revealed in the Church." Mays thought that two years "was not sufficient time to make an extensive and exhaustive study of the Negro Church," so he needed a person of Thomas's stature to serve on his oversight committee and assist him and Nicholson by providing "guidance and direction" at the onset of their work.[9] To expedite the study, Mays used his NUL connections with urban churches around the country.[10] With the support of Thomas, the local NUL affiliates, and the black press, Mays and Nicholson began to collect data and garnered publicity for the study from their office at Atlanta's Butler Street YMCA.

In the spring of 1931, Mays participated in a Yale University Divinity School seminar titled "Wither the Negro Church?" Upsilon Theta Chi, a black student society within the Divinity School whose motto was "Sacrifice and Service for Christ," sponsored the seminar. The faculty mentor to this student organization was Professor Jerome Davis. In the foreword of the printed proceedings of the meeting, Davis observed that the "Negro church has already made a profound impress on American life. If it can avoid the pitfalls of excessive absorption in worship and mysticism and unite, as Jesus did, an individual and a social passion—a love of God and a love of humanity—it may yet surpass other Protestant faiths." He presciently remarked, "Perhaps Negro ministers are peculiarly called of God to serve our country—to redeem all of our American nation, both white and black."[11]

Mays must have pondered the irony of his attending the Yale seminar. He had traveled a long way careerwise in the ten years since his Pullman porter days working the Yale-Harvard football game. He was now a national figure and one of seven male co-panelists: J. M. Ellison, professor at Virginia State College; George Edmund Haynes, secretary of the Commission on Race Relations of the Federal Council of Churches (FCC); Dr. Henry H. Proctor, pastor of the Nazarene Congregational Church, Brooklyn, New York; Frank T. Wilson, executive secretary of Colored Student Work, National Council of the YMCA, New York; and A. Phillip Randolph, general organizer and president of the Brotherhood of Sleeping Car Porters. The seminar was small and therefore permitted an intimate exchange among the panelists. The size also allowed panel members the time to make their presentation and to answer direct follow-up questions from the other panelists.

A. Philip Randolph was the first panelist to address the seminar. He contended that the Negro church had "no capitalist in it" and that Negro ministers were from a "working-class background." Randolph argued that "the time has come for the Negro church to take a long-range viewpoint and eschew a policy of temporary expedience and back financially and morally the bona fide trade union efforts of Negro workers to organize for new and better industrial opportunities, raise their wage scale, shorten their hours of work and support the national trade union struggle to secure liberal social legislation such as unemployment insurance, old age pensions, abolition of the injunction writ against labor, the five-day week, etc." Randolph's fellow panelists quizzed him about the benefits of aligning the Negro church with his labor effort. Randolph, whose work was being done in the most difficult years of union organizing, responded, "The greatest service the church can render is to keep up spirit . . . this is the kind of doctrine all Negro workers need. Even though [the Brotherhood of Sleeping Car Porters] is practically shattered, they need spirit or will to go back into the fight."[12]

Following up on Randolph's call for spiritual support, Mays remarked that black women work "very long, as long as twelve and fourteen hours a day and the wages $3, $4, and $5 a week." Mays charged that the church was implicated in the exploitation of these women because it raised a great deal of its money through its relationships with exploitative employers. Randolph responded that he "doubt[ed] whether you could have any organization in the form of a union among a group like that without some national direction, where you have a day-workers' organization."[13] Randolph was not very optimistic about the prospect of organizing female domestic workers.

Mays contended in his own presentation that none of the lofty goals his fellow panelists discussed could take place without leadership: "The direction in which an institution moves . . . the philosophy it develops and the technique it uses depends almost wholly upon the leadership of that institution."[14] Mays based his Yale address on two articles he had previously written that had appeared in both the *Crisis* and the *Christian Century*. His general point was that leadership coming from the black church had to adapt and keep up with the times. "In the main," he opined, "the church remains rather conservative and does not courageously grapple with basic wrongs inherent in our social and economic order." He suggested that maybe it was necessary to have fewer ministers and churches, reasoning, "If fewer ministers mean men of finer quality—intellectual, spiritual, social, and otherwise—prophets of the new day, fearless and courageous churches but better owing to consolidation, it may mean victory rather than defeat." It was important to him that men who were trained in the superior seminaries serve as church pastors. Despairingly he declared, "Many of our most outstanding ministers are teachers, social workers, or are engaged in some other phase of work."[15] Two years later, in 1933, with Mays serving as its primary author, *The Negro's Church* was published; in it were the same arguments that he outlined at the Yale seminar.

The Negro's Church painted a portrait of the Protestant church as one of the paramount institutions in the lives of black Americans. Mays and Nicholson had surveyed census data, made statistical analysis, and conducted oral interviews with clergy and others about the state of these churches. The main point from the study was that these churches were not fully attuned to their modern context. The book criticized black Protestant churches for failing to creatively meet modern circumstances and for leaving its believers, at times, mired in an irrelevant institution.[16] It argued that the weaknesses of these churches were not caused by some inherent deficiency of black people themselves or by their indulgence in excessive emotionalism, but rather that they reflected the greater failure of American Christianity that had been engulfed by racism. However, it insisted that black churches gave undue attention to eschatological themes about "life after death." This was, it contended, a survival technique that slaves developed to endure centuries of cruelties. This pattern of social adjustment, while helpful in the past, was not constructive for black congregations facing the twentieth century. *The Negro's Church* argued that if the church was to be a vital moral institution and improve conditions for blacks, it must become a vehicle for social change. Though the book was critical of the educational shortfalls of black Protestantism, it claimed that these congregations had an internal genius within them. That genius came from the essential spiritual and egalitarian values of freedom and democracy among its members. "This fellowship and freedom inherent in the Negro Church should be conclusive to spiritual growth of a unique kind," wrote Mays. "It furnishes the foundation for the Negro Church and the Negro ministry to become truly Christian and prophetic in the truest sense. . . . The Negro Church has the potentialities to become possibly the greatest spiritual force in the United States."[17] The church's inherent spiritual genesis could empower black Americans to claims of the promises of their faith in the here and now. This kind of faith would empower black people to make immediate claims to their rightful civic freedoms.

When *The Negro's Church* was released on February 20, 1933, Mays had returned to Chicago to complete his Ph.D. course work.[18] The book's publication came at a perfect time. Mays was a published author as well as a graduate student. In a letter to Jesse O. Thomas, Mays expressed his disappointed that the ISRR had not sent Thomas a reviewer's copy of the book so that he could write a review. According to Mays, the book had received a dozen reviews from both "Negro and white journals—they all speak in high praise of the book." He remarked proudly that "two Chicago professors have already reviewed the book and one of my major professors has just released a review which should appear in April. It is taking well here."[19] Mays had reason to be proud. Walter White of the NAACP reviewed *The Negro's Church* and summarized the importance of its publication: "Few American institutions have had greater influence in shaping the destiny and thought of a race and, in turn, influencing for better or for worse American thought upon a major problem than the Negro Church. At the same time no institution has received as little critical examination from either white or Negro students of social science. *The Negro's Church*, by Mays and Nicholson, is one of the few examinations of this sort and it is an important achievement in its understanding of all forces which have made [the Negro church] what it is."[20] Howard Thurman, reviewing the book in the *Intercollegian*, noted that the data in *The Negro's Church* was "a criminal indictment" of "the white man's religion" from which black churches developed. The story told in the book, he added, was "an eloquent dramatization of the tragedy of the segregated church." He concluded his sympathetic review with a scoff: "To preach the Kingdom of God from a segregated pulpit is one of the profoundest kinds of atheism. Loud must ring the laugh of Allah in his Mohammedan heaven as he beholds the spectacle of the First Baptist Church (Colored) and First Baptist Church (White)."[21]

While most reviews of *The Negro's Church* were favorable, at least one reviewer pointed out one of the great flaws of the book. Robert Sutherland noted that while the book was commendable, its "unbalanced method of 'sampling' gave a disproportionate attention to the highly organized and modernized 'white-denomination' churches and almost no attention to the second largest number of Negro churches, the Holiness sects." Sutherland generously attributed this omission to the short time span in which the researchers had to do their research, but it was significant. Mays, in fact, had his own biases against the Holiness/Pentecostal churches.[22] In spite of the criticism, the book was destined to become one of the mainstays of twentieth-century scholarship on black Protestant churches. Mays and Nicholson's volume was the third horse in a troika, taking its place alongside W. E. B. DuBois's *The Negro's Church* and Carter G. Woodson's *The History of the Negro Church.*[23]

Two interrelated biases informed *The Negro's Church*; the first was a status anxiety concerning the burgeoning black middle class, and the second was theological. These two prejudices informed one another. Did Christianity as practiced among black people sufficient appeal to the growing educated middle class? In the eyes of many, including Mays, the answer was reluctantly no. Black religiosity had to modernize with the times. This first bias then led to the second. For Mays, black Christians needed to discard the conservative theological orthodoxies because those orthodoxies led them down an eschatological path that did not sustain their struggles for justice and their resistance to white supremacy. To him, theological liberalism opened up important vistas that helped illuminate the faith of black believers and strengthened their commitment to build a more just society.

Theological liberalism, Mays believed, brought a relevancy to the practices of faith in a scientific era. It confronted hard questions about Christian faith that previously had been suppressed or ignored. For Mays, how could one hold true to the teachings of the Bible when biblical and linguistic scholars found inconsistencies throughout scriptural texts? How could one still believe in the centrality of the Christian teachings of Jesus as the resurrected Savior and God's final revelation when archaeology and other historical evidence pointed out that similar claims had been made about other religious figures in Jesus's time? All the more crucial was how could Christians continue to espouse the notion that God created the heavens and the earth in light of Charles Darwin's theorizing and evidence on evolution. For Mays, not answering such fundamental questions made Christianity totally irrelevant for modern life. Although Mays never described himself as such, he was a theological modernist.

Theological modernists adjudicated and resolved intellectual pitfalls within Christianity. They were convinced that in order to be reconciled to modern knowledge the Christian faith had to be rooted in the natural sciences and the realities of living in an industrial order. "Liberal theology is the child of two heritages," religious historian Gary Dorrien explains. "From its Enlightenment modernist heritage it has upheld the authority of modern knowledge, emphasized the continuity between reason and revelation, championed the values of tolerance, humanistic individualism, and democracy, and for the most part, distrusted metaphysical claims. From its evangelical heritage it has affirmed the authority of Christian experience, upheld the divinity and sovereignty of Christ, preached the need of personal salvation, and emphasized the importance of Christian missions." This intellectual tradition, which creatively fused "modernist and evangelical commitments," was foundational to the modernist theological viewpoint.[24]

The University of Chicago was the first university to move toward a theology less rooted in church doctrine and more in contemporary philosophy to address the nettlesome issues of religious belief. In the 1880s, the University of Chicago was a failing and little regarded Baptist institution, but in 1890 it was reorganized through the philanthropy of John D. Rockefeller and the imaginative leadership of William Rainey Harper. By the turn of the century, Chicago was a cutting-edge research university. One of the chief areas in which Chicago would achieve acclaim was in its research and instruction in the field of religion. President Harper, a Baptist clergyman and a scholar of the Old Testament, wanted the university's divinity school to advance the "scientific" study of religion as well as actively train clergymen. When Mays arrived at Chicago's campus in 1921 it was an established stronghold of liberal theology, and many religious intellectuals referred to it as simply the "Chicago School."[25]

By 1921, the Chicago School featured a variety of historical approaches to Christianity. One of its primary intellectual frameworks for the study of Christianity was "sociohistorical methodology," wherein religion was studied in the context of the broader environmental factors that influenced the evolution of religious practices. This approach eschewed any religious claims to supernaturalism and evaluated religious practices in terms of their overall historical milieu. In addition, the Divinity School was a vital academic center for the promotion of the Social Gospel. Shailer Mathews, the dean of the Divinity School, strongly believed that Christianity offered democracy invaluable ethical values.

Swift Hall, University of Chicago Divinity School, ca. 1925.
Courtesy of the University of Chicago Special Collections Research Center.

In other words, a properly interpreted Bible could help to make civilization more humane and help democratic practices flourish.[26] For Mays, the historical approach to Christianity and the evangelical missionary zeal that explicitly guided the social ethics of the Social Gospel fit an emerging pattern found among a small group of black theological modernists coming from university divinity schools.

Mays was not the first black religious intellectual to fall under the influence of the Chicago School. Richard R. Wright Jr., an African Methodist Episcopal clergyman, scholar, and bishop who preceded Mays by nearly twenty years at the university, was just one of many. Wright would acknowledge a deep and abiding debt to Professor Shailer Mathews throughout his long career.[27] Wright, too, had been influenced by Chicago's ethical activism in the teachings of the Social Gospel. The foundation for religious activism for Wright was a historical approach to biblical study. As a church leader, Wright exhorted his fellow clergy to "preach practical religion from their pulpits."[28] Like Wright, Mays espoused a religious modernism in which biblical scholarship and theology were guided by the evangelical principles found in the Social Gospel. An explicit mandate of the Social Gospel was the transformation of American society.

Shailer Mathews. Courtesy of the University of Chicago
Special Collections Research Center.

Mays attended the university off and on over a fourteen-year period, 1921
to 1935.[29] He was officially enrolled in 1921, 1924–25, and 1932–35. He was
awarded his Ph.D. on December 17, 1935.[30] He attended the Divinity School
first, when it was at the peak of its sociohistorical research on the New Testament.[31] The leading scholar during this period was Shirley Jackson Case.
As noted in Chapter 2, Mays had been introduced to Case's ideas while he
was a student at Bates College. Case published two notable studies on early
Christianity, *The Evolution of Christianity: A Genetic Study of First-Century
Christianity in Relation to Its Religious Environment* (1914) and *The Social
Origins of Christianity* (1923). Case's contribution to American New Testament
scholarship stressed the environmental factors in the evolution of Christianity.
Case believed that the textual criticism of the New Testament written up to that
point was important but inconclusive without a broader analysis of the Bible's
historical and cultural context. Like many modernist theologians of this period,
he was significantly influenced by philosophical naturalism. Case believed that
a biblical scholar had to give due consideration to science because the notions
of revelation were not sufficient to interpret early Christianity. Supernaturalism, which guided much of the Protestant church's teaching about the New
Testament, was impossible, according to Case, since it was not grounded in
historical reality. The scriptures did not simply drop out of the sky but rather

Shirley Jackson Case. Courtesy of the University of Chicago
Special Collections Research Center.

were shaped by an evolving interaction among culture, politics, and geographic location.[32]

The subject Mays chose for his master's thesis, titled "Pagan Survival in Christianity," reveals Case's influence. His thesis explored pagan practices related to such matters as the Virgin birth, the deification of Jesus, and the stoic philosophical influence on the writings of the Apostle Paul.[33] Mays contended that six notable factors influenced early Christianity: (1) the existence of a universal empire (which was begun by Alexander and completed by the Romans); (2) the growing spirit of cosmopolitanism and brotherhood, which Stoicism had done so much to inculcate; (3) a conception of a spiritual deity taught by philosophers; (4) the doctrine of immortality and other elements contained in the popular Greek and Oriental mysteries; (5) the Jewish ideal of a personal God, which succeeded in awakening the religious spirit where abstract notions of metaphysics had failed; and (6) a Jewish background (the canon of scripture and diaspora). He concluded, "Christianity was not destroyed because it was rooted in paganism." Mays argued "that Christianity was inevitably bound up with the environmental forces of the Roman world; that it is an evolutionary movement; and must be modified, as all movements are, by its environment."[34]

Mays further argued that Christianity was a social movement that took over the pagan world. Christianity, he wrote, "began in Judaism and, we may say, reached maturity in the Gentile World. In the main, the current beliefs of Judaism and the current views of Paganism were shared, in some form, by Christian converts. And in working out a distinct program of its own, it would naturally allow that Christianity would use to good advantage the essential elements of Pagan religions. . . . The Pagan elements were common possessions of the Gentile world at large. For example, the Christians were accustomed to emperor worship. They sought deliverance from present evils in some ruler sent from heaven. . . . This general idea of deliverer was shared and taken over by Christian teachers." Christians, he wrote, "made modifications." Their "program," he contended, "pertained to in the main, to the next world. This current Sa[v]iour-idea helped the Christians in the propaganda they spread. It was not the emperor, but the risen Christ who would bring deliverance."[35] He articulated a Case-like position well. Studying Christianity in the context of the history of religions and classical literature, he concluded that the Bible was not the fount of all knowledge. Rather, the Bible "primarily is a religious book, written for religious ends, and portrays the evolution of man's spiritual and ethical ideas in his quest for God and in his efforts to relate himself aright to God and man."[36]

Mays adopted Case's historical methodology and applied it to his own intellectual concerns about black religiosity. There is little doubt that Case's philosophical naturalism influenced Mays. He developed a theoretical "reservation" for cultural behavior that appeared to him to be "otherworldly." He historicized many aspects of black American religious practices and thought, attributing this behavior to issues of social adjustment in dealing with the long history of black oppression. In many ways, Mays viewed early Christians as he did black Americans. The early Christians were a defeated people who, with the execution of Jesus, turned the defeat of their social movement into a world-force for social change. He viewed religious faith functionally as a part of an arsenal for constructive transformation. He saw the possibility of harnessing the religious inclinations of black Americans, like those of the earliest Christians, to spur a modern social movement to reconstruct American society.

Another intellectual influence on Mays regarding the compensatory nature of black American religious behavior was the Chicago School of Sociology. Robert Ezra Park was one of the more prominent sociologists in the United States during the time Mays studied at Chicago. Two factors made Park influential on black intellectual thinking in this era. First, Park had worked as Booker T. Washington's secretary and ghostwriter prior to his storied tenure at Chicago.[37] Second, Park served as the academic mentor for two of Mays's contemporaries, E. Franklin Frazier and Charles Johnson.[38] Park believed that dominated people, such as black Americans, possessed little substantial organizational structure to overcome their oppression and thus relied too heavily on emotionalism and spontaneity as strategies for adapting to urban life.[39] Some of Park's assessments resonated with Mays's own concerns. Mays believed that black Americans could only gain the respect that they were rightfully entitled to as equal citizens if their institutions, particularly the church, served as a force for modernizing social change. Theologically, this meant that the church would have to construct a more modern set of religious tenets that addressed contemporary realities. All this was a part of Chicago's modernist appeal.

Mays thrived within the university because of its theological tolerance and intellectual rigor.[40] Most importantly, he valued the university's critique of society and its compelling vision for creating a more just society. As Mays delightfully recollected,

> One of the most fascinating courses I ever took at the University of Chicago was with a man whose theology I rejected. . . . He would sweep away all angels, Jesus Christ, God, heaven and hell. [A. E.] Hayden believed that man could build a world of peace, goodwill, and justice without relying on traditional Christian theology. I was attracted to him because of his firm belief in humankind and the fervor with which he defended his position. He did it with the zeal of the old-time Baptist preacher, of the kind I had heard in my Baptist community in South Carolina.

"*The life of one child is more important than all the buildings put on the campus of the university,*" Mays vividly remembered Hayden saying at the university's Rockefeller Chapel. "I said that if this man thought like that, I would take as many courses as I could with him, without neglecting the courses required in my major."[41]

The 1924 Scopes trial, the high-profile case over the teaching of evolution, was contemporaneous with Mays's time at Chicago. The trial was the catalyst for the irreparable schism between fundamentalists and modernist Christians over questions of science, cultural relevancy, and the significance of Protestant theology.[42] The modernism taught at Chicago was in sharp contradiction to the spectacle of the Scopes trial. For Mays, science and religion were not diametrically opposed to one another. The religious life was not antithetical to scientific discovery, whether in physics or evolutionary theory. The reality, however, was that black people fell on both sides of the issues of Darwin's evolutionary theory. Here was the crux of the concern about faith in God and acceptance of the theory of evolution: blacks "had a long tradition of belief in God's special providence for the poor and oppressed," and the worship traditions of many black churches "strongly identified the fate of the race with God's plan to liberate ancient Hebrews from the Egyptian bondage. Could black Christians throw away this trust in an immanent God who cares for his people in favor of modernists' abstract, intellectualized faith?"[43] The great fear was that in a godless world there would be no moral order or divine sanction that could protect the vulnerable and the dispossessed.[44] Mays found something positive in "the radical implications of evolution—the common origins of humanity and the importance of environment as heredity—and [he] believed that evolutionary science itself embodied the spirit of progress that would lift the race higher."[45] But this was not necessarily what the average church attendee believed. Mays realized that modernist theology had to be expressed in the evangelical language of American Protestantism. And for him that language was to be found in the Social Gospel.

In the 1920s, Chicago's Divinity School remained a strong proponent of the Social Gospel. Shailer Mathews, the dean of the Divinity School and author of one of the chief textbooks on the Social Gospel, titled *The Social Teaching of Jesus*: An Essay in Christian Sociology, largely dispensed with the notion that Jesus preached an apocalyptic version of the kingdom of God. Rather, Mathews taught the moderate view that the kingdom Jesus preached "was an ideal social order, progressively approximated through historical process, in which the loving fatherhood of God and the brotherly fellowship of humanity were affirmed."[46] However, for Mays, Walter Rauschenbusch's more incendiary ideas of the Social Gospel remained key.[47] In *A Theology for the Social Gospel*, Rauschenbusch contended, "The Church is the social factor in salvation. It offers Christ not only many human bodies and minds to serve as ministers of his salvation, but its own composite personality, with a collective memory stored with great hymns and Bible stories and deeds of heroism, with trained aesthetic and moral feelings, with a collective will set on righteousness."[48]

Mays derived many of his theological views about the societal function of the church from Rauschenbusch's theology. He understood that churches had a vital role to play in society by setting a religious agenda for change. Mays concurred with Rauschenbusch that the "saving power of the church does not rest on its institutional character, on its continuity, its ordination, its ministry, or its doctrine." Rather, "it rests on the presence of the Kingdom of God within her. The Church grows old; the Kingdom is ever young."[49]

One other important piece of historical scholarship was foundational to Mays in this period, although he never explicitly acknowledged it. In 1921, just as he began his graduate studies at Chicago, historian Carter G. Woodson published *The History of the Negro Church*. Woodson's volume painted the broad outline for much of the work Mays sought to do throughout his career as a dedicated churchman and theologian. Woodson's broad historical sweep of the experience of black Protestant Americans aided his thinking. Woodson's commentary about the history of black churches was source material for Mays's *The Negro's Church* and his future theologizing.[50]

As Mays completed *The Negro's Church*, he pondered the question of God in relationship to black life. In chapter 3 he keenly observed, "A man's conception of God may go a long way toward determining his conduct. The nation that believes that God is a God of war would hardly have any hesitancy in making all kinds of preparations for war, and may give little thought to the question of right. People who believe that God is a God of revenge would probably feel that it is quite all right to avenge the one who wronged them." Conversely, he added, "Those who actually believe in the kind of God that Jesus believed in would endeavor to regulate their conduct in the light of the God-idea as set forth by Jesus. But it is quite likely that those who believe that God will take care of them, that He will fight their battles if they will only pray, attend church, and pay their dues might take a do-nothing, *laissez-faire* attitude toward life and simply fold their hands at a time when real action is required."[51]

Mays continued this line of reasoning as he began study for his Ph.D., and at this time Professor Henry Wieman's views became significant in his thinking. Wieman was one of America's leading theologians at the time, though today he is rarely remembered.[52] It was Wieman who "whetted" May's "appetite" for philosophical theology and "taught him the philosophy of Alfred North White-head."[53] As a leader within the Chicago School, Wieman emphasized the need for a science of God. He was fond of saying that "man is hell-bent for God."[54] According to Wieman, in order to understand how human beings experienced God, one must evaluate how they conceived of God. This theological analysis must be based on an empirical methodology that was verifiable. Science, Wieman contended, lifted the veil of sentimentality from Christianity and removed the temptation to anthropomorphize or project superstitions onto God. Wieman believed that science not only enabled human beings to gain knowledge about God but also transformed the relationship between God and the human being. This changed relationship would result in new ritualized habits such as prayer and worship. The knowledge gained about God through scientific analyses allowed "people to commit themselves to the true God and not to some figment

Henry Wieman. Courtesy of the University of Chicago
Special Collections Research Center.

of their distorted needs."[55] Mays's lifelong struggle with God's justice converged with Wieman's intellectual concerns for a clearer conceptualization of God. This intellectual affinity stimulated Mays to reflect more broadly about what God meant in the collective experience of black Americans.[56]

Mays was still feverishly writing his dissertation when he took the position as dean of the Howard School of Religion. He worked himself to the point of exhaustion, both emotionally and physically, and was forcibly bedridden for months during the latter part of 1934 and early 1935. His dear friends and colleagues worried.[57] Howard Thurman chided him to "get a great deal of rest and let that thesis alone. ... There are other days in which you can work much more effectively without spending as much time on it."[58] Once he regained his health, Mays defended his dissertation, "The Idea of God in Contemporary Negro Literature," in December 1935. His dissertation adviser was Professor Edwin A. Aubrey.[59]

In writing his dissertation, Mays had been determined to represent the theological ideas of black Americans using source material that lay in plain view but remained neglected by theologians. While still in residence at the Divinity School in 1933, he had been warned that he should not expect to find more on the subject about the religious practices of blacks, since, according to some of his professors, *The Negro's Church* had sufficiently covered the subject. But Mays's proven intellectual abilities afforded him latitude in choosing his dissertation topic.[60] In a letter to Thurman in 1935, Mays expressed his pride in having defended his dissertation and received honors. "I came through as I had hoped that I would," he wrote, "with my head high above the waters for I have never wanted to be a border line case in anything. I would have preferred not to have had the degree if I had barely gotten by."[61]

While his boasting to Thurman was warranted, he might have also mentioned that it was Dorothy Porter, a brilliant Howard University librarian, who provided Mays access to a rich bevy of materials to use to complete his dissertation. And it was Sadie Mays's persistent encouragement and nursing when he suffered exhaustion that got him through his bedridden months. It was she who made him turn the dissertation into a book. It was quite satisfying for the both of them when the book was published in 1938. It had been a long road to Mays's becoming Dr. Mays, the twice-published book author.

With some revisions to his dissertation and a new introduction, Mays published the book as *The Negro's God: As Reflected in His Literature*.[62] In his study, he tried to clarify how black Americans historically conceptualized God. In his introduction he wrote, "Some people approach God through the sense of moral struggle against sin and evil [;] in which case God reveals himself in the struggle with man. Some approach God through the intellect as did Hegel; in which case God becomes absolute truth." But there was another way to approach God, "the ethical approach." He argued, "One may approach God by accepting the traditional views of God, taking God for granted as Jesus and the prophets did, but in an effort to achieve fullness of life, emphasizing those ideas of God that support one's desires and struggles to achieve the needs for existence. It is highly possible that the man who is suppressed and feels the injustices of society would emphasize the justice of God."[63]

Mays analyzed a variety of literary genres, including sermons, poetry, fiction, and essays, from two roughly distinct periods—during slavery from 1760 until 1860, and after emancipation, between 1865 and 1914, to categorized black literary production into two types, "mass" and "classical." Mass literature was the cultural production of ordinary religious believers: Negro spirituals, sermons, prayers, and Sunday school texts. Classical literature was primarily the written reflections of well-educated black writers, thinkers, and religious leaders. His broad typologies covered roughly.

His chief contention was that for the better part of American history black people's concept of God had been primarily "compensatory," one deriving from traditional readings of the Bible, with an "emphasis upon the magical, spectacular, partial, revengeful, and anthropomorphic nature of God as revealed in the Old Testament; the New Testament ideas of a just, impartial God; and those ideas of God that are being rapidly discarded in the age of science." The danger in a compensatory idea of God, Mays argued, was that it encouraged "a shallow pragmatism," or an approach in which any "belief or idea may be accredited as true if it satisfies our desire, *if it uplifts and consoles*; or if it makes us *happier to believe it* even though the belief or idea does not fit observed fact."[64]

Although he was critical of compensatory ideas about God, he did not view them as categorically bad. He observed, for example, that they gave comfort to people dealing with anxiety or grief. His chief concern was when "compensatory patterns" were linked to political struggle and social change. What worried him was the popularly held belief that God was omnipotent and wrathful and that God's sole purpose was to judge individual indiscretions as a litmus test for receiving the death benefit of heaven. This belief, he felt, did not empower anyone to change the negative social structures found in laws and government to make heaven real for their lives on earth. This kind of discourse about God, he believed, produced a "negative goodness in the individual based on a fear" of the afterlife and not a positive hope for his or her earthly life.[65]

Though Mays was silent about his past losses, his ruminations about God had a great deal to do with his most painful tragedies—the death of his first wife, Ellen Harvin, and the murder of his oldest brother, James Mays. Their deaths could not be simply washed away with easy words about God's loving kindness and the promise of everlasting life. At the core of his dissertation and subsequent book was his own intellectual and spiritual struggle to understand God, human suffering, and inexplicable evil. Like many black preachers of the nineteenth century, Mays grappled with questions of theodicy; that is, how were black people to think about arbitrary human suffering and God's Providence?[66] He attempted to discern, out of the various fragments of black people's own literature, a conception of God that would bring about social change and alleviate collective injustices. He maintained that blacks' idea of God had historically fluctuated as their freedoms and the social conditions changed. His study documented an unwavering fidelity to "God-talk" among blacks as a way to preserve community and as a way of responding to political injustices. The unyielding persistence of American racism was the thread that stitched his study together.

Mays saw the revolutionary upheaval in the aftermath of World War I as having created a new kind of culture of belief for black people. This shift dislodged an older faith, which slaves and former slaves employed to survive and sustain community. Mays's generation had grown disaffected with America's supposed innocence.[67] For Mays, this new intellectual climate posed a challenge. While rural dwellers and the emerging urban population continued to believe in God and attend church, their fidelity to religious orthodoxy had been called into question by a richly diverse group of cosmopolitan writers, thinkers, and political activists who challenged their belief.

Culturally, the Russian Revolution of 1917 spurred the revolt against Christian Victorianism. Black-owned journals and periodicals—*The Crisis, Opportunity, The Messenger*, and *The Liberator* among them—began increasingly to question the relevance of religion to black political struggle and cultural life.[68] Black newspapers around the country added to this rich discussion by reporting on the activities of black churches. The coverage helped to create an even more intensely critical climate regarding religious beliefs and practices. Meanwhile, perhaps for the first time, a cadre of young black intellectuals openly challenged theistic beliefs among black people without fear of reprisal. And both religious and nontheistic intellectuals alike critiqued what they perceived to be the excesses of black religious behavior.

A. Philip Randolph and Chandler Owens's socialist magazine *The Messenger* was one such forum for discussion of both liberal faith and atheism within the black community. Randolph, the son of an African Methodist Episcopal minister, was never an atheist but was highly critical of black churches. The magazine challenged the church's acquiescence to segregation and impoverishment and raged against traditional Victorian religiosity, which it said blinded black Americans to their struggles for living wages. The magazine's editors allowed for free expression and published the work of literary figures such as Claude McKay, whose poetry seared the consciousness of its readers with the message of God's death.[69] At the same time, however, Owens and Randolph published articles about the progressive political activities of black urban churches. Black people's faith persisted despite the intellectual criticism, and Mays understood this persistent faith from his own life's journey.

In the mid-1930, the sociological theory and the economic theorization of Karl Marx had put many black writers into a trance.[70] Marxism took hold of a small, boisterous group of writers whose works covered a wide variety of genres. They wrote using musical idioms from blues and folklore, and they attached themselves to the political ideology of communism or socialist economics. Writers and poets like Langston Hughes, Claude McKay, and later Richard Wright, directly challenged an older generation of black intellectuals for succession.[71] Hughes, McKay, and Wright had joined the Communist Party and subscribed to the party's atheism. Their writings openly challenged Christian belief. In this era of contestation for the hearts and minds of black people, Mays realized that if the black church was to retain its important historical place as a foundational institution in the lives of black people, the theology informing the community had to be updated to confront the strangle hold that racism and its twin tools—political disfranchisement and economic isolation—had on their lives.

In *The Negro's God*, Mays attempted to synthesize the Chicago School's emphasis on theological modernism into something relevant for the era of political radicalism and liberalism.[72] His "aim," he wrote in the book's preface, "is to tell America what the Negro thinks of God. . . . As strange as it may seem, this book represents the first attempt to study the development of the idea of God in Negro Literature." While providing a genealogy of blacks' ideas about God, Mays also countered the popular depiction of black religiosity as "over-emotional."[73]

In the spring of 1936, just as Mays began reworking his dissertation for publication, the popular Broadway musical *The Green Pastures*, with an all-black cast, was released as a film. The depiction of black American religiosity in *The Green Pastures* violated all of Mays's sensibilities. The Broadway musical opened in 1930 and had been well-received by both the black and white press. The musical presented blacks "as interracial ambassadors of goodwill whose charming flaws of dialect and naiveté allowed white audiences to admire their unthreatening dignity. For blacks, at least those who praised it, the play fulfilled an ambition that most black leaders, even the most nationalistic, had come to embrace—the eventual carving of a black place in American society based on dignity and merit." This may have been true of the Broadway show, but the film was received with considerably less enthusiasm, the responses ranging from skepticism to downright hostility. In the play, one of the central characters, Hezdrel, was depicted as a kind of New Negro radical. However, in the film, his role was diminished, and the other characters into minstrel stereotypes for mass appeal. The film's most important scene is when "De Lawd," played by Rex Ingram, presides over the heavenly fish fry.[74] Hollywood, it seems, adopted from its minstrel stage predecessor the nasty habit of cheapening the religious experiences of black people for laughs. From Hollywood's vantage point, black people did not "experience [the] true power of the divine in their lives." They only imagined that they did.[75]

For Mays, the religiosity portrayed in *The Green Pastures* was insulting. "It has been assumed by many people that the ideas of God expressed in *Green Pastures* are wholly representative of what the Negro thinks of God," he wrote in the preface to *The Negro's God*. "Although the author did not set out in this study to disprove anything presented in *Green Pastures*, the data themselves show that the Negro's idea of God is *not* now and has never been what *Green Pastures* may lead some people to believe."[76] His analysis of black literature, which he observed was written by "the best trained men of the race," confirmed that not all blacks considered God's will as an inevitable fate.

> The Negroes' ideas of God in this period are those of traditional Christianity, but they are the most lofty of the traditional ideas. The dominant ones are: God is just; He is love; He is no respecter of person; He is a God of peace; from one blood or species God made all mankind; God is on the side of the righteous and the oppressed; and God will eventually bring to judgment those who continue to violate His laws. It is clear, therefore, that these early Negro writers exercised a keen sense of selectivity and chose those of ideas of God that supported their claim for social justice and complete emancipation.[77]

Mays's rationale for the book was clear. He was "interested in the Negro race" and "the Negro represents one of the minority, underprivileged groups in American society."[78] His goal was to present black people's religious faith as a subject deserving respect and careful scholarly consideration. Their theological ideas were to be studied alongside of their "social and economic background" to see if their environment determined their theology. This was, Mays remarked, "a vital point because there are various approaches to a conception of God, and to see which approach the Negro has made is revealing in the light of the social situation in which he lives and of his minority status in American life."[79] Mays understood that there were a variety of ways in which scholars have approached God—intellectually, mystically, experientially, and through moral struggle. In Mays's mind, God could not simply be an aesthetically pleasing ethereal being but had to be a purposeful agent in the lives of black people for a greater ethical good.

Mays was intellectually torn throughout the pages of *The Negro's God*. Was God a human self-projection to help people deal with particular historical circumstances? This was a question he never quite answered in the book. However, he was firm in his conviction that no matter what moral force the universe called God, it was a force on the side of justice. Ironically, though *The Negro's God* was a theological exploration, its theoretical basis was grounded not in theology but in a facet of social psychology that examined defensiveness in a minority group's behavior. Mays based his conclusions on the scholarly literature outside of his field of study; however, one wonders why he did not more closely analyze his interpretive justification as he transformed the dissertation into a book.

Despite its shortcomings, the book was a seminal in terms of understanding black religious thought. In addition, it was a contemporary snapshot of the pressing issues of the day. For example, Mays expressed his appreciation for the work of Marcus Garvey. "Though not an American Negro," he wrote, "Marcus Garvey did spectacular work in America. His work was significant too. He called the colored man's attention to his numerical strength in the world." More important for Mays was that "he helped to develop race pride in the American Negro. He had much to say about God. He joined other Negro leaders in their efforts to convince the members of his race that they were not accursed people." Garvey "insisted that the Negro was created in the image of God and that in every particular race the Negro race is the equal of other races . . . it was Garvey who placed the emphasis on the conception that the Negro must see God not through the spectacles of white men nor yellow men, but through the eyes of Ethiopians." Garvey, Mays noted, used his ideas about God "to arouse the Negro to a sense of deep appreciation for his race. He used it, too, to stimulate the Negro to improve his social and economic conditions."[80]

While Mays was accepting of Garvey's religious nationalism, which appealed to his sense of manliness, he was unnerved by Nella Larsen's literary critique of black religiosity in her novel *Quicksand*. For Mays, Larsen's protagonist Helga Crane epitomized the crisis of faith among the black intelligentsia. According to Crane, Mays wrote, "what ailed the whole Negro race in America [was] the fatuous belief in the white man's God, this childlike trust in full compensation for all woes and privations in *Kingdom Come*." Although Mays agreed with this assessment, he took issue with Crane's view that black religious faith had succumbed to piteous and laughable defeat. "How the white man's God must laugh at the great joke He played on them," Mays charged. "Bound them to slavery, then to poverty and insult, and made them bear it unresistingly, uncomplainingly almost, by the sweet promises of mansions in the sky by and by."[81] Larsen portrayed the lives of women being bound by black religiosity, and Mays took issue with the Crane character's total disregard for any of the strengths of black religiosity. Mays's reading of the novel disregarded its insight into the gender politics of the era. "Larsen's own life and writings presented a model of modern black womanhood that challenged Mays's vision," historian Barbara Savage notes. His vision was based on unquestioned assumptions about male privilege. He viewed the black church as a social change agency led by a well-educated black clergy mobilizing the black masses in a struggle to win their civil rights. Nella Larsen's seemingly dismal view of black religion left him cold.[82]

The Negro's God never resolved many of the intellectual contradictions found in his dissertation. As social ethicist Gary Dorrien observed, "*The Negro's God* covered more material than its binary distinctions could handle."[83] This was the result of his extensive use of a purely descriptive historical methodology. He had been so heavily dependent upon historicity, fact-finding, and political mobilization that it actually constrained his reading of the literature he studied. The way he historicized black religious tradition almost caused him to undermine the very thrust of his theology. Mays did not analyze the rich cultural practices of black Americans or the ordinary language that they used to described God's meaningfulness in their lives, and thus he missed an opportunity to construct a positive theology. His understanding of theological modernism was too narrowly focused and bound by his desire to make a manly theology that presumably fought against domination. As a result, he ignored the actual modernity that was transforming black religiosity and black Protestantism. He also did not quite comprehend that black folk religion was sometimes a corrective to the blind spots of theological modernism. There were ways of thinking about God in relation to the experience of ordinary black people that needed to be illuminated. In this regard, *The Negro's God* did not completely fulfill Mays's lofty aspiration to unravel how the God-talk found in literature aided black people's efforts to gain full citizenship as Americans.

In his review of *The Negro's God*, historian Carter Woodson, pointed out some of these same flaws and stingily, and perhaps somewhat unfairly, criticized Mays for his overreliance on elite black literature. "[The] data set forth in the work . . . do not show as clearly as they should that the change in the Negro's conception of God did not result altogether from his persecution but was due to some extent to the changing conception of God among the whites themselves at the same time," Woodson wrote. "In a sense, therefore, the American Negro's conception of God is still that of those around him rather than any special contribution which he has made himself."[84]

Mays's Ph.D. mentor, Edwin Aubrey, who also reviewed the book, acknowledged that the book was "an important book on the history of American thought. . . . Dr. Mays has ably filled an important gap in the history of theological development in this country." However, he took issue with the breakdown of Mays's classification scheme after World War I. He noted, "It would have been valuable to compare these types of conception of God found in the last period with contemporary theological literature in general. As it stands this volume shows the weakness manifest in *The Negro's Church* by the same author: the disposition to make Negro thought too closely dependent on the social status of the colored race to the exclusion of influences affecting *all* Americans and producing equivalent attitudes in the religious thinking of whites as well." Aubrey pointed out other flaws in the book as well, though he presciently noted that one day as "the Negro" began to make a fuller contribution to American theological discourse, "his thinking will find a most valuable background in this book."[85]

Although Mays never returned to some of the seminal ideas found in his study, his book is one of the earliest forays into modernist theology by a black intellectual. Both *The Negro's Church* and *The Negro's God* were unabashed affirmations that black American religious life was worthy of serious academic study and theological reflection. They became the twin pillars of black modernist theology.

The centrality of the divine remained constant in Mays's thinking. "Though my ideas of God have changed mightily since my boyhood days," he wrote in 1961, "I still believe in God. I cannot believe otherwise."[86] "Yearning for the best and highest that man conceives," he continued, "[is planted by a higher power"—a power that he called God. Human beings, he opined, were "finite, weak and frail" and were prone to seek "strength in some source beyond himself." In surveying world history Mays affirmed a biblical anthropology. Essentially, he saw the human need to worship infamous heroes such as Hitler and Mussolini as a spiritual yearning for a greater security outside the self, which was his "proof that man needs a God." If man "abolishes the traditional Christian concept of God, he will create or find another god." In his scheme, "man must have something outside himself to which he can give ultimate allegiance."[87] Like Wieman, Mays continued to believe that "man is hell-bent for God."

However, unlike late-nineteenth-century religious liberals, Mays was never optimistic about progress in modern society.[88] Mays's humble beginnings were a prime example of human beings' capacity for evil and sinfulness, even in the name of God. The theological liberals who influenced him at Chicago, though intellectually stimulating, had not known what it meant to live with the daily brutalization and humiliation black Americans experienced. They had never felt the antipathy he experience as a racial minority or social exclusion. For Mays, evil intent and actions were a human reality. God, Mays believed, gave human beings freedom to make choices. They could make the wrong choices and as a result cause great harm to those around them, or they could make the right choices for the benefit of all. In his mind, the church had to be ever vigilant in standing guard against injustice and inhumanity.

While Mays always expressed hopefulness in God, he was pessimistic regarding humans' capacity to do what was fair and just. God, he repeatedly intoned, set the parameters of a discernable moral universe. "Man is a discoverer and not a creator. The scientist can do his work because the universe is dependable. . . . The universe belongs to God. If the universe were not orderly, the scientist could not function. The scientist did not make the universe orderly. The order came from God."[89] If the discernable moral order of God were violated, there would be negative consequences: "It is inherent in the laws of God that if man violates nature's law, he suffers."[90] God's laws should be followed for the good of the nation or the civilization. Mays thought that neither injustice nor exploitation was from God.

Mays also believed that Jesus "represents God, and God is absolute."[91] In his theological framework, Jesus is the Christ because he points human beings to what God would have them to do in life. Through the example of Jesus, God gave humanity an ethical imperative: "Jesus will not let our conscience be at ease. When we take advantage of the poor, the weak, and helpless, we meet Jesus." The universality of Jesus's prophetic message was inescapable. "He speaks softly but convincingly to us, telling us that when we take advantage of the helpless we take advantage of God, that when we hurt man we hurt God, that when we rob man we rob God, that when we kill man we kill God. Everywhere we turn, we meet this man Jesus. He will not let our conscience be at ease."[92]

Mays believed that a person's conscience was largely driven by faith. From this vantage point, what made Jesus the "Lord" was his "ethics and his belief that all wisdom flowed from God. Jesus represented God's highest ethical good. Mays interpreted Jesus's crucifixion as an unparalleled ethical sacrifice for God's cause. What made Jesus, the Christ, was the devotion to following his path through his teaching and understanding of the biblical prophets. "Approximately nineteen hundred years ago, a Jew of Palestine hung on a cross, dying between two thieves, because he dreamed a dream—that all men are sons of God, and when we hurt man we hurt God." According to Mays, Jesus was "the clearest relation of '*what God is like*'[;] through his teachings, crucifixion, and resurrection as revealed in the gospels, we get a glimpse of what God is like and his purpose for the world." For the church, Jesus was the master teacher. "In spiritual insight and in moral grandeur Jesus stands alone," said Mays. The church's task then was to proclaim him "the greatest teacher that ever lived."[93]

The religious modernism that Mays studied at Bates and Chicago must be seen in another context as well. Both schools were rooted in the Northern Baptist tradition.[94] Each school reflected the long history of Baptists in the United States, and particularly their belief in one's freedom to express one's individual conscience. To understand the modern symbiosis between black and white Protestantism, the denominational affiliation that connected them must be taken seriously. Any discussion of Mays's, or any other Baptist's liberal theology, must take into consideration the Baptist tradition in the United States. Being Baptist did not mean simply belonging to a voluntary denominational affiliation; it also meant adhering to an intellectual tradition that was derived from a theological meditation on the meaningfulness of God, the individual in society, and community.[95] It is important to understand that Baptists' disregard for some aspects of Christian creedalism also had an effect on how Mays viewed theological doctrine as a whole. Baptists always distrusted the statements of faith and ritual as the way to express one's faith in God and to be a community of believers. For Baptists, the most important response to God's saving actions in Jesus was the voluntary act of accepting God's divine grace in one's life and then becoming a member of the church through baptism.

It was therefore troublesome for Mays to reconcile collective agency with individual agency. Just as the explanations of race and society by the more radical economic determinists of the era were viewed with suspicion, so, too, were overarching dogmatic tenets of churches. The economic determinism preached by communists was a lot like the ancient creeds of the early church that did not leave room for individual agency. The antitheistic theories of many of Mays's intellectual peers did not comport with the notion of a sovereign God, which he and many ordinary black church-going people had come to rely upon in their daily struggle. The economist Abram Harris, a colleague of Mays's at Howard University, for example, argued in his book *The Black Worker* that church-affiliated colleges "infused southern education with religious zeal and with moral discipline." For Harris, black religiosity did not mobilize politically. In his estimation, this kind of education resulted in the black middle class looking to "heaven and philanthropy of benevolent whites for Negro salvation."[96] Unlike Harris, Mays viewed Christianity as having the power to mobilize black people and give them strength to fight injustices.

In February 1940, Mays presented a paper on the theological conception of grace to the Theological Discussion Group at the Yale University Divinity School. This scholarly group was comprised of leading American Protestant theologians such as H. Richard Niebuhr and Reinhold Niebuhr. The paper, titled "Nature, Grace, and Community," revealed his theological reasoning after the publication of *The Negro's God*. "Grace," Mays argued, "is God placing Himself at the disposal of man, which man may accept or reject. . . . It is the power of good which enables the individual to do what under ordinary circumstances he could not do. It is both dynamic and redemptive; but not irresistible." Mays's primary point was that grace is "a determinant in history." As World War II broke out in Asia and Europe, he was drawn to the idea that "communities are sustained not by the material resources, nor by the strength of armies and navies; but rather by virtue of the proper use of moral and spiritual qualities, which, although not man's creation, are nevertheless at his disposal." With this assertion Mays challenged the central tenet of philosophical naturalism, that "nature (including man) is all there is."[97]

Mays's theological contention with naturalism was predicated upon how he interpreted community. Drawing upon the scholarship of his Chicago mentor Edwin Aubrey, he defined community as "a certain 'mentality' of the people and a 'unity in social outlook.' By this general definition, there may be specific communities: international, interracial, inter-religious, inter-sex, and inter-industrial communities." The church was a special community. Quoting from Aubrey, he argued that the church "bases its authority upon an objective truth which reaches beyond the social milieu to the universe and beyond human adventure to the larger context from which man derives his meaning—the Church is a body of those who make a commitment beyond the range of social calculation." To Aubrey, accepting naturalism meant that human beings could not reach beyond themselves. Philosophical naturalism could make no argument for why human beings should not be self-absorbed and selfish. "The question must be raised, therefore, as to whether history proves that man's reason, taken by itself alone, can be relied upon to change selfishness into selflessness, hate into love as exists between man and man, group and group, nation and nation." The survival instincts in a human being "if allowed to go unchecked, become the basis of self-destruction." Mays grappled with the outbreak of wars from China to Europe and asked, "Why strive for an ideal community?" In this way of thinking, there would be no justifiable reason to do so "unless by chance, he finds himself [dependent] on the strong and powerful who determine what the purpose of existence shall be." Evoking a kind of social Darwinian logic, he asked, "If grace is not a determinant in history, what hope is there for the weak people of the earth who strive but to be swallowed up and exploited by the strong?"[98]

More importantly to Mays was that "under naturalism the Church as a distinct institution whose task it is to transform human nature into divine nature must cease to exist." The nineteenth-century Germanic idea that the church was only an indistinct cultural institution was false in his opinion. As an agent of community building the church was to redeem "a world that is torn to pieces by war" and individual impotence. For Mays, grace was a tool or a gift from God for remaking the world into a better community. In this sense, he challenged the rigidity of nineteenth-century Calvinist orthodoxy preached in Baptist doctrine about grace that led to fatalism and apathy.

Edwin Aubrey. Courtesy of the University of Pennsylvania Archives.

If grace is arbitrary and irresistible, there is likely to exist a kind of fatalistic indifference except for the preordained elect. In the very nature of things, religion tends to become highly otherworldly. Social action tends to be palliative rather than reconstructive, circumferential rather than central. Everything is in the hands of God; there is nothing that man can do about it. To the contrary, if grace is actually cooperative, redemptive, man is awakened to an inescapable sense of social responsibility. God through grace comes into him, lifts him, and gives him power to go forth with poise convinced that nothing unjust can permanently endure. Man is stimulated by a sense of divine impulsion. He is not alone in a struggle with sinful man. He arrives at and is sustained by a sense of corporate adequacy because he is a fellow-worker with God. If grace is God at the disposal of man, it means that God is also present as healer, lover, forgiver. . . . Without grace there can be no communion between God and man and without grace no community can be sustained.[99]

For Mays, God's grace supported the work of justice in the world. Those who received grace were righteous workers with God on the earth. Grace could never be meaningful if one's neighbors lived in oppression.

Mays's theological openness allowed him to ask questions about the Bible and God in an honest and critical way. His constant question was, how could

God stand on the side of the oppressed? It was this kind of intellectual honesty that aided Mays in sharpening his criticisms against the cultural and institutional structures of a racist society.

The intellectual sources of Protestant liberal theology helped plant the seeds of black modernist theology.[100] Mays's two books were central in that development. In this way, Mays anticipated the black theology movement, which began in the United States in the late 1960s.[101] Beliefs and practices about God in black communities were important to the struggle for human dignity and social justice. God-talk, Mays recognized, was powerful in the day-to-day joys and struggles of a community besieged by poverty and oppression. He had surveyed the range options and preachments within black communities about God in *The Negro's Church* and *The Negro's God*. God was everywhere! Turn any street corner in a black neighborhood and God was found in places like Father Divine's Peace Mission and Bishop Ida Robinson's Mount Sinai Holy Church of America, Inc., in the Moorish Science Temples, and in the various Pentecostal denominations that flowed upward from the southern deltas and bayous guided by holiness and spiritual exuberance. With the rich "God-talk" that prevailed in black communities in mind, he wrote many years after his books were published:

> It seems to me it matters *much* what one believes. In essence man
> is a bundle of beliefs and what he believes reveals what he is. We are
> what we do and what we believe. No one can live fully without a
> system of beliefs and convictions and no man can face the realities of
> life with confidence, poise, and hope without an abiding faith of some
> kind. The people who change the face of the earth are not cynics. They
> are men of faith. . . . The world moves forward on the feet of men who
> have faith. And faith must be big enough to command our complete
> allegiance.[102]

For Mays, if his argument about the meaningfulness of faith held true, then, the most important persons in fostering faith development were black Protestant clergymen. They were the leaders that were closest to the day-to-day struggles of ordinary people. However, as crucial as black ministers were as leaders, they were the least educated and professionally trained. In Mays's mind, they were the political agents needed to spiritually transform the black masses and inspire them to protest for civil rights. And in doing so, they would help black people gain a fuller humanity.

The Most Neglected Area in Negro Education

> Notwithstanding the fact that the Negro ministers, as a group,
> have lost prestige, it is still true that the Negro minister is the most
> significant leader of the Negro masses. This being true, the best trained
> men and women should be the leaders.
> —MAYS, quoted in *The Crisis*

In a 1933 article, "The Education of the Negro Ministers," Benjamin Mays summarized many of the conclusions he had come to regarding black clergymen in *The Negro's Church*: "Religion is non-competitive. Frequently it does not deal with social and economic needs. Often it projects its hopes in a distant future or dreams of a heaven where the values sought here, but unattained, will be realized in some far-off glory land." As a result, "it was much easier for the Negro to achieve freedom in religion than it was for him to acquire it in other fields. . . . It is far more difficult to keep a man, though a slave, from expressing and practicing his religion than it is to prohibit him from expressing and exercising his social and political views. Religion is as close to man as breathing." Ministers, he continued, were the "first to be accepted" among slaves, "primarily because of the nature of religion" and "partly because the minister was the first to be tolerated in appreciable numbers by slave owners." And lastly, Baptists and Methodists required "no special formal training in order to preach." Sociologically and religiously, black ministers were able to bypass the strictures of other professions because of ministry's open access. "As a special representative of God," he observed, the minister "was full-grown at the very beginning" and had "won his way into the hearts of the people." Black clergymen were indigenous ritual leaders within their communities. "He blessed the baby at birth, he married the adults, and in the hours of death and bereavement he shared the people's grief; he consoled them and brought them comfort. These are chief factors that gave the Negro minister a place of preeminence in the Negro group."[1]

The social status of black ministers was up for grabs. In a former time, Mays observed, "the minister was frequently the best and the only trained man of a given community." However, the "grand rush" in attaining "high school and college education" within black communities made the education of black ministers "urgent." He believed that the intellectual formation of black clergy was essential in addressing modern conditions. Mays sadly came to the conclusion that black theological institutions that trained ministers were the least progressive institutions. "As a result," he reasoned, "the best students in Negro colleges, who go into ministry, have found it necessary to pursue their training at the University of Chicago, Union, Colgate-Rochester, Harvard, Drew, Oberlin, Boston University, Yale and other Northern Seminaries." Bluntly he asserted, "Negro seminaries are, for the most part, so inferior in quality that Negro students are forced to take their religious training outside of Negro seminaries." A student's decision to attend a "Northern seminary should be a matter of choice rather than a necessity as now caused by the inadequacy of Negro seminaries." He realized that all institutions of higher education that served black students suffered from neglect. To him, this was especially true in theological education. Mays wrote, "There is no denying the fact that one of the next steps in Negro education should be found in Negro theological seminaries." These historically black seminaries, he believed, could be the "peer of any seminary in America." He observed, "If religion is to be respectable, challenging, and increasingly helpful to the group, we have no other choice than to concern ourselves more in the future with theological education among Negroes than we have in the past."[2]

There was one big problem. What theological institution would lead the charge in upgrading the professional education of black ministers? What black institution had enough resources to build a sustainable professional program? Most of the church-related private colleges had theology departments that were denominationally affiliated—for example, Fisk College in Nashville, Tennessee (Congregationalist); Johnson C. Smith in Charlotte, North Carolina (Presbyterian); Virginia Union in Richmond, Virginia (Baptist); Morehouse College in Atlanta (Baptist); and Gammon Theological Seminary in Atlanta, Georgia (Methodist)—but none of these schools had the quality of trained faculty to offer the graduate professional training that he envisioned. But all that changed in 1934. When Mays completed his Ph. D. course work at Chicago, Mordecai Johnson, the president of Howard University, asked him to be the university's new dean of the School of Religion. Here was his opportunity to build a rigorous graduate program for black clergy.

Howard University was once considered "The Capstone of Negro Education."[3] General Oliver O. Howard, who served in the Union army during the American Civil War and was the head of the Freedmen's Bureau, founded it in 1867. The scholarly advancement and rich productivity of the university's array of scholars made it one of the most exciting schools in the country, as well as one of the South's best universities.[4] In the South, there were very few institutions of higher education that openly challenged the doctrinaire opinions of their trustees. Howard University was different. Its faculty was allowed a greater degree of academic freedom than that exercised at many universities within the South. Its location in Washington, D.C., its openness, and its high-powered faculty made it the most desirable of all the black colleges and universities available. Mays joined a new generation of scholars at Howard—Abram Harris Jr. (economics), Ernest Everett Just (biology), E. Franklin Frazier (sociology), Ralph Bunche (political science), Alain Locke (philosophy), Charles Hamilton Houston (law), Sterling A. Brown (literature), and Rayford Logan and Charles Wesley (history)—all of whom were instrumental in shaping Howard's aura.[5] The history of Howard's changing status from a semisectarian college to a university was most evident in how the university sought to reconcile its larger educational goals to the Christian ministry.[6]

The School of Religion was formed during the Reconstruction era under a unique partnership between the federal government and the American Missionary Association (AMA).[7] The AMA, like most Protestant missionary organizations in the late nineteenth century, thought of themselves as serving the United States and the world by cultivating Christian faith through education. The School of Religion, under the initial leadership of General Howard, patterned itself along the lines of the AMA, having ties with the YMCA movement and cooperation with various Protestant denominations.

The school began modestly in 1872 with an emphasis on the practical training of black clergymen. James Bunyan Reeves, the school's first dean, was a black Presbyterian minister. When Reeves opened the doors of the theological department, it was comprised of "eighteen students of different denominations as well as four Methodist preachers from the city who attended when they could."[8] Reeves observed that there were educational disparities among the students in the department. He wrote, "Our students differ more in the amount of their previous preparation than in native capacity. . . . Respecting these students poorly fitted: We have received a few such; and think that by so doing we have pursued one purpose, for which the department was organized, and for which it will be greatly needed for some years to come. The dilemma was to receive them as they are or let them continue to preach as they are. I answer, receive them." They were received because black ministers were frontline leaders that protected the interests of the "newly emancipated freedmen." Black ministers sacrificially "held the trenches," encouraging education in the black community until other kinds of professional opportunities were available.[9]

Howard's theological department provided ministerial training on campus and via correspondence courses. In order to meet the educational needs of black Protestant clergymen in the early twentieth century, the university also instituted an annual convocation on topics germane to religious leadership. In 1918, under the direction of Dean David Butler Pratt, the first convocation of ministers was offered. Its title, "Effective Christianity in the Present Crisis," reflected the cultural and physical devastation of World War I. The featured speaker was retired chief judge of the U.S. Court of Claims and Howard trustee Stanton J. Peelle, whose talk was titled "The World War: Its Causes and Result."[10] In 1920, the theological department also began an annual Ministerial Institute in Kingston, North Carolina. These convocations and annual institutes served both the alumni of Howard's theological department and other interested clergy.[11]

Funding problems, however, plagued the theological department, especially after financing from the AMA and support from the local Presbyterian churches dried up. Financial woes kept the number of graduates consistently small. In addition, aside from its money problems, the school's model for theological education also stifled growth. The education offered at Howard was based upon New England college models, so the School of Religion was not set up to educate untrained and entrepreneurial clergymen who preached in black folk idioms. The New England model did not attract the attention of the kind of clergymen who traversed the southern countryside and traveled "up North," following their southern parishioners.

The Howard theological department had another problem: it was always looked upon as the university's stepchild. It was created inside a federally sponsored university, which meant the issues of religion and the state had to be kept separate. In essence, or at least in theory, government funds could not be used to train clergymen. And yet successive generations of the university's administrators supported the department, however meagerly, because of the college's ongoing ties to Protestant denominational funding and Protestant philanthropic networks. Subsequent Howard presidents hoped that the theological department would become a center for a learned black clergy, but they could not budget more money to that end.[12] However, in the late 1920s the university, including the theological department, found new dynamism.

That dynamism came in the university's first black president, the Reverend Mordecai Wyatt Johnson. In 1926, Johnson was selected to be Howard's eleventh president. Previously, Johnson was one of black America's most highly sought after public speakers and preachers. He was a successful pastor of the First Baptist Church in Charleston, West Virginia, and he was one of the great advocates of the Social Gospel. Like Mays, Johnson was a devotee of Walter Rauschenbusch's theological thought. Johnson had been educated at Morehouse College, the University of Chicago, Rochester Theological Seminary, and Harvard University Divinity School. He greatly influenced younger clergymen and religious intellectuals. Mays recalled that Johnson made a tremendous "impression on me when I first heard him speak while I was a teacher at Morehouse, and thereafter I had followed his career."[13] Johnson was only four years older than Mays but had already been a trailblazer in setting a theological agenda for social change among black Americans.

Although Johnson had been a much sought after public speaker on black college campuses, Howard's board of trustees' decision to hire him was not made without difficulty. Three factors made Johnson a favorable candidate: First, Johnson was an outsider. The university's board of trustees was split on the internal candidates from the Howard faculty. They felt if they chose a faculty member, there might be increased internal divisiveness among the faculty. They saw Johnson as a breath of fresh air. Second, Johnson was well connected to the Protestant establishment through his Baptist affiliations, his work with the YMCA, and his ties to Chicago, Rochester, and Harvard. Finally, students attending black colleges throughout the 1920s were demanding that they replace retiring white presidents with black ones, and Howard was no exception. Students demanded a change, and over time the trustees of these schools obliged.[14]

When Howard's trustees voted Johnson in as its president, it was big news in black communities across the nation. Johnson's election and ascension to the office was debated widely at South Carolina State, where Mays was teaching at the time. The biggest concern regarding Johnson was whether or not a black man could be successful as a fund-raiser and leader.[15] Johnson proved to be a successful, if not a controversial leader at Howard.

When Johnson accepted Howard's presidency, it was a university in name only, as many of its professional programs were unaccredited and the weight of the degree was little respected outside of the small circles of black elite. Johnson envisioned a university that would be a powerful resource for advancing the *race* throughout the world. His vision was in part derived from his religious catholicity. In one of his earliest sermons, Johnson noted, "Wherever you see the children of God in this world, they are people who are concerned about the sufferings of those who have no claim upon them."[16] It was out of this sense of humanity that he appealed to religious and nonreligious alike to join him in building Howard as a university. Though Howard's work was to be officially nonsectarian, religious belief and practice could not be neglected because they were bedrocks of black life.

In his 1927 inaugural presidential address Johnson highlighted the significant role of religion in the lives of black people; he especially highlighted the role of churches. "There are 47,000 Negro churches in the United States, and there are in the whole country today less than sixty college graduates getting ready to fill these pulpits," he reflected. "There is no organization and no combination of organizations that can, at this stage in the history of the Negro race, begin to compare with the fundamental importance of the Negro church. And yet we can see what is going to happen to that church if only sixty college men are preparing to enter the Negro pulpit." He had reached the same conclusion that Mays had reached about the education of black clergy: "The simple, unsophisticated, mystical religion of the Negro cannot continue to endure unless it is reinterpreted over and over to him by men who have a fundamental and far-reaching understanding of the significance of religion in relation to the complexities of modern civilized life." He further underscored the university's role in addressing issues germane to black Protestant churches and religion: "Here at Howard University we have the ground work laid for a great nonsectarian school of religion." The purpose of the graduate school of religion, he continued, would be to seek "the truth about the meaning of life without bias, endeavoring to deliver the people from superstition and from uncharitable sectarianism, binding them into an understandable cooperation, clarifying their vision, and releasing their energies for constructive service to the common good."[17]

By 1931, with Johnson's encouragement, the theological department began to be reconfigured. A year later, the department had been disbanded and its duties were subsumed under a new division, the School of Religion. In addition, Johnson recruited his fellow alumnus from Morehouse College and Rochester Theological Seminary, Howard Thurman, to the faculty.[18] Thurman accepted the offer because, he explained, "I was caught up in Mordecai Johnson's vision to create the first real community of black scholars, to build an authentic university in America primarily dedicated to black youth."[19] There was another internal transition taking place within the School of Religion. David Butler Pratt, a white New Englander, was near the end of his seventeen-year tenure as dean. Pratt was one of the last AMA holdovers from Howard's ties to the Congregationalist Church that began in the Reconstruction era.[20] Pratt had run the theology department and nurtured the Christian missionary impulse that had been at the heart of the university's earliest educational mission.[21]

Upon Pratt's retirement in 1934, Johnson sought to appoint a black man as dean of the School of Religion. He wanted someone with credibility and standing in the black community, especially in the South. If the School of Religion was going to be a credible force it would have to be guided by someone who commanded the respect of other ministers, who had superb academic credentials, and who could give the School of Religion academic standing. Johnson, a Baptist clergyman himself, knew the pitfalls of black ministerial education and desired a transformational leader at the helm of the School of Religion. Channing Tobias, who once more proved to be an able mentor and advocate for Mays, recommended to Johnson that he appoint Mays.[22]

When Mays finished his academic course work and exams at Chicago, he had initially accepted a position teaching religion at Fisk University in Nashville. However, later in that summer, Johnson offered him the job at Howard. Mays jumped at the opportunity to work under Johnson's leadership. As he explained, "I was eager to go to Howard for several reasons. I felt the challenge to make the School of Religion outstanding, to lift it, if possible, from its stepchild role to a place of respectability in the institution."[23] And no one had a better track record than Mays. He was the chief author of a seminal study on black churches and would shortly hold a doctorate in theology.

Professionally, Howard was more challenging and offered more varied resources than Fisk. Taking up his duties at Howard while still in the throes of dissertation writing, Mays had access to its small library along with its greatest asset, the librarian Dorothy Porter. He also had access to the vast holdings of the Library of Congress and felt that Howard was the place to be "as a black intellectual." His colleagues were first-rate, and that fed his competitive spirit. The city of Washington offered both Mays and his wife an opportunity for growth in their respective careers. There was only one sticking point: his commitment to Fisk. Mays traveled to Nashville to ask Fisk's president, Thomas Jones, directly for permission to be released from his contract. Jones was gracious. Upon being released from his obligation to Fisk, he and Sadie excitedly packed all of their things in Atlanta and moved to Washington.

As Howard's new dean of the School of Religion, Mays faced a unique challenge. Unlike his theological counterparts who were at private, formerly church-affiliated universities or denominational seminaries, he had to walk a fine line regarding the separation of church and state since Howard received most of its funding from the U.S. government. This funding base was always paradoxical. Howard needed the congressional financing for growth, and yet racially based public policies kept the university's mission at bay. Howard faculty members had to be grateful to their donor base yet critical of its social agenda.[24] The School of Religion, as a Christian seminary, had an even greater set of funding problems than the university as a whole.

The School of Religion was independent and thus received no financial support outside of meager church funds, philanthropic foundation money, and the partial revenue that the university provided for the maintenance of its building and faculty. When Mays arrived at school, he found both its physical facilities and academic curriculum inadequate. "Prior to 1934," he noted, "the School of Religion had been mainly an institution for graduating men with the Bachelor of Theology degree, one that required only two years of college and two years of theological training." It was Mays's idea that the school be a professional one. "In 1934," he reported, "the B.Th. Degree was being phased out with the goal of making the School of Religion a full-fledged professional school, accepting only college graduates. My predecessor, Dean D. Butler Pratt, was very apprehensive about making the School of Religion a professional school. President Mordecai Johnson had his misgivings also. They doubted that such a School of Religion could attract enough college students to justify its existence." Mays, however, never was in doubt that he could meet the challenge.

He inherited no prestige at the university when he became the dean of the School of Religion. As he remembered, "The School of Religion was housed on Sixth Street in a shabby frame building. The library holdings were grossly inadequate. The school did not have any prestige of the other professional schools in the university community: medicine, law, dentistry, and engineering. The fact that the School of Religion was as old as the university itself added no luster to its reputation." But there were two things about the School of Religion that made the work worthwhile for Mays: "the challenge to improve it, and the opportunity to work with Mordecai Johnson."[25] The School of Religion's enrollment was "twenty-eight students—fourteen with college degrees in the graduate school and fourteen who were combining two years of college with two years of theological work."[26] Nothing proved to be more difficult than transforming the School of Religion into a professional program.

Mays went to work. He identified six objectives for the School of Religion: (1) It would "produce ministers of character and social imagination superior to those of the average citizen." (2) It would "strive to produce ministers who are the intellectual equals of men in any profession." (3) A minister not only must be intellectually sound but also "must be able to present and interpret his message in a convincing, sincere fashion[;] . . . to this end the School of Religion of Howard University [would lay] great emphasis upon the preparation and delivery of sermons." (4) Social caste, "whether built upon the basis of color, intellect, wealth or ancestry[,] is both vicious and ungodly, and certainly has no place among those who claim to represent God on the earth. It is, therefore, the aim of the School of Religion of Howard University to produce a group of ministers who will draw no fundamental distinction between 'high' and 'low,' 'rich' and 'poor,' and none between the 'learned' and the 'unlearned,' realizing that position, prestige, power are largely accidental possession." The most important thing the school had to achieve was "to graduate young ministers who look at life in the light of a thoroughgoing respect for personality and individuality." (5) The school would aim "to produce men who can interpret religion and theology in a changing world so as to make religion an effective agency in developing personality and a vital force in perfecting social change. . . . If the role of theology is definitive and if it is to aid in the cure of 'sick' souls, the modern theologian must clarify religious concepts (God, sin, salvation, et cetera), so as to make them constructive in the life of the individual and functional in the life of the group." (6) The School of Religion needed "to produce men who have a passion for preaching." Mays observed, "Young men go through our leading seminaries and come out with no passion for preaching."[27] He believed that passionless preaching resulted from the dry pedagogy of scholars who critiqued the Bible in such a manner that the narrative was flattened. In this regard, Mays hoped to bridge biblical scholarship with the art of black narrative preaching. To him, being erudite did not have to mean being dry. Great oratory was a necessary tool in organizing and creating a heightened social consciousness among black churchgoers for social change. Any school instructing a cadre of black clergy had to make the art of preaching a pivotal part of its education. Mays, Thurman, and Johnson were strong models for their students of what powerful black intellectual preaching could be like. This trio of black male churchmen was intent on inserting black clergy squarely in the intellectual and political debates taking place on civil rights.

Mays's drive to make the School of Religion highly academic and thoroughly professional also reflected the inherent tensions within theological seminaries in the first half of the twentieth century. In the wake of William Rainey Harper's ingenuity in structuring the University of Chicago as a research university with an academic divinity school, other divinity schools and seminaries were torn between the needs of professional training for Protestant clergy and making theology, as an academic discipline, a respectable field in the wider orb of the research university.[28]

In 1934, the Institute of Social and Religious Research (ISRR) and the Conference of Theological Seminaries co-published *The Education of American Ministers*, a four-volume study on the problem of theological education in the United States. Seminaries and university divinity schools were worried about the diminishing prestige of Protestant clergymen. The study sought

Benjamin Mays (far left) and Mordecai Johnson (center), ca. 1975. Courtesy of the
Moorland-Spingarn Research Center, Howard University.

to evaluate how theological education measured up against other kinds of professional education.[29] William Brown, the author of volume one, explained, "We find that the standard of requirement in the best professional schools had been very rapidly rising. It takes longer preparation and requires harder work to graduate from a first-class law or medical school than it did twenty years ago. If the ministry is to hold its own with the leaders of other professions, it is essential that the graduates of the best theological schools should be subjected to a discipline no less rigorous."[30] If the educational status of white Protestant clergymen had diminished, then the formal training of black Protestant clergymen simply had never gained currency. Mark May, the author of the second volume in the series, noted, "Clearly the educational status of colored Protestant ministers is much lower than that of white Protestant ministers."[31]

Mays was part of the ongoing national discussion regarding the prestige and professionalization of the Protestant clergy.[32] Like his theological counterparts, he wanted to raise academic standards and secure the School of Religion as a fully accredited school recognized by the American Association of Theological Schools.[33] Mays, however, also wanted to do this because he believed black clergymen were central to black people's fight for civic freedoms. Nothing in the three volumes on *The Education of the American* had ever suggested that clergymen be educated for societal change. In this regard, Mays stood out from his peers in theological education. Howard's School of Religion, under his leadership, was to educate clergy to be a part of the wider middle-class insurgency against Jim Crow.

The chief problem Mays faced was the recruitment of students. There were plenty of men, and some women, going into ministry, but, among black people, the call to the ministry had very little to do with formal education. Mays had to organize the school in order to attract prospective college graduates who felt themselves called to the ministry and who were willing to attend a divinity school or a seminary instead of going directly to a church. By 1937, the School of Religion's mission statement, which appeared in its catalog, read:

> The purpose of the School of Religion is to prepare men and women for Christian service; it aims to produce ministers and Christian workers whose integrity of character and social imagination are superior to those of the average citizen; to produce leaders in religion who are the intellectual equals of men in any profession; to graduate men and women who are able to interpret the Christian message in a convincing manner; to educate men and women who will draw no fundamental distinction between men recognizing the fact that caste built upon color, intellect, wealth or ancestry is both vicious and ungodly; it aims further to produce men who can interpret religion and theology in a changing world so as to make religion an effective agency in developing personality and a vital force in perfecting social change; finally it is the purpose of the School of Religion to turn out young men who have a zeal and passion for preaching—men who preach because they must.[34]

The catalog also indicated that the school, "open without discrimination to men and women," was "inter-denominational . . . students are taught the great fundamental doctrines common to all evangelical churches. The result is that they are made not less loyal to their own denominations, but better able to see the loyalty of all to the one common Saviour and better able to join in hearty co-operation with their brethren for the advancement of a common cause."[35] Another benefit to attending the School of Religion, the catalog pointed out, was the amenities to be found living in Washington, D.C.: "[the School of Religion] is in contact with a large colored population, so that students have ample opportunity to participate actively in work in local churches, social settlements, and other institutions. There are in Washington nearly

150 Negro churches, representing all of the important denominations, so that each student can keep close relationship with the church of his choice."[36]

One of Mays's chief anxieties was the nation's cultural perception of the South.[37] Many white northerners, for example, associated the South with rural underdevelopment, ignorance, and brutality, of which black people were the prime example. The problem was that "all things southern" were intimately linked to black southern religiosity. For Mays's, then, if black ministers were going to serve as agents of intellectual modernization, there was an even heavier burden placed on the education of black clergymen. Black clergymen, as leaders, had to be vanguards of education and social activism in order to dispel the mythic cultural perception that southerners, especially black southerners, were overly simplistic and emotive. Howard University's level of theological education would help move black southern Christians out of what Mays called "otherworldly faith."

The sheer numbers of black southern migrants who made their way to large cities made the training of black clergy an imperative in Mays's mind. Some of the old religious habits of the South, he constantly felt, were insufficient to sustain religious belief. He had little faith that black laypeople could adapt to the changes that were occurring in the city and the country without strong, well-trained, and educated clergy. Indeed, there were many inadequacies attributable to the black ministers. However, black clergymen were no more deficient than their white untutored counterparts in the South. Yet Mays joined the editorial chorus emanating from the black press that feared that black Christian religiosity would not be helpful to blacks in assimilating quickly into the urban middle class. He worried that, without a socially engaged faith, black people would continue to be vulnerable in their fight against racism. Nevertheless, black ministers anchored "their folk" by helping create community in unfamiliar cities and by spiritually strengthening them as they endured the daily humiliations of racial bigotry.

It was also Mays's goal to loosen some of the denominational loyalties that black people held, loyalties that were tied to familial relationships, community building activities, and southern regional ties. While being a Baptist was important to him, he did not want his denominational and theological affinities to get in the way of serving the overall needs of black people. He was concerned that excessive denominational loyalties prevented churches from coming together for the common good. As Mays explained to students at the start of the 1937 school year, "We do not minimize the value of denominations. We are not trying to abolish the denominational emphasis. For example, I was born into the Baptist Church and I plan to die in the Baptist Church." He placed a greater emphasis on broad Protestant ecumenical efforts and cooperation, such as he had been a part of in the YMCA. "For a long time yet, and perhaps forever," he continued, "there will be denominations. But, we, in this School of Theology, claim to conserve all that is valuable in the denominations and at the same time expose our students to that richness of life which accrues to one who moves with ease among those of other faiths and who enriches his life by imbibing their culture and appreciating their differences."[38] In order to build effective black churches, Mays believed, black clergy had to steer clear of rigid denomi-nationalism. He recognized that discarding denominational affections would not happen quickly but believed that the ecumenical formation of "men" in their theological studies would help in the long run to end the legacy of black denominational divisiveness. More cooperative black churches were stronger agents for social betterment. Black clergymen, united across denominations, would be better able to both serve the religious needs of black laity and provide a formidable spiritual institution for social change.[39]

Mays took pride in being open to women in the School of Religion. Though the School of Religion was open to educating black women, they could only be secondary leaders in the black church. Women would mainly assume the role of Christian educators and wives, not preachers.[40] And women college students were not recruited in the same way Mays vigorously recruited male students. The irony of this is that large urban centers like Chicago "provided arenas where black women became principal agents of change in conceptions of reli-gious authority, worship, and social outreach."[41] Even more ironic was the pre-dominance of black women in Protestant denominations. At Howard's School of Religion, Mays and his faculty recognized female agency to a limited degree. Women, though important to the institutional function of black church life, served "a decorous function only."[42] Outside the respectable religious main-stream, black women assumed agency for themselves and re-created the tra-ditions of black women's religious empowerment not readily acknowledged by Mays. Although the School of Religion did not accord women the status as clergy, its openness allowed women to make their own intellectual claims on their faith. Nineteenth-century Victorian attitudes about proper Chris-tian women continued to have currency even in theologically liberal divinity schools. The School of Religion was not alone in its manifestations of male exclusionary practices—the much-heralded Howard Law School also margin-alized women, too. In fact, the law school had fewer women students in its classes than the School of Religion.

In spite of this grave and rather typical omission concerning women in the ministry, Mays fervidly recruited college graduates who desired to go into

Christian ministry. His previous work as a National YMCA staff member, along with his preaching and teaching, were beneficial in this regard because these activities gave him connections to most black colleges around the country. The School of Religion was also the beneficiary of Mordecai Johnson's presence, as Howard's president-preacher, and Howard Thurman, who had become a much sought after lecturer and preacher. These three men—Johnson, Mays, and Thurman—slowly began to give the School of Religion an intellectually intoxicating aura that attracted students. Steadily, the School of Religion was constructing a cadre of students committed to their calling as Protestant clergymen and civic religious leaders.

The civil rights activist and Howard School of Religion graduate James Farmer, whose father, James Farmer Sr., joined the School of Religion faculty in 1938, remembered the city of Washington as being highly segregated in the late 1930s.[43] Farmer noted that the excitement of being on Howard's campus, what he termed the "black Athens," was incomparable. He vividly recollected the atmosphere inside the School of Religion in an era "before religion occupied a central role in the black struggle, and before religious thinkers became intellectually respectable among the austere rank of black scholars." He observed that Howard students' perception of religion was based on the appearance of "the facility in which the school was housed: a dilapidated old frame house, in need of paint, across the street from the main campus." Though housed shabbily, the school had a remarkable faculty. "Its faculty members . . . were not inferior and would hold their own with those of any theological seminary in the country," Farmer recalled. "My father, of course, would have been a star any place. Benjamin E. Mays, the dean who also taught church history, was a fine scholar, administrator, speaker and writer." With delight he remembered, "There was also Paul T. Lutov, a White Russian from the Russian Orthodox Church, who taught Old Testament and Hebrew and was more at home with the language he taught than with the English in which he taught it. (Sometimes he would strain so hard in silent search for the right English word or phrase that we thought he was going to burst a blood vessel; even his neatly trimmed beard seemed to turn red. Then, he would shrug and speak Hebrew words, which sent us to our Hebrew-English dictionaries.)" And finally, Farmer added, "there was the incomparable Howard Thurman. Mystic, poet, philosopher, preacher, he was professor of social ethics and dean of the chapel. When Thurman occupied the university pulpit, Rankin Memorial Chapel was packed. Though few but theologians and philosophers comprehended what he was saying, everyone else thought if only they *had* understood [,] it would have been wonderful, so mesmerizing was his resonant voice and so captivating was the artistry of his delivery. Those who did grasp the meaning of his sermons were even more ecstatic."[44]

Farmer added that the School of Religion was a challenging intellectual environment for students. Biblical criticism, liberal theology, and ethics were challenges to those "coming to the seminary with a devout and dogmatic Sunday school theology." He recalled that "one first-year seminarian came to class one morning red-eyed and falling asleep; he had been up all night crying and praying for his professors' souls. Two others packed up and went home the first month." He also remembered that "the professors were critical scholars, but they were very devout."[45] More important to Farmer was that the school directed its students to be agents of social change.

The model for democratic social change that Mays and his Howard University colleagues aspired to came from India, where Christianity was practiced by only a fraction of the Indian population. The independence movement led by Mohandas Gandhi became the model for a constructive political movement for social change. Gandhi's struggle in India was the counterpoint to what occurred in Russia in 1917, where communist government had achieved power through violent coercion. The politics of Gandhi and the prophetic pronouncements of Jesus offered a different and more just way to revolt against oppression and to usher in social change. "If one book stood for this new movement," according to scholar Daniel Immerwahr, "it was *The Christ of the Indian Road* (1925), penned by E. Stanley Jones, whom *Time* would later call 'the world's greatest Christian missionary.'"[46]

In the 1930s, black internationalism thrived at Howard.[47] For Mays, it grew out of Protestant missionary societies. His primary exposure to world politics had come through his work with the YMCA. Several of his friends and acquaintances had been exposed to the world via their connections to the YMCA, YWCA, and other Christian student movements. John Hope and Mordecai Johnson had preceded Mays and Howard Thurman in traveling abroad and coming into contact with future religious and political leaders through their networking with international Christian organizations.[48] In fact, it had been a long tradition among black Americans to take part in these enterprises that dated back to the eighteenth century.[49] Arguably, the black religious diaspora has lasted longer than many other social networks described by scholars between black Americans and those in Africa and Latin America.[50] Though black internationalism had roots in Protestant missions, it has received far less scholarly attention than the diasporic links rooted in political radicalism.

Socialism, and even more so its radical cousin, communism, was highly attractive to many black intellectuals.[51] Infatuation with radical politics placed black Americans who were formally educated and Christian into a political as well as intellectual quandary. In the face of the violence routinely carried out against blacks in the South, black Christian intellectuals looked for ways to respond. Religiously, they needed social action that comported with their evangelical faith, which emphasized the notion that God respected the equality and individuality of persons. This emphasis gave most Protestants a high respect for democratic governance. Communism's tendency to invert the evangelical emphasis in favor of collective empowerment and its atheism proved to be unacceptable to Christian thinkers like Mays. However, in an era when so many black intellectuals romanced communism and the Communist Party, black religious thinkers had to provide a social justice alternative.

Under Mays's leadership, the School of Religion's eighteenth opening convocation was an attempt to construct a theological perspective on social change. The theme of the three-day assembly was "The Contribution of the Church to Social Reconstruction." The presenters were ecumenical in every sense of the word. Rabbi Edward L. Israel of the Har Sinai Congregation of Baltimore, Maryland, gave three lectures: "Danger Zone in the Social Order," "The Rise of Hitler," and "The Rise of Mussolini." The following day, the convocation heard from the author of *Religion and Communism*, Dr. Julius Hecker, who gave two addresses: "The Philosophy of Communism" and "The Actual Operation of Communism." Howard faculty member and political scientist Ralph Bunche presented an address titled "The Philosophy of the New Deal," while Robert Weaver, a U.S. Department of Interior adviser, gave a speech titled "The Actual Operation of the New Deal."

Mordecai Johnson gave the banquet address on Mahatma Gandhi. "Dr. Johnson pointed out," according to the *News*, the School of Religion's newsletter, "that for the first time in history political power, economic exploitation, and military domination have been challenged by the power of the Spirit. It is the first time that 'Soul force or *non-violent* coercion' has been projected into the political area as a technique of the under-privileged for achieving social ends." He continued, "The modern political powers are so accustomed to brute force as the means of gaining their objectives that they are hardly prepared to deal with spiritual forces embodied in the work of Mahatma Gandhi. The Indian Saint releases to the world a new method of dealing with intrenched [*sic*] power, and the 'Gandhi Way' will no doubt prove more effective and permanent than the brutal way of military power or the domineering way of the dictator."[52]

While Johnson's address was the climax of the convocation, the final day of the event was devoted to subjects of historic Christianity and contemporary Christianity. These sessions were led by prominent black church leaders, including Dr. William Lloyd Imes of the St. James Presbyterian Church in New York City; Dr. J. A. Martin, the general secretary of the General Board of Religious Education of the Colored Methodist Episcopal Church; and the Reverend Marshall Shepard, pastor of the Mt. Olivet Baptist Church in West Philadelphia, Pennsylvania. After hearing Johnson's talk, these leaders and the School of Religion faculty had their marching orders to rethink what it meant for the black church to be at the forefront of a worldwide freedom movement based on a Gandhian model. Howard Thurman later recalled the optimism of that moment: "There was a stirring in the wind that we recognized." Mordecai Johnson's "authentic tribute to the journey into freedom chartered by this *little brown man*" would be a catalyst for a theological investigation of Christian ethics and nonviolent social change.[53]

By 1935, the School of Religion had become the university's academic hub for discussion on Gandhi's political methodology. This discussion could be traced back to the annual YMCA conferences at King's Mountain (see chapter 3) and to the 1929 International YMCA meeting held in Mysore, India, which was attended by Max Yergan,[54] the only black American YMCA field worker in South Africa from 1921 to 1936, and Frank T. Wilson and Juliette Derricotte of the national YWCA.[55] Wilson and Derricotte's trip was notable because the YMCA and the Student Christian Movement were being challenged to tackle the issues of racism and colonialism.[56] Wilson and Derricotte were regularly invited to the School of Religion to give talks at Howard's Rankin Memorial Chapel on Gandhian methodology.

Howard Thurman should be credited for making his colleagues at the School of Religion see the theological connection between Gandhi's philosophy and political movement and their own religious and political concerns.[57] Through his efforts, many important Gandhi allies—including two notable British women, Miriam Slade and Muriel Lester—lectured at the university.[58] Thurman had visited India and met Gandhi through the auspices of the International YMCA in 1935.[59] Thurman's trip was tantamount to a conversion experience, especially after Gandhi pointedly inquired of him as to why he was Christian and not Muslim, given the discrimination and oppression that black Americans had experienced.[60] Mays had wanted to join Thurman on this first trip to India, but he was still in the throes of dissertation writing and handling the administrative duties of the School of Religion; he would make his own journey to India the following year.

Mays's trip to India was also transformative. YMCA leader Channing Tobias arranged for May to be a delegate to the YMCA international gathering there along with himself. Mays left the United States before the Christmas holidays so that he would arrive in New Delhi, India, before the 1936 Mysore conference and have time to attend the Indian National Congress and to meet with Gandhi. He briefly met with Jawaharlal Nehru, an independence leader and the future first prime minister of independent India, and Mrs. Vijaya Lakshmi Pandit, Nehru's sister. Mays skipped out on a tour of the Taj Mahal to secure an interview with Gandhi. "For a very long time," he wrote, "I had wished to see and talk with this ninety-pound brown man who had done so much to make Indians proud of their history and culture; who had identified himself with fifty million untouchables, determined to lift them to a place of dignity and respectability in the life of India; and who had started a movement for India's independence which would eventually lead to the dissolution of the British Empire."[61]

Mays and Tobias spent ninety minutes interviewing Gandhi. Mays asked him three questions: First, he asked him to explain what he meant by "passive resistance." "Passive resistance," Gandhi asserted, was "a misnomer for nonviolent resistance. It is more active than violent resistance." The genius of nonviolence, according to Gandhi, was its invisibility. Violence, though highly visible, never had the last word. It is illusory and transitory. The effects of nonviolent action grow with age. "And the more it is practiced," Gandhi reasoned, "the more effective and inexhaustible it becomes, and ultimately the whole world stands agape and exclaims, *a miracle has happened.* All miracles are due to the silent and effective working of invisible forces. Non-violence is the most invisible and the most effective."[62]

Mays's second question to Gandhi was about discipline and strategy. "I have no doubt in my mind about the superiority of non-violence," Mays said, "but the thing that bothers me is about its exercise on a large scale, the difficulty of so disciplining the mass mind on the point of love. It is easier to discipline individuals. What should be the strategy when they break out? Do we retreat or do we go on?" Gandhi's reply was interesting and counterintuitive. He explained to Mays, "People do not gain the training by preaching. Non-violence cannot be preached. It has to be practised." Violence, Gandhi noted, was symbolically portrayed throughout all society. He also noted that violence excluded those who were disabled. He told Mays, "The maimed and the blind and the leprous cannot join the army of violence. There is also an age limit in the army. For a non-violent struggle there is no age-limit; the blind and the maimed and the bed-ridden may serve, and not only men but women also. When the spirit of non-violence pervades the people and actually begins to work, its effect is visible to all."[63]

Mays third question was about the abolition of the caste system. Gandhi viewed the caste system as simply a social-class strata or a division of labor. In

Gandhi's estimation, people in the lower caste did important jobs for society; what he condemned was the notion that individuals were untouchable because of the job they occupied. In India, the Dalits, or untouchables, were socially bound to occupy the most ritually impure jobs in Indian society, the occupations that involved handling animal carcasses, cleaning up human feces, and any other duties that were considered debased. The untouchables were also forbidden to marry outside their caste. Similar to black Americans, the untouchables in Indian society carried out essential tasks but were ritually defined as impure and discriminated against throughout the society. Mays learned from Gandhi that caste status of untouchables gave them no social protection in terms of respect and rights. "All [upper] caste men could with impunity step on and spit upon the untouchable. So Gandhi had cast his lot with the man farthest down, the untouchable."[64] Although Mays came away from his interview understanding Gandhi's perspective on caste, he never really grasped the significance of the dispute regarding caste taking place between Gandhi and one of his political rivals, B. R. Ambedkar, an untouchable, in the Indian nationalist struggle.[65] Mays's interview with Gandhi gave him plentiful thoughts to contemplate.

Mays left Gandhi to travel to Mysore in southern India to attend the Twenty-first World Conference of the World Alliance of YMCA.[66] "Mysore," he recounted, "was my first World Conference, and having been segregated and discriminated against most of my life, I found it interesting to be in a World Conference where members of different races and nations met on a plane of absolute equality."[67] However, he was to discovered a great deal about the global nature of the color line.

One of his more startling moments in Mysore was his visit to a school for untouchables: "While at Mysore I was invited by the headmaster of an 'untouchable' school in a neighboring village to speak to his students. I asked him why, since there were thirteen US delegates, he had chosen me. He replied that he wanted a Negro; and when I told him that Channing Tobias was also a Negro, he answered that Tobias was too fair complexioned to do what he wanted done." Having accepted the invitation, Mays went to the school and dined with the students. "After dinner," he recalled, "I was introduced as an untouchable who had achieved distinction. The headmaster told them I had suffered at the hands of the white men in the United States every indignity that they suffered from the various castes in India and that I was proof that they, too, could be 'somebody worthwhile' despite the stigma of being members of a depressed class." Mays was initially "horrified, puzzled, angry to be called an untouchable." His indignation was short-lived as he realized that his situation in America was somewhat analogous to that of the untouchables in India: "In my country, I was segregated almost everywhere I went, always in the South and often in the North. . . . I—just as they—through the mere accident of birth, was indeed an untouchable!"[68]

For the first time, Mays recognized that color lines and ethnic discrimination were common to all human beings. He also recognized that the kind of social respectability that he had achieved through education was something all people desired. The students he met saw in him, a black American, the possibility to achieve distinction through determination and perseverance. In this moment, Mays gained a perspective outside the United States about what it meant to live constricted by arbitrary factors such as caste, color and, or, ethnicity. This awareness pushed him further in the belief that God did not limit human beings, but rather other human beings placed limits on one another out of irrational hatred or fear and greed.

Mays also saw the limitations of the Mysore conference. He realized that international religious gatherings resolved very little. They did not alleviate the political situations of various oppressed people. They did, however, provide safe spaces for anti-imperialist and antiracist religious adherents to gather and inform one another about their respective struggles. The international YMCA and the Student Christian Movement provided a forum for people of different faiths to affirm their commitment to justice when other avenues, outside of radical politics, were closed, to them. At the Mysore meeting, Mays was "elected as a member of the World Committee Y.M.C.A., the post formerly held by the late John Hope," the former president of Morehouse College. The selection of Mays to replace Hope in this position was perhaps providential.[69] In any case, his election at Mysore placed him on the international stage.[70]

Mays returned to the United States eager to incorporate his experience into his theological agenda. He reported on the Indian independence movement in numerous periodicals, and he began looking to India's political situation for ideas that might work in aiding blacks in resisting racial segregation. By explaining what he saw and learned in India, Mays believed that he could stimulate conversations about what an effective movement for social change might look like among blacks.

In March of 1937, Mays wrote an article about his trip overseas for the *Journal of Negro Education*. The titled of the article, "The Color Line Around the World," was evocative of W. E. B. DuBois. He explained to the journal readers what he learned about himself and that racial thinking was endemic to the Europe's imperial orders. He noted the growing tension between Arabs and Jews, as more Jews immigrated into Palestine, commenting on the discussions he had with Jews regarding the persecution of Jews in Germany and Austria, and related the difficulties that black South Africans were having with being racially segregated in their own country. Readers learned the nature of the YMCA conference at Mysore. He described how an appointed international commission—led by Channing Tobias, head of the Colored Division of the National YMCA, and Dr. Edgar Brooks, secretary of the South African YMCA— brought before the conference body for its approval a policy on internal racial discrimination in the YMCA. He wrote that the "commission declared that racial discrimination on the part of the Y.M.C.A. is contrary to the will of God and that failure of so-called Christian people to witness with courage and devotion the will of God in race relations, as in other areas, explains in part the winning of youth to materialistic non-Christian movements." While the commission unanimously adopted the recommendation that "no association should adopt a racially exclusive membership policy or close any of its activities to any man on the ground of his race or color," it meant very little. Specific national localities— like the American South, South Africa, and Germany—determined their own policies, irrespective of an international declaration. Mays also sardonically observed, "The most theologically correct people in the Conference were the representatives from Germany. They, more than the rest of us, insisted the theological 'i' and 't' be dotted and crossed rightly." They held up committee reports until proper theological protocol had been met. "But," as he wrote, "there was no correlation between their theology and their treatment of the Jews. In private conversation they justified what Germany is doing to the Jews."[71]

Mays wrote about the complexity of Indian society and the class, ethnic, and religious factionalism that made the independence struggle so difficult. "The British rule in India would be an entirely different brand of imperialism were the Indians white people," Mays pointedly observed. Racism allowed the British to justify their "contention that the Indians are incapable of self-government." He added, "Though imperialism knows no color line, it is inclined to be less lenient and considerate in its treatment of colored people." For him, Gandhi's resistance of British imperialism and racism did two things that black Americans desperately needed. It fought back against the racial strictures of the imperialist order, and it empowered the Indians to believe in their own abilities. Mays's commentary on Gandhi was prescient. "The world is too close to him to appraise him adequately," he wrote. "Certainly my knowledge of him is too meager for me to speak of his influence with finality. But I believe that the future historians will record among his contributions to India something like the following: 'He did more than any other man to dispel fear from the Indian mind and more than any other to make Indians proud to be

Indians.' That the non-violence campaign was a failure, no one has a right to say. All the evidence is not yet in." Nevertheless, Mays continued, "the fact that Gandhi and his non-violent campaign has given the Indian masses a new conception of courage, no man can honestly deny. To discipline people to face death, to die, to go to jail for the cause without fear and without resorting to violence is an achievement of the first magnitude. And when an oppressed race ceases to be afraid, it is free. The cardinal principles of non-violence are love and fearlessness."[72]

Mays's travels provided him with more nuanced and layered ideas about the levels of worldwide racism and ethnic chauvinism. Although he made stops in China and Japan, he did not comment on the growing level of animosity between the two countries and the subtext of racial inferiority that accompanied Japanese imperialism. However, he did compare the plight of black South Africans with that of black Americans: "What happens to the natives in South Africa seems just as incredible to those of us who are unfamiliar with the situation there as the fact of lynching and segregation of Negroes in the United States seems to the people of India." He was also troubled and perplexed by the near total resentment toward Jews from various regions in Europe. He noted ominously that repression of Jews in other parts of the world was being used to justify the Jewish takeover of Palestine. "There is great danger, even if less cruel and inhuman, that the Jews will do to the Arabs in Palestine what the Germans are doing to Jews in Germany," he commented. It was evident to him that "wherever colored and white people live together in large numbers and compete economically there seems to be a definite racial consciousness that eventuates in some kind of racial discrimination or resentment." He observed on his trip through Asia and a small portion of Egypt that there was no racial discrimination in accommodations in these countries. He naively concluded, "It is therefore most difficult for colored people of these countries to understand the racial discrimination in the United States and South Africa."[73]

Mays wrote about his trip in the *News* as well, making many of the same observations about India and Gandhi's contribution to the Indian independence movement that he had in the *Journal of Negro Education*. In addition, he wrote a series of seven articles for *Journal and Guide*, a regional black-owned newspaper published in Norfolk, Virginia. Five of the articles explained the history and politics of the Indian independence movement. The sixth article described the growing tension between Arabs and Jews in Palestine. The seventh article explained how American racial discrimination was perceived in other countries as a reflection of the United States policy toward people of color in other countries—a viewpoint that black civil rights leaders would later take advantage of at the height of the anticommunist repression and the Cold War era.[74]

In the summer of 1937, Mays traveled to England as a delegate to the Oxford Conference on Church, Community, and State, an international theological gathering dominated by Americans and Europeans. This trip would be significant for him because the conference was the foundation of what came to be the World Council of Churches. One of the more important voices at the conference was the American theologian Reinhold Niebuhr. Also attending the meeting was John Foster Dulles, future American secretary of state. The gathering was held in light of the growing crisis in Germany, Italy, and Spain, and because of concerns about a prospective war in Europe. Most delegates at the conference were aware of the schism that occurred in the German Protestant Church led by the theologians Martin Niemöller and Dietrich Bonhoeffer, who criticized the Nazi regime and broke away from the German state church, the Lutheran Church, to form the Confessing Church. They resisted Nazism by disclaiming, in a letter, that the mission of the church could not be synonymous with that of the German state.

When Mays returned to the United States, he wrote a series of articles for the *Journal and Guide* to inform its readers about what had occurred in Oxford. He explained that the Oxford conference had tried to delineate the role of the political state and the role of the church. For the church to function at its highest level, it needed to be free of state intervention. He also reported that the conference challenged Christians to be careful of wedding religious faith to any particular economic order. One of the church's primary tasks was to hold all economic systems accountable for respecting the lives and labors of human beings. At Oxford, the conference delegates expressed openly their worries about social disintegration in their respective countries and the growing secularization in Europe. Mays keenly observed in one of his articles the delegates' concern about war. "Historically speaking," he wrote, "the organized Christian church has supported all major wars of history. And I fear will continue to do so for quite a while yet. Individual Christians here and there will refuse to participate in wars, but the organized church is too much a part of this world and too un-Godly for it to stand against the state in time of war."[75] Mays also informed his readers that the Oxford conference pronounced that "brotherhood" was key to the Christian life, which he wholeheartedly supported. However, he warned, "I believe the world is trending toward disaster. I cannot see any hope for a world where every nation on the face of the earth distrusts every other nation."[76] Echoing Reinhold Niebuhr, he noted, "The world is morally and spiritually bankrupt. As long as the material forces of the world undermine and subordinate the spiritual forces, we are in for tragic days."[77]

In his last article for the *Journal and Guide*, titled "Hitler Would Be 'God' to Germans, Asserts Dr. Mays," Mays discussed *Mein Kampf*, Hitler's disjunctive autobiographical account, and the intense racial hatred that was evident both in the memoir and in Germany. From the memoir, he noted, readers could learn how Hitler sought to replace religion with a nationalist ideology dominated by a perverse racial theory and hatred for Jews. He observed that even if Hitler retracted his racial position, the German state would still require supreme loyalty under his proposed regime. And he observed correctly that the German church would go along with the Nazi regime, even if Hitler declared war on Jews. He commented that the sixteenth-century theologian Martin Luther held that there were two kingdoms in the economy of God—the earthly kingdom and the spiritual kingdom. The earthly kingdom was the realm of politics and commerce and was the provenance of political rulers. Drawing the Apostle Paul's injunction and early modern political statecraft, Luther understood that the believer's role was to acknowledge the earthly kingdom and conform and give deference to its leaders as a sign of Christian obedience. However, it was in the spiritual kingdom, the one of belief and faith that was at the core of what the New Testament taught, that Christians did not need to bother with earthly politics because God had ordained leaders who were accountable to a higher sovereign. Social conformity was at the root of German Lutherans' understanding of church-state relations. Mays thought that Hitler would go the route of his counterpart in Italy, Mussolini, and make peace with the German state church. However, he eerily noted, "what the outcome will be we can only guess."[78]

In the October 1937 issue of the *Crisis*, Mays explained that the Oxford conference was the scene of a heated debate about capitalism, led by Reinhold Niebuhr, John MacMurray, and R. H. Tawney. The conference, he wrote, challenged "every aspect of the existing economic systems." Although he believed Oxford was a grand gathering in terms of its Christian fellowship, he wrote, "I could not help but feel that what we did at Oxford would have *no* significant bearing on world-situations and nothing that we did there would in any way change world policies and thus ward off the catastrophe toward which the world is inevitably drifting." He had concluded that nothing the Christian church did in a worldwide conference would stop Japanese aggression, Hitler's warfare against Jews in Germany, or "Italy's ambition to reestablish the Roman Empire. The communists and fascists in Spain will continue to fight despite what we said at Oxford." Mays seemed to have left Oxford with clarity about the limits of the church as a vehicle for social change. The "Oxford reports had much to say about the church repenting of its sins," he observed. "I fear that for the most part, the church will not repent except verbally and that it will continue to live in the same old way and that it will continue to move in the same old beaten paths. Segregation in God's church will continue in America and in South Africa after Oxford." Prophetically, maybe sensing the work of the Confessing Church in Germany and the work of the black Church in America, he penned, "When the church truly repents, let us not deceive ourselves; it will be a *suffering* church."[79]

In December 1937, Mays wrote another theological assessment of the Oxford conference in a Christmas meditation titled "Christianity in a Changing World." Using his ideas regarding necessity of historical change, he came to the conclusion that there was only one constant in Christianity. Referring to the gospel of love, he argued that "the findings of science cannot repudiate, wars cannot invalidate and a materialistic world cannot ignore" it. Love was at the center of the teachings of Jesus and at the center of the church. "The organizing principle in life is love. These are the timeless elements in Christianity and they will stand in the midst of ruin and change." Highlighting some of the accomplishments of the Oxford conference, he told his readers that "the Christmas Season . . . can be celebrated in the Spirit of the Christ only if we make articulate in our own lives these eternal qualities of his religion: *love, brotherhood, peace.*"[80]

The conferences at Mysore and Oxford opened up the world to Mays. It put him at the forefront of the political and social upheaval taking place on the eve of World War II. In 1939, just forty days before World War II fully escalated in Europe, Mays and a few students in the School of Religion traveled to Amsterdam for the First World Conference of Christian Youth. The theme of the conference was "Christus Victor." For readers of the *Crisis* and the *Journal and Guide* he once again analyzed the fate of the world and how a Christian assembly in the midst of the gathering storm was important but too late in light of the inevitability of war. Mays reported in the *Crisis* that the conference participants, who hailed from all over the world, discussed the problems of race and religion. He noted that the colonial representatives were from Africa, Asia, Australia, and New Zealand and that race as a category of division in the colonial world—a world filled with strong nationalist state ideologies—was germane as a worldwide issue. Mays highlighted just three issues that were discussed by the commission on youth and race—"The Jewish Issue," "Dutch for Segregation" in South Africa, and the "Intermarriage Bugaboo." He noted that many young people attending the conference lived in denial that some

Benjamin Mays (first row, second from left) at the First World Conference of Christian Youth, Amsterdam, Holland, ca. 1939. Courtesy of the Moorland-Spingarn Research Center, Howard University.

of their fellow citizens were being forcibly marginalized through state power. Mays found that they used biblical passages in a slipshod and escapist manner to avoid the brutal realities of racism in Europe and elsewhere. He concluded that young people were no more progressive on issues of race than their elders who were driving their respective countries into war. Mays concluded that he was "convinced more than ever before that the biggest problem facing the world today is the problem of race. Christian people the world over cannot continue to seek avenues of escape and ignore the problem. . . . To declare that 'we are all one in Christ Jesus' and deny, at the same time, the reality of that proclamation in the church and in everyday living is to deny God and repudiate the Lordship of Jesus Christ."[81]

Through his travels, Mays began to see that black American political struggles were just one aspect of those of the world's.[82] As Leonard Terrell, a School of Religion alumnus, observed about Mays's travels in India, "Dean Mays is discovering how the needs of the rest of the world are linked in a very organic way with our needs in America. Fundamentally, the solution of our problems is the same whenever the problem raises its head." Students expected, on the basis of what Terrell wrote, that Mays would "be able to inform us how the rest of the world is attempting to solve its problems; that is to say, those who believe that permanent solutions must develop on a basis other than physical force or the clashing of arms." Mays's travels and publications prompted within the School of Religion serious and intellectually charged discussions about American Christianity and Christianity around the globe.[83]

Samuel Gandy, a student in the class of 1938, noted Mays's absence during his travels to India: "Yes, the Dean is sharpening the issues of India. We knew that the Dean would hold his own in the great struggles of world issues. We miss him here, but we look forward to his return this spring when we shall again discuss in our usual manner the role of theology." Gandy understood that students were expected to support the School of Religion's internationalism. Mays's travel opportunities brought prestige to the program and created the sense that the School of Religion was a part of the global struggle. As Gandy proudly explained to his fellow students, Mays's accomplishments were their accomplishments, too. "After all," he noted, "the fellowship of our school means that whatever is done by one member is representative of the whole; so that the Dean is actually going places for us."[84] And Gandy got Mays's message absolutely correct. Following Mays's lead, students attended numerous conferences, from YMCA meetings to the National Negro Congress.[85] Critical reflection on the world was an important part of being a student at the School of Religion.

Mays repeatedly told new students who entered the School of Religion that the school was developing "men of character, thought, information and a passion to preach the gospel of Christ." Mays wanted the School of Religion not only to promote serious discussion but also to provide a warm and nurturing environment. The seriousness came first. He warned students, as Amos Ryce, a School of Religion student, described, "to accept the friendly overtures of the faculty outside of the class room but pointed out the danger of taking this fellowship as a substitute for scholarship lest they be disappointed at the day of reckonin.'" The School of Religion was a warm and collegial setting for students and faculty, but the dean demanded a high level of achievement from the student body. As one student explained, at exam time, the students fell under the "spell of Mays."[86]

Although the total student enrollment of the School of Religion was much smaller than the rest of the university's professional schools, its students began to produce a body of critical literature. For the first three years of Mays's deanship, each graduating student was expected to produce a thesis. The theses that were produced included "An Investigation of Certain Factors Related to Juvenile Delinquency among Negroes in Three Census Tracts of the District of Columbia"; "The Use of Religion for Social Control in American Slavery"; "A Historical Study of Legally Sanctioned Religious Education in Maryland Public Schools"; "A Critical Study of Two Minority Techniques in the Light of Christian Principles"; "A Study of Religious Beliefs and Attitudes among Colored Students"; "An Examination of the Doctrine of the Second Coming of Christ"; "Religious Education in Ancient India"; "A Critical Study of the Rise and Development of Second Century Gnosticism and Its Contributions to the Development of Christian Theology up to 325"; and "A Historical Study of the Church Union among Independent Negro Methodists." What Mays desired was intellectually razor sharp men and women serving the church.[87]

Mays told every graduating class that "intellectual honesty and moral integrity obligate one to preach only that which he sincerely believes; that which he can swear by and, if need be, die by. This is the only way to preach with persuasion and power. Preach a positive gospel and never air your negatives in the pulpit."[88] The small number of men and women who came through the School of Religion under Mays's leadership understood his point as they rigorously prepared to lead a freedom struggle with black church folk.

In a 1938 *Crisis* article, "The Most Neglected Area in Negro Education," a shorter and updated version of an piece he had written in 1933, Mays acknowledged once again the difficulty of educating black ministers. "The million dollar library of Howard [U]niversity, now in process of completion, probably represents many, many times the amount of money spent for the physical improvement of theological education among Negroes since 1912."[89] Since his arrival at Howard, he had tried to increase the scholarship money available to his students and improve the School of Religion facility. The building of the million-dollar library, today the Founders Library, was a boon, since the vacated Carnegie Library building would immediately become the home of the School of Religion.[90] For the first time in its history, the School of Religion would be housed on Howard's quadrangle, not in a shabby house on Georgia Avenue. Faculty members would have better offices, along with more classroom space, and a bigger library. The more attractive its facilities were, Mays knew, the more attractive the School of Religion would be to college-educated students thinking about attending seminary rather than choosing another professional career. The loss of prestige of the black clergy could be recovered, he believed, with "an increased number of vitalized and intelligent leaders" who could "save the values inherent in religion and the Negro church. . . . The Negro minister is the most significant leader of the Negro masses. This being true, the best trained men and women should be the leaders." He was persuaded that "the next great advance in Negro education should be in the direction of improving the religious and theological training among Negroes."[91]

Mays's years at Howard were rich. He began building a cadre of theologically conversant students to serve black churches. He was able to travel abroad for the first time in his life, and he was privileged to work with some of the very brightest academics among the black intelligentsia. Yet he also experienced loss. During these years, both his father and mother died. The loss of his mother was the most significant to him. He tenderly remembered Louvenia Mays in the School of Religion newsletter. "She came along at a time when Negroes had little or no opportunity to be educated," he wrote. "She never attended school a day in her life. But like most Negroes of the early period, she had great faith in what education might do for one." As he would in his memoir later in his life, he explained that his mother "did not wholly comprehend the restlessness that characterized me as a boy when I kept pleading that I be sent away to school that ran three or four months a year. Nor did she understand thoroughly why I kept going to school so long—to high school, college, and university. But she believed in me and somehow felt that if I wanted to go on, it was the thing to do. At no time in her heart did she discourage me." She was selfless and gave him "sympathy, encouragement, and prayer" and physically toiled "in the field with the hope" that he would be able to attend school. It was the depth of his mother's spirituality that he emphasized in his latter recollections about her: "For more than fifty years she prayed at least twice a day. . . . It was no doubt this deep religious faith that enabled her to endure hardships without breaking under the load."[92]

He never linked the kind of spirituality that he saw in his mother's slave religion—her prayer life and her ability to love in spite of societal hatred—to his affinity for a supremely just God or to his inquiries into Gandhian nonviolent social resistance. What he learned from his mother—her forbearance and loving patience—was always the shaping force in his life, a deeper part of his combative spirituality than he gave credit.[93] His mother's practices of Christian charity, nonviolence, and determined steadfastness had a spiritual depth and power to them that were a subtext in his theological thought. As he moved on with his career, he recognized that his mother represented the best that God had to offer the Negro's disenchanted and often tragic world.[94] Interestingly, Mays's father would die just three months after his mother. Mays did not write Hezekiah Mays a tender remembrance as he had done for his mother.[95]

Mays's work to transform Howard University School of Religion into a premiere theological training center for black clergy was left unfinished. In his six years at Howard, he achieved most of his objectives. The School of Religion received accreditation from the American Association of Theological Schools.[96] In addition, the School of Religion's library was significantly enhanced with the purchase of a part of the defunct Auburn Theological Seminary's library.[97] Unfortunately, at the time of his departure, there simply were not enough talented leaders groomed to his level. Mays's replacement to the deanship was William Stuart Nelson, the well-regarded theologian and former president of Shaw University.[98] Nelson lacked Mays's charisma and inherited a program that was still fragile and trying to establish its place among modern nonsectarian universities. We will never know what other major accomplishments the School of Religion might have achieved under Mays's energetic leadership because, in 1940, the board of Morehouse College, in desperate need of his leadership, called him to be their president.[99]

Schoolmaster of the Movement

A college must be judged not only by excellent teachers, but by the spirit
and philosophy which permeates it from top to bottom.
—MAYS, *Quotable Quotes of Benjamin E. Mays*

On Saturday, May 11, 1940, the *Atlanta Daily World* headline proclaimed,
"Dr. Mays Elected President of Morehouse." The article informed its readers
that "Dr. Benjamin E. Mays, Dean of the School of Religion of Howard
University, and formerly a member of Morehouse College faculty, Friday was
elected president of Morehouse College. Dr. Mays was the unanimous choice of
the board of trustees, which met in annual session here." Among black Baptists,
Mays's selection to the presidency of Morehouse College was bigger news than
the selection of Winston Churchill as Britain's wartime prime minister. The
announcement about Mays even dwarfed the other headline story regarding
the election of the bishops in the African Methodist Episcopal (AME) Church,
which, among *Daily World* readers, might have held just as much intrigue
as Churchill's precipitous rise in the wake of Britain's prime minister Neville
Chamberlin's resignation. However, among black Atlantans on May 11, neither
the politics of executing the war in Britain nor the backroom political dealings
of AME bishops rivaled the importance Mays's appointment as Morehouse's
sixth president. In 1940, the college remained the most significant college in
the United States dedicated solely to educating black men.[1] The person taking
the helm of Morehouse was major news in Atlanta.

While the *Atlanta Daily World* presented Mays's selection as a foregone
conclusion, he had not actually accepted the position. He would not accept
the offer until May 31, 1940. He explained that John Hervey Wheeler of Durham, North Carolina, a member of the Morehouse board of trustees, had in-
terviewed him early in 1940.[2] He viewed his chances of getting the job as quite
remote and he was content with his successes at Howard's School of Religion.
Sadie Mays, however, predicted that the offer would be made to him. "On May
10, 1940," Mays recalled receiving "a long-distance call from Trevor Arnett,
a Board member, and former president of the General Education Board," informing him that he had been selected as the president of Morehouse College.

Mays had known Arnett since his days working for the YMCA and the Institute of Social and Religious Research (ISRR). He told Arnett that he would consider the offer but that he would first have to discuss it with Mordecai Johnson. Mays had a strong inclination that Johnson would approve of him taking the helm of Morehouse, Johnson's alma mater. In addition to talking with Johnson, he also traveled around the country—to Atlanta; Muskegon, Michigan; Durham; and back to Washington, D.C.—assessing the academic and financial status of Morehouse and his support among key faculty members and alumni. When he finally accepted the offer, he carefully outlined the key issues, such as faculty salary, that he thought the Morehouse's board of trustees needed to address. The trustees agreed with Mays that all the issues he outlined needed to be addressed.

Although the *Atlanta Daily World* reported Mays appointment as great news for the college, not everyone was pleased. Benjamin Mays "is a notorious modernist," charged the Reverend D. D. Crawford, a Morehouse College alumnus, in the May 15, 1940, issue of the magazine, *The Georgia Baptist*. "He believes in everything in general and nothing in particular. He is a scientific Christian not a religious one." Crawford expressed his fear that his alma mater had made a grave mistake in hiring Mays as its president. From its inception, Crawford contended, Morehouse had been a college led by "thorough, orthodox" Christian leaders until the appointment of Mays. He also feared that the board of trustees' appointment of Mays would "wipe out every vestige of what Negro Baptists hold dear." Crawford predicted that the board's action would "enforce upon us, what they call a liberal religion." Crawford's shrill charges were ignored, but he was correct in arguing that Mays was not a traditional "Negro Baptist."[3]

Mays had come full circle. It had been nineteen years since his meeting with Morehouse president John Hope in the library of the University of Chicago in 1921. The Morehouse College he prepared to return to was weaker than when he taught there; it had been crippled as a result of the 1929 economic collapse and a vacuum in leadership. A succession of leadership woes plagued the college. First, there was the death of former president John Hope, followed by the retirement of Hope's successor, Samuel Howard Archer, and, finally, there was a three-year interim presidency that accomplished very little. Morehouse's trustees were in desperate straits. During the 1930s, Morehouse College's stature had been diminished and usurped by the presidents of Atlanta University and Spelman College in an evolving collaborative plan among Atlanta's historic black colleges and seminaries.[4] As Dr. Hugh M. Gloster, Mays successor as president of Morehouse, later observed, "When Dr. Mays assumed the Presidency in 1940, Morehouse was a weak and failing school."[5] Morehouse needed a president who possessed administrative skills, political acumen, and public stature.

The Morehouse trustees did in fact consider a number of their alumni for the position; however, for one reason or another, they could not or did not fill the position with one of their own. Morehouse alumnus Mordecai Johnson was in no position to leave the presidency of Howard, and Howard Thurman, Mays's colleague in the School of Religion, did not have any desire to be a college president. There were other possibilities, but none had the charisma, administrative talents, or the kind of connections to the Protestant establishment that Mays had fostered throughout his career. In addition, he had the blessing of Johnson, who had cultivated Mays's career by appointing him to key university committees during his time at Howard. And finally, Mays would be the first president of Morehouse to have a doctorate degree. Sadie Mays's intuition about Morehouse trustees offering him the job as president was on target. She knew, like the Morehouse board came to realize, that he was the best man available for the job.

Mays had two reasons for accepting the position. "I had not been asked, before receiving the offer, whether I would accept it if offered," he explained. "Nevertheless, the news broke in the press that I had been elected, and the news releases implied that I had accepted . . . to decline would lead the public to believe that I had made a commitment and reneged on it." However, what he found to be the "more persuasive factor was the challenge of the job." Morehouse graduates were making vital contributions in society. "I [had] found a special, intangible something at Morehouse in 1921," he recalled, "which sent men out into life with a sense of mission, believing that they could accomplish whatever they set out to do. This priceless quality was still alive when I returned in 1940 . . . instilling in Morehouse students the idea that despite crippling circumscriptions the sky was the limit."[6] The challenge for May—as it had been at Howard's School of Religion—was to shape a cadre of students for leadership.

In accepting the Morehouse presidency, Mays had to forgo other professional and personal options. One of his difficulties in accepting the Morehouse presidency was his planned one-year sabbatical from the School of Religion to go to South Africa. He had been eager to learn about South Africa and make some comparisons between conditions of black Americans and black South Africans. He had learned much about South Africa through Max Yergan's writings and lectures, as well as his attendance at international conferences. The departure of Yergan from the staff of the World Committee of the YMCA in

South Africa in 1936 had opened the door for Mays to temporarily replace him. Mays, John Mott, the YMCA chairman; Tracy Strong of the International YMCA; and officials from the South African YMCA had been in negotiation for nearly nine months before he was invited to accept Morehouse's presidency. The problem for all of them was the outbreak of war in Asia and Europe. As Tracy Strong informed him, "As you foresaw in your letter of September 5th the war is affecting not only the work of the World's Committee, but every National Movement involved in the war. All the countries of Europe are living under a strain and most of them are mobilized." Mays thought it might be wise to postpone his sabbatical, if necessary, which would have begun on July 1, 1940. His hope was to "join the staff of the World Committee for approximately eighteen months or two years."[7] Even though the war was a hindrance, it did not deter him or Mott from continuing to plan. As late as March of 1940, Mays was still trying to clarify with Mott the specific time of his departure for South Africa and the salary he would be paid. In a letter to Mott he noted, "Financial obligations to our families and the four nieces and nephews that we are helping in college must be arranged for before we leave."[8] Although the onset of war prevented him from going to South Africa during the summer of 1940, in the end, his acceptance of the Morehouse presidency mattered to him the most.

In another letter to Mott, Mays revealed the depth of his feelings and his prescient sense about his role at Morehouse: "I have spent many days—in fact three weeks—trying to decide whether I should accept the presidency of Morehouse College. After much agony of soul, in meditation and prayer, I have come to the conclusion that I should accept the presidency of Morehouse College." "For approximately three years now," he continued, "Morehouse College has been without a president. The General Education Board has a conditional gift offer which terminates the first of July, 1942—that is, they will give Morehouse $400,000. These two factors, the urgency of the endowment and the fact that Morehouse has not had a president for some time, make it impossible for them to release me to serve this year in South Africa." He added, "But in the light of the whole situation and in the light of what I visualize for my life during the next twenty-five years, I think I am making the right decision."[9] Though he realized the trip to South Africa might never occur, he submitted a memorandum accompanying his letter of acceptance to Morehouse's board of trustees noting his unfulfilled obligation. "I am accepting the presidency as of July 1, 1940," he wrote, "knowing full well that I am obligated to carry out my contract with the World Committee of the YMCA."[10]

Never one to shirk on his commitments, he appealed to the Morehouse board of trustees for a sabbatical in 1946 to go to South Africa and do the work he had promised.[11] Morehouse was still in too fragile a state to allow its president to go away for an entire year, and his dream of going to South Africa was dashed. One wonders—had Mays been able to go to South Africa after the end of World War II, would it have radicalized him to the extent that it radicalized his good acquaintance, Max Yergan, who put his theology books aside and looked to communist revolutionary philosophy to achieve social equality?[12] The rise of South Africa's Nationalist Party in 1947 and its installation of apartheid would surely have made Mays ponder what kind of strategy could be used in the country to combat its increasingly brutal and racist regime. The apartheid regime fostered troubling dissonances in Yergan, so that he lost faith in Christianity, the church, and institutions like the YMCA. It was perhaps fortunate that Mays did not go to South Africa because he might have lost his faith, too. In hindsight, it was his faith that propelled him to promote the virtues of Morehouse College and to preach a public theology of racial justice, a theology that emboldened black students to be part of a global movement for racial justice.[13]

Another difficulty he and Sadie faced together was being back in the city of Atlanta.[14] Atlanta was as segregated as Washington, D.C., but Atlanta felt even more so. While living in Atlanta in the early 1930s, Mays had witnessed the trumped up charges and abuse of state power against Angelo Herndon for sedition based upon his choice of reading material and his communist affiliation. In fact, Sadie Mays served on the committee to free Herndon. Atlanta in 1940 remained a deeply parochial southern city.[15] Whites still refused to use formal titles when addressing Benjamin or Sadie. It was much easier for whites to call Mays "Dr." or "Reverend" than "Mr."[16] When Mays returned to Atlanta as Morehouse's president, the city was still rigidly bound to racial hierarchy. Washington, in contrast, was a bit more tolerant, and there was progressive thinking and an sense of rebellion among the intelligentsia gathered around Howard. Howard's faculty was at the center of New Deal social activism. Students had initiated the "Don't Buy Where You Can't Work" campaign, which had been used in Harlem and elsewhere. They had begun to exercise the tactics of noncooperation campaigns, and Marion Anderson's legendary concert in front of the Lincoln Memorial foreshadowed the 1963 March on Washington. Even if black Washingtonians were equally segregated, the urban ethos was different. Washington, though segregated, had a cosmopolitan air, attracting people from all over the world. Nevertheless, Mays returned to the deeper South for a cause—the empowerment and education of young black men.

On September 18, 1940, Mays gave his first address to the incoming freshman class at Morehouse College. He welcomed them into the rich institutional legacy of the college. "When I welcome you here, I am welcoming you to a great institution, an institution with great traditions," he told them. "If Morehouse College stands in any danger," he warned, "it is the danger that threatens all outstanding institutions and all successful individuals. We may come to feel our past achievements are so great that we can move along on past reputation. Nothing could be more damaging or demoralizing." Challenging the students, he stated, "If Morehouse College is to continue to be great; it must continue to produce outstanding personalities. We welcome you, therefore, to an institution whose achievements have called forth the respect and the admiration of the thinkers of America. It is our task to continue and increase this high regard which they hold for us." He recalled how he first came to Morehouse in 1921, as result of John Hope's offer for him to teach, and because of his need of money. The three years he spent at Morehouse were significant. "Though not a Morehouse graduate," he said, "I am marked as a Morehouse man all over the country. Somehow I have the mark of a Morehouse person." Wryly he commented, "Since the Board of Trustees did not see fit to call a President from Morehouse men, they came as near to doing that as they could without actually doing so."[17]

Mays wanted this incoming class, scheduled to graduate in 1944, to be aware of the tremendous task before him. "As I stand here talking to you this morning, I do it with considerable fear and trembling," he said.[18] He had to alert students, in a positive way, to the dire financial predicament of the college. It needed to raise money for its endowment, faculty salaries and housing, academic buildings, chapel, gymnasium, and student scholarship money.

The outbreak of World War II in Europe and Asia and the imminent entry of the United States into it made Mays circumspect. One of the first articles he wrote after arriving back in Atlanta was for the *Atlanta Daily World* on September 1, 1940. In it he urged black men to stay in college instead of joining the armed forces. He quoted from a letter that all college and university presidents had received from the armed forces: "Young people should be advised that it is their patriotic duty to continue the normal course of their education, unless and until they are called, so that they will be well prepared for greatest usefulness to their country."[19] A shortage of college-age males, given Morehouse's financial straits, could have closed its doors. Mays's great fear was that the armed forces might prove attractive to young black men who in ordinary times might have enrolled in college. Mays's concerns, though warranted, did not align with most black men's view of military service. Many poor, working and middle-class black men assiduously tried to avoid being drafted in a segregated army. What kept a young men, even academically talented ones, from attending Morehouse was pretty simple—they lacked money.

Though the size of the enrollment and the number of students who could pay tuition were central to the ultimate success of the college, what mattered most to Mays creating an atmosphere where strong instruction was linked to the continuous development of moral integrity. "I know what a great responsibility it is to try to direct the thinking and to develop the character of young people," Mays told the first freshman class under his presidency. "It is serious enough when times are normal, but it is far more serious when the entire world seems to be going to pieces, when lying is a virtue, when the murder of women and children is right, and when hypocrisy is considered normal procedure." The burden of being a college president was trying in normal times, he asserted, "but in times like these it is enough to make one shudder."[20]

"My success here," he reflected, "depends not only upon myself but upon factors beyond my control. It depends upon the confidence, moral support, and good will that I am able to evoke from the public, both local and national." The challenge of his presidency, he stated, would be to "determine the good will, the cooperation, the financial and moral support of friends and graduates of Morehouse College. But more than that, what we do here will be determined in large measure by the attitude of the members of the Board of Trustees—their attitude toward me and the college."[21] He needed the cooperation of the board of trustees, but he also needed the support of the school's partner institutions in the Atlanta University complex. And he wanted the students to understand that he needed their support and confidence, too.

In the sermonic conclusion of his address, he made a simple pledge to the students to offer his best to the college: "I promise you before my Maker, before God, that I will give to Morehouse College all that I have. I will give to this institution and to you the best of my mind, heart and soul. I will give to this institution my money until it reaches the sacrificial point." "In other words," he continued, his voice rising, "I will serve you and I will serve this institution as if God almighty sent me into the world for the specific purpose of being the Sixth President of Morehouse College. I will not cheat on you. I will not work by the clock. I will do more than draw my breath and my salary." Thundering, he promised, "I will serve you with the same dignity and with the same pride that Franklin Roosevelt serves the people of the United States. This is all that I can promise you. When I reach the point where I cannot serve you this way, when the time comes when I cannot give you the best of my mind, soul, heart, time and energy, I will pass my resignation in to the members of the Board of Trustees. I pledge you this on the 18th day of September 1940; and, God helping me, I can do no other!"[22]

It was no coincidence that he concluded his first talk with an oratorical flourish in which he quoted Martin Luther, the sixteenth-century Protestant Reformer. He knew that Morehouse students, steeped in the tradition of black Baptist preaching, would love the rhetorical device, and he knew that good preaching let the audience depart on an inspirational high and ready to commit themselves to the cause of building Morehouse. The Morehouse presidency was not simply a job to Mays—it was his pulpit on the national and world stage. Underlying his preachments to students was a philosophy of education rooted in his principled democratic beliefs and an ethical theological vision.[23]

Mays had long held that education was more than professional certification. In 1928, in a speech before a YMCA gathering in Tallahassee, Florida, he gave a talk titled "Ear Marks of an Educated Man." He told the young men gathered that to be educated is to be radical. A radical person is one who thinks for himself by getting at the root of an issue, and in the case of the black man, radicalism prompts him to acknowledge that the "Negro is not an inferior." The second mark of an educated man was "an open mind." It was important in life to always learn and seek out new truth. The third mark was the "courage of conviction." To act on a belief, whether it was the Christian faith or not, required courage. If a person believed in a desegregated society, he proclaimed his belief without equivocation. Jesus, for example, died for his convictions. The fourth mark of an educated man was restlessness. He urged his audience members never to be satisfied or complacent. Self-satisfaction was always disastrous. Easy contentment never brought out the best in a person or lead to high achievement. The fifth mark was "an appreciation for all values and all knowledge." It was important for students to understand that knowledge was vast and wide and came from many places. He emphasized that the goal of education was to instill in a people an appreciation for different philosophical and cultural values as they shaped their own lives. The final mark was sensitivity to "social and economic injustices." It was important that an educated person be sensitive to the needs of the most vulnerable in society. For Mays, it was not enough for an educated individual to serve his own needs; education was a privilege requiring that an individual serve others. Being truly educated, he believed, meant that one should practice altruism and self-sacrifice.[24]

His educational philosophy struck a middle ground between that of Booker T. Washington, who advocated industrial training, and W. E. B. DuBois, who promoted classical or liberal arts education. What Mays found appealing about Washington was that he gave black people pride in the accomplishments and building of Tuskegee Institute. Black people, with their own labor, built an institution of significance with a black leader at the helm. On the other hand, he agreed with DuBois on the virtue of the liberal arts education, especially in training leaders for the freedom struggles of black people. Like DuBois, Mays had been trained in a liberal arts institution that taught that religion and classical studies were foundational to shaping democratic institutions. Mays, as did all Morehouse leaders, viewed the school's mission as shaping the whole person. Mays believed that the task of educators was to spiritually uplift students and to turn their minds toward noble ends.[25] A liberal arts education should prepare an individual to act on his or her convictions.

In July 1940, Mays wrote an article for the *Journal of Negro Education* titled "The Religious Life and Needs of Negro Students." The article specifically dealt with the religious dimension of black student life but also gave insight into how Mays viewed the needs of black college students more broadly. He asserted that students needed a better historical understanding of the black church and, more generally, the history of Christianity. He concluded—from surveys taken on many black college campuses—that most black students claimed to be Christian and to have some type of church affiliation. However, from experience, he knew that many of these students had little understanding of their own churches' history or even general knowledge of American church history as a whole. For example, it was important, in Mays's estimation, that students have some historical knowledge of American Christianity as it related to slavery. The "searchlight of Christianity could not shine forever upon the institution of slavery without dissolving it," he wrote. And the "Negro would have been in a sad plight after emancipation if the Christian church had not come to his rescue educationally and religiously." For good measure, he added, "Christianity has been and still is one of the most powerful weapons the Negro possesses with which to press claims in American life. It cannot be denied, therefore, that the Negro's heritage in America is a religious one."[26]

Just as black students needed to learn more church history, they also needed to have more historical knowledge of the Bible, though Mays felt that students were not solely at fault in their ignorance. He blamed college and university administrators for the problem. "In many of our colleges," he claimed, "there is no opportunity afforded the student to select courses in which religion is taught, the teachers are too often less qualified than the teachers who teach in other areas of the college." Teaching religious literature and tradition allowed students to make up their own minds about religion's role in human history. Religious history was just as vital to the college or university curriculum as the natural sciences. "If education is to deal with the whole of culture," he opined, "the college can no more escape its responsibility in the area of religion than it can escape its responsibility in the area of literature and mathematics."[27]

Interestingly enough, though Morehouse was nonsectarian, Mays believed that his faculty members were all religious practitioners. For him, "the religion which students see demonstrated in the lives of teachers and administrators have more significance than all the preaching and compulsory chapel services combined. Teachers in their treatment of students should meet the high test of religion." Fundamental to a good educational institution was the premise that students were not simply the means to financially support the institution; they were the ends.

Mays also believed that college students needed institutional structure, authority, and guidance as they developed into ethical decision makers. "Ethics and morals may be relative terms," he explained. "But the student, if he is to count, must build up for himself a system of ethics which for him is the final authority. And this system must be an ever-expanding system but always built up in the light of the highest and the best he knows." The models for this kind of behavior were the college instructors and administrators.[28]

As he reflected on the religious needs of black students, he recalled the significance of his mother's "slave religion." He wrote, "Somehow, and I do not know how it is to be done, Negro students need a faith for their day equivalent to that of their enslaved ancestors. They had the religious faith that brought them through when times for them were far more precarious than the times are for us." He saw slave religion, for all of its faults, as resolute. And while he believed that slave religion was not to be idolized, students needed to learn from slaves' faithful determination to overcome obstacles. "This faith in our day would need to be modified in the light of changed conditions and in the light of what science has revealed," he wrote. "But if the Negro student's intellect could be saturated with a religious faith that could do for him what faith alone did for their ancestors, it is difficult to imagine what could be accomplished. A religious faith coupled with brains and intelligence would go a long way to save Negro students from despair and cynicism."[29]

At the core of slave religion was a righteous God, he believed. Students facing obstacles had to have a sense that religion would "give direction to life—a direction that is neither communistic nor fascistic—not even the direction of a capitalistic individualism. Slave religion, as Mays interpreted it, "recognizes the judgment of God in history—a faith in God would not be shaken even if economic structures collapsed altogether, if governments the world over were destroyed, and if ecclesiastical systems came to ruin one by one." What made this kind of faith so important was its steadfast hope and perseverance to believe against all odds. This deeply rooted belief system would give students an unswerving determination to fight against social injustice. A college such as Morehouse that promoted such a faith was foundational to producing indefatigable students of character and principle. Students would need such a faith to thrive in a society and a world that constantly heaped indignities on black people. Evoking St. Augustine and Psalm 43 of the Hebrew scriptures, he explained that "with such a conviction one will strive for the establishment of a righteous order; but he will understand that if the righteous order is not established, both the unrighteous and the more nearly righteous will suffer. And on the ruins of unrighteousness he will try again to build the City of God. This kind of religion, therefore, would give direction to Negro life—security in the midst of insecurity."[30]

In 1943, Mays directed the Morehouse faculty and administration to publish a student-recruiting pamphlet, which could also be distributed to philanthropic donors. Titled "What We Seek to Achieve at Morehouse College," the pamphlet did not have Mays's name on it, but the goals it listed for the college could have been lifted directly from his 1940 article. "Morehouse College," the pamphlet read, "must continue to strengthen its emphasis of developing students of sound integrity.... The trouble with the world lies primarily in the area of ethics and morals. It will not be sufficient for Morehouse College ... to produce clever graduates; ... rather [it will be] sufficient when it can produce honest men, men who can be trusted both in public and private life—men who are sensitive to the wrongs, the sufferings, and the injustices of society and who are willing to share the responsibility for correcting them." The pamphlet was full of the high idealism found in Mays's educational philosophy. It acknowledged the technical skills that a Morehouse student should possess when he graduated, but it added, "The Negro student needs other skills— skills in how to remain poised and hopeful and jubilant in an environment that is not always friendly to his ambitions and strivings. He needs the mind of the scientist, the wisdom of a philosopher, and the religious faith of the Negro slave."[31]

Morehouse College's goals were part of a much larger freedom movement. "However learned the Morehouse College man may become," the pamphlet, as conceived by Mays, read, "his destiny is tied up, and inevitably so, with the great mass of people who do the ordinary work of the world and need their souls lifted by contact and fellowship with the more privileged among us.... A community-minded college would go a long way toward assisting the student to move away from the erroneous conception of absolute freedom of the individual—the old idea that the 'selfish interest of the individual' is alone to be taken into consideration." The pamphlet concluded, "There must be no wide gulf between the educated and uneducated at Morehouse College. The college is not training men for *special privilege* but for honest sincere service. . . . This community mindedness must not be wholly racial, even if one is forced to live in a bi-racial civilization; it must include all races, all nations and the world."[32]

Mays wanted Morehouse to be in the thick of the debate concerning contemporary social issues. This debate included the wider democratic movements that reverberated through the politics of Henry Wallace, the labor movement, the black-led civil rights struggle, and anticolonial resistance in other parts of the world. By the end of World War II, Mays thought of Morehouse College as "an experiment in democratic living." It was essential to him that black people practice democracy in the areas they controlled. The Morehouse pamphlet stated, "If the essence of democracy is to develop responsible people, the only way to produce them is to give them opportunities to carry responsibility. Though the Negro has been denied complete freedom a long time, he must not interpret what little freedom he has to mean license to dominate others. If freedom carries responsibilities, it seems clear that student participation in all programs that shape the destiny of Morehouse College will go a long way in helping him to experience the meaning of freedom and responsibility in a democracy." Mays premised these ideas about democratic practices with the belief that a dedicated faculty would lead students by example. It was their duty to shape Morehouse men into democratic citizens.[33]

Mays's educational philosophy was visionary. However, the implementation of this vision was constrained by the school's economic and social realities. The first issue was sustaining enrollment at a men's college during a time of war. The Depression and World War II had almost completely crippled the institution. From 1940 to 1945 Morehouse College enrollment averaged around 355, with an all-time low enrollment of 272 during the 1943–44 academic year.[34]

The second great obstacle was simply paying the bills. The challenge for most black college students, as it had been for Mays when he was a student, was financing college. He had to require that students pay all back bills. Morehouse did not have enough money to sustain itself without the students' tuition dollars. The enrollment numbers were not large enough to provide the school with a financial cushion and its endowment, and the endowment itself was paltry. Realistically the college could not afford not to collect past-due accounts.[35] Added to tuition collection, the college had a difficult time getting money from its alumni in any sustained way to build its coffers. Unlike Howard University, which had some largesse from the federal government, Morehouse continued to rely solely on the munificence of churches and northern philanthropic organizations and individuals. Morehouse, therefore, was still very much dependent on the declining financial support of the American Baptist Church and the Rockefeller Foundation and on the small gifts inconsistently coming in from its alumni base. Given the financial realities of running a small private college, Mays concluded that "there were only two ways of getting more money: (1) Raise it; and (2) do a better job of collecting fees." The latter of the two ways earned Mays the affectionate moniker "Buck Benny."[36]

Mays's difficulty raising funds reflected the down side of the emerging black middle-class consumer culture. Initially under John Hope, and more so through Mays, the notion of being a "Morehouse man" developed currency as a way of instilling pride and praise for the achievements of the student body and alumni. This sense of pride, Mays believed, should have spurred financial gifts to the college. But, as he came to realize, Morehouse alumni were not very forthcoming with contributions to their beloved institution in any significant or sacrificial way. Morehouse alumni, though poorer than their white counterparts from comparable colleges, had achieved some economic success. Many had become big-city clergymen, lawyers, and teachers, but they had not demonstrated a long-term commitment to donate what they could to the college. Of course, there were individuals who consistently gave to the college, but generally speaking, Mays solicited everyone—"students, faculty, trustees, alumni and friends" of Morehouse to contribute.[37] The emerging black middle class in Atlanta and Morehouse graduates in general reflected a larger American reality of economic behavior, driven more by consumer culture than the ethics of sacrificial giving.

Adding to Mays's obstacles in managing Morehouse were other cultural contradictions within the black middle class. The city of Atlanta's historic black colleges' role in building a sizable middle class is a wonderful legacy. These schools not only offered formal education to black people, they germinated ideas and culture. Mays repeatedly noted the relative intellectual freedom that the church-related institution offered his students. He was well aware of the leadership and political roles these institutions played as building blocks for a political movement, and, given that these kinds of colleges did not receive substantive support from politically controlled state agencies, they could more overtly prepare and encourage students to be engaged citizens. He wrote, "Citizenship as it relates to the Negro and the ballot can never be fully realized until there is intelligent concern and intelligent leadership emanating from Negro colleges." It was incumbent upon black liberal arts colleges to see that

Negro students know thoroughly the history and development of the American Government and how this Government functions. . . . Of all students in American colleges, the Negro students should be conversant with and understand every item in the Constitution of the United States. Negro students should have at their fingertips a complete knowledge of every decision the United States Supreme Court had handed down in behalf of minorities since the founding of this country. The Negro liberal arts colleges should study and understand thoroughly the State Constitutions. Compulsory courses to this end should be required of every student.

In making these kinds of courses mandatory, black colleges would "share in an effort to develop a real democracy in the United States." This responsibility the colleges could not escape.[38]

While black liberal arts colleges were essential to the larger freedom struggles, they were also entrenched in a middle-class culture that was highly racialized and socially stratified, where black skin was often associated with economic impoverishment and lack of beauty. As a dark-skinned man, Mays joined this middle-class circle by virtue of his educational achievement and his marriages, as both of his wives were light-skinned. This is not to say that Mays or his wives ever accepted stereotypes, labels, or conventions as normative, but the reality was that Mays traveled among a black elite that believed that a light skin was a signifier of beauty and status. While Mays disdained many of the black middle class's regressive attitudes, he had no choice but to operate and negotiate within the racial hierarchies found on black college campuses.[39] And there is no doubt he often felt the personal sting of these attitudes even though he was given a pass because of his status as president of Morehouse. Nevertheless, his role as a college president mandated that he work with alumni and local black civic leaders of all types in Atlanta, many of whom were deeply ensconced in these negative attitudes that equated one's value with one's pigmentation. Whether he liked it or not, this was the divide in the black world, which he could not escape.

Despite the glaring pigmentocracy within these institutions, we must not overlook the fact that Atlanta's black middle class had a more impressive tradition of progressive reform politics than their white counterparts. Atlanta's black middle class led a local political insurgency to undo the southern exclusionary laws in their city and successfully fought to establish a more fully inclusive Atlanta.[40] Black middle-class professionals benefited from access to federally created jobs through segregated New Deal programs that accorded

The presidents of Atlanta's five black colleges, ca. 1950. Courtesy of the
Moorland-Spingarn Research Center, Howard University.

them responsibilities in overseeing the limited programs directed toward black
Atlantans. Ironically, the interests of this small group of middle-class professionals were often conflated with the interests of the majority of poor blacks
in the city.[41] Conflicts over whose interests were actually represented affected
the local politics of Atlanta, as class divisions in the black community grew
wider.[42] Mays hoped to challenge the prevailing assumptions about skin color-
ation equating to social class standing that so defined black Atlanta, and at the
same time build Morehouse.

The reality was that the black middle class was constricted in terms of mobility
and political power, no matter where they turned. When Mays tried to get white
business leaders to meet with black civic and business leaders in the 1940s, he
found little success. According to the Reverend Martin Luther King Sr., although
the meetings Mays held were laudable, "very little came out of the initial meetings. . . . The white businessmen who were with us saw little need to interfere with
the *gracious Atlanta way of doing things*."[43] Nevertheless, Mays had to be diplo-
matic to maintain cordial relationships with Atlanta's white business community.

Mays did not receive many financial contributions for the college's endowment from Atlanta's largely white-owned businesses. In an interesting and

ironic twist, he secretly established a relationship with the novelist Margaret Mitchell, who had written southern plantation life into American mythological lore in the 1936 novel *Gone with the Wind*. Its 1939 film adaptation, starring Clark Gable and Vivian Leigh, would establish this vision of the American South in the American imagination as thoroughly as its cinematic predecessor *Birth of a Nation*.[44] Mitchell made contributions to Morehouse for some of the college's students to attend medical school. Mays swallowed hard on accepting these funds. Surely if he had despised the film *Green Pastures*, the depiction of slaves in *Gone with the Wind* surely left him demoralized and frustrated. Yet if he wanted some of the college's better students to attend medical school, he had to do what all black college presidents did: hold his nose and take the financial assistance with all the dignity he could muster.[45] For the most part, though, the white business establishment of Atlanta ignored this small, all-black liberal arts college. Therefore Mays realized early on that he had to generate publicity about Morehouse College in order to raise money and recruit talented students, just as he had done at Howard University. His success at the college depended upon inspiring the very brightest black male students to attend Morehouse and build on its tradition of producing leaders.

Mays carried out this duty by trying to be an exemplary model of ethical leadership; he embodied elegance, an aspect of his life he assiduously honed.[46] As Russell Adams, a Morehouse alumnus, recollected, Mays's stylishness was a great influence on all the young men in his class. Mays was "always dressed *Gentlemen Quarterly* style," he recalled, "usually some version of pin-stripe gray suit accentuating his height and lack of body fat. He was camera ready."[47] Adams also pointed out that the deep connection Mays had with students was partly due to his life experiences. Adams recalled that Mays's "precisely selected words lovingly and rhythmically enunciated" told the story of black struggle. When Mays reached the crescendo in his sermons, Adams observed, "any line between Mays the elegant messenger and Mays the kinsman in struggle disappeared, *his* language ennobling our cause."

And finally, there was Mays the living example of what these young men could do with their lives. Students, Adams reflected,

> saw what a black man could be when they saw Mays, whose high fluting
> style contrasted with his forthrightness about his family background:
> he could talk about picking cotton—he was once a South Carolina
> cotton picking champ; he could talk about painting houses—he was
> an expert with the paintbrush and bucket; he would say things such as
> "neither my mother nor my father could read; but I am here." Virtually

every year, Mays returned to his home town and gave a standing room only to audiences made of sharecroppers, maids, and underpaid school teachers. . . . Onetime, he introduced one of his semi-literate brothers to us in Sale Hall Auditorium, saying, "My brother gave everything he could spare to help me stay in school." I remember going back to my room, Graves Hall, Room 452, and crying without restraint at the sheer nobility of the gesture.

Mays's embodiment of black manliness, characterized by integrity, nobility, and eloquence, pulled his male students toward a larger vision of their humanity and what they could accomplish.[48]

Mays's leadership signified the position to which civically engaged black men might ascend in American society. However, in spite of Mays's example, there were other, sexual dimensions of black manliness expressed at Morehouse. It was Mays's duty to project and an overarching ideal of how black men should behave, but no matter what his presidential duties were, it did not prevent students or faculty members from being libidinously homosexual or heterosexual, or in some cases a combination of both.[49] Mays did not speak openly about this aspect of college life, for in a highly racialized and stratified society, to discuss sexuality publicly in the 1940s would have been threatening to the college's religious donors, frightened its base in the black Baptist Church, and given a hostile patriarchal southern community yet another excuse to destroy an institution that provided opportunity to black men. Whatever concerns Mays had about these aspects of the college remained closeted and discussed internally among the faculty, staff, and students. For even Mays did not fulfill the masculine ideal by fathering children.

One of the disappointing personal realities for the Mayses was that they never had any children. Sadie Mays had a tubular pregnancy, which required emergency surgery to save her life while they vacationed in Cuba in August of 1941.[50] Mays did not reveal his personal pains and heartaches; one cannot assess his or Sadie Mays's emotions about their childlessness or how it affected their marriage. As a result of Mayses not having any children of their own, the Morehouse students became their de facto children. They also took on the additional responsibility of funding their nieces and nephews' college education. After the death of Mays's parents, the couple quietly supported his older sister Susie as she and her husband struggled through the New Deal's farm policies that put black farmers in the South at an even greater economic disadvantage than they had been previously.

The Mayses' freedom from parental responsibilities meant that they never had to worry about their children causing embarrassment to their work at

Benjamin Mays and Sadie Gray Mays attending a state dinner at the White House, 1962.
Courtesy of the Moorland-Spingarn Research Center, Howard University.

Morehouse College or measuring their own successes or failures against those
of their parents. In a system of southern oppression—under which the social,
economic, and personal lives of black Americans were even more susceptible to

life's unseemly compromise to protect and rear children—not having children actually gave the Mayses more personal liberty. No matter how disappointed they might have felt about this absence in their relationship, being free of parental obligations allowed Mays to devote his time to his students and to social advocacy through writing and public speaking. As a couple, they never allowed their personal grief about their childlessness to incapacitate their positive vision and hopes for black children.

In an article titled "Improving the Morale of Negro Children and Youth," Mays argued that the morale of Negro children needed significant improvement. "By morale," he penned, "we mean spirit, confidence, hope, enthusiasm, aspiration, ambition, and freedom from fear." The only way to encourage the morale of black children, he concluded, was to defeat legalized segregation and the cultural apartheid that existed in America, south and north. As a childless couple, the Mayses were able to use their time and resources to be unwavering advocates for the full inclusion of black children into a democratic society.

The two major intellectual issues that remained constant for Mays as Morehouse's president were democracy and Christianity. Central to his thinking as a public theologian was the idea that democratic institutions played a vital role in Protestant Christian social witness, and that Christianity was best exhibited in the fair play of democratic practices. He argued that Christianity, if it were going to be believed in, had to be a force in the church that allowed all people to be full citizens. This, he believed, exhibited the kingdom of heaven on earth. World War II and its atrocities made Mays's Social Gospel even more radical.

He remained principally democratic in his political ideology. In an era in which many black intellectuals flirted with Communism or joined the Communist Party, Mays's religious intellectualism seemed unfashionable. However, his distrust of Communism was based on the belief that no group of people should ever hold complete political power. The dictatorship of the proletariat, or the party's vanguard, to use V. I. Lenin's terminology, violated the Baptist egalitarianism that considered all human beings to be equal in the eyes of their Creator. As he once explained, "I have no love for communism. I hate its atheism and I deplore its denial of freedom. I hate all forms of totalitarianism in which the individual exists for the state."[51] Theologically speaking, Mays believed that all people were sinful and were prone to abuse their power when given unlimited power. He simply did not believe that a small group of leaders with all the political power, no matter how well intended, would have the wisdom not to abuse it. Furthermore, Mays felt that if white southern Democrats so egregiously violated democratic precepts, the Communists, with no civil limitations, might do worse. More importantly, Communism declared open war on religious beliefs and the church. To Mays, a political system that mandated disbelief was even more dangerous than the inefficiencies and abuses of American democracy.

He was, then, a committed democrat, and he preached democracy side by side with his Christian beliefs. He deemed that religious beliefs along with democratic principles could, in fact, reshape American politics. He believed the more effective rhetorical use of Christian ethics would ultimately defeat defenders of segregation. When the Swedish economist Gunnar Myrdal examined American race relations in his study *The American Dilemma* in 1944, he came to the conclusion that the problem in America was that the majority of white Americans had not lived up to the American creed. The American creed, according to Myrdal, in what was a generous reading of American history, was in essence that Americans believed in fair play for all citizens and that racial prejudices in America were contradictory to the overall societal impetus. This kind of talk of creed and faith in democracy was the language of the black Social Gospel that Mays had been preaching. It should be noted that while Myrdal gets the credit for describing American race relations in terms of a dilemma between belief and action, this language was co-opted from the theology that Mays and others had already been advancing.[52] Mays's advocacy of the religious principles of brotherhood and democratic ideas of equality as twin ideals was not new. He often promoted civil religion in his efforts to challenge both blacks and whites to be more democratic in their thinking about American racial injustice.[53] Christianity and democratic practices were wedded together as though the one informed the other. In his social analysis, he contended that the heritage of the United States was the Judeo-Christian tradition and, as a result, citizens of the country could be morally persuaded to act justly. They were vital moral agents in helping to build the case for a moral authority to challenge injustice and achieve social change. And for this reason he held on to his faith in American democracy even when it was clearly evident that up to this point the American style of democracy was used to exclude and disadvantage black Americans economically and politically.

Mays understood that the Constitution had not been written to fully include blacks as citizens, but its laws and procedural processes gave "the Negro hope" to fight for their citizenship rights. This, he argued, was because "the Constitution is democratic in principles and ideals, the American people are obligated in the name of democracy and in the name of national honor to implement them into every area of American life." The Constitution, he held, stood "as a beacon light to pass judgment upon all that we do. Without the principles set forth in the Constitution, the Negro would be hopeless and would have no protection in law." To him black people had no alternative but to fight for their constitutional rights.[54]

The United States' entry into World War II brought the constitutional question to the fore. What would it mean for black people to be full participants in a war effort without sufficient guarantees of their legal rights at home? He questioned whether the war would be beneficial to blacks without what he called the "will to justice." To him, only righteous actions and moral fortitude by the American public would change the black disenfranchisement. Was America ready to exercise its moral capacity to make democracy a reality for all of its citizens, he asked. He was uncertain whether the war would tip the scales toward black social advancement, but he unhesitatingly supported the war. He believed "that nothing interferes with our united effort to win the war." According to him, the war required two things from black and white leaders: truthfulness and courage. Black leaders had to realize that their patriotism would "bring no appreciable change in racial attitudes on the part of the dominant American mind as a result of the war." He recognized "that Georgia will still insist on its white [Democratic] primary; that there will be no more liberality after the war than now, on the question of allowing Negroes to be trained for jobs and permitting them to work on parity with white workers." His insistence that black leaders recognize this truth was a bitter lesson learned from World War I. During the First World War, W. E. B. DuBois endorsed the United States' entry into the war based on the hopes that President Woodrow Wilson would defend the citizenship rights of black Americans. DuBois's public support for the war did not change the Wilson administration's segregation policies one iota. As a result, a great deal of disillusionment was fostered among the masses. Mays thought that broken promises only hurt progressive political efforts and increased cynicism and self-defeat.

Mays's political pragmatism in regard to the war came perilously close to acquiescence to political power. He did not support a Gandhian approach of non-cooperation against war mobilization, which Bayard Rustin of the Fellowship of Reconciliation strongly supported. Nor was he a political rejectionist like Elijah Muhammad—of the burgeoning Nation of Islam (NOI)—who refused to participate in the war. His viewpoint could have been an easy mark for criticism by more radical religious adherents in the black community. Both Rustin and Muhammad served time in federal prison for being conscientious objectors to the war. But Mays's earlier travels helped him understand the limited choices that blacks had. His journey through both Japan and Germany in the late 1930s gave him a different perspective about what was going on in those countries. His astute observations of the total disdain and absolute hatred of minorities exhibited by their political regimes convinced him that black Americans had little choice but to support the United States. Ever the realist, he knew that whites, while appreciative during the crisis, would never voluntarily give blacks democratic freedoms as result of their patriotism.

History had taught Mays that blacks' fight for justice would have to include more than being cooperative in the war. He believed that building a sustainable political argument on behalf of black citizens required an appeal to moral and religious principles. But in the interim, he counseled cooperation and sacrifice to defeat the Axis forces. He felt that "deep-seated prejudices that have been centuries in the making are not destroyed because of a war that extends over a period of three or five years, or because Negroes have fought for democracy on foreign fields." He also realized that if blacks did not participate they would lose moral authority in making the argument before the nation for full citizenship rights. Thus he hoped that espousing this kind of realism would "help to save Negroes and other minorities from disillusionment and despair," especially in the postwar years. He knew the struggle to achieve democracy was going to be long and difficult.

White leaders, Mays also recognized, had to face a different truth: they should not expect black people to be satisfied with the status quo after the war. Black leaders "should make it clear to white people," he stated unambiguously, that they could not expect blacks to "share the dangers of war" without sharing "correspondingly the fruits of democracy." It was up to white leaders to tell the rest of the country "that Negroes have a right to expect the ballot, a right to want an opportunity to work, to be promoted on the job, to want equal pay for equal work, and a right to desire the good things that all Americans desire." Two important questions remained unanswered: "Does America want a democracy that includes all people? Do we want the Christian religion to function so that brotherhood will be a reality?" He asserted:

> The Church and Christian America could avoid hypocrisy and maintain integrity of soul only by striving earnestly to do in practice what they advocated in theory. As long as the Gospel of Christ is preached in America and as long as we have a Constitution that guarantees equality of opportunity to all of its citizens and a supreme court to interpret the spirit of that Constitution, the Negro can accept whatever responsibility his country lays upon him. As a minority group in the American commonwealth these are the most powerful weapons the Negro has at his disposal.[55]

The way Mays articulated the issues of war and democracy resonated with many black men and women making their way "up North." His views about Christianity and its relationship to democracy had a strong appeal among black people who flocked to church on Sunday morning both in the North and in the South. His faith was a fighting one.

His convictions about democracy and Christianity had wide appeal on black college campuses. One of his most widely cited addresses, "Democratizing and Christianizing America in This Generation," given at Howard University's commencement in 1945, received accolades and praise from the general public and students alike. Mays told the students that they had a responsibility to challenge the antidemocratic forces in the United States. He believed this could be done "without violence or revolution." Why? Because the United States, by virtue of the "Federal Constitution and by virtue of its Christian pronouncements to become Christianized and democratized," would rationally compel Americans to be just. To him, the country would have no other choice; if Americans were not just President Franklin Roosevelt's claims for the four freedoms for all people in the world—"freedom of speech and expression," "freedom of every person to worship God," "freedom from want," and "freedom from fear"—that justified World War II, would be declared duplicitous by the court of world opinion.[56] This justice was vital for America "to maintain integrity of soul" and avoid hypocrisy before other nations. He argued that the students' challenge in life was to make America true to its constitutional promise and its religious foundations. The greater challenge, he said, was to live morally principled lives and to be committed to overturning the injustices. He told the graduating class of 1945 that the task before them was not simply intellectual but "ethical and moral." Their generation's job was "to make men good as well as intellectual." He emphasized the importance of being responsible people. "Representing a minority group as you do," he proclaimed, "you can not afford to join the exploiting class, because you are the exploited.... He who cries out against undemocratic principles should be democratic. We whine the loudest, and justly so, but for that reason alone we must be exemplars of justice."[57] The students at Howard University were not the only recipients of Mays's charge; Morehouse students were also frequently treated to the same sermonizing, challenging them to be social contributors, democratic citizens, and just Christian men.

The war years shrank Morehouse's student body. Inventively, the college began its early admission program for high school students, which was modeled after the University of Chicago. The idea was to attract the most promising male students to begin their scholastic journey before they completed high school. In this way the college could attract not only young men from families who could afford to pay tuition but also those who were academically gifted. The early-entrance program was also reminiscent of the high school program at South Carolina State. In 1944, because of this early-entrance program, Martin Luther King Jr. entered Morehouse at age fifteen.[58] Young freshman, like King, would help stave-off the ruin of the college. When the war ended, Morehouse received an influx of new students, including some veterans, which increased enrollment and solved some of the college's financial woes. Veterans, who returned to college as more worldly and experienced, interjected a new kind of militancy and seriousness into the student body at Morehouse.

In this environment, Mays was intent on shaping the ideological dimensions of student life. During his tenure, he used the Tuesday chapel services to offer students a time for insightful meditation, a practice he had inherited from John Hope. Mays used this time to inform his students about religion, personal decorum, and democratic engagement. One of the distinct advantages of Morehouse being a private, church-affiliated liberal arts college was that moral guidance was seen as essential to the students' preparation. The Tuesday morning chapel talks were extended examinations of the question of leadership in all of its dimensions—religious, political, academic, and social. He constantly infused his students with his theological and social views, hoping that the young men would incorporate ethical leadership into their respective roles serving black communities.

His concerns about leadership went beyond the school's walls. The central problem facing black people was how to create and sustain ethical leadership. What would keep black leaders—and leaders in general—from using the needs of black people to their own advantage? Mays knew firsthand that this was an important practical area to address from his ongoing connection to daily black church life. He also knew how difficult it was to get principled, honest, and civically engaged leadership from the ranks of the burgeoning middle class. He contended that the problem of effective leadership, no matter what the race, was partially due to the absence of moral fortitude, integrity, and courage. These leadership characteristics, which he attempted to nurture in the Morehouse students, were the same ones needed throughout America.

Mays tried to exemplify ethical leadership in his civil rights actions as well. In Atlanta, he joined local coalitions and the national NAACP's effort to gain blacks the right the vote.[59] In addition, he and his more politically cautious friend Gordon Blaine Hancock planned and participated in the Durham

Conference in 1942, where black southern leaders came together to make an appeal for goodwill from the southern political establishment by addressing racial economic and educational funding disparities. Mays's role in the conference was to push cautious black leaders to be more vigorous in their demands for greater civic freedoms; his lone dissent to the conference's halfhearted remarks against segregation did not make it into the "The Durham Manifesto," the final document that the conference produced. The statement was more tepid than Mays wanted. The conference pushed white southern moderates and cautious local black leaders to see that the fundamental principles of democracy were at stake as the world tackled Nazi racism. The conference prepared the ground for the Southern Regional Council.[60]

In another important civil rights action, in 1947 Mays filed a federal lawsuit against the Southern Railway Company, one of the train lines he consistently rode, for racial discrimination and violation of the federal transportation statute. Representing Mays in this case was the NAACP legal team headed by Thurgood Marshall. Although the case never made it through the federal court system, he wanted to add his name to the list of plaintiffs against racial discrimination on interstate trains and buses.[61] His legal protest was not as daring as Bayard Rustin and the Fellowship of Reconciliations' 1947 "Journey for Reconciliation," in which whites and blacks defied the laws of segregation by riding interstate buses throughout the South, but a black college president, publicly expressing dissent about a private corporation was unusual.[62]

Mays resolved to stand for what was just and fair, and he deliberately shaped Morehouse as an incubator for critically engaged leaders. He explained that Morehouse provided a community that was above the fray so that its students could thoughtfully and objectively examine themselves and the world around them.[63] He expected Morehouse students to achieve distinction. He demanded that they make their mark in all areas of their endeavors through hard work. Just as his parents instilled in him a proud work ethic when he was a boy toiling in the cotton fields, he annually challenged Morehouse graduates to "do your work as if God sent you into the world at this precise moment in history to do this work."[64]

In these years, Mays seemed indefatigable. In addition to everything else he did, he was one of the key behind-the-scene brokers among his fellow black college presidents in the creation of the United Negro College Fund in 1943.[65] Not only was Mays a notable black college president and a well-regarded black clergyman; until 1955, Mays was arguably the most well known black educator and educated black clergyman in the United States. His weekly opinion column, "My View," began appearing in 1946 in the nationally syndicated, black-owned *Pittsburgh Courier*. His column ran opposite that of George Schuyler, who at the time was the most satirical and politically famous black conservative columnist in the United States.[66] Just as he had done in the 1930s, he regularly informed readers about their constitutional rights, their need for skills and education, his religious perspectives, and foreign policy concerns. In writing this weekly column, he kept intellectually attuned to the current events affecting black communities, especially in the South. Throughout his career he had tried to inform black people who lacked access to powerful elites about pressing local and global concerns. He was cognizant that movements for social justice and independence, which were occurring the world over, were intrinsic to the black freedom movement in the United States.

By the late 1940s, Mays had been honored by both Bates College and the University of Chicago Divinity School as a distinguished alumnus. In October of 1949, the University of Chicago Divinity School recognized his extraordinary leadership as an educator, "a churchman of the ecumenical movement . . . a humanitarian . . . a preacher and teacher; a lecturer and contributor to learned as well as various representative journals of thought and opinion; an alumnus. . . who served faithfully the needs of his fellows, and illumined the contemporary relevance of the Christian faith." It was an honor that both he and the entire college were grateful to have bestowed on him.[67] What was ironic about him receiving this accolade from Chicago was that if he had wanted to teach there, he would not have been hired. Two prominent white scholars, Robert Hutchins, the president of the university, and William Ogburn, a member of the faculty publicly opposed the hiring of blacks on the faculty.[68] While other scholars in higher education were not as vocal about their opinions regarding opening the doors of the academy to nonwhite scholars, their silence spoke volumes.[69] Nevertheless Mays graciously accepted these honors as signs of progress in the ongoing struggle to recognize and sustain black achievement.

When Morehouse graduate Leronne Bennett looked back on Mays's years as president of Morehouse, he declared him one of America's "Last Great Schoolmasters," which was by no means an over statement.[70] Measuring Mays's presidency within the context of his own historical moment from 1940 until the U.S. Supreme Court ruled on *Brown v. Board of Education* in 1954, we might take Bennett's description a step further. In many respects, it would be more accurate to call Mays schoolmaster to the movement, which a later generation of activists would call the civil rights movement. No other American college president, black or white, matched his intense moral commitment to or his eloquent demands for democracy and social justice in this period. To his students, "Buck Benny" inspired hope, built confidence, and encourage societal change in every venue where he was allowed to speak, write, and preach. From 1940, when he became Morehouse's president, until 1954, he was unrivaled in his principled democratic stand; he laid the intellectual groundwork for social change throughout the South among black churchgoing college students. His constant coalition-building for a fully inclusive society in both black and white circles was unmatched among his peers. He never relented in his belief that racism, which was deeply embedded in American Christianity, reduced the Christian faith to pious platitudes and delegitimized democracy in America.

Seeking to Be Christian in Race Relations

I would tremble for the Christian cause if 50 Negroes were to enter an average local
church in this country on a Sunday morning and ask to become members. Fundamentally we are afraid . . . to practice the Christian Religion.
—MAYS, quoted in *Time* magazine

In 1946, Mays authored a twenty-five-cent booklet titled *Seeking to Be Christian
in Race Relations*. It was part of a trilogy called "The Christian and Race,"
which also included Ethel Alpenfels's *Nonsense about Race* and Margaret C.
McCulloch's *Know—Then Act*, published by the United Methodist Women's
Friendship Press.[1] The United Methodist women played a crucial, yet unsung,
role in facilitating the distribution of this and other important civil rights
literature.[2] According to Mays, their role was equal to that of the NAACP in
educating the American public about ending "an uncivilized era" of racial
intolerance.[3] His small book was part of wider effort to address American
Christianity and the problem of race relations in the late 1940s. Beginning in
1946, Mays sustained an ongoing public theological critique of American racism, which he saw entrenched in churches, domestic institutions, and foreign
policy.[4] With a black prophetic and oppositional viewpoint, Mays's theological
writings and weekly *Pittsburgh Courier* column over a ten-year period—1945
until 1955—challenged the Cold War intellectual consensus that dominated
much of American public discourse in this period.[5]

It is crucial to recollect that American Christendom—both Catholic and
Protestant—had been shamed by the evils of racism as the United States discovered a funhouse-mirror image of itself in the horrors of the Nazi regime. In
every American city, interracial religious alliances worked together through the
auspices of local congregations and ecumenical alliances—like the YMCA, the
YWCA, and religiously based civil rights organization such as the Fellowship of
Reconciliation (FOR), the Congress on Racial Equality (CORE), and hundreds
of other regional groups to confront the ugliness of racial hatred. The Federal
Council of Churches (FCC), which had begun promoting "Race Relations Sundays" among its member denominations in 1922, had an even greater impetus
to fight racism in light of Nazi atrocities.[6] But even before the war had ended,

the outbreak of race riots in 1943 across the United States—from Harlem to Detroit to Los Angeles—signified the depth of racial animus among Americans.

In 1944, the FCC elected Mays as its vice president, the first time a black person filled this position.[7] *Time* magazine reported Mays's FCC election with this amusing mischaracterization of Mays: "Elected the Council's first Negro vice president . . . is quiet, earnest Dr. Benjamin Elijah Mays, 49, Baptist minister and president of Atlanta's Morehouse College. A firm believer in education and patience as cures for racial discrimination, Baptist Mays is himself so tolerant that he has never once tried to proselytize his Methodist wife."[8] It was true that Mays respected Sadie's Methodism, her family's denominational tradition. He respected her as his equal and saw no need for her to become a Baptist simply because he was one. However, he was far from being a mid-twentieth-century reincarnation of Booker T. Washington, as the *Time* reporter implied.

In his position as the FCC's vice president, Mays tried diligently to enhance and strengthen the FCC's position on racial justice. He exerted a great deal of effort trying to achieve more principled compromises concerning the issues of race relations and Christian understanding as a part of the FCC's stated positions. Beginning in 1943, before his election, Mays served on an FCC commission on race and religion, which was "given a charge to gather facts about the relations between blacks and whites, between Jews and Gentiles, and between recent immigrants and other Americans." What was revealed in the commission's discussions was that most white members were more afraid of interracial marriages between blacks and whites than they were about condemning racial segregation. Mays and other black members fought to protect the right of black and citizens to intermarry. "In a democratic and Christian society such as we dream of in America," they wrote in a draft of the commission's report, "there can be no legal limitation, based on race, creed, or national origin alone, upon free relationships among people." However, the language that Mays and his colleagues offered did not make it into the final version. According to historian Barbara Savage, "When the council adopted its final commission report on the conferences on race and religion in 1946, it included no mention of the intermarriage issue. All reference had been marked out in the penultimate draft with the simple notation 'eliminate.' The final statement merely condemned segregation as 'a violation of the gospel of love and human brotherhood and proposed more study to work on an unsegregated Church and unsegregated society.' "[9] Although Mays and his cohorts pushed the issue, racial fears and sexual taboos were stubbornly fixed and reinforced by both the church and society. Nonetheless, desegregation, continued to be seen as the hallmark of progress against such barriers.

Although 1946 was just as harsh as previous years in terms of the black struggle, there were a few hopeful signs of progress.[10] Jackie Robinson was in the minor leagues, soon to be brought up to play for the Brooklyn Dodgers. The NAACP's legal defense teams spearheaded civil rights cases and were steadily winning trials that were overturning legal precedents that enforced racial segregation. One of the most important legal victories won by the NAACP in the U.S. Supreme Court was *Smith v. Allright*, which challenged the all-white Texas primary. The victory inspired voter registration drives in many southern cities, including Atlanta, in 1944.[11] For Mays, however, one of the most galvanizing events for black people was the ending of the war.

During the war, Mays connected the war's campaign rhetoric of freedom to black people's freedom struggle. Exposure to the wider world through war gave black Americans new impetus to fight for their civic freedoms at home. War must be fought based on ideals, Mays asserted, and those ideals must be all-inclusive. "I am convinced that our WWII pronouncements stimulated Negroes in the United States," he wrote, and impelled those "who believe in freedom" to insist that the federal government fully implement democracy for all people.[12] *Seeking to Be Christian in Race Relations* was written in the context of a changing global order and shifts in American domestic politics.

For Mays, a book written for the church was a great vehicle through which to attack racial segregation. He realized that American racism was not simply a topic of discussion for a select group of sociologists and academic theologians. Local churches were where municipal decision-makers and everyday people found guidance and solace week after week. His theological insights on racism were intended to foster moral discourse inside local congregations on the issues of Christians and race. It was his hope that this discourse would challenge the prejudices and actions of churchgoers and prick their conscience, thereby spurring their social concern to action.

Ethical beliefs, Mays believed, must be consistent with actions. In a lecture given at Yale University Divinity School in 1952, he stated:

Beliefs are not theoretical things divorced from action. Beliefs always find expression in action. It is psychologically impossible to believe something and to act constantly contrary to that belief. . . . Knowledge is never ours until we have acted upon it. It might be said that we know only that which we have experienced, and our beliefs are confirmed only by our actions. Beliefs are more than intellectual assents. They involve convictions, and convictions involve action. We believe what we do, and we are what we do.[13]

Mays, who by the mid-1940s, had reached the status as one America's premier churchman was able to step into diverse Protestant congregations throughout the country and reach white society in ways other black civil rights activist could not. Because of his firsthand knowledge of how extensive a clergyman could affect a believer's understanding, he viewed theological argumentation, preaching, and teaching as crucial in defining the pathway to black American freedoms. Local churches could encourage its members to think and take action about issues that other institutions could not. Churchgoers therefore needed to be theologically prepared to create a religious ideological groundswell against segregation. Mays's theology was written so that it could be grasped at the congregational level. Having been a pastor, he knew how important it was to help people overcome the fear of change. He intentionally sought to touch the heart—which he understood as the seat of the moral conscience—in order to move churchgoing persons away from their psychological fears about a racially integrated society. This idea of convicting the sinner ran deep in American culture beginning with the First and Second Great Awakenings, the great religious revivals that spread through American society in the eighteenth and nineteenth centuries. Religious revivalism empowered individuals and communities to cope with societal upheaval, face changing social conditions, and challenge formidable societal institutions. It was Mays's conviction that southerners needed a revival in the form of "a new god." "Segregation," he explained, "spelled with a capital letter" was their god and they worshipped at the altar of race. Their creed, he declared, was "*Keep the Negro in his place.*"[14]

Seeking to Be Christian in Race Relations was foundational to the calls for religious renewal that ignited the civil rights movement throughout the country.[15] Mays's theology was intended to justify reformist protests and social actions based in Protestant congregations. He tried to shift carefully the scope of Protestant church teachings away from ones that were exclusively concerned with creeds and personal behavior to an ethic that examined collective behavior. It was not that Mays was not concerned about personal morality; he was. As a theological advocate for civil rights, he thought more emphasis had to be placed on the church's collective moral understanding in response to the collective immorality of racism.

Mays first formulated his theology of American race relations in a lengthy article titled "The American Negro and the Christian Religion," which appeared in the *Journal of Negro Education* in 1939.[16] He argued that Christianity was not synonymous with the organized church. He defined the church as "the organization whose task it is to carry forward the work of Christ and to strive to bring the world to Jesus Christ. This may be individual Protestant denominations, the Eastern Orthodox Church, or the Roman Catholic Church. And yet, it is not the aim here to confuse the institution with the Christian religion, though at times the institution and the Christian religion may be identical." When the true church "stands for the Fatherhood of God and the brotherhood of man and for the Christian emphasis set forth by Jesus that the supreme values of the universe are human values and exemplifies these ideals in service, practice, and fellowship, then the Church and the Christian religion become one."

The church as a human institution was a contradictory agency, led by contradictory agents, especially concerning race in the United States. "In every area of American life," Mays asserted, "the Negro is discriminated against. in government, in business, in politics, in industry, and in education." Both laws and customs upheld the arbitrariness of racial selectivity. And for the most part, he highlighted, discrimination was "sanctioned by religion" and practiced by people who called themselves Christians. "Now and then religion registers its protest against these discriminations," he stressed, "but not often." Segregation was total. "Organized Christian religion [was] no better at this point than social, political, or business enterprises. Whether in the North or the South, Christian fellowship is almost wholly within the confines of race."

The great paradox of American Christianity in history, Mays observed, was that "some people who called themselves Christians believed in slavery and some sought to justify it on Christian grounds; others sought to have it abolished on the basis of Christian principles." And the same thing could be said about segregation: "There are people who say they are Christians who would give anything to perpetuate segregated economy; there are other so-called Christians who would give much to have it abolished. The Christian religion as it has functioned in America has been both the friend and the foe of the Negro." "Despite the paradoxes and the feebleness with which it is practiced in the American Social Order," Mays prophetically observed, "it is potentially, and at times actually, the most powerful weapon a minority group has to press its just claim for equal opportunities for survival."[17]

Although Mays thought that Christianity could be a potent weapon for social change, he was concerned that it would be the Christians outside of the institutional church that would be most effective at using it.[18] More worrisome to him was the growing cynicism among blacks due to the racial contradictions found in American Christianity. "The Negro," he wrote, "is more critical now of the potency of the Christian religion than at any time previously. He believes in Jesus, what he did and said and what he stood for. But he does not believe that a sufficient number of people will take Jesus seriously enough for it to make an appreciable difference in social and economic affairs." He added, "Many able Negroes actually believe that they can expect very little help from the Christian religion in the solution of the complex problems that confront them as a minority exploited group."[19]

Historically, Mays observed, "social changes occur with exceptional slowness. One cannot expect much change in the status of the American Negro with reference to the Christian religion in so short a period as ten years. The segregated schools and churches will be deeply entrenched in 1950 as they are now." What will have changed is that "fellowship across racial lines will continue to increase and by 1950 Negroes will not have to sneak and hide as much as they do now." He believed that young people would push churches toward being more socially engaged in the problem of race. In the end, he asserted, "Negro churches will be forced for their own sake to become more interested in the problems of labor."[20] But Mays foresaw no revolution in the churches in 1939 because

> the Christian forces would need to be willing to sacrifice position,
> prestige, and power by going out on a Christian crusade to abolish
> all dualism in American society especially in those areas where the
> Christian religion is supposed to have the last word. . . . The people who
> maintain dualism in secular life are the same people who embrace the
> Christian religion. The people in secular life, therefore, are the members
> of the Christian churches. They pay the bills. They are the members of
> the choir and chairmen of the deacon boards. They are the masters of
> finances. So there will be no revolution in Christianity by 1950.[21]

By 1946, when he authored *Seeking to Be Christian in Race Relations*, however, Mays was cautiously optimistic. This forty-seven-page book would prove to be his clearest statement of his antiracist theology. "I believe," he penned, "that in seeking a basis for the elimination of race prejudice and discrimination, we must find that basis in something other than man. It is not enough for us to call upon races to be decent toward one another for the mere sake of humanity." In addressing racism, he asserted, human beings had to acknowledge their dependency on God. At the heart of all good human relations was the acknowledgment that a mysterious God, with loving intention, set human beings at the helm of creation as one of his creatures. "For this reason," he wrote, "it is a foolish notion to think that man has greatness in himself or that he has status because he belongs to a special race or nation." Whatever power or beauty or knowledge or wisdom human beings possess comes from the transcendent creator.[22]

In his estimation, it was a creator God who gave all persons their common DNA.[23] "From the standpoint of the Christian faith," he argued, "man has a common father, God. From the viewpoint of science man has a common ancestry." The implicit base of Christianity as a religious faith for him was "that all men are brothers because God is father of all." This, he believed, was a fact on which science actually concurred with religion. To Mays, this fact linked all humans together. In a statement that his student Martin Luther King would later co-opt, he observed, "The destiny of each individual wherever he resides on earth is tied up with the destiny of all men that inhabit the globe." Christian belief, Mays argued, placed supreme value on the life of each individual: "If God is holy and sacred, and if man is born in God's image, the life of each human being must also be sacred." As the children of God, all people were entitled to a full life within God's creation.

He was convinced that the love of God and the love of one's fellow human beings were inseparable. Therefore all human relationships were a reflection of the love of God. Central to Mays's thinking was the idea that "[you] should love the Lord your God with all your heart, and with all your soul, and with all your mind, and your neighbor as yourself" (Luke 7:10). Integral to his understanding of Jesus was that he acted on his full belief in God by believing in and loving people. "Few people," Mays stated, "recognize the fact that Jesus got into trouble not so much because he believed in God as because he believed in the sacred worth of the individual soul. If Jesus had gone throughout the Palestinian or Greco-Roman world merely talking about God and doing nothing to help man, he would hardly have got into trouble because almost everyone in the Greco-Roman world believed in God or gods. Jesus got in trouble because he believed in man." The purpose of a Christian life was to act on Jesus's great dictum to love God and one's neighbor as one's self. He explained, "When Jesus sums up the law and the prophets by urging man to love God first and his neighbor as himself, he is trying to get man to dethrone himself and put God and his neighbor at the center of his life."[24]

In his estimation, Christianity was a "God-Man Centered Religion"—a phrase he borrowed from the liberal preacher Harry Emerson Fosdick. By this he meant that Christianity was neither wholly God-centered nor wholly man-centered. If Christianity is only God-centered, he reasoned, "it is likely to become highly other-worldly, a religion whereby we seek mainly to save ourselves from a burning hell or to win a place of heavenly rest after this earthly life has ended. [But] when our religion becomes wholly man-centered we risk committing the unpardonable sin" of idolatry. "We are likely to deny the existence of God in whom Jesus believed and the God whom the Christian is supposed to worship."[25]

Jesus, Mays believed, struck the perfect balance as a believer: "[The] religion of Jesus might be described as a triangular religion, and equilateral triangle at that. The three sides of the triangle were God, man, and Jesus. In our case the three sides are God, man and self."[26] In Mays's mind, Jesus's humanity made him most appealing; his humanness was deeply embedded in a calling from God. Jesus's radical character was to be found in his ethics of love in action, and the spirit of Christ that flowed through human beings would be found in acts of selfless love.

Mays did not think human beings could practice such selfless love in action without conversion. Human beings, he argued, had contradictory impulses, both divine and demonic. God gave human beings freedom, and they are free to decide what impulses or attitudes will dominate their lives. Mays deemed that the hope of humanity was found not in knowledge, although being knowledgeable was helpful, but in the free acceptance of God. "The Christian faith not only maintains that conversion is possible through the power of religion," he wrote, "but it insists further that man is not, as some people think, a creature of his environment wholly shackled and chained by custom, law, habit, tradition, and by what other people say and do. It declares that man can break the bonds of his environment, rise above it, and transform it." Knowledge alone was not enough to transform the human condition. The power of God alone could break the bonds of tradition and the slavishness to social custom. "As pessimistic as the Christian may be about man," Mays declared, "he can never deny the power of the Christian to make men better."[27]

Mays was relentless in his focus on the radical calling of Jesus. To him, Jesus's beliefs and actions were synonymous. Jesus's praxis came from his deep, abiding trust in God. Jesus was willing to die for his convictions. The irony, Mays noted, was that most adults who urged young people to be like Jesus were unwilling to bring scorn on themselves as Jesus had done. One who attempts to live like Jesus, he wrote, "is likely to find the going hard. It may not mean a physical death, but it may mean less social, economic, and political success."[28] He recognized that Jesus left no definitive social program like the Communists might promote, but true Christian faith was a call to act. "It matters not how unyielding the social pattern, how unbending the law, how terrible the possible ostracism," he asserted, "the Christian who really believes in God and man will do something about his belief."[29]

In 1945, Mays gave drafts of the book to two of his theological peers, Edwin Aubrey, his divinity school dissertation mentor and the president of Crozier Theological Seminary in Chester, Pennsylvania; and Albert Outler, a professor at Duke University Divinity School. Aubrey, after first praising Mays for his thoughtfully written work, criticized his conceptualization of human freedom, particularly as it related to "freedom from determination of our thought by prejudice (this for the whites particularly), and second, as it concern[ed] freedom to live creatively."[30] Albert Outler also praised Mays for his thoughtful work. He wrote, "You can scarcely doubt, after having heard my lectures that I would be in whole-hearted agreement with your approach of putting a concrete ethical problem like race in its wider, supporting theological context. . . . I am glad for such distinguished support, proud to profess pretty much the same faith with you." Outler also provided Mays with a chapter-by-chapter outline of questions he had about the draft. More importantly, Outler questioned Mays's "statements concerning the crucial relations between Jesus and God and Jesus and Man. . . . Here is where we are the farthest apart doctrinally. I certainly wouldn't ask you to accept my own rather 'high' Christology but it might be helpful to look over your formulations to be sure you've said *all* you can or mean to."[31]

Mays always believed that Jesus's humanity was more significant than his divinity. His core convictions were God-centered. He wrote: "The basic issues of life are not political or economic but are religious: God, man, ethics and spiritual values. A belief in God and in man as revealed by Jesus is the most important thing facing the world today. If we could ever get the proper attitude toward God and man, we could more easily settle our political, economic, and social questions. I am talking about a belief in God that expresses itself in action. The true Christian not only has faith that leads to action, but he has faith that the results of his action ultimately will be good."[32]

Although he firmly believed that Christians had to be catalysts for social change, he was not sanguine. He reflected that Christian pronouncements are louder than their actions. Having just a true trust in God was not enough. True belief in God required "risk taking," especially in the area of "race relations." Racism demonstrated American Christians' incomplete trust in God. Fear, he believed, held Christians back from acting on their belief in God. He opined, "The human mind can always justify what we do, or what we fail to do because we are afraid."[33] This, he argued, was not the faith that Jesus showed. "One of the deepest facts of spiritual experience lies in the ultimate success of apparent defeat," he observed. True Christianity requires that one set aside fear and "act on [one's] belief and trust God for the results."[34]

Realistically, Mays knew that *Seeking to Be Christian in Race Relations* would not spark a wholesale revolution in racial attitudes. He acknowledged: "When segregation is abolished, we will take a long stride toward real democracy and true Christianity. . . . The abolition of segregation will make discrimination more difficult; but it will not eliminate it no more than the non-segregation of women has stopped men from discriminating against women."[35] He understood the need for more long-term systemic changes, but in the interim he steadily pushed ahead with the understanding that calls for spiritual renewal would galvanize American society to tear down racial segregation.

However, the larger society's brief postwar optimism quickly evaporated. Giddiness was replaced with anxiety. Cold War ideological debates and the advent of nuclear weaponry created a highly distrustful world. Here Mays departed intellectually from his much more heralded peer, theologian Reinhold Niebuhr. By the late 1940s and 1950s, theologians like Niebuhr had lost faith in Christianity's radical power to spur social change.[36] Germany's genocidal aggression and Soviet totalitarianism had chased away their hopefulness and made them democratic ideological supporters of U.S. power and aggression. Niebuhr, and other Christian Realists who supported U.S. action against the Soviet Union, failed to consider that two-thirds of the world's people lived in abject poverty and had been colonially exploited. Niebuhr's theological ethics, while insightful, trapped in notions of Western cultural superiority. Niebuhr's theological ethics showed little sympathy for emerging anticolonial political states. By 1950, Niebuhr had become America's public theologian to the liberal political establishment, supporting the Cold War and America's racialize foreign policy. Niebuhr's version of theological realism would eventually make him ambivalent about a black-led American civil rights movement.

Mays, having dealt with a variety of liberal whites throughout his career, warned blacks about the kind of ambivalent political liberalism that Niebuhr and others exhibited. Their acquiescence to racism at home and its colonial form abroad was readily apparent to him. He felt that black people ought to be wary of white "liberals" regarding the politics of race: "We have seen many persons elevated way beyond their achievement because we have not been discriminating at this point. When we become too gullible and give too much credit to a member of another race because he seems liberal, then discover we have overrated him and that he is not what we took him to be, there is danger of our losing faith and confidence in White people."[37]

Many of Mays's white intellectual contemporaries, though well meaning, exhibited downright ignorance about the struggles of black Americans. In his estimation, they were not committed enough to stand alongside black people in the fight for their political freedoms. His work with the FCC had taught him that white churchgoing liberals had a limited understanding of democracy, which tended toward paternalism and was inconsistent with what black people truly desired.[38] He knew they simply could not share the daily pain and ostracism of being alienated from society's resources.[39] On the other hand, Mays constantly bemoaned the fact that many black leaders often lacked the courage and moral conviction to be candid about the social realities that blacks faced. If black leaders were reluctant to address their own situation, it stood to reason that others who held mainstream power, like Niebuhr, would be even more so. He recognized that eradicating racial injustices did not prompt the same sense of urgency in white religious intellectuals that it prompted in their black counterparts.[40]

To Mays, only through the dogged persistence of "slave religion," and its eschatology of hope, could racial justice be achieved. This viewpoint had a great affinity with some of the best of mainstream theological thought. "The Christian is a citizen of two worlds," Mays wrote, echoing some of Reinhold Niebuhr's best thoughts. "The world that now is and the world that ought to be. . . . He is part of the existing order with all of its imperfections, shortcomings, and brutality. Yet he can never accept the present order." To be Christian meant being "[loyal] to something that transcends this earth. . . . The Christian's ultimate allegiance is to the God of Jesus Christ and not to any particular economic, political, national, racial, or denominational order."[41] To start a movement required a determined and combative faith to keep hope, which was global in scope, alive. Mays realized that the desire for democratic freedoms and the need for self-determination that motivated black Americans to fight for civil rights came from the same inherent human spirit for freedom.[42]

Throughout 1947 into 1948, Mays commented on international events, especially the democratic movement coming out of India. For him, India exhibited the spirit of a new era. "Despite India's poverty, illiteracy, caste and utter military weakness," he wrote, the independence movement had managed to free itself from the grip of the greatest empire of the world, Britain. "India was not and India is not now able to win her freedom by force of arms, as we won ours in the Revolutionary War. Here we have the greatest empire in history yielding before the intangible army of spirit." India was able to accomplish independence because of extraordinary and unselfish leaders, he asserted. They employed "spiritual power," which, he argued, was a new force in the affairs of nations.

He contended that it was "the moral and spiritual power of non-violence [that] restrained the British when they might have used more violent means of keeping the Indian people in subjection." He concluded that it might be well for black Americans to study Indian methodologies "[to supplement] our efforts to be free, by resorting more and more to the spiritual and moral powers that we could so effectively use if we had the sufficient faith and religion and direction."[43] Mays saw in India a burgeoning spirit, the eschatological hope, of a true democracy arising from impoverishment and colonialism.

In his 1948 *Courier* column, Mays recollected his meeting with Gandhi in 1936. The column sketched out Gandhi's long, patient struggle to achieve independence in India. He now saw Gandhi's model as an alternative to nuclear arms buildup. He recalled Gandhi's instruction that "non-violence required valor of a different kind. Violence is self[-]defeating, and the repercussion from non-violence will never be hatred and revenge." Gandhi's most important lesson to him was about handling fear: "The non-violent man must be absolutely fearless." Nonviolence was a courageous choice. "If one refuses to use violence out of fear, it is not only not non-violence but the person is a coward. It would be nobler to use violence and fight it out to the death than to practice the non-use of force because of fear." To act nonviolently was an act of great faith, a kind of faith that truly coincided with democratic values.[44]

U.S. policymakers, however, did not share Mays's faith in nonviolence. The Cold War was driven by political fears. Unwavering loyalty became the litmus test for American patriotism. Many black Americans who expressed critical views of U.S. domestic and foreign policies became targets of governmental suppression. This was especially true for those with connections to the Communist Party. Although Mays rejected communism as a governmental philosophy, he publicly acknowledged that Russian Communism, at least in theory, was perhaps more egalitarian toward its racial minorities than the United States was to its own (a view that seemed to completely disregard Stalin's purges, gulags, and ethnic cleansing). The Communists, with their vision of equality and their strong support for anticolonial movements, were having an impact. He felt that the threat of Communism had created pressure on the United States to change its policies. Mays wrote, "It is utter stupidity for Christian nations to allow atheistic and humanistic Russia to set the pace." He believed American policymakers misunderstood the impact of the democratic victory in World War II. The victory of the Allied forces against racist imperialism in Europe "helped India, made the Africans restless, and stimulated Negroes in the United States," Mays observed.[45]

Mays put forward a more daring public theological challenge than he had previously expressed to the militarization of American foreign policy in his disapproval of the Korean War. He believed that the ensuing battle over communism and liberal democracy would not be settled by fighting in North Korea. Accordingly, he wrote, "the United States and Russia cannot continue the *cold war* without eventually fighting. I do not believe it can continue forever. Either the cold war stops or there will be a third world war." His theologically position was, "War is against God and whatever is against God will destroy itself."[16] It was his opinion that emphasis on militarism detracted from the United States' more powerful message about the virtues of a democratic society. The Cold War's communist rhetoric and saber rattling would cause untold damage to the innocent and undermine the claims of democratic governance. Mays felt that the terms of freedom under communism and that under democracy ought to be "spelled out" and compared and contrasted in relation to "economics, human relations and religion." He thought it important to know the principles that were at stake as the two powers clashed in Korea. For him, racial exclusion remained a litmus test by which the rest of the world judged the United States. When black people were fairly included in all aspects of American government as equal citizens, then other nations would see America as a truly democratic role model.[47]

The political reality was more complicated than how Mays painted it. The House Un-American Activities Committee's draconian investigations and southern red-baiting had changed the country's political discourse.[48] Black political activists and civil rights organizations as well as organized labor feared being labeled as surrogates of the Communist Party. Labor and civil rights organization leaders were often placed in an untenable and defensive position by Cold War rhetoric. They had to perform a balancing act to advocate against labor and social injustices and at the same time affirm loyalty to the government. The NAACP and its local chapters scurried to drape themselves in the American flag and to distance themselves from black activists with radical viewpoints to protect the overall goals of their organization. In the process, the very principles of democracy that their respective organizations espoused were compromised due to their fear of being labeled communist.

Mays, a lifetime member of the NAACP, believed that it was one of the country's most democratic organizations. "The NAACP aims only to further the cause of democracy in areas where it is weakest," he wrote. The organization's mass appeal among black Americans dwindled, however, as anticommunism attacks took its toll on all black American organizing efforts. He urged black people to support the work of the NAACP. "The support for an organization like the NAACP must come mainly from the people it seeks to emancipate." Mays also used the prevailing anticommunist rhetoric to urge his readers to support the organization and to placate powerful southern politicians who used the communist label to weaken black civil rights momentum: "It is a great tribute to the leadership of the NAACP that it has not allowed Communist infiltration which would weaken its influence and destroy its effectiveness."[49] He attempted to change the course of the public debate about the evils of communism by arguing positively for the moral virtues of democracy.[50]

However, in southern electoral politics, labeling someone as a communist was like accusing him or her of being a heinous murderer or a rapist. It was the 1950s equivalent of waving the bloody shirt, and it discredited the legitimacy of political dissent. Mays and other black Georgians were denied access to the Mid-Century White House Conference on Children and Youth sponsored by President Truman because Georgia's governor, Herman Talmadge, blocked the appointment of any black Georgians who participated in White House conferences. Luckily for Mays and other black Georgians, the White House administrators found other ways to circumvent Talmadge.[51] But Talmadge was not beyond cunningly besmirching Mays or any other black leader in Georgia with the communist label to stop their access to political power.

Mays openly discussed the dangerous manipulation of political rhetoric against communism. While he adamantly disagreed with communist ideology, he did not believe that undemocratic means should be used to defame the character of American citizens. In 1949, he came strongly to the defense of Paul Robeson, a vocal critic of the U.S. government's response to lynching, in the controversy that ensued after the press misquoted a statement Robeson made during a benefit concert for the Civil Rights Congress in Peekskill, New York. During the concert on August 27, Robeson reportedly said that, as a result of lynching, "Negroes won't fight for the U.S." What he actually said was, "It is unthinkable that American Negroes will go to war in behalf of those who have oppressed us for generations . . . against a country (the Soviet Union) which in one generation has raised our people to the full dignity of mankind." Robeson's misquotation went across the wire services and created an instant backlash.

The attacks on Robeson's views were numerous, and everyone associated with Robeson was suspect. This all came on the heels of government investigators rounding up black members of the Communist Party, including Robeson's dear friend New York City councilman Benjamin Davis. On September 4, Robeson was scheduled to give another concert in Peekskill. This second concert brought out Robeson supporters and counterdemonstrators. When the concert was over and the crowd was dispersing, a riot broke out. State reports exonerated many of the counterdemonstrators, but an American Civil Liberty Union (ACLU) investigation found that the counterdemonstrators had deliberately provoked a fight with those peaceably attending the Robeson concert. Their findings did not matter; the mainstream media discredited Robeson as being "red."

In his October 15 *Courier* column, Mays defended Robeson's right to criticize the U.S. government: "There are those who say that Robeson should stick to his art singing and acting. . . . I think this criticism is irrelevant because in a supposedly free country Paul Robeson has the right to speak if he wants to speak. Those who say that he should not speak are simply saying they do not like what Robeson is doing." Mays repeated Robeson's misquotation in his column. He thought Robeson's sentiment wrongheaded. "For good or ill the destiny of Negro Americans is tied up with the destiny of this country," he wrote. But it did not matter whether he agreed or disagreed with Robeson's politics. Robeson's freedom of speech was too important to the larger cause of democracy and should not be squelched. Robeson, he continued, "is symbolic of what is possible for an extraordinary Negro to achieve in our country. . . . Negroes may or may not agree with what Robeson is doing. Nevertheless, every sane, honest Negro must admit that Robeson is fighting against racial injustice and exploitation, which any American who believes in justice and democracy should be fighting against." "I believe Robeson is sincere," he concluded. "I believe he loves his people. I believe he has identified himself with suffering humanity everywhere. I think America should so radically amend her ways on the question of race that it would be increasingly impossible for Robeson, or any other Negro, to feel the necessity of doing what he is doing. Simply to damn Robeson is to deal with the symptom and not the disease. Let America eradicate the disease."[52]

In Mays's thinking, the right of conscience remained paramount. As a defender of the prerogatives of faith and political freedom, Mays would later criticize the antidemocratic practices of the House Un-American Activities Committees. The strength of a democracy, he wrote, lies in the fact that "the individual has rights with which even the government must respect and cannot violate. . . . We have never believed in this country that government can do no wrong." He asserted, somewhat naively, that individuals who were being called before the House Un-American Activities Committee should waive their First or Fifth Amendment rights and use instead simple honesty rather than their duly constituted legal protections.

Mays also frankly acknowledged that the Communist Party was, by law, not illegal as a political party. "It is not a crime to be a member of the Communist party," he penned. "Isn't it contradictory to go out on a Communist hunt while at the same time we recognize the legality of the party? It doesn't make sense to me to talk about robbing a Communist of his citizenship, while at the same time we recognize the legality of the party." The process of investigating Americans, Communists, or otherwise had to be principled and transparent and "not Fascist." Taking stock of Senator Joseph McCarthy's prosecutorial style, he observed that if his "committee, or any other committee, can trample at will on the rights of innocent people, especially innocent 'little people,' [then] we are beginning to destroy the freedom and democracy which we fight to defend."[53] This situation emphasized for Mays how mass fear and lack of faith could undermine democratic institutions.

Interestingly enough, Mays never directly experienced the governmental hostility and humiliation that public figures like Paul Robeson or W. E. B. Du-Bois experienced. Perhaps Mays's brand of Christian criticism against segregation and against global inequities did not appear threatening, because at no time did Mays lead an organization that could, in theory, bring the masses to the streets. Had Mays been criticizing U.S. domestic and foreign policies as president of the National Baptist Convention, perhaps there might have been an investigation into his affiliations and associations. Mays was able to shield himself from the threat of communist mudslinging. He opted out of events that appeared to have overt communist support in order to protect the interest of the college. And fellow *Courier* columnist George Schuyler called him to task for supporting the efforts of the Civil Rights Congress, who Schuyler accused of protecting communists like Robeson.[54] In the face of these accusations, Mays quietly withdrew his endorsement of the group. Nevertheless, Mays continued to be an outspoken critic of the country's antidemocratic tolerance of racial segregation. As a Baptist, Mays believed that freedom of conscience required that the freedom of speech be protected. In Mays's mind, protest was the only way to revitalize oppressed people's sense of their own humanity. The integrated society was one that dignified everyone as citizens worthy of respect.

As a clergyman, Mays understood the power of language, and he cleverly aligned the black struggle for freedom with the freedoms enunciated in the Constitution and dominant Protestant culture. Like nineteenth-century reformers emerging out of the Second Great Awakening, Mays believed that Christianity had a direct impact on the nation-state, which enabled him to make an even more effective moral argument against racial injustice in this era of political recrimination. His rhetoric helped many black activists and educators undermine the South's political hold on the language of morality and faith. It denied southern political leaders the room to use the threat of communism as a strategy to delegitimize black dissent. Mays's Christian rhetoric gave space for civil rights activism in the Protestant church culture of the American South.

In his view, resisting segregation was not only about gaining political representation but equally about alleviating those in power from their own forms of racial bondage. He observed that resistance, even limited resistance to segregation, created new conditions between the oppressed and the oppressor. Overturning segregation, he wrote in the *Courier*, eased the pressure on both blacks and whites. He believed that resistance to segregation was necessary because it was spiritually transformational for the body politic. He wrote that resisting segregation had two virtues: first, it would be "good for [black people's] souls," and, second, it would force "the white people of America [to] respect us and admire us in a way now undreamed of."[55]

Mays chose to positively define integration.[56] Living in an integrated society included the right to choose one's direction in life and to do whatever one wants to, within reason. No one needed to be constrained by arbitrary characteristics like physical features. Being fully human required that an individual "be free to associate with his friends of whatever nation or race." Advocating for integration was, for Mays, equivalent to exercising the freedom of conscience. All human beings are born free. Integration, Mays emphasized, was not to be pursued because one felt insecure or inferior, which indicated that one was bound by an enslaved mindset: "[I]f one seeks integration because he feels insecure; if he seeks it because he discredits everything the segregated group has done; because he thinks that nothing built up or owned by Negroes is worth saving in an integrated society; if he seeks it because he thinks another race or group is better than his own; or because he feels that he will enhance his own worth or lift his social standing thereby—if these are the reasons, they are definite signs of inferiority and integration will not do anything to help such an individual." In Mays's thinking, someone seeking integration with a slavish mindset would miss the point. His Christian conviction was this: "Whatever restricts, binds, or circumscribes one on the grounds of race, whether [or not] in a segregated society, is a denial of the rights which God gives every man. Character, mind, fair play, social visions and the ability to get along with others are the only standards by which a man should be judged."[57]

To live freely meant that one had to continue to practice democratic behavior. He was quite critical of the Truman administration's decision to give arms to developing countries based upon the idea of defending democracy against communism.[58] He argued that more arms "will not guarantee democracy and it will not keep away communism or fascism. The best way to spread democracy is for the United States to be democratic. It cannot spread it by lynching Negroes, segregating them and hating Jews." Democracy, he believed, could be guaranteed only by example. "If we cannot make it work at home," he warned, "we will never be able to establish it abroad. Loyalty, like love, cannot be purchased with money."[59] In this vein, Mays opposed both the North Atlantic Treaty Organization (NATO) and parts of the Marshall Plan.

Mays wanted the United States to negotiate with the Soviet Union and not set them on the defensive by arming the U.S. European allies, which he felt NATO had done.[60] He also thought it senseless to give money to the Fascist leader of Spain, Francisco Franco, out of fear of communism. Furthermore, it outraged him that Congress had not appropriated money to equalize the educational standards of black children in the South. He noted: "It is for the best interest of national defense that we provide the best possible education for our children. To improve the educational facilities of our public schools is a national emergency."[61]

Mays also believed that in order for democracy to be affirmed as a positive system of governance, racism had to be defeated first in the churches. He persisted in critiquing American churches—especially white southern churches—in this regard. In one of his 1947 columns, Mays reported that white North Carolina Baptists had retreated from one of their official reports indicating that they had voted to eliminate segregation in the church. Many of the state Baptist convention delegates claimed that they were unaware of the entirety of the report and therefore had to reread and vote over again. In effect, they continued to support segregation. The report, Mays observed, simply stated that in God's eyes all persons were equal. "They were simply stating a Christian axiom and they were not even advocating, except by implication, that segregation should be abolished," Mays scornfully noted. "I wondered what would a group of North Carolina scientists have done if they had set forth in objective fashion, as the churchman did, the most enlightened, up-to-date findings of science on the question of race." He dismissed these Baptists as being tepid and not aware of current scientific findings about race. To him, white Protestants were willing to obfuscate using words like "discrimination," but were unwilling to condemn racial segregation itself. "As long as segregation remains intact," he wrote, "there will be many who will decry discrimination, but who do not seem to understand that wherever segregation exists, discrimination follows as the night the day. He who believes in segregation believes in discrimination."[62]

Mays viewed white southern Christianity as discrediting the religious faith. In 1946, in Monroe, Georgia, two black men and two black women were pulled out of their car and shot with a barrage of bullets at close range in the middle of the day for attempting to register to vote.[63] The investigating authorities, including the FBI, were unable to apprehend anyone for the crime. This unresolved crime was a shortcoming of local, state, and federal governance. He saw this brutality as a problem of religion, too. He wrote with uncharacteristic bluntness that the crime in Monroe meant that "millions of people in America" condoned lynching. He maintained, "In this sense, many of us good people, church people, university professors, educated people, legislators and congressman are a part of the mob." Angrily he deduced, "When one is lynched, it is not much worse than if a dog had been killed. If his soul is cramped, his mind circumscribed, his body segregated, it doesn't matter; after all, he is nothing but a Negro." He summed up the Monroe travesty using overt evangelical language: "This is a religious problem. It will never be settled on any other basis. The vote, good jobs, educational opportunities, justice in the courts, improved health facilities are necessary, and we must fight for them in order to save ourselves and in order to save the soul of America—but unless we can see men as men and not as colored, red, white or yellow men, we will not be able to resolve this difficulty."[64]

It mattered little to Mays that in May of 1947, the Southern Baptist Convention (SBC) adopted a more moderate stance toward black Americans in one its statements, which supported President Harry Truman's initiative, *To Secure These Rights*. The convention statement said, "Encouraging progress is being made . . . . The right of all men to vote in government . . . has been upheld again and again in the high courts of the South. . . . The right of all American citizens to equal recognition in employment has been confirmed in recent significant cases. . . . The right to equal opportunity in education has gained considerable support. . . . [It is] the undeniable truth that the South, of its own volition, is moving in the direction of the objectives which were recommended by the report of the President's Committee on Civil Rights."[65]

Written by moderates in the convention, the statement meant nothing to Mays. He knew that the SBC could not force churches to adopt the policy, let alone compel them to be racially inclusive. The denomination's mandates were strictly voluntary, and local churches were more likely to uphold the status quo of "southern race relations" than to fully advocate for racial equality. The fact was that most local congregations openly supported segregation, or they tacitly supported it through their unwillingness to speak out against it. Mays considered statements great only when they were followed up by actions. The SBC's statement was found wanting by its inactivity and that of most of their city and rural congregations.

The SBC did not meet the theological mark, so Mays focused upon a Baptist theology that did. In 1950, Mays published an edited volume of Walter Rauschenbusch's writings titled *A Gospel for the Social Awakening*, a book that received only one cursory review.[66] The selected pieces convey Mays's ideas of church activism. Rauschenbusch, who had long been ignored and dismissed by both orthodox and neoorthodox theologians, had been reborn in Mays's unheralded publication.[67] In a world where white evangelicals were marking their assent to public prominence once more through the preaching of a charismatic newcomer, Billy Graham, Mays's book signaled that there was a different kind of evangelical faith, one focused not solely on the personal spiritual transformation of individuals but on societal transformation.

Mays's publication of Rauschenbusch's Social Gospel ideas was a black theological counterforce to white Protestant schools of thought at that time. On the one hand, there was Reinhold Niebuhr, who had publicly promoted a new ethic called Christian Realism that took a much more cautious approach toward utopian visions found in political movements in the wake of World War II, the Holocaust, and Stalin, and in the new nuclear order. In books like *Children of Darkness, Children of Light* (1944) and *The Irony of American History* (1952), Niebuhr began cautioning against the totalizing utopian ideas inherent in Christian eschatology and political movements. Evil could be perpetrated through the most noble of intent. On other hand, there was Billy Graham preaching individual salvation, personal virtue, and heaven like a revivalist of the Second Great Awakening. But while Niebuhr was an ambivalent intellectual ally of the black freedom struggles because of his understanding of human aggression and evil at the beginning of the atomic age, Graham ignored them, emphasizing individual salvation with no social justice component. Of these two variants in Protestant thinking, Mays saw the mass appeal of the highly visible Graham as possibly more consequential to black civil rights than Niebuhr's Cold War theology.

In March of 1955, Mays explained to *Courier* readers that, after seeing a television interview with Graham on *Meet the Press*, he was pleased to hear Graham reject segregation on principle but that he had, as a Christian, come to his position too slowly. He remembered Graham coming to Atlanta in 1953 and abiding by the rules of segregation. Black ministers thus refused to attend or support his citywide revival. Mays sharply observed, "A man coming to preach the Gospel of Christ must come with an un-segregated heart. In Christ there is neither Jew nor Greek, bond nor free, male or female, for we are all one in him." Graham "was on the spot. He could not tell the world that he believes in segregation. It would be contrary to the Gospel he preaches." Graham courageously, though quite cautiously, heeded the challenge to integrate his revivals, but his fellow SBC clergymen did not support his views on desegregating their churches.[68] In Mays's view, both the SBC and Graham had taken too long to take action against segregation. He saw Graham's inaction as similar to moderate Christians in Europe who went along with Nazi policies until it was too late. For Mays, Graham's unwillingness to fully confront segregation was an affront to Christian principles.[69]

The enormity of Jewish persecution and genocide baffled Mays and troubled him deeply. Having traveled to Germany and Holland in the late 1930s, he understood the kind of persecution that European Jews were under but could not fathom the Nazi regime's systematic extermination of Jews and other minorities in Europe. He realized the extent to which unfounded, mythic prejudices could lead human beings to commit barbarous acts, including lynchings and genocide, but the sheer number of Jews slaughtered was staggering. But he saw parallels between the experiences of European Jewry and those of black Americans.[70] The experience of European Jews was a dire warning to blacks: even if blacks were successful in ending segregation, they would still face discrimination and insecurity. The long history of the Jews was a stark reminder of how unexplored prejudices could be politically manipulated if leaders were not held accountable. He publicly ruminated that what happened to the Jews could possibly be the fate of black South Africans, if world leaders were not watchful. In his mind, European Jewish history had much to teach black people about their struggles in America.

Mays felt it was important that all Christians acknowledge the centrality of Judaism. He urged his fellow Protestant believers not to be anti-Semitic. He pointedly stated that "the great paradox" of Jewish-Christian relations is that "the people who produced the Old and New Testaments are the ancestors of the modern Jew whom so many of us hate, despise and kick around. The man whom we worship as God, and declare *no salvation without Him*, is one of the ancestors of the present-day Jew." He found this paradox to be a mystery. He believed that Jews as an American ethnic group were a model for blacks: "Let the Negro people observe the Jew and be wise. Let us make every contribution we can to the world and let us develop to the full every gift God has given us. But we must not be defeated nor frustrated when we find doors shut in our faces despite our great contribution to humanity and to the world."[71]

Although Mays believed that Jews were role models for blacks, there was much he left unsaid about the relationship. At the day-to-day level, the realities that blacks and Jews faced were difficult, not necessarily just because of religious prejudices, but also because of the differences in social class levels. For many readers of his *Courier* column, interactions with Jews were such that class conflicts were unavoidable. Many Jews in cities and towns were small retailers, landlords, and jewelers. The competing interest between the two ethnic groups often played out angrily in local communities where blacks were economically poorer and felt exploited. And in the South, where Jews were an even more distinct minority, many Jews dared not challenge the prevailing system of Jim Crow out of fear of being singled out for punishment themselves.

Many southern Jews in cities like Atlanta felt they had no choice but to adopt southern mores in order to be accepted. Seeking a way to ease tensions, Mays became involved in the National Conference of Christian and Jews, and he urged brotherhood and theological understanding.[72]

Though he was committed to the building of bridges between Protestants and Jews, he continued to harbor ambivalence about Israel as a nation-state. As he had seen in his travels in the late 1930s, Jewish émigrés into Palestine were aggressively moving in on Arabs in the region, which he feared might one day erupt into hatred and civil war. In 1947, he once again addressed the dilemma in his *Courier* column. "The Jewish-Arab problem is almost beyond solution," he explained. "The Jews are convinced that it is their national home. It has been theirs since Bible time and the Bible gives them the right to it. The Arabs feel that the Jews have not possessed Palestine for many centuries and that they, the Arabs, have been there for approximately thirteen centuries." Given the tiny size of the land itself, the interactions between Arabs and Jews was inevitably bound for conflict. The Nazis' attempted extermination of European Jews only aggravated the situation in Palestine. Mays thought the best solution would be to allow more Jews from Europe to immigrate into the United States rather than to support their building a nation-state. He once again reminded his readers of the great contribution that Jews had made to all humanity, and he opined that the people of the United States must actively seek to alleviate the situation in the region.[73]

Though he had reservations about Israel as a political state, Mays thought that being Christian in race relations meant ridding the church of anti-Semitism. Jews and Christians alike worshipped the same God. And it was the special responsibility of black Protestants and Jews to advance the cause of civil and human rights. This political alliance was born of the realities of world politics in a nuclear age. In a speech before the Conference of Christians and Jews in November of 1954, he stated, "The more deadly our weapons of destruction, . . . the more urgent that we live in brotherly accord. There is no time for the erection of national, religious, and racial barriers. . . . We need all the time at our disposal to tear down the barriers which for centuries we have been erecting."[74] And great leaders were needed to meet the crisis of the age.

Vigorous ethical leadership was needed to promote social justice and progressive actions. In his mind, Mary McLeod Bethune was an ideal model of leadership. She possessed graciousness and dignity in resisting the overall affects of segregation that few in her generation, male or female, could emulate. He noted that she was in fact "queenly" in bearing. She had educated black children in Florida and started a historic black college, served with great political effectiveness in the Roosevelt administration, and had led the National Council of Negro Women (NCNW) as an important advocate for civil rights. He was dismayed with black college graduates because few were willing to choose a path of leadership like Bethune had. Mays reminded readers that when Bethune retired, her replacement as president of the NCNW was significant to the civil rights struggle. "The next president of the Council," he wrote, "should be as Mrs. Bethune, a woman who has already built herself up by a noble record of past achievements." There was something transcendent in Bethune's leadership style. "The successor to Mary McLeod Bethune should have both *mass* and *class* appeal," he noted. "It is not enough to appeal to the so-called *classes* or the *intellectuals*. . . . A truly great leader must appeal to the *masses* and champion the cause of the *masses*." All great leaders had mass appeal. "One of the greatest compliments ever passed on to Jesus is the one which says, 'The common people heard Him gladly.' Wherever he went to speak, *the little people* were there." Perhaps Mays did not mean to, but he inadvertently passed judgment on the black leadership class of which he was a part. Few of these leaders who were dedicated to the causes of human freedom, with the exception of Bethune or A. Philip Randolph, had mass appeal.[75]

Leadership, as Mays well understood, meant headaches, heartaches, and at times unwarranted ridicule. It was very easy for those who sat on the sidelines to lob barbed criticisms at leaders. Over the years, Bethune had taken her share of criticism from political radicals, sexist men who believed women should not be public leaders, and those who thought she was generationally out of touch. However, what made Bethune so admirable to him was her willingness to take on a mantle of leadership and serve others, which she effectively did in spite of these criticisms. It was Mays's hope that more young women and men would imitate the selflessness and the grace that she exhibited as a leader. He believed that men who ran civil rights organizations had not given Bethune's leadership enough consideration. But Mays felt her true genius as a leader came from her commitment to selfless service, which made her compelling and created for her a loyal following. In his way of thinking, this made her one of the great Christian leaders in the country.

For Mays, being Christian in race relations meant having a vision of the world; looking at human suffering as a reality; having steadfast courage to challenge injustice; and working deliberately and patiently to re-create a broken and hurtful world. Christian leaders not only represented middle-class interests but also provided a voice for the voiceless. Leaders had to be willing to sacrifice for what was right and just, even in the face of opposition. These were the theological and governing principles Mays believed in and espoused publicly.

Mays expected leaders of faith to be catalysts in the civil rights struggle. He felt that only leaders of great faith could lead and help to sustain a powerful social movement.

An interesting historical irony is that in 1956, W. E. B. DuBois found it surprising that a young, educated black Baptist clergyman named Martin Luther King Jr. was at the epicenter of the awakening of national protest for civil rights. DuBois had always been respectful but critical of black churches, and he had his doubts about the young clergyman's commitment to a true Gandhian approach.[76] Mays, on the other hand, expected the kind of leadership that King had begun to exhibit in Montgomery. He had tried to be an example of what he believed engaged leadership ought to look like. Perhaps DuBois's astonishment was warranted given the cultural conservatism and political vulnerability of most black ministers, but most black ministers did not have Mays as their mentor. Mays was pleased that King had taken up his ideas as he stepped into the public spotlight. That is what he expected and urged all of his students to do! Through his actions as a churchman, his institution-building, and his writings, he had helped to prepare the way for King's generation of religious activists in a "Third Great Awakening." But what astonished Mays most was the alacrity and moral courage with which the generation of young adults he had nurtured and encouraged took up his clarion call for democratic social change throughout the United States.

I Have Only Just a Minute

Every man and woman is born into the world to do something unique and
something distinctive and if he or she does not do it, it will never be done.
—MAYS, *Quotable Quotes of Benjamin E. Mays*

During his tenure as president of Morehouse College, Mays constantly recited
to his students an anonymous poem titled "God's Minute":

I have only a minute.
Only sixty seconds in it,
Forced upon me—can't refuse it.
Didn't seek it, didn't choose it,
But it's up to me to use it.
I must suffer if I lose it,
Give account if I abuse it.
Just a tiny little minute—
But eternity is in it.[1]

He consistently encouraged them to use time wisely, because time was fleeting.
For Mays, the ephemeral nature of time required that each person be deliber-
ate and wise. Throughout the 1950s he used his own "minute" to vigorously
promote his Christian vision of American society. He promoted religious
and civic engagement in the struggle for human rights in the United States,
as well as in South Africa, and he continued to invest himself in building
the institutional infrastructure of theological education for black clergy. Time
was precious.

Nothing captured the moment for Mays more than the U.S. Supreme Court's
ruling in *Brown v. Board of Education*, on May 17, 1954.[2] Mays had been president of Morehouse College for fourteen years, and he, like everyone, highly
anticipated the ruling. In February 1954, just three months prior to the ruling,
Mays wrote an article on the case for *New South*, the journal of the Southern
Regional Council, titled "We Are Unnecessarily Excited." In it he analyzed the
legal and social ramifications of the case from a global and ethical perspective.
"We here in the deep South are unnecessarily excited over what the decision the

United States Supreme Court may hand down in the cases before it involving segregation in the public schools," Mays wrote. "I believe we are confusing the issue. Some of us think that the chief issue before the Supreme Court is whether or not Negro and white children will be allowed to attend the same public school." Of equal importance was the "moral issue" underlying the case. *Brown* was "not [just] a local issue affecting only those of us who live in the deep South." The Supreme Court's decision held global implications, "either for good or for ill." The case, he asserted, would either win or lose the allegiances of "the peoples of Africa and Asia."

Even with a positive Supreme Court ruling, Mays continued, the process of desegregation would be "much slower than we think." Mays cited four reasons why implementing this ruling would be slow. First, the ruling would apply only to the local cases lumped together under the rubric of *Brown v. Board of Education*—cases in Clarendon County, South Carolina; Prince Edward County, Virginia; the District of Columbia; Topeka, Kansas; and a case in Delaware. After the ruling, he believed, some states would immediately outlaw segregation as they had already done in higher education, and the remainder of the states might have to be ordered by the courts to comply. Second, black parents would be cautious about the decision: "They will not risk their children being embarrassed and for that reason they will not rush in just because the Supreme Court has voted against segregation." It would, in Mays's estimation, take a while for black parents to be comfortable even after formal segregation was declared unconstitutional. "We all know that legalized segregation is a badge of inferiority," he wrote, "imposed by one group upon another. It stigmatizes the Negro as being unfit to move about as a free human being. The Negro wants the stigma removed so that he, too, can walk the earth with dignity. No man wants to be penalized for what God made him. The Negro wants equality before God and equality before the law." However, the legal stigma of being a racial inferior would be removed. Third, even though blacks desired integration, they would not feel pressured to integrate because they enjoyed their own institutions. An example was the famous Riverside Church of New York City, which had "been opened to Negroes for decades and yet the Negro churches in Harlem are packed to capacity with only a few Negroes in the membership at Riverside." He thought this would also be "the case in public schools" if the black school was already considered "first rate." And finally, residential segregation in both the North and the South would be a significant barrier to easy integration. Mays recognized that the racial makeup of schools followed demographic and residential patterns; as a result, schools would be less "integrated for sometime to come."

Although Mays knew how difficult it would be to achieve racial integration, he was still able to place a politically positive spin on the situation for the mainly white readership of *New South*. Mays wrote, "Desegregation will be easier than we think because it has been in process fifteen years or more and no calamity has fallen upon the South." Rhetorically, he put the best face on the South's political possibilities: "When the white primary was declared unconstitutional, Negroes voted and there was no revolution. When the Supreme Court made it possible for Negroes to eat unsegregated in the dining car and to travel as interstate passengers unsegregated, the traveling white public accepted it. When the federal courts ruled in favor of Negroes attending white universities in the South, the Negro students were enrolled and there was no revolution down South." Mays was hopeful that the "prophets of doom," who predicted catastrophe in the South if integration were to come, would be wrong. In early 1954, Mays's optimism was at its highest. "I suppose I have more faith in my native South than most Southerners," he wrote. "If the United States Supreme Court rules against segregation in public schools, I believe the Southern people will meet the challenge with dignity, poise, and calm."

Mays revealed one caveat in this optimistic scenario: southern politicians. "If our leaders are cool, calm, and collected, and if they lead in the spirit of democracy and the Christian religion, the people will follow and we will prove to the world that we not only talk democracy but we live it; we not only talk Christianity but we walk it." For the most part, however, southern political leaders did not stay "cool, calm, and collected." They followed the lead of South Carolina's Strom Thurmond and the Dixiecrats of 1948 and the political leadership of the South was overtaken by reactionary racist politics. They formed White Citizens' Councils throughout the South in an attempt to stave off integration at all cost. Mays knew this but persisted in challenging white southern leaders to do what was morally right and in the best interest of the South. But in the mind of the white southern ruling class, the only thing that was morally right was keeping political control of the South, no matter what the Supreme Court ruled.[3]

As he pondered the impending *Brown* decision more, he told readers of his *Pittsburgh Courier* column that even if the Supreme Court should rule against the plaintiffs, segregation was going to fall under its own weight for two reasons. One, the United States would lose prestige and moral authority in the court of world opinion in their current era of anticolonial independence movements. And, two, as a practical matter, "a decision of this kind will be tantamount to saying to the nation that you must *spend billions of dollars* and spend it quickly to try to do the impossible—make two things equal in every area of our life." Although segregation was weakening at the time of the Court's deliberations, he observed, "its back" was "still strong and rugged." "The first great step towards integrated citizenship," he concluded, "will be taken when segregation's back is completely broken."[4]

When the Supreme Court issued its ruling, Mays deliberated on how it would affect the leaders and alumni of historic black colleges. In a speech titled "Our Colleges and the Supreme Court Decision," given at Lincoln University in Pennsylvania, he was ebullient. "You are sharing with us in tonight's Convocation an occasion of [a] great moment," he said, ". . . an occasion that has been one hundred years in the making. . . . You are sharing with us tonight, then, the beginning of a new century in our history—a day in which the American ideal of equality of opportunity for all people has taken on new meaning." Mays contended that the *Brown* ruling ought not to be perceived as a threat but seen as opportunity. The thirty-one colleges that made up the United Negro College Fund, he emphasized, would continue to fulfill their mission. To him, historic black colleges like Lincoln (founded in 1854) never were "segregating institutions" and their charters "were all[-]inclusive from the beginning." Black and white cohabitated on equal footing on black college campuses, and both black and white faculty "lived with the Negro students and taught them with great affection and love." Further, the integrated faculty "saw their students not as sons and daughters of slaves but as sons and daughters of God, as human beings, of intrinsic worth and value." The interracial character of black colleges was one of their defining features. It was these colleges that "carried the torch of freedom and interracial good will for the whole South."

Ironically, Mays insisted that the end of segregation would allow black colleges to freely compete for students: "The Supreme Court decision will enable these colleges, in time, free in soul, heart and mind, to do fully what up to now they have been forbidden to do: open their doors to all qualified students who seek admission." With the end of segregation, Mays asserted, black colleges would "be judged on the basis of the quality of their work," not their racial composition. He saw no reason that black colleges would not be able to meet these challenges because blacks could be meritorious. Additionally, Mays felt that there would be a need in the United States for the kind of education historic black colleges provided because they supported some of the most vulnerable students in society.

As inspired as his words were, his enthusiasm was tempered by the economic disadvantages that segregation placed on the shoulders of black people.

"As wonderful as the decision of the Supreme Court is," he opined, "it cannot remove the fact that at present, and unfortunately for a long time to come, the Negro will be a disadvantaged economic group." Therefore, colleges that served black students had to keep their tuition low. "It will take a long time for a group which started behind in the race of life to compete economically with a group that began the race centuries ahead." Perhaps, overtaken by the moment, he naively uttered: "An understanding American public will not forget this fact when our society is completely integrated."[5]

Following the *Brown* decision Mays wrote another article on the case in the YWCA *Magazine*, titled "The Supreme Court Decision and Our Responsibility." He described three different groups' reactions to the Supreme Court's decision. The first group "did not believe that any one clothed in his right mind would dare to abolish one of the nation's false gods—segregation. These people plan to do everything in their power to circumvent the decision." The second group—which he initially belonged to—viewed the *Brown* decision "with great joy." He penned, "These people want to see the decision implemented—not in the next twenty-five years, and not in the next ten years; but the movement to integrate should begin, now, all over the nation." Though he did not mention who made up this second group, it is safe to assume that many were black. Mays characterized the third group as "the gradualists." This group contended that "segregation was a blot on the nation's democracy and should be abolished; but they believe it should have been left to each state to [abolish it] its own way." Though the gradualists did not agree with how the court rendered its decision, "they were willing . . . to go along with the decision and to see ways and means of implementing it."

Mays concurred with the gradualists' opinion that institutions move slowly. But he did not share their belief that integration could be achieved "without federal intervention." He noted that "Arkansas and Kentucky moved toward integration in higher education without federal intervention," but no other state where segregation was vigorously enforced had done so without being sued in the federal courts. Public schools that served black children were unequal to their white counterparts in every way. It "would have been unnecessary," Mays believed, for the country to force the South during Reconstruction to universalize and equalize education since "integration would have evolved imperceptibly." He concluded that even though the gradualists had a point, in the end, their position was "unhistorical and unrealistic." Keenly he reflected, "If one group has all the power and wields it, makes all the laws and administers them, has all the tax money and distributes it, it is too great a strain on the goodness of human nature to expect that group to deal as justly with a minority group, which is not represented, as it does with its own. Human nature is not good enough to do that in the year of our Lord 1954."

He encouraged readers of the YWCA *Magazine* to look at the *Brown* decision from a moral vantage point. Vehemently arguing once more that democracy had ethical requirements, and that the world needed to see America's democratic leadership, Mays stated, "Through the orderly process of law as laid down in our Constitution by our founding fathers. This is the American way. The rights of the weakest minority and those of the humble citizen can be protected or sustained through the Supreme Court." He repeated that the *Brown* decision was more than a local issue; it had both international and moral implications. "The soul of American democracy was on trial," he asserted, "and our people should be made to see" this in the implications of the court's decision. The ruling held liberating possibilities. "The minds and souls of all Americans, will be freed, in time, from the chains of prejudice and the prison house of ill-will."[6]

At the behest of the directors of the Phelps-Stokes Fund, Mays joined other presidents of black colleges in Hot Springs, Arkansas, in October of 1954, to discuss the meaning of the *Brown* decision for their respective institutions. The college presidents wrote a statement that asserted, "The Constitution is our sovereign authority.... Our cause has always been the Constitution." The signatories rejected Communism and wrapped themselves up in patriotic fervor. The statement read as though it had been lifted directly from Mays's writings. "We are convinced that there is a fundamental sense of fair play in the South," it read. "Southern people have accepted previous decisions of the Supreme Court and the social changes resulting there from, such decision as the abolition of the white primary, and the admissions of Negroes to white universities. . . . We believe that the South will likewise accept the decision of May 17. . . . It is our hope that all of the colleges and universities of the South[,] Negro and white[,] will immediately implement the spirit of the Court's decision[,] accepting, irrespective of race, all qualified students who seek admission."[7] While the presidents of black colleges exhibited restraint and accepted the Court's decision, most southern politicians stepped up their attack on it. It did not take Mays too long to realize that the system of Jim Crow was not going to voluntarily whither away through reasoned arguments. The escalated racial politics would have to be confronted in another manner.

If the *Brown* decision was the central domestic issue concerning America's black and white citizens in the 1950s, racial politics continued to be part and parcel of geopolitics at the apex of the Cold War. For Mays, nothing

Benjamin Mays at the World Council of Churches meeting, England, July 1949.
Photograph by Larry Burrow/Time & Life Pictures, Getty Images.

demonstrated this more than South African apartheid. As the representative
of the National Baptist Convention (NBC) on the Central Committee of the
World Council of Churches (WCC), he was in a unique position to challenge
the theological foundations of apartheid.[8] For him, apartheid and American
segregation were hardly distinguishable in their net effect of isolating and
marginalizing black people.[9]

Beginning in 1950, Mays had begun a running debate with Dr. Ben J. Marais,
another member of the Central Committee who represented the Dutch Re-
formed Church in the Transvaal region of South Africa. Marais believed that
apartheid, though not biblically sanctioned, "was a practical necessity" and
that the Central Committee "should send an all white-delegation to South
Africa to help seek a solution to the racial situation there," a position Mays
categorically opposed. Mays felt that it "was absolutely mandatory that [he]
oppose him." As he explained, "I knew only too well what racial discrimination and segregation meant, and I knew that the World Council of Churches

could not afford to be a party to racism in South Africa."[10] He elaborated in the *Buffalo Evening News*:

> Since 1937, in seven world conferences, I have heard the story of South Africa. . . . It's the same old story. The only new element today is apartheid (segregation). . . . To say that apartheid is not segregation but separate development—to say that it is for the good of all—is almost blasphemy. To say that it is in the interest of Bantu or the black man is a terrible thing to say. Why not let us be frank and say apartheid is a system that has been worked out because two million Europeans feel if they do not have apartheid they will be swallowed. . . . It disturbed me that the outstanding ecumenical body of Christendom should even raise this question. . . . I think the Central Committee is a little too timid. I don't believe the situation in South Africa will grow worse if this committee speaks a word of protest in the name of God. . . . It is for us to speak what we believe to be the voice of God and leave the consequences to God. I make no apologies for the racial situation in the United States; God knows it's bad enough. But we can honestly say that it is not getting worse, as it is in South Africa.[11]

Thus Mays advocated for sending an ecumenical interracial delegation to South Africa.

Although Mays was able to convince the Central Committee to agree to sending an ecumenical interracial delegation to do a fact-finding mission, the motion was approved with the caveat that the white Afrikaner church must be consulted first. This effectively ended an interracial delegation from visiting the country. For Mays, however, the debate was not over. He would restate his objection to a theology that supported racial exclusion in another international church forum, the Eighth World Baptist Congress (WBC) that met in Cleveland.[12] Although his speech against racial injustice there was enthusiastically received, he realized that "nothing would really change as a result of the address. . . . But, like the Hebrew prophets, one must make his witness even though we do not repent."[13]

In August of 1954, the WCC met on the campus of Northwestern University in Evanston, Illinois. In front of the entire body of delegates Mays offered his most important theological rebuttal to apartheid in South Africa. Preceding his speech, Ben Marais once again made the argument for the practical necessity of segregation in South Africa. Marais continued to espouse the notion that, though not biblically sanctioned, apartheid was for the good of all in his country. Mays countered Marais's argument in an address titled "The Church

Amidst Ethnic and Racial Tension." The point of his address was "to indicate that the only basis the church has for its segregated policy is the wickedness of church people themselves."[14]

At the same time that Mays was condemning the white South African church's support of apartheid, Mays was making one of his more definitive statements about the theology that supported racial segregation in the United States. His address was given just three months after the *Brown* ruling. Here was the moment he had been waiting for, an opportunity to drive a stake in the heart of the very theology that undergirded racism. Mays, no doubt, calculated that he would receive maximum press coverage both nationally and internationally at this assembly and counted on the largely mainstream white media to deliver this important message around the world. He also knew that since the assembly was being held just north of Chicago, his speech would receive enormous attention from the black press as well. In July 1954, *Ebony* magazine, a national monthly serving black Americans, had named Mays as one of the ten leading black clergymen in the country.[15] He was guaranteed to get positive notices from the national black press, including the *Pittsburgh Courier.*[16] His shrewd calculation prove to be correct.

His objective was twofold: first, to dispense with the notion that the Bible sanctioned racism and, second, to empower black people on the African continent and in the United States by instructing them that there was no theological justification for their political subordination. Mays told the assembly,

> Within the past quarter of a century, Christians have been forced to think about the bearing of their faith upon the problem of racial discrimination, and upon the meaning of the races in human history. Wars involving mankind, the rise of atheistic communism, the development of the Nordic theory of racial superiority, the struggles of the colored peoples everywhere for freedom, and a new emphasis on the meaning of the gospel in our time have made us embarrassingly aware of the wide gulf that frequently exists between our gospel and our practice . . . [but] members of your Commission, supported by the best biblical scholars[,] concluded that anyone who seeks to shelter in the Bible for his defense of racial segregation in the church is living in a glass house which is neither rock nor bulletproof.

He went further, turning Marais's concession that there were no biblical grounds for racial segregation against him: "My distinguished colleague, B. J. Marais, sought the thinking of the fourteen leading theologians of Europe on this subject, including Emil Brunner and Karl Barth. They all agree that we can find no justification in the Bible for a segregated church based on race or ethnic origin. . . . So if there are those among us who seek support in the Bible for segregated churches based on color, race, caste, or ethnic origin, they must turn elsewhere for support."

The heart of the argument was whether or not the church could actually organize itself to move against the oppressive practices of racial exclusion. Mays asked the assembly, "If the modern churches cannot practice Christian fellowship in worship and membership, how can they preach the prophetic word to secular organizations that discriminate on the grounds of race, color, and caste? . . . At this Assembly, the people will want to know whether the church has any responsibility as an organized group for the alleviation of racial injustice in social and political, and economic life."[17] He offered no specific formulas as to how churches were to address this question. However, Mays had accomplished what he had set out to do; he had put to rest the argument that biblical theology supported racial apartheid. The assembly interrupted his speech ten times with applause. He received extensive coverage—on the radio and in newspapers—and hate mail.[18] Ignoring the criticisms and threats, he preached a moral imperative of "brotherhood" to every audience he was asked to address. A year later, Mays would have another opportunity to eloquently make his case in front of another influential audience.

He had one of his most stellar moments—in a long career of many stellar moments—when he was invited to speak before the Southern Historical Association (SHA) in the fall of 1955. He had been invited to Memphis to be on a panel with the Nobel Prize–winning novelist William Faulkner and Nashville lawyer Cecil Sims to discuss the *Brown* decision and its implications for the South's future.[19] Mays's invitation to the panel had been arranged by the historian John Hope Franklin, one of the SHA's few black members, and advocated by young white members of the organization, all of whom taught outside the South.

Because of Faulkner's presence, the audience grew so large that the meeting, which was being held at the Peabody Hotel, had to be moved from an afternoon session to an evening session in the Grand Ballroom. Officers of the SHA worked diligently to keep Faulkner, who was well known for his alcohol abuse, sober and lucid throughout the day. In addition, the Peabody Hotel management was terribly anxious about the session. It kept members of the press out of the meeting, fearing that a photographer would capture Mays on the main dais with Faulkner and Sims or the thirty other blacks integrating the SHA meeting. Given the rise of White Citizens' Councils in Memphis and elsewhere, the hotel management worried that photographs of blacks and whites comingling as equals might be interpreted as an endorsement of desegregation, which would damage the hotel's business. It also demanded that Mays enter the hotel through the kitchen, rather than the front entrance. The hotel's largely black kitchen staff watched him walk, quietly and dignified, through the kitchen and into the auditorium to intellectually champion full citizenship for black Americans. And he did not disappoint them.

Mays, in fact, stole the moment. He repeated what he had been saying during his travels around the country for nearly fifteen years. He informed the audience that segregation was "a great evil" and that if this evil institution was not abolished it would be a denial of America's covenant found in the Declaration of Independence. He added that the sacred books of the Bible did not support segregation and cast moral judgment on all people. With striking oratorical skill, Mays asserted that the problem of segregation undermined governmental leadership among the world's people. "If we lose this battle for freedom for 15 million Negroes," he cautioned his audience, "we lose it for 145 million whites and eventually we will lose it for the world. This is a time for greatness." At the end of the speech, the five hundred historians in the audience rose to their feet and gave him a prolonged, thunderous, ovation.

It was ironic that Faulkner's talk, which he delivered in a soft whisper and later would be reprised in his 1956 *Harper's Magazine* essay "On Fear," was, in fact, a disappointment to members of the SHA. The media coverage, however, both local (in the *Memphis Commercial Appeal*) and national (the *New York Times*) indicated that Faulkner's address was the most significant at the gathering. Mays, on the other hand, received no publicity other than the SHA's publication of the speech, which it published without its imprint. But the thirty black participants seated in the audience and the Peabody Hotel's black service staff knew what had occurred; Mays was the true star at SHA's panel. He had spoken forcefully as well as eloquently of the moral imperatives of the *Brown* decision and about the deeper, more insistent quandary that racism posed as America projected itself onto the world stage.[20]

The meeting of southern historians was a positive start to a direly needed discussion of how to reasonably implement the Supreme Court's ruling and constructively integrate southern institutions. But the *Brown* ruling was met in most southern political quarters with vitriolic speeches and shrewd political plans for resisting the implementation of the law. Mays knew, as he informed his weekly column readers, that it was imperative for black people to do more public protest. Human dignity required that black people be treated fairly. Mays educated *Courier* subscribers, for instance, that the law allowed black people to act against the enforced segregation on trains and buses since the U.S. Supreme Court had outlawed segregation in interstate transportation.

"I know that many Negroes are afraid to protest," he wrote. "Some lack poise and cannot protest without blowing up; others are like the blind mule. But those who are blessed with the ability to raise questions calmly without emotional display should protest more." He challenged his readers to at least write letters of complaint to railroads. But he also acknowledged that many black people feared making their complaints public for fear of economic reprisals. Mays pointed out that the problem was with railroad officials and not necessarily with the white passengers. The ultimate reason black people should protest was to protect their dignity as persons. "I behave as I do," he concluded, "because I know that as long as I am treated as a Negro, a caste man, this thing isn't right and until my dying day I shall insist first on being a human being and incidentally a Negro. In my protest, I am not fighting to be with anybody. I just want to be human and be allowed to walk the earth with dignity."[21] When he wrote those words, he was unaware that the tipping point had been reached; mass protest in the South was just a few months away.

On August 1, 1955, Mays turned sixty-one. He was a senior statesman as a college president and a civil rights activist. He had spoken and written so many times about the relationship between American Christianity and democracy, and in so many venues, one wonders if he got tired of it. We will never know because he continued like a faithful Hebrew prophet waiting for the day of God's judgment. He continued to point out the patent injustices piled against black citizens. But nothing struck home like the senseless murder of fourteen-year-old Emmett Till in Money, Mississippi, in 1955 by John William "J. W." Milam and Roy Bryant for whistling at Carolyn Bryant. For him, Till's death was irrational and hateful, but it also showed that "segregation, the cause of most injustice, is hobbling along on crutches on its way out." He believed that "decent white people will be more determined now than ever before to see to it that America—all America—becomes a decent place for all to live—even Negroes."[22] It must have appeared providential that within a few months of Till's death and of his triumphant speech before the SHA Rosa Parks made her dramatic stance on a Montgomery, Alabama, bus and Martin Luther King Jr., a Morehouse graduate, a son of Atlanta, a child of the black Baptist Church, rose to prominence. Nothing prepared Mays for King's thrust into history's spotlight as a civil rights leader in 1955.

By 1956, Mays was publicly overshadowed by his former student. King was then the twenty-seven-year-old elected president of the Montgomery Improvement Association (MIA), the organization in charge of leading the Montgomery bus boycott. King was young, articulate, and perfectly camera-ready for the emerging television news media. Although he had some promising political skills, he was hardly the mature person or leader the media made him out to be. King realized that he had been drawn into a political vortex that put unimaginable demands on his life. In those earliest days in Montgomery, when he was initially drawn into the national spotlight, he needed a persona with more gravitas than his young age afforded him. The persona that he appeared to have adapted for his use in order to establish himself with the image of a serious thinker and political leader was that of Mays. In this way, King was able to present himself as a more mature leader, and he was successful.

Mays, as King testified, had been significant in his life and influential in his calling to be a Baptist minister. Mays was also one of the clergy members who listened to his trial sermon and ordained him. When King decided to attend seminary in 1948, at the age of nineteen, it was Mays who had written a key recommendation on King's behalf. Although King was a very young and academically middling student while at Morehouse, Mays wrote to Crozier Seminary admissions officers that King had a "good mind" and he believed him worthy of admission.[23] In addition, Mays had a special relationship with the seminary's president, Edwin Aubrey. Mays knew that King would get the very best and most rigorous introduction to modernist theology under the administration of Aubrey. Crozier was not Union Seminary in New York City, University of Chicago Divinity School, or Yale Divinity School, which at the time were the top Protestant academic seminaries that educated the clergy, but it was a very good Baptist theological seminary where a youthful King could develop more academic discipline in preparation for his career in ministry. Mays believed Crozier was an ideal place for King, and King, in fact, excelled there. He then followed in Mays's footsteps by seeking a Ph.D. in theology.[24]

During King's doctoral studies at Boston University, his academic inquiry focused on the question of God. King paid homage to Mays by writing a dissertation along similar lines as Mays's dissertation, comparing the concepts of God in the respective theologies of Edgar Sheffield Brightman and Henry Wieman. King's study of Henry Wieman's conceptualizations of God was a nod to Mays's influence as well. He was familiar with Mays's book *The Negro's God* and perhaps wanted to be recognized by his mentor as being a serious theological thinker, a great preacher, and a contributor to the cause of black freedom.[25] Like Mays, King wanted to be able to build bridges between academia and the life of ordinary black believers.

King also had other significant mentors in the Morehouse circle, including his religion professors George Kelsey, Melvin Watson, and the venerable Morehouse alumnus Howard Thurman. Although Howard Thurman—who was appointed to be the first black dean of Marsh Chapel at Boston University in 1953—and others were confidantes of King, it was Mays's model of the

Benjamin Mays and Martin Luther King Jr. at the Morehouse College graduation, 1957.
Courtesy of Morehouse College Archives.

minister as social activist that he followed. As the saying goes, imitation is
the sincerest form of flattery, and King, without question, modeled his earliest
public persona after Mays. He needed Mays's words and counsel to stave off
his own concerns and an overbearing father. He also needed Mays for spiritual support as he faced the burden of being perceived as the personification
of black America's hopes and dreams. It was Mays who held the job as King's
consigliore over the next fourteen years as the death threats against him grew
more ominous and the public battles more dangerous.[26]

In his column in February 1956, Mays offered one of his first public assessments of the Montgomery bus boycott and King's leadership. He wrote
as though he had no personal relationship with King and had not been intimately involved behind the scenes in the boycott. The column recounted the
reasons for the Montgomery protest and King's election as the president and
spokesman for the organization. He also noted the limited goals of the MIA.
"Negroes," he wrote, "are requesting three things: better treatment of Negro
passengers, a first come first serve regulation on the buses, and Negro bus

drivers in predominately Negro areas. All three are within the Southern pattern of segregation and they are not willing to grant them." Mays thought this spoke volumes about how much white civic leaders of Montgomery wanted racial submission, not merely segregation. Mays also commented on the purpose of unity among black people in carrying out the boycott: This unity had a backlash because whites resented "Negroes showing solidarity and manhood," he offered. Mays expressed pride in Montgomery's black citizens for carrying out their protest "in an orderly manner." And more importantly, he told his national readership that "the stature of the Rev. M. L. King Jr. has increased tremendously since he urged the crowd at his house, after the bombing, not to get panicky and/or resort to violence."[27] King had shown extraordinary calmness and fortitude in the face of threats against him and his family.

At the age of sixty-two, Mays was more than happy to give King the kind of support he needed as he took the national spotlight as one of the leading fig-ures in the black freedom struggle. In addition, King's initial activism brought invaluable national attention and prominence to Morehouse College. In the spring of 1957, Mays saw to it that the young King was awarded an honorary doctorate of humane letters for his courageous leadership in the yearlong Montgomery bus boycott.[28] Mays said in his commendation:

> You are mature beyond years, wiser at twenty-eight than most men at
> sixty; more courageous in the righteous struggle than most men can
> ever be; living faith that most men preach about but never experience.
> Significant is the fact that you did not seek leadership in the Montgom-
> ery controversy. It was thrust upon you by the people. You did not betray
> the trust of the leadership. You led people with great dignity, Christian
> grace, and determined purpose. While you were away, your colleagues in
> the battle for freedom were being hounded and arrested like criminals.
> When it was suggested by legal counsel that you might stay away and
> avoid arrest, I heard you say with my own ears: "I would rather spend ten
> years in jail than desert the people in crisis." At that moment, my heart,
> my mind, and my soul stood erect and saluted you. I knew then that you
> were called to leadership for just such a time as this. . . . On this our 90th
> anniversary, your Alma Mater is happy to be the first college or univer-
> sity to honor you this way.[29]

As King contemplated his mission and the future of the civil rights move-ment after Montgomery, he would turn to Mays time and again for advice as the politics of the movement became tempestuous and surged onto the streets of America. In forming the Southern Christian Leadership Conference (SCLC),

King relied heavily on Mays's conviction that ministers were significant grass-roots leaders in the fight for civil rights. The SCLC's motto, "To Redeem the Soul of America," was a phrase that Mays had quoted from Walter Rauschenbusch's work.[30] Additionally, it was Mays who stopped the young King and the president of the NAACP, Roy Wilkins, from bickering over Wilkins's concern that King was encroaching on NAACP work in the early days of the SCLC.[31] Mays understood the fundamentally different approaches taken by the SCLC and the NAACP. Their respective strategies for ending segregation were rooted in the intraclass and professional politics of black America, as he explained years later in a 1978 interview. "The NAACP was and is composed of lawyers and they don't march in the streets," he observed. "They feel that the first thing you've got to do is have the United States Supreme Court to declare this thing [racial segregation] illegal, and that's logical."[32] Mays was a lifelong member and a trustee of the NAACP, but he realized that the push for civil rights needed different methods of protest that included not solely legal briefs but street-level boycotts and marches. However, what Mays did not mention was that there was a distinct anticlerical prejudice among some black civil rights activists, who viewed black ministers, especially those not formally educated, as not being the best representatives of black people's interests. Ironically, King's SCLC would demonstrate many of the autocratic leadership flaws of the black clergy.

From the Montgomery bus boycott forward, Mays would publicly advocate on King's behalf.[33] He explained to both white and black audiences what King was trying to accomplish socially and politically, and why the states of Alabama and Georgia felt it necessary to charge King with felonious trumped-up legal charges.[34] Mays would remain steadfastly committed to King throughout his life.[35] King, we can infer, was the son he never had.

King was just one example of the kind of minister Mays had hoped to educate. In fact, black people craved more activist ministers in their communities.[36] Although the demands of the Morehouse presidency slowed him, it did not deter him from keeping his dream of creating an educational center where black clergymen could be professionally educated. He stubbornly held on to the idea that black people needed a significant theological training center and a place of inquiry where black churches and religion could be studied. Immediately after his appointment as Morehouse's president in 1940, he began a conversation with other church-affiliated colleges about their theological training programs and how to combine efforts for the professional training of black clergymen. It would take him approximately seventeen years, until 1957, to negotiate and gain funding for a new graduate center for the training of black clergy in the Atlanta University Center.

Morehouse College was still a black Baptist preachers' training school when Mays took over. The Morehouse School of Religion did not have the requisite size or faculty to do what Mays had done at Howard. However, the combined church-affiliated colleges, all of which had a theological curriculum, would only be enhanced if they were brought together. In Atlanta, there was Morris Brown College, which housed the African Methodist Episcopal Church–affiliated Turner Theological Seminary; Gammon Theological Seminary, which was affiliated with the Methodist Episcopal Church (today the United Methodist Church); and, of course, Morehouse. If these three schools could establish a strong cooperative relationship, Mays thought, they could build a competitive graduate school for ministers. In 1948, with the encouragement of the Rockefeller General Education Board, a proposal was put forth to solidify the relationship. It would take the next eight years for the three schools to move away from their denominational turf battles and settle on making a brand new institution, the Interdenominational Theological Center (ITC). Mays's experiences at Howard convinced him that a Protestant seminary that brought together black clergy from various denominations would bode well for building socially engaged black churches. It would be an added bonus for the black community to have solidly educated ministers serving them.

His next big concern was finding the best person to lead the ITC as the academic dean. In a series of letters, Mays gently tried to convince George Kelsey, a former professor of religion at Morehouse and one of Mays's most trusted colleagues, to come back to Atlanta. In a letter dated November 17, 1958, Mays took great care to provide Kelsey with all the details: "The ITC has its own Board of Trustees. The Dean over the Center is not responsible for finance. It is to be a quality seminary, one of the best . . . we hope to be able to pay well. . . . This is a combination of Morehouse, Gammon, Morris Brown, Turner and Phillips School of Theology at Lane College. . . . I think a strong Baptist should serve as Dean."[37] Although Kelsey allowed his name to be put in for nomination for the position, he ultimately declined the job. He had accepted a position teaching theological ethics at Drew University in Madison, New Jersey, which he felt offered him a better opportunity for teaching and publication.[38]

Dr. Harry Richardson, the stalwart president of Gammon Theological Seminary, became the ITC's first president. Richardson and Mays's relationship dated back to the late 1930s when Richardson was the chaplain at Tuskegee Institute. These two old friends shepherded this new institution into existence through all the headaches of black denominational politics, which could be contentious.[39] Mays and Richardson had found a ripe political moment to establish the ITC.

Mays wrote in his *Courier* column how pleased he was with the formation of the ITC. It was an important moment for black people and their churches. The black church, he argued, was the one institution that black Americans fully owned and the ITC would be a training center for a new generation of black ministers to lead black Protestant churches around the country. The center would do what he had hoped to do at Howard University: equip black clergymen, through intellectual dialogue and scholarship, to better educate and serve black Protestant congregations. It would focus on sharpening students' analytical skills and encouraging critical consumption of new concepts and trends in theological education. Black Christian communities throughout the country would be the beneficiaries of this new ecumenical institution.

Mays was hopeful that the ITC would produce many more progressive black ministers like Martin Luther King Jr. He was convinced the ITC would forge stronger bonds between black denominations and clergy and lead to partnerships between black denominations and organizations like the National Council of Churches of Christ (NCC) and the World Council of Churches. The "faculty of the new seminary," he asserted, "will be interracial and interdenominational from the beginning" and it "will pay special attention to the application of Christian principles to the economic, political and social problems of the area."[40]

Mays's grand dreams and hopes for the ITC were in stark contrast to the political realities of black churches. More specifically, his denomination, the National Baptist Convention, presented a formidable problem to advancing his ITC objectives. In the 1950s, the NBC was considered to be the largest black denomination in the United States. Although the NBC was numerically sizable and powerful, its social change strategy for black America was not as progressive as Mays wanted it to be. The NBC was a conservative institution whose traditions endured. As black southern migrants moved north, many Baptist country preachers with entrepreneurial ingenuity, talent, and plain old gumption had secured large congregations. Migrants had also taken leadership positions and made powerful alliances within their respective churches and denominations. Clergy appointments to large churches or important committees were often politically motivated. Mays knew the politics well from his brief time as an assistant to Lacey Kirk Williams, the pastor of Olivet Baptist Church in Chicago. Williams, who presided over the NBC for eighteen years, appointed Mays as the NBC's representative at various international church conferences. Williams's successor, David V. Jemison, pastor of Tabernacle Baptist Church in Selma, Alabama, who served from 1941 to 1953,[41] also appointed Mays to represent the NBC on the WCC's Central Committee.[42] Mays had firsthand experience with the operations of the NBC, and it taught him that the denomination had not evolved very much since its beginnings in the 1890s, during the height of racial segregation. He concluded that the NBC needed to adapt to the contemporary situation.[43] He was convinced that with transparent and democratic leadership, the NBC could be a powerful force of change by unifying black Americans in their larger struggle to attain more education and secure civil rights.

He was initially pleased that one of his contemporaries, the Reverend Joseph H. Jackson, had been elected president of the NBC in 1953, replacing the venerable David V. Jemison. Jackson and Mays had many things in common. Jackson was born in rural Mississippi in 1900 and, like Mays, had worked hard to attain an education. He was also educated in modernist and Social Gospel theology at the Colgate Rochester Divinity School. As the corresponding secretary of the Foreign Mission Board, Jackson wielded considerable political power in the NBC. Like Mays, he was a key representative of the NBC at international church gatherings.[44] In 1939, Jackson received a great deal of attention for breaking the color line when he preached at the World Baptist Alliance in Atlanta. Additionally, Jackson, like Mays, believed that black clergy should be better educated theologically. By all measures, Jackson should have been a model of effective pastoral leadership. Upon taking the reigns of Olivet Baptist—then the largest NBC congregation in the United States—Jackson guided the congregation out of debt and to an increased membership. A report from the University of Chicago unabashedly described Olivet under Jackson's leadership as "one of the best organized Protestant Churches in America."[45]

It was reasonable to Mays that under a more open and democratic process, Jackson was elected to be the NBC's president. However, Mays did not realize how calculating and shrewd Jackson was in maintaining his lock on power. Jackson had been undemocratic and autocratic in the churches he served. While Jackson might have had modernist theological training, he was an old-style dictatorial political church boss. His style of leadership was more in keeping with the rough-and-tumble political environment of Philadelphia and Chicago. In 1953, Jackson falsely promised the convention that if he were elected president he would accept the convention's decision to limit the term of the presidency to just four years. Almost immediately after being elected, Jackson balked at that pledge.[46]

By his third year, in 1956, he used procedural tactics to help him undo the presidential term limit. Having appointed key allies to the subcommittee charged to review the term limit of the presidency, Jackson knew that the committee would be deadlocked on the issue. He therefore summarily ruled on the issue as president of the convention, asserting that "there is no tenure in the Constitution of the Baptist Convention," and, in effect, declaring the past tenure decision "null and void." NBC members overwhelmingly supported his decision. Jackson's autocratic behavior justified their own dictatorial leadership in their respective congregations. As one Baptist minister, the Reverend M. W. Whitt, observed at the 1956 convention, leadership in the Baptist Church was not determined "on the basis of a static rule or law"—inferring it was rather by a call of God.[47]

For Mays, Jackson's decision was undemocratic and deceitful.[48] He believed that this kind of behavior alienated young black people and made them increasingly more cynical about the church's mission and clergymen's leadership. More importantly, Mays felt that it threatened the democratic struggle that was being waged by blacks throughout the South. From his perspective, Jackson's leadership style had to be challenged for the sake of the church's mission.

There was one thing that Jackson clearly understood and that Mays underestimated: Not everyone in the NBC affirmed the kind of theological modernism that these two men had been taught as students and that Mays explicitly embraced. Most black Baptist ministers were either theologically conservative or fundamentalists in their doctrinal understandings. For them, Jesus was their Savior, not a historical figure who died for his convictions, and the church's primary function was to provide a spiritual and ethical home where believers could gather together for worship and be guided by strong pastoral leadership. Ironically, Jackson's autocratic style derived from the theology that a minister was called by God to preach and no one could challenge his calling.

Mays politically miscalculated. In contrast to Mays, who had served a congregation for only three years, Jackson had been a preacher all his life and had "learned how to manage the convention's black populist ethos in order to accommodate" his power, and "he always ran on the platform that he was the defender of the preachers from the small congregations," which constituted the bulk of the NBC.[49] As a scholar and a clergyman himself, Mays understood many things about black churches, but he took too lightly the ambition of his fellow clergymen and the lengths to which these determined men—most of whom garnered respect only in the confines of their own churches—would go to gain and hold on to prestige and status. They saw in J. H. Jackson, a southern migrant to the North and pastor to large urban church, the fulfillment of their own ambitions.[50]

Jackson's usurpation of presidential power at the NBC convention so offended Mays that he would later join ranks with a group of young ministers, including King, to attempt to oust Jackson as its president, a move that Jackson never forgave or forgot. After the success of the Montgomery bus boycott, King wanted a political base within the NBC to help lead a campaign of direct action against segregation. Both Mays and King found Jackson's leadership quite undemocratic and considered his unwillingness to present a plan to the NBC to become a full partner in nonviolent social action to be a religious failing. How could the NBC not use its numbers to support a socially moral cause to undermine the vestiges of legal racial bigotry around the country? The fact that the NBC did not fully support education in a manner he thought fit for a denomination its size disturbed him even more. He observed in his *Courier* column, "[The] main difficulty with the National Baptist Convention Inc., and I am not speaking solely of the present administration, is the fact that the leadership through the years has played politics and has been more concerned with perpetuating itself in office than it has been in launching a real constructive program." With ire, he noted, "The National Baptist Convention, Inc., has never had a national program of education." Mays thought this was embarrassing. Scornfully he wrote, "If the [white] Southern Baptists withdrew their support from the National Baptist Seminary in Nashville, it would be difficult for it to maintain itself." He accused the NBC of failing to systematically recruit men with integrity to the Baptist ministry and to place them after they left the seminary. Nor were there any plans "to provide scholarships for brilliant Negro Baptists who otherwise could not go to college."[51]

In fairness to Jackson, he had hosted a conference on Baptist education at Morehouse College in the late fall of 1956.[52] To Mays, however, the conference was a sham because the meeting put no real plan forward to address funding black Baptist students in college. It seemed as though the Morehouse conference was set up for the sake of appearances and to mute political criticism from progressives in the NBC. Five years later, in 1961, Mays continued to be frustrated by the NBC's lack of financial stewardship for either education or civil rights protest.[53] The regime that controlled the convention needed to be removed.

Mays had hoped that the convention, which was to meet in Kansas City, Missouri, would be orderly. He concurred with a suggestion made by one of the stalwarts of the convention that mediation be brought in to resolve the divisive issues surrounding the election of the president. He wrote in his column, "Wouldn't it be wonderful if the first act of business at Kansas City would be a fair election, with delegates voting by states for the candidate of their choice?"[54] Young progressives like King and Gardner Taylor of Brooklyn, New York, planned to unseat Jackson in Kansas City, an act that Jackson scornfully remembered as the "March-In."[55] Mays had pledged his support for, if not explicit endorsement of the Taylor faction in his column.

In September of 1961, Taylor was summarily defeated by the political wizardry and steely determination of Joseph H. Jackson. Tragically, at the 1961 convention, in a pushing and shoving incident, one of Jackson's supporters, the Reverend Mr. Wright, was accidentally pushed off the stage and fell to his death. Jackson immediately told the Associated Press that it was King who had been the mastermind behind the protest strategy, which led to Wright's death. He would later retract this statement in the *Chicago Sun-Times* by saying that King was the mastermind behind the civil rights movement, not the fight over tenure at the convention. However, the damage to King had been done; the national press had run away with the story without fully checking the facts. What was interesting about this challenge to Jackson's presidency was that he and Martin Luther King Sr. had been longtime friends and NBC political allies. Mays, in his subsequent *Courier* articles sought to protect King, and by extension the civil rights movement. He liberally quoted from King's telegram to Jackson asking for a retraction of his comments.[56] The political battles for control of the NBC left Jackson a bitter foe of the King faction. In petty and significant ways, Jackson worked hard to ensure his national and international prestige to stave off the threat of King's coalition.

After 1961, Mays would leave the NBC, along with two thousand other clergymen, to form the Progressive Baptist Convention.[57] The political battles within the NBC just proved to Mays that a theological training center was necessary for the future of the black church. His hope was that a more thoroughly educated and progressive black clergy would provide the kind of leadership black churchgoers deserved and needed.

Jackson's antics stung Mays deeply. In 1962, to ensure that fellow NBC clergy understood his authority, Jackson arranged to have an audience with Pope John XXIII in Rome on his way back from a WCC meeting. He was able to do so through his connections with Mayor Richard Dailey of Chicago. He would be the first black Protestant clergymen to have that honor. Though Mays had been a key leader in the WCC for many years, he never had the opportunity to have an audience with the pope.[58] He would ultimately attend John XXIII's funeral as a part of the delegation accompanying Vice President Lyndon Johnson. The level of the rivalry between the two men is uncertain. But the politics of the NBC would later have other ramifications for the civil rights movement.

In 1960, black college students met at Shaw University in Raleigh, North Carolina, and formed the Student Non-Violent Coordinating Committee (SNCC). Ella J. Baker, a veteran civil rights activist who had worked for both the NAACP and the SCLC, counseled them. Baker would instruct students to shy away from the black Baptist ministers after her experience working with King's newly formed SCLC. She felt that the patriarchal leadership style of black ministers reflected in NBC politics did not always serve black people or the movement to end social inequality well. In contrast to Mays, Baker was unconvinced that black clergymen were the best grassroots leaders for a movement for social change in America. Neither Mays nor his protégé, King, saw sexism, whether in the NBC or in the SCLC, as problematic as it really was.[59] As it evolved, SNCC, a far more progressive and inclusive organization than either the SCLC or the NBC, would confront sexism among its members, too.

Mays, though always personally broad-minded in his attitude toward women, and toward women leaders, did not publicly articulate a view about sexism until the early 1970s.[60] Baker, however, clearly knew from her cumulative experience that a leadership cadre dominated by conservative men in the black churches and civil rights organizations like the NAACP was too hierarchical to empower the local people, many of whom were women, to develop leadership and organize nationally from the grassroots level.

Baker cautioned students to keep their organization independent and to stay away from the autocratic, charismatic leadership style especially associated with black clergymen. Just as Baker had counseled, student activists throughout the South outflanked black clergymen and mainstream civil rights leaders. While their elders feuded in organizations like the NBC, they took another direction in organizing black communities, making their elders' internecine political squabbles seem irrelevant. These young people refused to wait on the approval of religious leaders whose fighting would not usher in the kingdom of heaven on earth or get anyone served at lunch counters across the South.[61]

As the drama behind the civil rights movement unfolded in the second half of the 1950s, Mays felt confident his persistent role as an intellectual mentor had begun to bear fruit. He had spent his "minute" preparing the way institutionally for social change. He, like Ella Baker, had become a wise elder giving guidance to a courageous group of young people who took to the streets with a fervent and youthful moral righteousness to protest America's historical wrongs.

This Is Not a Short War, This Is a Long War

No man is really free who is afraid to speak the truth as he knows it,
or who is too fearful to take a stand for that which he knows is right.
Every man has his Gethsemane.
—MAYS, *Quotable Quotes of Benjamin E. Mays*

On February 1, 1960, the Greensboro sit-in, carried out by four male freshmen from North Carolina A&T, caught everyone by surprise for its boldness and its simplicity. Within weeks of the Greensboro sit-in, black students all over the South were feverishly participating in acts of civil disobedience. By March, students in the Atlanta University complex of colleges were also swept up in the tide of sit-ins, civic demonstrations, and street protests throughout the city. Nothing prepared Mays for the next eleven years, from 1960 to 1971, with the advent of sustained public civil rights protest throughout the country.[1] These years were an emotional roller-coaster ride for him; they were filled with momentous highs and great lows. During these years he continued to be nationally recognized, albeit as a key mentor to Martin Luther King Jr. He also experienced great personal grief and losses as he reached his senior years, including King's assassination and the death of his wife, Sadie. Yet, wonderfully, he had lived long enough to see a mass national democratic movement on behalf of civil rights—a movement that he had vigorously cultivated—come to fruition. It was indeed gratifying for him to see this movement led in part by several of his Morehouse students, including Julian Bond, Lonnie King, and Hamilton Holmes, who were at the forefront of the student-led phase of the civil rights movement in Atlanta along with Spelman student Marian Wright (Edelman).[2]

As students made their plans for sit-ins, Mays and Rufus Clement, the president of Atlanta University, encouraged them to first state their concerns publicly and then helped them pay for a public advertisement in the *Atlanta Constitution*. The students formed a committee and published a document titled "An Appeal for Human Rights." It outlined the difficulties black Atlantans faced both socially and economically. The students concluded their pronouncement with a declaration, which read like a portion of Mays's Social Gospel theologizing. They declared:

WE HOLD THAT:

(1) The practice of racial [segregation] is not in keeping with the ideals of Democracy and Christianity.

(2) Racial segregation is robbing not only the segregated but the segregator of his human dignity. Furthermore, the propagation [of] racial prejudice is unfair to the generations yet unborn

(3) In times of war, the Negro has fought and died for his country; yet he still has not been accorded first-class citizenship.

(4) In spite of the fact that the Negro pays his share of taxes, he does not enjoy participation in city, county and state government at the level where laws are enacted.

(5) The social, economic, and political progress of Georgia is retarded by segregation and prejudices.

(6) America is fast losing the respect of other nations by the poor example which she sets [in] the area of race relations.

It is unfortunate that [the] Negro is being forced to fight, in any way, for what is due him and is freely accorded other Americans. It is unfortunate that even today some people should hold to the erroneous idea of racial [segregation] despite the fact that the world is fast moving toward an integrated humanity.

The time has come for the people of Atlanta and Georgia to take a good look at what is really happening in this country, and to stop believing those who tell us that everything is fine and equal, and that the Negro is happy [and] satisfied.

It is to be regretted that there are those who still refuse to recognize the over-riding supremacy of the Federal Law.

Our churches which are ordained by God and claim to be the houses of all people, foster segregation of the races to the point of making Sunday the most segregated day of the week.

We, the students of the Atlanta University Center, are driven by past and present events to assert our feelings to the citizens of Atlanta and to the world.

We, therefore, call upon all people in authority—State, County, and City officials; all leaders in civic life—ministers, teachers, and business men; and all people of good will to assort [sic] themselves and abolish these injustices. We must say in all candor that we plan to use every legal and non-violent means at our disposal to secure full citizenship rights as members of this great Democracy of ours.[3]

In this appeal, the inclusion of language about God and country, which Mays had so carefully crafted, became a powerful ideological tool for black students around Atlanta as they prepared to take action and publicly dramatize just how antidemocratic and inhumane legally enforced segregation was throughout the South. The white southern Protestant elite, who had once justified and couched their actions and attitudes in a form of civil religion, had now been surpassed by a new generation of young black people whose moral claims echoed those Mays had been making in his speeches before they were born.

Though he was proud of the students' activism, Mays also became fearful for their well being as violent reprisals worsened as the civil rights protest generated a headwind. Ernest Vandiver, governor of Georgia, had told protesters in Atlanta, who planned a commemorative march for the sixth anniversary of *Brown v. Board of Education*, that "they would be sorry" if they demonstrated in front of the state capitol. State troopers, he warned, were readied to stop any protest to protect the capitol building.[4] Having witnessed the violent political repression through his years, Mays wanted the students to be cautious. He requested a meeting with one of the student leaders, Morehouse student Lonnie King, in hopes of talking him into postponing the march. In the meeting, in a role reversal, the more determined King instead held Mays accountable, using the same words that Mays had used to inspire students in his Tuesday chapels. King reminded Mays of one his chapel talks titled "Never Sacrifice a Principle for Peace." King told Mays that by trying to postpone the march he was "asking [the demonstrators] to sacrifice the principle of [full equality] that we're trying to fight for so that we can have peace. There will be no peace as long as there is segregation." As King recalled, Mays paused and simply responded, "See you at Wheat Street."[5] King and the marchers never made it to the state capitol because Atlanta chief of police stopped them two blocks before they reach the capitol building and turned the demonstrators back, hoping to avert a confrontation with state troopers. Though this particular demonstration did not fully succeed, Mays was proud of King's steadfast resolve and leadership.[6]

Atlanta's young warriors, as Mays affectionately called them, had gotten the message, and it was now their time to act. It was their turn to push back against segregation using the lessons and wisdom they had received from Mays. His role now was to work in the background to protect the protesters as much as possible and keep the NAACP informed about the students' activities. When the Atlanta sit-ins began, Mays wrote to Roy Wilkins, the national president of the NAACP, informing him of the direction of the protest. He reported, "A group of students outside of the organized bunch did go to Kress [a national chain store] but the Atlanta sit-down protest was directed against restaurants in public places, particularly those serving the public like the railroad and bus stations and like government buildings." While Mays was totally sympathetic to the students' cause, he wanted them to direct their protest at public sites and institutions that clearly violated federal law, a tactic in line with the NAACP's legal strategy.[7]

The NAACP's strict adherence to political lobbying and legal strategy, however, seemed to students to be too politically conservative in challenging the power structure of the South. Mays eluded to this perception in another letter to Wilkins. "I am very glad to know that the Legal Defense Fund of the NAACP is defending the 83 Atlanta students [who had participated in sit-ins and demonstrations] through Attorneys Hollowell and Walden." Donald Hollowell and A. T. (Austin Thomas) Walden were prominent black attorneys in Atlanta whose defense work on behalf of the demonstrators anchored the local student movement.[8] "This, as you see, puts the NAACP and the Legal Defense Fund directly in the fight," he discreetly noted to Wilkins. "Although you no doubt are aware of this, I thought you should know that this is the situation, and the people in the community believe definitely that the defense of the students should come about in this way."[9] Mays, who stood publicly and principally in defense of the students' right to protest and boycott businesses that discriminated, was the most beloved president among those of Atlanta's historically black colleges, as Marion Wright Edelman recalled. According to Edelman, "He inspired and taught and stood by us when we challenged Atlanta's racial discrimination. Some of his teachings I wrote in my college diary. Others, I internalized, and like many others who heard him frequently, I shared his words with others."[10]

Throughout his career, Mays stood with and listened to black students, encouraging them to engage and make changes in their world. The changes he pushed for beginning in the late 1920s (see chapter 3) were finally becoming a reality through Atlanta's young warriors and other young people participating in civil rights organizing. In his *Courier* column on March 26, 1960, Mays eagerly supported the students and set out to define for his readers the historical significance of what the students at A&T and the Atlanta University Center (AUC) had begun. He tied their actions to the larger history of black struggle in America and the global struggle for human rights. What students were accomplishing was "part of the world struggle on the part of the suppressed peoples everywhere—Asia, Africa, North and South Americas—to breathe the air of freedom and justice."[11]

He continued his advocacy for the student protesters in his columns. Mays encouraged not only students but also adults to participate in the protest. In March 1961, he wrote a column titled "Adult Responsibility" in which he praised students for their efforts. Mays then cautioned them, using a biblical allusion, that they were "not fighting against flesh and blood, but principalities and powers and wickedness in high places," in order to temper student exuberance and give them a longer perspective on their protest. "When they win the lunch counter battle," he wrote, "they will need to move on to something else and from that something else, and so on. Throughout the whole of their lifetime, they will be fighting—if not segregation, they will be fighting against discrimination on the basis of race and color. This is not a short war, this is a long war." Mays also warned that activism was not solely the duty of student activists. "Older people" could not afford "to drag their feet in this fight," he asserted.

> If students can go to jail for the cause, certainly older people should not
> only be willing to support the students by contributing heavily to the
> cause, but they should help by not spending their money in places dis-
> criminating against Negroes on the basis of race and color. . . . We can-
> not win the battle whether students stay in jail without bail or whether
> they are bailed out unless the adult community is so organized that it
> will support the students' efforts by not spending their money where we
> are discriminated against on account of race. . . . Some of us have been
> sticking our necks out a long time trying to get segregation and dis-
> crimination abolished. It seems that there is something every adult can
> do to support the student movement morally, financially, going to jail
> if necessary, and certainly by supporting those establishments that are
> more decent in their treatment of Negroes and other colored people.[12]

Many black college presidents, especially those of public institutions, feared the financial backlash of student activism on their campuses, but Mays, as a president of a private college, felt free to stand up with students and protesters in public based upon his long-held democratic beliefs. This is not to say that his Morehouse trustees were not wary about the activism on the campus. Mays's views about the value of student activism prevailed, however, and the respect for him grew. And the momentum of the movement grew, too.

In the summer of 1962, Mays was asked to chair the Conference on Religion and Race to be held in Chicago on January 14–17, 1963. He was especially gratified because this was a gathering "of more than seven hundred religious leaders[;] the conference marked the first that Protestant, Catholic, and Jewish religious bodies had gathered for the express purpose of attacking racism in the United States at all levels of society, including within the religious bodies themselves."[13] Though optimistic, he had limited goals for the Chicago meeting. The meeting was set as a religious commemoration of the one hundredth anniversary of the Emancipation Proclamation, which was the perfect time to build a coalition of religious leaders across a wider spectrum of beliefs to further the goal what CORE, SCLC, SNCC, and the NAACP had accomplished legislatively: tougher enforcement of the federal civil rights statues. He opened the meeting with words that Martin Luther King Jr. would echo several months later at the March on Washington: "We come this week to think together, to work together, to pray together and to dedicate ourselves to the task of completing the job which Lincoln began 100 years ago." He declared, "This conference will create in us a new sense of urgency to do in the next ten years what we failed to do in the past 100 year—abolish from among us racial discrimination and prejudice."[14] Politically, Mays aimed to create a broad-based religious coalition that would sustain protesters in the South and pressure nationally elected politicians. He wrote in his *Courier* column a few weeks later that it was his hope that the religious alliances would "work against racial bias at the local level." Not everyone was pleased.

Anna Hedgeman, a longtime political activist and organizer from Harlem who attended the Conference on Race and Religion, thought Mays missed an opportunity to represent black people's history and the history of the black church at the meeting. She criticized Mays for not making the most of the Chicago conference. She was disappointed that there had been "no presentation of the Negro church, no basic realization that the Negro church had left the balconies and other segregated parts of the major denominations in order to find dignity for its members and their worship. There was no realization of the structure, which the Negro church had built; or its distrust of the Christianity of the white communions." She chastised Mays because at the meeting there "was no presentation either of the storefront church or the cults which have arisen among lonely Negro refugees. Dr. Mays, who is an authority on the Negro Church and who has theological training, might well have told the dramatic meaning of the Negro Church to the total church and nation." She continued, "He might have presented the way in which the Negro church too has a developed structure and power. Dr. Mays could easily have indicated that there would be need for such conversation between Negro and white church leaders, for the only real power the Negro leader has ever had has been within his own church." She wanted Mays to ask more searching questions. "Would the Negro be willing to play a secondary role if churches merge? Could he have confidence in the leadership of the white churches? These questions were not discussed at Chicago. Negroes at the Conference on Religion and Race were talked to and about, but we ourselves did not speak of our faith, which *passeth all understanding*."[15]

Hedgeman had a point about the wider issues concerning the black churches and what the changes in federal laws would mean for them. There is no doubt Mays could have addressed these issues. In addition to these criticisms, Hedgeman would also decry, like Ella Baker, the sexist attitudes and behavior of male civil rights leaders.[16] Despite her rightful rancor, she devoted her energy to organizing the March on Washington to support upcoming civil rights legislation. That the march had to be a success among the American public was something she and Mays did agree on.

Nothing proved Mays's point about the efficacy of protest than the March on Washington.[17] On August 28, 1963, just some twenty-seven days after his sixty-ninth birthday, Mays was seated on the steps of the Lincoln Memorial as a program participant in the March on Washington. It was during the march that participants learned of the death of the scholar and social crusader W. E. B. DuBois, who was a founding member of the NAACP. DuBois had been a great influence on Mays's life, especially in the years when he edited the *Crisis* magazine. "When I was a high school student in South Carolina," Mays explained in a tribute to DuBois, who had just turned ninety-three, "I began reading the *Crisis* magazine. I read it eagerly because Dr. DuBois was saying what my immature young mind wanted said, but had neither the ability nor the channel through which to say the things that he was saying." Although he was dismissive of DuBois's turn to Communism, as well as his seminal book, *Black Reconstruction*, written in 1935, Mays respected DuBois's lifelong dedication to the cause of black people's freedom.[18]

DuBois's body of writings and scholarship had built the academic foundation that Mays laid claim to in his own thought. And it was DuBois who recognized Mays as a potential young leader in the *Crisis* and who published one of his first articles.[19] DuBois was never a personal mentor to Mays, but he had been a public role model for him and many others as a intellectual. Ironically, DuBois's death coincided with the international spotlight glaring on the March on Washington and King. As Mays reflected on DuBois's legacy, he compared him to Booker T. Washington, DuBois's onetime nemesis. He wrote that Washington had been accepted into the American "Hall of Fame," a position DuBois would most likely never hold because of his uncompromising views. However, he thought that the appreciation for DuBois would "increase with time" because "he spoke for the future."[20]

Benjamin Mays seated next to Sammy Davis Jr. at the March on Washington. Courtesy of the Moorland-Spingarn Research Center, Howard University

But not even DuBois's death could detract from the monumental moment. Here Mays was, back in Washington, D.C., in front of the Lincoln Memorial, where he once attended Marion Anderson's Easter Concert in 1939, which set the precedent for the March on Washington. Patiently waiting on the steps of the Lincoln Memorial for the events to unfold, surrounded by Hollywood celebrities, labor activists, and many of the country's leading clergy, he must have reflected on his own career advancing civil rights through religious understanding with some delight.

Just like the more than 200,000 marchers on the mall that hot summer day, Mays, too, would stand in rapt attention listening to King's magnificent oration that closed the demonstration. He no doubt beamed with pride knowing that he had a small part in nurturing King and seeing him deliver one of the most compelling speeches for American justice ever given. The "I Have a Dream" oration contained a message that reflected his own sermonizing throughout America. He must have thought to himself that, finally, in front of the entire world press, all of America could hear what he and his forbearers had been trying to convince America of—the nobility of its own democratic principles. And just like Mahalia Jackson, the great gospel singer, whose singing had warmed up the audience for King, Mays, too, was compelled to say "Amen." Proudly, he gave a swift benediction after his protégé's most famous oration. As he noted in his column a couple of weeks after the march, "It was a beautiful scene. From the Lincoln Memorial to Washington's Monument there was a mass of humanity. So far as one could see to the left, nothing but people and a similar sea of faces to the right. A great day!"[21]

Mays felt gratified by black students' democratic activism. His years of labor as an advocate for and inspiration to young people were now yielding results. At the sit-ins, planned boycotts, and demonstration marches taking place all over the United States, his students were being purposeful in their actions and principled in their concerns for democratic freedoms for black people. Not everyone shared Mays's viewpoint, however. The civil rights movement and Morehouse College's close relationship with it created all kinds of strains for him. He was still the president of a college that was quite economically vulnerable and therefore dependent on the generosity of national foundations and corporate leaders. Additionally, there was concern that the school would not be able to obtain financial support from the federal government. After all, the movement was challenging social, religious, and political institutions, which had failed in the past to serve black Americans. It was a precarious time in the life of Morehouse. The college needed the largesse of the federal government, which funded science and technological education at American colleges in the wake of the Cold War. Morehouse also needed corporate support to build its endowment. He frequently found himself walking a tightrope. As a college president, he had to simultaneously maintain the financial viability of Morehouse and support, advocate for, and, increasingly, protect student protesters.

Mays knew all too well that students' nonviolent battle was being fought against reactionary southern politics—which sanctioned terrorist violence.

News of the violence was strewn across the headlines. The riot ensuing after the enrollment of James Meredith at the University of Mississippi; the murder of Medgar Evers, a NAACP staffer in Mississippi; the bombing of the Sixteenth Street Baptist Church in Birmingham, Alabama, killing four young girls; and the assassination of the president of the United States, John F. Kennedy, were vivid reminders to Mays of the violence opponents of civil rights were capable of inflicting. This time around, though, the entire country would publicly witness the type of violence that undergirded racial segregation in the United States. Violence toward the protesters, exposed by news media in the 1960s, was the same kind he recalled from his earliest childhood memory. And this time around, the frequency of terrorist acts did not silence or repress democratic participation or kill the protesters' spirit as it had back then.

The civil rights movement went forward in spite of the violence, but the tensions created by both personal ethics and political demands strained the personal relationship between King and Mays. King had been desirous of a seat on Morehouse's board of trustees, and King's father, a thirty-year trustee, had urged Mays to put King's nomination forward. Some of the trustees considered King's activities too controversial for him to serve as a trustee. One can only speculate that King's dalliances with women outside his marriage had also become a problem for members of the board of trustees. Although it has not been fully documented, it is likely that the Federal Bureau of Investigation (FBI) had begun to inform some of the trustees of King's personal indiscretions, doing whatever it could to discredit his leadership. Whatever the case may have been, the board of trustees voted against King's placement on the board, leaving Mays with the unpleasant and awkward duty of explaining to him why he was not elected. King was stunned and aggrieved that his mentor had not been able to be more persuasive with his trustees.[22]

Mays nevertheless vigorously defended King in his *Courier* column when the FBI director, J. Edgar Hoover, called him the "most notorious liar in the country." And he turned the spotlight back on the FBI's slow investigations of heinous hate crimes against black Americans all throughout the South.[23] When King was awarded the Nobel Prize for Peace later in 1964, many of the trustees who had been reluctant to elect King as a member became quite a bit more disposed to appointing him as a Morehouse trustee.[24] There were tensions felt even inside the Mayses' household as the movement pressed forward. According to Ralph Abernathy, one of King's top lieutenants, Mrs. Mays was none too happy about King's repeated use, in his public addresses, of phrases, wholesale quotes, and parts of speeches authored by Mays without giving him credit for them. She wanted her husband to be given the credit that he rightly deserved. She found it unseemly and questioned King's character. Mays remained quiet about his wife's complaints, however, not wishing to be a distraction to King and the larger aims of the movement. He knew that black preachers, like their counterparts in the music world, were famous for borrowing stylistic innovations and rhetorical flourishes without attribution. However, Sadie felt that King's international reputation as a famed preacher was based on her husband's words, and her loyalty was first and foremost to him as a wife, not to King as a movement leader. If King was one of the spearheads of the movement, Mrs. Mays thought, he should fully acknowledge that the ideas he preached were his mentor's, not his own.[25]

Even in the midst of calamitous times and tensions created by the civil rights movement, Mays looked ahead to the next generation of black college students, the post–civil rights generation, who would enter college as he retired in 1967. Politically he felt that it was incumbent upon him to address the future they faced. In February of 1964, Mays addressed the students and faculty of Livingstone College in Salisbury, North Carolina, for their Founders' Day observance. There were no reporters from CBS television news or the *New York Times* in attendance to give him national recognition for his talk at a small historically all-black college. By now the more quotable people in this era were Malcolm X, James Baldwin, King, Wilkins, and Whitney Young as well as the many other local activists who were all vying to get their viewpoints heard and faces on the airwaves. Mays's speech would not be quoted in the east coast intellectual journals or magazines such as *Atlantic Monthly*, *Commentary*, the *Nation*, or the *New Republic*. But he continued to give speeches behind the segregated veil of all-black institutions of higher education. Few major white institutions of higher education, steeped in elitism, had really considered admitting black students to their campuses en masse until the late 1960s. And none of these institutions saw a need to address the intellectual and educational needs of black students. Throughout the 1960s, Mays's publicity outside of Atlanta receded to the back pages of national newspapers, and he received little major television coverage. In the world of black colleges, however, he was still a giant.

He gave his speech at Livingstone College the day after U.S. Congress voted 290–130 in favor of the Civil Rights Act of 1964. Although the Senate had not yet debated the bill, Mays believed that it would support passage as well. Seizing the moment, as the civil rights bill was winding its way through debate, he wanted to explain what the last ten years of court decisions, street protests, voter registration drives, and boycotts meant as the United States moved toward legal desegregation. The goal of desegregation for blacks was not simply "to be with white Americans," he explained. Integration, he contended, was a spiritual state in which barriers of "nationality, race, or color" are transcended for the goal of a common purpose. The goal of desegregation was "to unshackle the minds of Negro youth, loose the chain from the Negro's soul, free his heart from fear and intimidation so that he will be able to develop whatever gifts God has given him and share the fruits of his mind and soul with humanity around the globe, in business and industry, in medicine and law, in music and dance, and in painting and sculpture." Desegregation would allow black people the birthright given to them by God. Always the preacher and theologian, he told his audience that the goal "of desegregation is to free the mind and soul of Negro people so that Negro youth can reach for the stars and grasp after the moon."[26]

For him, the goal of desegregation had another dimension: it was also to free "the mind of the white South." Desegregation would free not only the South but the entire nation. Mays acknowledged that these efforts to desegregate the United States came with some form of coercion, either through the courts or on the streets of America. So in his Livingstone address, he warned both students and alumni in the audience that the battle to desegregate American society was a worthy cause but it required them to shoulder the heaviest responsibility. The fight required a three-pronged attack: they had to meet great academic challenges, demonstrate in the streets, and fight legal battles in the courts. With an omniscient soberness about American society, he informed his Livingstone audience about the realities black Americans faced as legally supported racial discrimination would come slowly but inevitably to its demise:

Desegregation and eventually integration present a special challenge to Negroes and especially to Negro youth. No allowance will be made for our shortcomings because for two hundred forty-six years our ancestors were slaves and for another one hundred years we were enslaved again through segregation by law and by custom. No allowance will be made for our poverty even though the average income of the Negro family is only about 55 percent of that of the average white family. . . . What am I trying to say? I am trying to tell you with every ounce of my one hundred seventy-seven pounds that you, with low income, poor academic backgrounds before college, unfortunate home conditions, handicapped ancestors for three and a half centuries—you are now required to compete in the open market with those who have more favorable circumstances than you for several centuries. Our inadequacies will be printed in the press, flashed over the radio, and screened on television. Nobody will explain the reason for our shortcomings.[27]

He spoke with candor as he had many times before within the safe confines of all-black audiences. As early as 1954, shortly after the *Brown* decision, he began warning black churches and civic groups alike that the end of legal racial segregation would not mean full freedom for black Americans. He believed that the end of legal discrimination would be accompanied by a backlash of covert racial discrimination and black economic impoverishment in the coming years.

He realized that the social problems he and Sadie had tried to address in the late 1920s while working in the city of Tampa, Florida, had only grown worse. As a frequent visitor to Cleveland, Ohio, where his brother's family lived, Mays observed in their lives in the industrial belt of the Great Lakes region the kinds of discrimination that black southerners faced. He worried increasingly, both privately and publicly, about the insufficient academic preparation many black students in high school received, as reflected in the Morehouse freshmen classes coming from all over the United States.

Mays understood the sociological problem well. He knew how difficult it was for young black people to attain a college education. Their experiences were reminiscent of his own earlier struggles. He continued to appeal to his students' personal pride and ambition to excel academically. But Mays's inspirational messages were not always enough. Although Morehouse had put in place academic remediation programs, they were insufficient to deal with the enormity of the problem. Morehouse's institutional challenge was like that of a double-Dutch jump-roper; it would have to jump over two ropes simultaneously—high achievement and remediation—and without financial support. Mays's prophetic theology and his belief in an academic meritocracy would be sorely challenged by the continuing reality that public education in most American cities was failing black children. The educationally impoverished legacy of South Carolina schools, which stifled him as a youngster, had followed black people on a migratory path from rural villages to big urban cities in both the North and the South. Additionally, in the wake of the civil rights movement, the most gifted and best-prepared black students were slowly but steadily being siphoned off to wealthier public and private universities.[28]

Substandard academic preparation of black students was only one of many difficulties facing black Americans as legalized Jim Crow ebbed. In Atlanta, for example, all around the black colleges were the symptoms of growing urban decay. By the 1950s, the growing economic disparities between blacks and whites were hastened by the flight of the white middle-class to the fast-growing suburban rim of Atlanta. Figuratively, a new type of noose was gradually being tightened around the necks of Atlanta's black poor, even as social activists attempted to address the issues of unequal access to education and housing and bleak job prospects. Federal social policy and the changing demographics of Atlanta had a deep effect on the West Side neighborhood where the AUC and Morehouse were located. The vitality of the AUC neighborhood was eroding steadily due to a combination of ill-considered federal legislation, public policies, and racism, in what simply became known as urban renewal.[29] The combined effect of white flight, urban renewal, and poor delivery of education wreaked havoc through the core of American cities like Atlanta, spreading like a ubiquitous cancer.

Throughout the 1960s, the presidents of Atlanta's black colleges, like Mays, were quietly and justifiably worried about the deterioration of their neighborhood. Mays and his colleagues understood their colleges' vulnerability in the evolving black ghetto, but felt inadequate do anything about it as they struggled just to keep their own poorly funded colleges afloat. They feared the random street crime that slowly crept up to their gates. Not knowing what to do about it, many retreated in fear, making ill-considered derogatory remarks about the black poor, who were, more often than not, also the victims of street crime and deleterious social policies.[30]

At times, more radical community activists, following the lead of the Nation of Islam (NOI) minister Malcolm X, accused black college presidents of being part of the problem of the ghetto. To some, the solutions these leaders proposed were based solely on individual achievement, and did not effectively address the collective needs of the ghettoized black community. They interpreted their statements as little more than platitudes reflective of their bourgeois cultural mores, which to them did not address the cultural deprivation blacks suffered in a racist society. Nor did these advocates feel that such sentiments, like using a traditional approach to education, empowered the black poor to have agency in their own communities. According to these critics, many of whom had been students at black colleges, these institutions were too steeped in bourgeois cultural sentimentality, which led them to unwittingly imitate the same behavior of America's white power structure that kept black people oppressed and ghettoized.

Mays appreciated these young critics, but he did not appear to fully grasp the cultural shift resulting from Malcolm X's challenge to black civil rights leaders to affirm Black Nationalism as a positive force for organizing poor and ghettoized black communities. When Malcolm X was assassinated on February 21, 1965, Mays noted his death by paraphrasing Martin Luther King Jr.'s comment that "we must face the fact that Malcolm X was murdered by morally inclement climate. It reveals that our society is still sick enough to express dissent through murder." King's observation led Mays to reflect on what X might have become if he had not been forced to live such a harsh life that included incarceration for robbery. In the conclusion of his commentary, Mays questioned the nature of a society that prevented a brilliant individual like Malcolm X from living up to his full potential simply because he was unable to have access to resources and education in his adolescent years. He wrote, "Supposed he had lived in a society in which all men are treated equally and with respect, instead of the 'sick' one to which he was born and in which he died under a fusillade of bullets."[31] Though thoughtful in his reflection, Mays failed to acknowledge Malcolm X's real impact. Malcolm X had re-stoked Black Nationalism and Pan-Africanism in the imaginations of black Americans. His murder was a reminder to younger black activists that black Americans, especially black men, could be killed with impunity throughout America's ghettoes. Malcolm X's angry and strident cultural affirmation of black people's dignity with combative cries for black self-defense instead of nonviolence fueled a new political rhetoric that pointed to the growing disenchantment of black people located in the urban core of American cities.[32]

Nothing captured the moment more than when in 1966 Stokely Carmichael, a SNCC field organizer, encouraged protesters to use the term "Black Power" in support of James Meredith's solitary protest march, the "March Against Fear." Meredith commenced his march on June 5, 1966, in Memphis, Tennessee, and while marching to Jackson, Mississippi, he was wounded on a Mississippi highway by an attempted assassin.[33] SNCC and SCLC organizers worked together to plan a march that would demonstrate solidarity with Meredith's sole protest. During the march, in Greenwood, Mississippi, Carmichael timed the shouts of "Black Power!" to be captured on the evening news and in newspaper headlines. Its use surpassed what he had hoped to achieve. The expression carried with it a powerful rhetorical message and signaled deeper disenchantment about America's failed promises to black Americans. The term also revealed the need for more a systematic analysis of the problems of the black poor.

As was the case with King, it would take Mays a while to discern exactly what Carmichael and others meant by Black Power. In February 1967, the AUC hosted a debate at Clark College where Carmichael and the Reverend Samuel Williams, an important local civil rights leader and teacher, publicly debated the ideas surrounding Black Power.[34] Had it not been for his upcoming retirement and Morehouse's centennial anniversary, Mays, the old college debater, would certainly have relished taking on the challenge of debating Carmichael.

At first Mays reacted somewhat defensively to the angry young critics of America and the black establishment. He thought that they were a bit hasty and perhaps even reckless in using the term "Black Power" in a provocative manner without a clear political purpose.[35] To him, the expression implied revolutionary violence and racial separatism. Through his experiences over more than seventy years, he had come to believe that violence solved very little in the long term and would resolve nothing for the cause of black freedom.[36] As a thinker in the Christian tradition, Mays could not accept a separatist ideology as a matter of religious conviction. Religion, by its very nature, called humanity to be spiritually one.[37] Throughout his career, Mays had indicted white Protestants on moral grounds for their racism and worked to dismantle all religious justification for racial segregation. Principally, he could not advocate for any form of black separatism. In his opinion, the Black Power slogan, without a clear philosophical or theological framework to back it up was simply a needlessly provocative phrase with no real political plan attached to it to alleviate the condition of what he called the "average and the below-average man."[38]

Black Power, in fact had historical antecedents going back to Marcus Garvey and beyond. This ideology was actually built on the pioneering work of many of the New Negro intellectuals. However, in this formulation, Black Power advocates went beyond that of their predecessors and questioned the very foundation of Western culture itself. Social analysis put forward by notables such as Frantz Fanon—the psychiatrist and anticolonial intellectual from Martinique, whose volume *The Wretched of the Earth* was published in English in 1965—radicalized the way many black intellectuals and social activists assessed the protracted issues of race in America in a way Mays had not grasped. The changing secular consciousness of black writers that concerned Mays in the late 1930s had evolved.[39] Even though he viewed the call for Black Power as being inherently separatist, some of the long-term outcomes, debates, and academic publications that began with the calls for Black Power were undoubtedly surprising and pleasing to him.

Black Power also troubled Mays because of its decidedly anti-Christian sentiment. Christianity had always been a source of tension for many black intellectuals and social activists. It vexed them that black churches had the ear of ordinary black people more than any other organization, including labor unions. They castigated black churches for engaging in what they deemed nonprogressive activities as they tried to assume the mantle of authority with ordinary black folk to lure them away from black churches.

Nevertheless, black religiosity continued to be an essential ingredient in the making of the civil rights movement. Ironically, revivalist religiosity, which helped to spawn the civil rights movement and came from the same black folk culture that promoted the "otherworldliness" that Mays had theologically criticized, galvanized black people to protest (see chapter 7).[40] Many of the successes of the southern civil rights movement were heavily dependent upon those people who lived ordinary lives and found solace in their churches. It was the religiously committed people who were essential to the success of boycotts and protests and who provided the financial support for the lawsuits. Black churchgoers provided the communication network so desperately needed by movement activists to execute cohesive protest plans, provide information, and make financial appeals.

Yet, despite the church community's active participation and critical support in the civil rights struggle, Mays observed, hostility toward black ministers persisted. Just as Mays feared, the new generation of activists considered them too cautious and too self-aggrandizing.[41] Attacks against black ministers and churches, were repeated on college campuses, in bookstores, and even on street corners. These intellectual tensions continued to grow between 1963 and 1967 as the civil rights coalition splintered ideologically, with one faction embracing a religiously motivated, and racially inclusive, social activism and the other espousing the politics of cultural nationalism and/or pragmatic ethnic power politics in the calls for Black Power.

Mays was never one to shy away from a good debate. He wanted his opinions to be heard in the fierce discourse about Black Power. In a column written in the *Chicago Defender*, he argued that Black Power had to be defined by more than sloganeering and youthful political posturing. Black Power could only be gained through achievement—academic, business, and political.[42] His argument fell on deaf ears. To many Black Power supporters, Mays's "old-fashion" building-block solution did not address the immediate needs of an impoverished urban population. It was too reformist, too bourgeois, and not radical enough. This is why he felt the need to write his memoirs.

Mays turned to what he had done best with young people; he entered into a dialogue with them by narrating the history of the black American struggle through his own life's story. His narrative would be more historical than *The Autobiography of Malcolm X* or Claude Brown's *Manchild in the Promised Land*, both published in 1965, which gave gritty urban views of black life. His story would provide a longer descriptive account of how the black struggle had evolved from the end of the nineteenth century and throughout the twentieth. He hoped that the baby boomers would better understand the broader context and impact of Black Power contextually.

Benjamin and Sadie Mays, Howard Thurman, Hugh Gloster, and Yvonne King
Gloster at the Morehouse Centennial, 1967. Courtesy of the Moorland-Spingarn
Research Center, Howard University.

Morehouse College celebrated its centennial anniversary in 1967, and Mays
finally retired, just short of the age of seventy-three. Just as he had promised
to Morehouse students in 1940, he had given the college and the students his
very best.[43] Though he had wanted to retire earlier, in 1964, Morehouse's board
of trustees asked him to stay on longer while they searched for the right person to build on his legacy. It was fitting that Mays was able to continue in his
duties and then relinquish them at the college's one-hundredth—anniversary
celebration. He had overseen Morehouse College for twenty-seven years and
sure-footedly guided it through some of its most difficult days. He had inspired
many students to face their handicaps, dig in, and do their very best.

The year 1967 would prove to be significant in other ways, too. Antiwar
protest against the Vietnam War spread and in April, King publicly joined it.
He gave one of his most eloquent appeals, and arguably one of his greatest
speeches, at New York's Riverside Church. King's speech resonated with the
growing climate of uncertainty about the war's purpose and its adverse impact
on poverty at home. When critics, including the editor of the *Courier* and Jackie
Robinson, the former major league baseball star, attacked King's position on

the war, Mays wrote a strong rebuttal in his weekly column defending King's right to link the civil rights violations at home to human rights violations in Vietnam.[44] Mays contended that King had a right to speak out against the war. It was reminiscent of his own dissent in the 1950s regarding the Korean War.[45] "I do not agree with the leaders who criticize Dr. King on the ground he should stick to civil rights and not mix civil rights with foreign policy," Mays asserted. Mays held that there was a greater human rights movement around the world and King, as a leader, could not keep silent for the sake of political expediency, as many other civil rights leaders and politicians wished him to do. He took a long-range view on King's critique of U.S. actions in the war. "He may be right in his stand on Vietnam," he opined, "and he may be wrong. History will finally record the verdict." What was certain for him was the criticisms being leveled at King because of his position on the war in Vietnam were "not convincing."[46]

Antiwar sentiment spread like wildfire. Black students entering colleges and universities in the fall of 1967 were more and more aroused by the multiple meanings of the chant "Black Power" and more sympathetic to the growing disenchantment across America with the war in Vietnam. An unpopular war intersected with increased discontentment with urban domestic policies, creating tense relationships between civil rights organizations and the Johnson administration.[47] The idea of the patience and patriotism associated with the "Double V" campaign of World War II was lost to students. Noting immaturity, intellectual confusion, and campus unrest, especially on black college campuses, Mays asked students in his weekly column: what did they hope to gain from their protests?

In July of 1967, Newark, Detroit, and a host of other American cities were inflamed by riotous social unrest. In that year, the collective anger of black people living in major northern cities raged wildly against political and economic marginalization and state-sanctioned police brutality. For Mays, the summer of 1967 was a stark contrast to 1898, when the Phoenix riot and other mob actions coerced black people into political submission throughout the South. It was as though northern urban black folk were getting their revenge, even if it meant maniacally setting their own poor communities aflame to protest. Even still, he did not condone the actions. Mays noted with ire that, though social inequities were persistently prevalent, "nothing that the Negro is suffering justifies arson, looting and murder." The rebellions, as some young radical activists called the urban unrest of that year, in his opinion, did not advance the cause of civil rights nor would it end persistent racism and impoverishment.[48]

After twenty-seven years of faithful service, it was good for Mays to step down from the presidency of Morehouse. He wanted and needed the time to write a fuller account of his thoughts than his weekly column in the *Courier* allowed. It was his strong desire to elevate the discussion and bring some sanity and reason to the anger and recrimination acted out in the streets and in the classrooms. By the end of 1967, the young warriors had grown weary of protest politics, which had been couched in a civil religion.[49] The persistent and aggressive violence used against civil rights activists had reached the tipping point. Some activists viewed nonviolent strategies as being unrealistic in light of the outright terror that had been organized against them. But, in Mays's opinion, the militant turn in the rhetoric used by activists, who he felt were losing sight of the longer-term battles still to be fought, was too extreme. Certainly he understood how they felt, and he knew of the terror they experienced. Nevertheless, he remained committed to the nonviolent approach as the only legitimate way to gain the moral high ground and delegitimize racist terrorism.

Though he understood the social activists' outrage, nothing drove home his point more than the Orangeburg massacre, which occurred in February of 1968, when students at South Carolina State University, his alma mater, were protesting a segregated bowling alley. As the protest heated up, the students started a bonfire on campus. When law enforcement officials arrived to put out the fire, a banister thrown by a student allegedly hit one of them. In an effort to control the crowd, a law enforcement official fired into the air. Reacting to the gunshot, other law enforcement officers opened fire on the entire crowd, killing three students and injuring twenty-seven. Officials would later claim students fired upon them, even though there was no evidence to support the claim. The incident troubled Mays deeply—and infuriated him. He believed that through the courts, not revolutionary violence, was the best way to resolve problems.[50] Unfortunately, as was the case in the Orangeburg incident, whites that exercised violence against blacks were seldom tried, and if they were, they were acquitted.

In the aftermath of the Orangeburg massacre, on April 4, 1968, Martin Luther King Jr. became yet another martyr in the civil rights struggle. This was the proverbial last straw for critics of nonviolent religious social activism. King's death showed the raw brutality of the American political order, and it required a response based on political and even military power. King's assassination reflected the hypocrisy of white Christians, and some argued that it proved the failure of a movement directed by love. From their perspective, white Americans, whether directly or indirectly were complicit in the political violence and guilty of trying to quash black Americans' freedoms. Kings murder, viewed in the light of the Vietnam War and the political calls for "law and order" by Barry Goldwater, Richard Nixon, and their political minions, created deep skepticism about a mass political movement rooted in religious idealism.

The assassination of King devastated Mays. King had figuratively grown up in the Mayses' home since the age of fifteen. The King who Mays knew was a decent and publicly principled man, faced with a historically burdensome responsibility of being the country's most visible civil rights leader. For the thirteen years of King's public career, Mays had served as one of his closest confidantes. King had often shared with Mays his premonitions about being killed.[51] In a 1963 letter Mays wrote to King shortly after the assassination of President John F. Kennedy, he cautioned King about his own vulnerability. He emotively wrote, "President Kennedy's death was almost more than I could take. If they hated him, they love you less. I hope that you will take every precaution as you move around."[52] His letter was hauntingly prescient. According to Coretta Scott King, Mays came to visit her the night of her husband's assassination. She told him, "You know, Dr. Mays, Martin always said he wanted you to do his eulogy." To which Mays replied, "I always wanted him to preach mine."[53] Stoically, Mays accepted the duty of eulogizing his spiritual son.

Over the course of his lengthy career, Mays had eulogized numerous prominent figures within the circles of black colleges and black communities, from Benjamin Brawley, long-standing dean and literary scholar of Morehouse College, to his own mentor, Channing Tobias.[54] King's eulogy, however, was different in scale than any of these. It was to be given before the glaring spotlights and television cameras of the national and international press and would be beamed via satellite to audiences around the world. Before a world audience, he would have to restrain his own angry brokenheartedness. He had been given the responsibility to affectively move the nation and to provide a balm to forlorn and angry black citizens, some of whom set aflame cities in riotous unrest around the United States. His task was difficult. He had to give tribute, provide comfort, and buoy the struggle for justice.

ON A HOT spring day, April 9, 1968, with the temperature soaring into the high 80s, King's funeral was held at the Ebenezer Baptist Church. Usually on Sundays, Ebenezer, a church founded by ex-slaves, normally overflowed with black members and visitors. However, for the first time in the church's history, members were forced to stand outside of their own sanctuary as the crowd of mostly white dignitaries occupied their seats for King's funeral. King's funeral plan also included a silent march from Ebenezer to the grounds of Morehouse College, where an open service would include all who wish to attend.

The five-mile march and the sweltering heat that day diminished the energies of the marchers and those who waited for the procession to arrive. It ran an hour late. The crowd was tired, and many suffered heat exhaustion as the huge entourage escorting King's mule-drawn coffin walked onto Morehouse's campus. When the King family arrived, shortly after the processional ended, the crowd turned a bit raucous and angry. According to Ralph Abernathy, Martin Luther King Sr., sensing the restlessness of the crowd, commanded Abernathy: "Get Mays up there, Ralph, so we can end it." Cutting out many other preachers who were expected to give addresses, Abernathy introduced Mays so the program would come to a close. The crowd could barely hear Mays as a result of a poor sound system; however, he delivered the most memorable tribute, other than King's own recorded version of the "Drum Major Instinct," given that long, hot day.[55]

Mays deployed all of the great rhetorical devices he had gleaned as a public speaker; he captured the moment, the deep sense of hurt and the outrage of the audience. He bellowed out to the hot and exhausted crowd how Martin Luther King Jr. had been purposeful and constructive with his life. He reminded them of their own duty to do the same:

> If we love Martin Luther King, Jr., and respect him, as this crowd surely testifies, let us see to it that he did not die in vain; let us see to it that we do not dishonor his name by trying to solve our problems through rioting in the streets. Violence was foreign to his nature. He warned that continued riots could produce a Fascist state. But let us see to it also that conditions that cause riots are promptly removed, as the President of the United States is trying to get us to do. Let black and white alike search their hearts; and if there be prejudice in our hearts, let us exterminate it and let us pray, as Martin Luther King, Jr., would if he could: *Father, forgive them for they know not what they do.* If we do this, Martin Luther King, Jr., will have died a redemptive death from which all mankind will benefit.[56]

His eulogy was brilliant. With his impassioned words, he prodded blacks to turn their collective grief and outrage into hope for the future.[57] The reality of the matter was that King was dead, and from that moment, the intellectual landscape that governed the civil rights movement, which Mays had powerfully influenced, would be changed. The theology that Mays articulated and used to help build an interracial religious coalition on behalf of civil rights died alongside of King on the balcony of the Lorraine Hotel. Rage and cynicism ran rampant among young black people toward the country where a person who advocated Christian love and constructive social policies could be assassinated. The coalition of faith fragmented.

In reality, even before King's assassination, rebellion and revolution were in the air. Nonfiction books authored by black men had a healthy and fashionable run between 1965 and 1970. Besides *The Autobiography of Malcolm X* and Fanon's *Wretched of the Earth*, there was Carmichael and Hamilton's *Black Power: A Politics of Liberation*, Harold Cruise's *The Crisis of the Negro Intellectual*, Eldridge Cleaver's *Soul on Ice*, and William Grier and Price Cobbs's *Black Rage*, to name just a few. Even Mays's good friend Jesse O. Thomas, the Urban League's southern regional field director, wrote his memoir titled *My Story in Black and White: The Autobiography of Jesse O. Thomas*, in 1967. Male authors such as these dominated the narrative about black life in this era.[58]

A crop of younger religious intellectuals and clergymen, under the umbrella of the National Committee of Black Church Men (NCBCM), also joined the published voices with their own viewpoints. For them, American Christianity needed to be theologically reframed to bring justice to the black community. Whether Mays liked it or not, Malcolm X's indictments against Christianity had struck a chord with them. The NCBCM's political and social call for Black Power pushed black Christians to consider the ways in which Protestant Christianity reinforced oppressive political practices and in so doing undermined the self-esteem of black Americans. The NCBCM contended that genuine Christian reconciliation required empowerment of the self. Reconciliation could only be achieved when black people claimed a new positive self-image as individuals and as a historical group. "As long as we are filled with hatred for ourselves," the NCBCM stated, "we will be unable to respect others." Echoing Mays's theology, it asserted: "Too often the Negro church has steered its members away from the reign of God in *this world* to a distorted and complacent view of *an otherworldly* conception of God's power."[59]

In 1969, no black religious intellectual seized this moment better than a young theologian by the name of James Cone, who taught at Union Theological Seminary. Cone created a tidal wave in academic theological circles with his stinging critique of American Christianity. In his 1969 book, *Black Theology and Black Power*, Cone argued that the purpose of black theology was to critique the historical abuse of black Americans by American Christianity. He also argued that the true Christians in North America were not white but black Americans who had endured and fought back against racism and oppression. He emphatically declared that God was on the side of the oppressed. This resonated with the idea Mays expressed in *The Negro's God* (see chapter 4) that the oppressed could not be free unless they were theological enabled to assert their freedom. Cone's analysis was more blunt. He explained that in order for white Christians to be reconciled with their faith, they must join the struggle to liberate oppressed people. In the case of North America, that meant joining the faith and political struggles of black Americans.[60] In this respect, Cone

Benjamin Mays delivering the Michigan State University commencement address, June 9, 1968. Courtesy of the Michigan State University Archives and Historical Collections, East Lansing, Michigan.

made explicit many of the ideas Mays had only inferred in the late 1920s through the 1950s.

Mays's religious idealism and prophetic criticism of Jim Crow were by the late 1960s passé to the exponents of Black Theology. The generational differences were telling. In Mays's estimation, it would be sinful and tragic if a person did not give his very best effort to change his dire social circumstances. In Cone's view, it was the dire circumstances themselves that were sinful and tragic because they overwhelmed the individual. Cone stressed that the church had to be the revolutionary agent in the effort to tear down those barriers of oppression that kept individuals mired in impoverished conditions. Mays would agree but would argue that individual agency was paramount to God's work on earth. As a result, individual human beings were historical actors in effecting social change. Although the new generation of black religious intellectuals had great respect for Mays, they did not think his critique of the church had gone far enough.

This new generation of black religious intellectuals, while building on Mays's critique of the Negro church, had moved away from his emphasis on the individual. In Atlanta, other religious intellectuals, most notably historian Vincent Harding, director of the Institute for the Black World (IBW) tried to build a cadre of activist-scholars to provide a careful study of the systemic issues confronting black America. Harding, however, appreciated Mays's legacy and wrote the introduction to *The Negro's God* when Athenaeum Press reissued it in 1969.[61]

Mays not only found challenges by new radical intellectuals, but he also saw a growing religious pluralism within black communities emerging that challenged black Protestantism. The Nation of Islam (NOI) became a formidable alternative to black Protestantism. The NOI developed in many urban areas, initially in the Great Lakes corridor from Detroit to Chicago, and from there spread out to the rest of the country. This was especially due to Malcolm X and the heavyweight boxer Muhammad Ali's ardent popularization of the NOI's theological message. Elijah Muhammad, the leader of the NOI, characterized Islam as the black man's true religion. He appealed to the black poor by describing whites as the devil. Malcolm X spread this message until 1964, when he left the NOI. Though Malcolm X did not live long enough to organize his own mosque and political movement, his charismatic appeals to black pride and self-determination resonated with many different sectors of the black community. Malcolm X's assassination in 1965, and the popularity of his autobiography, made his message about black pride even more romantic among some young people than when he was alive. Additionally, Muhammad Ali's courageous resistance to the draft during the Vietnam War heightened the NOI's stature among black Americans.

These new views—with an emphasis on politics, culture, and religiosity—struck against the heart of Mays's ethical beliefs. The promotion of the black community as the first order of religious faith left him in a bit of a quandary. Although he took pride in being part of an ethnic collective, like most in his generation, he upheld the individual as primary. He had not fully developed a theological or political language with which to express the collective ideology of black pride. His generation had not quite figured out how to promote both the individual and positive communal self-identity, self-interest, and political power apart from racial assimilation. The religious arguments he advocated had now been augmented.

But Mays, at age seventy-two, continued to have vigorous energy. He dedicated himself to writing and publishing the memoir. He felt it was necessary to complete his book while he was still in good health. As soon as he and Sadie settled into their new house off-campus, he organized himself to write his autobiography. He received a grant from the Ford Foundation so that he could hire student assistants who would visit South Carolina and Georgia state archives and records to compile as much sociological and historical detail as possible to supplement his recounting of his experiences in the states. Without question, he wanted to make sure that readers, long after he was dead, would not be misled about American history in his lifetime. His book would be supported by verifiable historical facts.

Mays also wanted to spend more time with his wife without the distractions of administering a college. Sadie's health had begun to decline in the early 1960s. Although they had sought the best medical care and made regular visits to the Mayo Clinic in Rochester, Minnesota, her health conditions worsened. Unfortunately, her treatments did not stave off Mrs. Mays's deteriorating medical condition. Taking care of her was now his chief priority. He hired personal assistants to help with her care while he continued his work. He nursed Sadie and tried his best to continue his intellectual agenda. In addition to researching and writing his memoir he was working on his collection of sermons titled *Disturbed about Man*, which was near publication.

While Mays's student assistants were gathering information in Georgia and South Carolina, gleaning significant details about black life throughout the South in the first half of the twentieth century, Mays was interviewing people of his generation who had grown up in the South. He drove to South Carolina to interview his eldest sister, Susie, then near the age of ninety, to get more details about his own family history.

To make sure his facts were historically accurate, Mays regularly corresponded with Dr. John Hope Franklin, a professor of history at the University of Chicago, who was by then the most prominent black historian in the American academy. Mays asked Franklin for a detailed commentary on Mays's interpretation of past events. Dr. Franklin, ever the great history professor, also advised Mays on stylistic matters and provided his own observations about black history.[62]

He also corresponded with one of his more beloved Morehouse students, Samuel DuBois Cook, and his wife, Sylvia. Cook had become one of the first black American professors hired by Duke University in the political science department. Mays regularly sent them chapters of his memoir for their review and comments over the course of 1968 and 1969. In fact, Cook had also been instrumental in Mays's receiving a Ford Foundation grant. While on leave from Duke University, Cook served as a Ford program officer in the late 1960s. In December of 1968, in one of her earliest responses to one of Mays's chapters, Sylvia Cook insightfully wrote that the work he had done throughout his life had served as a prelude for the work that Martin Luther King Jr. attempted to accomplish.[63]

By 1969, when Mays was a trustee at Morehouse student protests were taking place on college campuses across the country. And Morehouse was no exception. There would be no peaceful rapprochements between students and college administrators as there had been in the early 1960s when students consulted with Mays about their protest plans. In the spring of 1969, Morehouse students stormed into a trustees' meeting to demand that their proposal for black studies be acted upon. Although Mays had always advocated for student concerns, some of the students' indecorous behavior incensed him. He believed in the democratic process, and students making their claims through using physical coercion offended everything he held dear. He was unaware that many students who supported the lock-in protest were reluctant to hold Mays hostage. Though he was retired, students still widely respected and revered him. For Mays, the students' anger and rash actions made it all the more urgent that he complete his autobiography.[64]

Meanwhile, Sadie Mays's health declined more rapidly than Mays had anticipated, and she was placed in Atlanta's Happy Haven nursing home, a nursing home she had vigorously worked to build and transform on behalf of the aged, sick, and homeless.[65] Mays's writing, speaking engagements, and research slowed to a halt that summer, as he shuttled back and forth from his home to the nursing home, dutifully checking in with her and staying by her bedside. And as if 1969 had not been tumultuous enough, with Mays writing his memoir and still grieving over the death of King, Sadie Mays died in October, leaving him with more grief and sadness. For over forty-three years, they had been partners in the work of bolstering students and attempting to redress the social ills of the black community. She had supported him, challenged him, calmed his fears, read his work, and been his political sounding board.[66] Mays knew he would have been a lesser man without her. Her departure left an irreplaceable void in his heart. With condolences arriving from colleagues, former students, fellow Atlantans, and well-wishers all over the country and the world, Mays valiantly continued his life without her. Grief stricken, he returned to writing the autobiography.

Mays was driven to complete his memoir in order to address the chasm between his generation and what would have been his grandchildren's generation. In a letter to a representative of the Rockefeller Foundation, which provided him an additional grant to complete his memoir, he said he felt compelled to finish the project because he believed he was a witness to the black experience in twentieth-century America.[67] His story was a testimony to what spiritual hope and perseverance could do in any person's life. His individual journey, he knew, was the same long struggle for basic civic freedoms that all black Americans of his generation had endured. He declared that his experiences were the experiences of every black person born at the nadir of racial exclusion. His autobiographical remembrances fit into a long pattern among black intellectuals.[68]

In the preface to his earliest completed draft of *Born to Rebel* Mays wrote,

This volume may . . . help to bridge the wide gap in thinking and experience between my generation and the present generation and thus give
our youth a sense of history. Young people born just before and since
World War II, and certainly since 1954, do not have the faintest idea
what Negro-white relations were like in the South and in my native
South Carolina in the days of my youth. . . . Young black Americans
have made great contributions to improve human relations through sit-
ins, boycotts, and demonstrations which those of us who are older could
hardly have made in our time; and yet the present generation of young
people have built on foundations laid by their elders through "blood,
sweat and tears," and through the innocent death of millions of Negroes
who lived a long time ago.[69]

In a letter to one of his assistants, Robert Allen, a former Morehouse student and the author of *Black Awakening in Capitalist America*, published
in 1969, Mays noted that he was uncertain about whether to title his book
"Born to Rebel or The Black Experience."[70] He settled on *Born to Rebel*, which
Scribner's Press published in 1971. Like a sagacious grandfather, Mays recounted his past in the context of other black people's experiences, and he
illuminated the hardships blacks faced in the Jim Crow South. Throughout
his life he had used his autobiographical narrative in sermons, speeches, and
articles. With the publication of the book, he could permanently leave the
story he had frequently shared in bits and pieces. The book's aim was not
simply to look at the past but also to give wise counsel to the post–civil rights
generation.

His concluding chapter assessed the deeper historical meaning and impact
of Black Power in a pluralistic society. Mays wrote that, historically, black separatist strategies had been disappointing at best and delusional at worst. Contrary to the trendy rhetoric, he argued that there was no silver bullet to end the
complex problems of race or the social and economic situation that confronted
black Americans. He surmised that, whatever the future held, a combination of
structural governmental actions and black economic and philanthropic initiatives would be necessary to end the long-term effects of past racial discrimination. Mays acknowledged that advocates of Black Power had a point about
voting black representatives into political office. He had always believed that
without the vote, black people were virtually slaves. Moreover, like the black
studies advocates, he felt that black people should know the history of their
community as a matter pride. He was, after all, a child of parents who had

been born American slaves. However, Mays knew that knowledge of history or black studies alone could not reshape the contours of American society or end racism in the future.[71] What black people needed, he believed, was better education and skills in order to participate in a competitive society, as well genuine opportunities to do so. He opined that in the long-term, mainstream liberal efforts, not revolutionary ones, were more beneficial to black people in terms of gaining collective power through the vote, providing a sound education, and building institutions, such as Morehouse, for the future.

What is interesting about Mays's conclusions about Black Power in *Born to Rebel* is the absence of religion. After all, Mays had spent a better part of his life preparing clergymen for black churches. He had also spent much of his intellectual energy. One can only speculate that in Mays's haste to complete the book, he was not able to take up the challenge to address black theology. Nevertheless, Mays recognized and appreciated many of the claims of the new generation who were responding to their moment on the stage with the ideology of Black Power. He never shied away from the controversy surrounding Black Power or any of the other contentious issues of the times. His columns in both the *Courier* and the *Chicago Defender* were replete with his opinions about social matters of the day. He fully engaged his God-given minute, offering understanding, criticism, and concern about the fate of ordinary black people. With characteristic courage and intellectual honesty, Mays never departed from his Christian principles.

Mays recognized that his life story represented not only black people's political and social struggles but also the greater struggle of humanity in securing civil protections and human rights. More than anything else, he wanted readers of *Born to Rebel* to find hope and spiritual strength from his story. His intellectual pilgrimage began when he was a frightened child witnessing his father's personal humiliation and political terrorization. Building on a strong theological foundation, he found the courage and the will to resist the kinds of social conformity expected of him. The will to rebel against society's expectations had been nurtured in him from listening to his mother's prayers and believing in her God, an ethical God whom he encountered in the biblical narratives and in the lives of the politically oppressed black people who worshipped in a small Baptist church on a rural road in Greenwood County, South Carolina.

When *Born to Rebel* was published, Mays was hopeful that his rich life would inspire others to fight against despair and achieve great things. As for him, the long war continued, and he continued to grapple with the issues of politics, education, and impoverishment that occupied Atlanta throughout the 1970s.

Lord, the People Have Driven Me On

> We ought not to seek greatness; we ought to seek to serve and
> when we seek to serve we will bump into greatness along the way.
> —MAYS, *Quotable Quotes of Benjamin E. Mays*

When *Born to Rebel* was published, Mays was nearly seventy-seven. Though aged, he never relented in his struggle to achieve full democracy for black Americans. Segregation in American society was simply wrong religiously or otherwise. He had written journal articles, newspaper columns, and books urging both blacks and whites to rethink their understanding of Christianity in order to end white supremacy. He thoughtfully engaged with and challenged American society. Along with his black theological peers, he helped to reformulate American civil religious discourse to aid black freedom struggles.

"Benjamin Mays is one of those persons in America who understood long ago that racial prejudice and discrimination were problems of the human spirit," wrote Mays's friend theological ethicist George Kelsey in an unpublished paper. Kelsey observed in Mays's ideology that if answers were to be found for the problem of racism then the "human spirit must be taken into account." For Mays, Kelsey assessed, God, first and foremost, cared about the person, and it was up to the individual to freely accept or reject God's love. God's love held the possibility of heroic action for everyone. As a result of God's love, each person had the potential to achieve and serve in spite of difficult circumstances of life. Kelsey concluded, "If one should inquire as to what the fundamental ground of Christian moral decision in the thought of Benjamin Mays is, his search will lead to a faith that is trust. Faith is first, last, and always act. When it is not act, it is not alive and therefore is not."[1] As Kelsey critically reflected, Mays's emphasis on faith as action proved to be an intellectual joist in civil rights mobilization.

By the late 1960s, however, Mays's theological idealism seemed outdated to a new generation of black Americans activists who challenged the intellectual pieties of Christian theology that grounded his thinking. His viewpoint on racial injustice and exclusion did not speak to the level of resentment and discontent that young black Americans felt, particularly after the assassination of

Martin Luther King Jr.[2] He believed that the ends of religion and democratic politics were always human freedom and spiritual unity. Black religious intellectuals and their nonreligious counterparts parted company on whether notions of the spirit or love had anything to say in addressing political power structures. Religious thought as social critique was politely dismissed and became relegated to a handful of seminaries and divinity schools where strands of liberation theology—Latin American, Black, and Feminist—were being taught. How strange, because Mays argued consistently that religion and religiosity were crucial to shaping black political actions. He knew that black people found solace, hope, and joy in faith, church, and religious institutions. It was therefore paramount for him that all black intellectuals attempt to analyze and appreciate the significance of black religious faith. Yet, consistently, scholars and critics understate the religious dimension of black life and its influence on the civil rights struggle and black activism.[3]

In 1971, the writer Ishmael Reed reviewed *Born to Rebel* for the *New York Times Book Review*. Reed wittily observed that Mays's life "exemplifies a tradition of excellence, illustrated elsewhere by Ralph Ellison's 'Long Oklahoma Eye,' Satchel Paige's 'Hesitation Pitch,' the legendary black man who built a whole town with 5 million handmade bricks, and Marcus Garvey's tenacity." Reed continued, "In this book, Mays directs his message to a young generation of Americans. What he seems to be saying is, 'You're not the first to come along with black pride and a quest for dignity. My generation possessed all of these qualities and what is more we had it *worse*."[4] Reed pointed out that the generational differences that were publicly heralded in the news media were not as substantive as headlines screamed they were at the time.[5] Reed picked up on Mays's point that black life was more expansive than contemporary commentators would have one believe it was. He noted that *Born to Rebel* was a helpful reminder to the "younger generation that 'the black experience' is a galaxy and not the slave-pen many whites and blacks desire it be."

Overall, Reed was generous in his appraisal of *Born to Rebel*. The one matter he took critical exception to was Mays's reliance on classical references "to get his story across." He observed that Mays's "generation of scholars was firmly grounded in the Western tradition." Provocatively, he stated, "It seems that Mays' generation of Greek-speaking Phi Beta Kappas never questioned the reading list. They merely passed all the "tests" of Western scholarship and achieved 'degrees.' The younger generation in many ways has modified the reading list or in some cases thrown it out altogether and substituted its own; the new generation seems to have decided that self-determination begins with the head."[6] Mays likely would have disagreed. With the publication of *The Negro's Church* and *The Negro's God*, Mays was in fact modifying the predominately white academies' reading lists. He altered the "canon" by contributing literature that explored Protestant religious thought and institutions from a black perspective.

Perceptively, Reed understood that central to *Born to Rebel* was the idea of respectability. He implied that Mays's social ambition was to be generally accepted without question according to the standards of conventional American middle-class norms and behavior. He interpreted Mays's viewpoint about respectability rather narrowly. Mays's view was not a facile uplift ideology. It was religiously grounded in metaphysical claims about transcendence and faith. Mays's goal was never merely to be accepted into white America. What he insisted upon was a wholesale spiritual transformation of American society, a society in which all human beings were dignified as persons.[7] His understanding of respectability was never blind to the entrenchment of white American racial privilege and racism's global power. He was well aware of the structural dimensions of black struggle. This is why, in his estimation, it required faith and love to persevere and to keep oneself from getting lost in self-destructive hatred. True love required a clear-eyed analysis of the societal issues facing black Americans and a determined faith that social impediments could be overcome.

In 1950, Mays wrote an article for the *Pittsburgh Courier* under the rubric "The Negro in the Next 50 Years." He insightfully told readers how the first half of the twentieth century was a fight to achieve basic humanity "for Negroes." However, he thought that by 1975 all segregation would be abolished in all public places and, most notably, that "segregation in the house of God will be a thing of the past." He rightfully predicted that by the year 2000, black Americans would make their way into public office throughout the country, even in the Deep South, and they would be enrolled in public universities throughout the country. But he also recognized that "inferior public schools," which doggedly persisted in black communities, would reduce the number of blacks who were able to academically compete in a less segregated society. The lack of "opportunity to become more competent on the job and complete exclusion" meant that the percentage of highly qualified blacks would be smaller than the percentage of highly qualified whites. Mays predicted, "The damaging effect of slavery and segregation will flow into the whole of the next half century. . . . Thus the second half century will hold competition galore" for blacks. Therefore, he cautioned, blacks "must compete" with people who have had more social advantages.[8] He was prescient in his understanding of structural deficits that black American would face.

Nearly twenty years after his prediction, in 1969, Mays was elected to the Atlanta School Board. He was the board's first black president. Though a senior citizen, he remained energetic and fought steadfastly over eleven years to improve the educational attainment of the black children of Atlanta against the backdrop of white flight.[9] He believed in an old Calvinist adage that said learning was a way of instilling faith and hope. Leading the Atlanta School Board, however, challenged his belief.[10] In a democracy, he contended, reasonable people could disagree, but that through good leadership, compromise would be reached for "the good of the whole." It was disappointing to him that the issues at stake in the 1954 *Brown v. Board of Education* decision were not fully resolved by the mid-1970s. The racist attitudes and political actions surrounding school desegregation in Atlanta and elsewhere were deeply troublesome to him. It left him angry and somewhat disillusioned.[11] Mays, always a hopeful person, lost some confidence.[12] Black liberationist theologian James Cone's indictment of American society began to resonate with Mays more and more.[13] For Mays, America's failure to diligently work at racially integrating America's schools was a sign of the country's lack of spiritual commitment to its own principles of democracy.

There was another reason for his growing despondency. The civil rights movement's carefully crafted theological platform that tied Christianity to democracy and governance had been usurped following Martin Luther King Jr.'s successful political mobilization of black churches in the South. White southerners and politically conservative evangelicals began organizing using religious rhetoric to support their more conservative causes, too. By the mid-1970s, organizations such as Jerry Falwell's Moral Majority and later Pat Robertson's Christian Coalition began co-opting both the moral theological platform and the church-based mobilization strategy of the civil rights movement for their own political ends.[14] The evolving Christian Right soon formed a larger coalition of political conservatism that was intent on limiting the kind of political and cultural liberalism that the civil rights movement had inspired.[15]

This waning of political liberalism was also a part of the demise of Protestant mainline churches.[16] These churches were the institutional basis of Protestant liberal theology and ones in which Mays had cultivated as important allies in the civil rights movement. A new era of political conservatism, which evolved in the rising Sunbelt cities of the West and the South, slowly became dominant in both religious and public life. Nevertheless, civil right legislation enacted in the mid-1960s still had a moral claim on the nation's conscience. Even the most conservative preacher or politician could not deny the moral and historical basis for the enactment of legislation that ended racial segregation. The legal

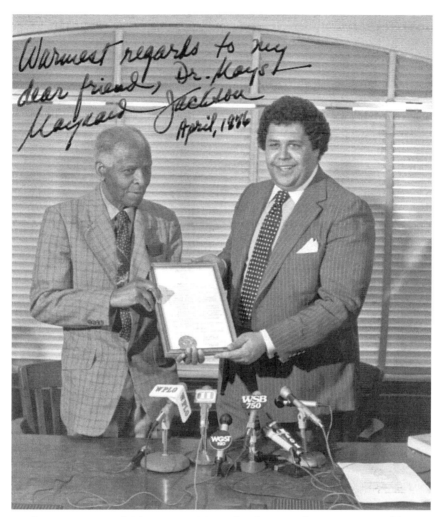

Warmest regards to my dear friend, Dr. Mays. *Maynard Jackson. April, 1976.*

Benjamin Mays and Atlanta mayor Maynard Jackson, April 1976. Courtesy of the Moorland-Spingarn Research Center, Howard University.

end of racial segregation allowed blacks around the country to vote for black candidates into all levels of government in record numbers. As a result, cities like Atlanta were politically transformed.

Throughout the 1970s Mays served as the pastor, wise elder, and senior consigliere to an emerging national black leadership and black Atlanta's newly elected politicians. Many of them were organizational leaders in the civil rights movement, including Whitney Young, Vernon Jordan, Andrew Young, and John Lewis, and notable Morehouse alums like Julian Bond, Maynard Jackson, and Lonnie King.[17] Aspiring civic and political leaders sought

Benjamin Mays and President Jimmy Carter, 1980. Courtesy of the Moorland-Spingarn Research Center, Howard University.

out Mays's counsel and his endorsements. His national standing gave him influence, which he tried to use discretely. In addition to black politicians, Mays would also consult with post–civil rights white southern politicians, most notably Jimmy Carter, who was elected governor of Georgia in 1971. In his bid for the 1976 Democratic presidential nomination, Carter, with Mays's endorsement, gained the support of black politicians and voters around the country. Some point to Mays's endorsement of Carter as a major factor in his election as president in 1976.

Although politicians sought to curry favor with Mays, his first priority continued to be black students of all ages. He publicly worried about the spiritual and academic well being of black children as he observed the growing disparate socioeconomic conditions in black communities. And nothing was more vexing to Mays than two tragic events the occurred in the late 1970s. The first was the infamous Jonestown massacre, in 1978, where over nine hundred people, mostly black Americans, died in a cult suicide and/or murder in Guyana. The second was a series of child murders that rocked Atlanta's black community over a two-year period. From the summer of 1979 to the spring of 1981, roughly thirty children and young adults were found near one of Atlanta's poorest black communities. These events, along with retrenchment on desegregation, left him disheartened. He nevertheless summoned up the courage to speak to the crises of his final years with prophetic urgency.

In a speech titled "Meeting Tomorrow's Challenges Today with Academic, Moral and Spiritual Preparation," Mays tried to put what he saw happening to black children in perspective. Ironically, this speech was given at the time of Jimmy Carter's presidency and the slow expansion of the black middle class. "People can be academically competent and yet completely lacking in morality and spiritual preparation," he observed. Referring to a handful of infamous historical figures—Herod the Great, Nero, Napoleon, and Hitler—he cautioned his audience to remember, "These were well-trained men. But they had no morality, no spirituality." Academic preparation alone was not enough. Black people, he argued, "must bring morality and spirituality to America. I doubt if the White community can." (Mays did not explain how students were to be spiritually and academically prepared for leadership. Perhaps the pressing plight of blacks in the urban core had overwhelmed his thoughts.) Noting that the level of federal, state, and local government aid to the poor, especially the black urban poor, was dropping, he urged black leaders to challenge this trend. His speech foreshadowed a more conservative turn in American politics away from governmental solutions to inequality. With exasperation, he proclaimed: "Why should White people care if in the next century or two the Black race is completely blotted out because of their affliction? The race problem could be resolved without dropping bombs. I am convinced if this were the White race in this predicament, the President of United States would be working on it, all Congress would be concerned, all business people in the United States would be spending their monies to alleviate the situation. Budgets balanced or not, Congress would shell out of the money."[18] "Unless Black people in the United States arouse everybody in this country to the plight we are in," he concluded, "nobody else will. . . . This is our mission. . . . *It is urgent.*" Black Americans had to be the guardians of democracy and faithful to their Christianity if justice were to be equitably served in America.

During his last decade of life, people continued to seek him out for counsel and the honors continued to roll in. Universities awarded him honorary degrees, and civil rights and religious organizations all honored him. Even Mays's home state of South Carolina would pay great tribute to him by placing his portrait in the statehouse. His tiny home in Epworth, South Carolina, would also become a designated state historic landmark.[19] Mays did not worry about the banquets, the honorary degrees, or the plaques. Though elderly, Mays continued to think about what contribution he could make to society. In 1975, in an issue of the Howard University School of Religion's *Journal of Religious*

Thought was dedicated to his career, Mays wrote the closing comments. He noted that he was gratified by his friends' appreciation. Their appreciation, he wrote, was "challenging because from my childhood years the people have driven me on. . . . To me praise, recognition and honor have never been things to bask in, to sit on, to decorate walls and brag about." They always challenged and motivated Mays to do more, even at eighty.[20]

In 1981, having resigned his position on the Atlanta School Board, he authored a shorter version of *Born to Rebel* for students, which he aptly titled, *Lord, the People Have Driven Me On*. He wanted students to know of the faith and hope that shaped his life. Even though he was dismayed by the failure of government to fully enforce the *Brown* decision and eradicate poverty, he continued to have faith that God had placed him on earth for the world's betterment. As his health declined and his memory became eroded by dementia, Mays remained defiant about the matters he believed in, even giving a stirring address to the National Baptist Convention USA from his wheelchair![21]

On March 28, 1984 Mays died in Atlanta at the age of eighty-nine.[22] He bequeathed a modest sum to Morehouse College.[23] He also left a small inheritance for his nieces and nephews and their descendents. More enduring than the monetary and material gifts he left to his family and Morehouse College was the rich legacy that was organic to the religious concerns and political struggles of black Americans. Mays's career as a churchman was formative in ideologically shaping the southern civil rights movement.[24] His impact as an educator and a theologian can still be felt in institutes of higher education and theological institutions all over the United States.[25] Martin Luther King's referring to Mays as his "spiritual and intellectual father" was not simply hyperbole; Mays was one of the black religious intellectual giants that laid the foundation for King's path. Additionally, Mays's compelling philosophy that high achievement in formal education was necessary for both the spiritual enrichment and political empowerment of oppressed people is one that should never be forgotten. Mays maintained an unwavering faith in the potential of black Americans as individuals and as citizens of the United States. Sociologist Hylan Lewis, a fellow student of Mays's at the University of Chicago in the 1930s, off-handedly remarked in an interview that Mays "wrote to the servants."[26] Indeed, Mays did write and preach to "the servants." It was their struggles, their religious faith, and their rich possibilities that inspired him. Conversely, wherever he traveled and spoke, he inspired all people to reach for greatness within themselves.

It was the totality of Mays's experiences from his rootedness in the black Baptist church, his academic training, his national and international leadership in the ecumenical church, and his leadership as the president of Morehouse

College that gave him a unique way of connecting the dots of theology, social justice, and the struggle for civil and human rights. He was not the first or the only person to point out that Christian faith was an integral force for social change in the United States, but as one of America's leading churchman of his era, Mays was able to preach his unique brand of black prophetic theology not only from the pulpit but also in the halls of the academy and in the corridors of power to call for justice and spiritual renewal.

Over twenty-five hundred people from all over the country gathered on Morehouse's campus to attend Benjamin Elijah Mays's funeral. They came to remember a man whose parents were born in American slavery and who had made herculean strides to attain a formal education and become a national leader. But even more so, they came to honor a humble man of integrity, a leader who's religious and intellectual honesty was inspiring. The crowd that jammed the campus chapel came to pay homage to a man who had remained faithful to the deepest concerns of his students and the highest aspirations of black people throughout the United States. He had been an intellectual and spiritual mentor to black America's hopes. He accomplished this by rebelling against the forces of spiritual and political segregation in his own life and by challenging his students and young people everywhere to rebel against the forces of bigotry, ignorance, and poverty in their own lives. In his eulogy, Samuel DuBois Cook, Mays's former student and friend observed,

> Dr. Mays was born free. He lived free. He died free. Always coura-geous, he was a prophet to the core of his being—always emphasizing the creative tension between the "is" and the "ought," promise and fulfillment, the Kingdom of man and the Kingdom of God. He never forgot the prophetic responsibility to speak "truth to power." He was always his own man, always a man of great moral courage, rebellion, and affirmation. Fierce independence and individualism, nobility, and supreme integrity were hallmarks of his great life. "Never sell your soul" was a central theme and imperative of his teachings and life. His soul was never for sale to anybody at any time for any price. In a world of constant pressures and counter-pressures, he had supreme integrity, character, and incorruptibility.[27]

The *New York Times* seconded Cook's assessment in a small opinion piece titled "Educator of the Spirit": "Less visible but just as important to the civil rights movement as any political operative were the leaders who offered inspiration and education. Dr. Benjamin E. Mays . . . was one of the best of these. . . . He struggled to integrate all-white colleges but also championed predominately black schools like Morehouse College in Atlanta. There for 27 years, he inspired a new generation. . . . Teacher and preacher: It was a noble and powerful combination."[28]

Mays the democratic activist, the religious intellectual, the eloquent preacher, the educator, and the student who always strove to be at the top of his class had kept faith in his ethical God and remained steadfast in his solidarity with black America and the struggles of the globally disfranchised. He never forgot that he had once been an American untouchable. And by keeping faith, he gave those who followed in his footsteps a shining example of what principled, democratic, and religious leadership might look like in a world struggling to surmount avarice, ethnic hatreds, unreasoned prejudices, terrorism, and the destructive violence of war. In a world of darkness, his light continues to shine.

Notes

ABBREVIATIONS

ADW	*Atlanta Daily World*
BEMP	Benjamin Elijah Mays Papers, Manuscript Department, Moorland-Spingarn Research Center, Howard University, Washington, D.C.
CD	*Chicago Defender*
CDS	University of Chicago Divinity School, Department of Special Collections, Chicago, Illinois
GKP	George Kelsey Papers, Drew University Archives, Madison, N.J.
JRMP	John R. Mott Papers, Yale University Divinity School Library Special Collections, New Haven, Conn.
NAACPP	National Association for the Advancement of Colored People Papers, Library of Congress, Washington, D.C.
NCC	National Council of the Churches of Christ in the United States of America–Division of Home Missions Records, Presbyterian Historical Society, Philadelphia, Pa.
News	*The News* (Howard University School of Religion)
NULP	National Urban League Papers, Library of Congress, Washington, D.C.
PC	*Pittsburgh Courier*
PCP	Pullman Company Papers, Newberry Library, Chicago, Ill.
RFAC	Rockefeller Foundation Archive Center, Sleepy Hollow, N.Y.
YDS	Yale University Divinity School Library, Special Collections, New Haven, Conn.
YMCAA	Kautz Family YMCA Archives, University of Minnesota Libraries, Minneapolis, Minn.

INTRODUCTION

1. Martin Luther King Jr., "Statement Regarding the Retirement of Benjamin E. Mays," King Center Archives, Atlanta, Ga., 1967, 1; Linda Williams, "Molding Men: At Morehouse College, Middle-Class Blacks Are Taught to Lead," *Wall Street Journal*, May 5, 1987, 1, 25; Frank J. Prial, "Benjamin Mays, Educator, Dies; Served as Inspiration to Dr. King," *New York Times*, March 29, 1984, D.23; Flip Schulke's photograph of Mays can be found in *Time* magazine, April 19, 1968, in the article titled "King's Last March," 18.

2. Bruce Kuklick, *Churchmen and Philosophers: From Jonathan Edwards to John Dewey* (New Haven, Conn.: Yale University Press, 1985). White male churchmen in the American academy of the eighteenth and nineteenth centuries dominate Kuklick's study.

He traces them from their foundational base in Protestant theology at the end of the nineteenth century to Dewey's social science pragmatism. The argument can be made that Mays developed his idea of the churchman from what George McKenna describes in *The Puritan Origins of Patriotism* (New Haven, Conn.: Yale University Press, 2007) as a Puritan model. Unfortunately, McKenna's splendid study omits African Americans' religious views as being a part of the Puritan tradition. Mays's theological thinking was rooted in the activism of the Second Great Awakening of the nineteenth century. He, and other churchmen like him, gave a decidedly new twist to the Puritan motif that McKenna discusses.

3. Lerone Bennett Jr., "The Last of the Great Schoolmasters," *Ebony* 32 (December 1977): 74–79.

4. Cornel West, *Prophesy Deliverance!: An Afro-American Revolutionary Christianity* (Philadelphia: Westminster Press, 1982).

5. Paul Tillich, *The Protestant Era* (Chicago: University of Chicago Press, 1948), 230. I am very grateful for the article by James Melvin Washington, "Jesse Jackson and the Symbolic Politics of Black Christendom," *ANNALS of the American Academy of Political and Social Science* 480 (1) (July 1985): 90–91, for bringing Tillich's theological insight to my attention.

6. I am indebted to Lawrence Levine's observation that "religion is more than institution, and because Protestant churches failed to protect the slave's inner being from the incursions of the slave system, it does not follow that the spiritual message of Protestantism failed them as well. Certainly the slaves perceived the distinction. Referring to the white patrols which frequently and brutally interfered with the religious services of the slaves on his plantation, West Turner exclaimed: "Dey law us out of church, but they couldn't law 'way Christ" (*Black Culture and Black Consciousness: Afro-American Folk Thought from Slavery to Freedom* [New York: Oxford University Press, 1977], 54).

7. David L. Chappell, *Stone of Hope: Prophetic Religion and the Death of Jim Crow* (Chapel Hill: University of North Carolina Press, 2004), 102.

8. Joseph Crespino, *In Search of Another Country: Mississippi and the Conservative Counterrevolution* (Princeton, N.J.: Princeton University Press, 2007), 12.

9. Dwight Billings, "Religion as Opposition: A Gramscian Analysis," *American Journal of Sociology* 96 (1) (1990): 6–7.

10. Benjamin Mays, "A Negro Educator Gives His Views," *Christian Science Monitor*, January 19, 1957, 22.

11. These volumes on the religious dimension of the civil rights movement are indispensable. The richness of this literature began with Robert Wiesbrot's study *On Father Divine and the Struggle for Racial Equality* (Urbana: University of Illinois Press, 1983), which was followed up by Jill Watt's book *God, Harlem U.S.A.: The Father Divine Story* (Berkeley: University of California Press, 1992) on the same subject. Ralph Luker's *The Social Gospel in Black and White: American Racial Reform, 1885–1912* (Chapel Hill: University of North Carolina Press, 1992) is indispensable in this discussion. Other rich studies are Judith Weisenfeld, *Hollywood Be Thy Name: African American Religion in American Film, 1929–1949* (Berkeley: University of California Press, 2007), and, most

recently, Wallace Best, *Passionately Human, No Less Divine: Religion and Culture in Black Chicago*, 1915–1952 (Princeton, N.J.: Princeton University Press, 2005); Cynthia Taylor, *A. Philip Randolph: The Religious Journey of An African American Labor Leader* (New York: New York University Press, 2006); and Edward Blum's two volumes, *W. E. B. Du Bois: American Prophet* (Philadelphia: University of Pennsylvania Press, 2007) and *Reforging the White Republic: Race, Religion, and American Nationalism, 1865–1898* (Baton Rouge: Louisiana State University Press, 2005), as well as Paul Harvey's *Redeeming the South: Religious Cultures and Racial Identities among Southern Baptists, 1865–1925* (Chapel Hill: University of North Carolina Press, 1992) and *Freedom's Coming: Religious Culture and the Shaping of the South from the Civil War through the Civil Rights Era* (Chapel Hill: University of North Carolina Press, 2005).

12. This study of Mays owes a debt to several fine historians and four important works. Paul Harvey, in *Freedom's Coming*, explains that "theological racism" was at the heart of the struggle between blacks and whites throughout the American South. He defines theological racism as "the conscious use of religious doctrine and practice to create and enforce social hierarchies and privileged southerners of European descent, who were legally classified and socially privileged as white, while degrading southerners of African descent, who were legally categorized and socially stigmatized as black" (2). Harvey notes that this system was deeply entrenched but contested by multiple readings of the Bible. He concludes, "In the twentieth century, this theology of race was radically overturned in part through a re-imagination of the same Christian thought that was part of its creation. By the 1960s, segregationists defended Jim Crow more on emotional ('our way of life'), practical ('tradition'), and constitutional ('states rights') than theological grounds. In doing so, they lost the battle to spiritually inspired activists who deconstructed Jim Crow" (2). I argue in this book that no one was more important to the task of "spiritually" deconstructing Jim Crow than Benjamin Mays. Mays was at the top of a most distinguished class of religious radicals, "such as Howard 'Buck' Kester, Myles Horton, Modjeska Simkins, Ella Baker, Gordon Blaine Hancock, Lillian Smith, Nelle Morton, Charles Jones, Virginia Durr, Glenn Smiley, Septima Clark, and Jo Ann Gibson Robinson," to name only a few (49). This study explores the linkages between the civil rights movement as a movement for democratic social change and its religious dimensions by putting a black religious intellectual more fully into the historical record. We should remember, as historian Dennis Dickerson has so cogently reminded students of American civil rights history, that religiously grounded intellectuals like Mays helped shape the civil rights movement ideologically long before Martin Luther King Jr. arrived on the scene.

Mays was also a part of a generation of American liberal theologians who spoke to the wider American public, as historian Gary Dorrien has shown in his histories of modern theology in the United States, most especially *The Making of American Liberal Theology: Idealism, Realism, and Modernity*, 1900–1950 (Louisville, Ky.: Westminster John Knox Press, 2003). This generation of theologians, though modernist in orientation, maintained ties to American Protestant denominations as worship leaders, preachers, and public intellectuals. Mays's peers included Harry Emerson Fosdick, the Niebuhr brothers, and Paul Tillich. But Mays, living under legal and cultural segregation in the American South, could speak only to issues primarily concerning the conditions of black Americans. Mays presented his theological criticisms in whatever forum he was allowed to speak or write. Mays urged both black and white Americans to resist the rule of white supremacy in the United States and throughout the world. He was firmly convinced that his brand of theology, derived from the human experiences of black America, was important not only to Americans but also to the people of the world, especially in the emerging democracies in Asia and Africa. In this regard, Dorrien brands Mays as a public theologian because much of his work involved achieving social justice within the bounds of Protestant theology. Unlike his white peers, Mays did not receive as much scholarly attention inside academic seminaries and in the white-dominated mass media, but Dorrien recognizes his theological writings and sermons as having had far more currency than is widely appreciated.

By placing Mays's public theology back into the historical picture, we get a broader perspective of how the civil rights movement and other social struggles were ideologically actualized. It is unfortunate that many fine studies on the American civil rights movement that consider religion, and especially as it relates to the movement in the late 1950s through the 1960s, do so by only looking at Martin Luther King Jr., and they curiously associate King only with the legendary, if not overrated, neoorthodox theologian Reinhold Niebuhr without ever acknowledging that King was introduced to Niebuhr through a mediating lens of black religious thinkers. A side effect is that many King scholars have not looked for sources emanating out of black religious institutions to support their narratives because they have not dug deep enough into the written record of black religious thought. Therefore, readers of American history are often left with a prevailing narrative that Reinhold Niebuhr's thought was central to Martin Luther King Jr.'s analysis of American theology and American racism. Unfortunately, this linear narrative fits too neatly into an already existing paradigm of anti-intellectualism that scholars unwittingly employ to describe the activism that black Christians used in redressing larger social inequities. In this regard, Niebuhr is given too much credit and black religious thinkers like Mays have been given too little credit.

The third book to which this study owes a very big debt is Barbara Dianne Savage's *Your Spirit Walk Beside Us: The Politics of Black Religion* (Cambridge, Mass.: Harvard University Press, 2008). Savage places Mays in a fuller context of black intellectual thought in her discussion of the role of "the Negro Church" in the civil rights struggle. Her study puts Mays back into a larger context of black thought with many of his contemporaries—Mary Macleod Bethune, W. E. B. DuBois, E. Franklin Frazier, and Nannie Burroughs, to name only a few—regarding what role black religiosity and black Protantism played in shaping black communities in their democratic struggle. Savage underscores what became apparent to me as I culled through Mays's writings about black religious faith, black Protantism, and the struggle for civil rights, which was that more was expected of "the Negro's Church" and its clerics than any one organization or group of leaders could bear. Religious formulations—moral suasion and prophetic jeremiads—did motivate people to be socially engaged in changing exclusive legal structures, but religion by itself was inadequate to address larger endemic problems in the society as a whole.

The fourth book that informs this biography is Curtis J. Evans's *The Burden of Black Religion* (New York: Oxford University Press, 2008). The significance of Evans is its important intervention on how religion has been used as a marker of blackness in American culture. "Black religion," he writes,

> became the chief bearer of meaning and status for the nature and place of blacks in America because of questions raised by the early conversion of Slaves to Christianity.... 'Black Religion,' whether conceptualized variously by whites and blacks as an amorphous spirituality, primitive religion, emotionalism, or actual black churches under the rubric of 'the Negro Church,' groaned under the burden of a multiplicity of interpreters' demands ranging from uplift of the race to bringing an ambiguous quality of 'spiritual softness' to a materialistic and racist white culture. (4–5)

CHAPTER ONE

1. Benjamin E. Mays, *Born to Rebel: An Autobiography* (New York: Scribner, [1971]; reprint, with a revised foreword by Orville Vernon Burton (Athens: University of Georgia Press, 2003), 1. For more on the Phoenix riot from another African American, see Raymond Gavins, *The Perils and Prospects of Southern Black Leadership: Gordon Blaine Hancock, 1884–1970* (Durham, N.C.: Duke University Press, 1977), 6–7.

2. Mays's birth year is debatable. Census records, he says, record him as being born in 1894. His parents had informed him that he was born in 1895. It was fairly typical among rural families where children were born at home to have disputable dates of birth. I have accepted Mays's account that the census records corrected the year he was born.

3. On Benjamin Tillman, see Stephen Kantrowitz, *Ben Tillman and the Reconstruction of White Supremacy* (Chapel Hill: University of North Carolina Press, 2000); and Randolph Werner, "'New South' Carolina: Ben Tillman and the Rise of Bourgeois Politics, 1880–1893," in *Developing Dixie: Modernization in a Traditional Society*, ed. Winfred B. Moore Jr., Joseph F. Tripp, and Lyon G. Tyler Jr. (Westport, Conn.: Greenwood Press, 1988), chap. 10.

4. Moore, Tripp, and Tyler, eds., *Developing Dixie*, app. A, 323–48; also see Michael Perman, *Struggle for Mastery: Disfranchisement in the South, 1888–1908* (Chapel Hill: University of North Carolina Press, 2001), 94–95.

5. See H. Leon Prather Sr., "The Origins of the Phoenix Racial Massacre of 1898," in Moore, Tripp, and Tyler, eds., *Developing Dixie*, chap. 5; and James Hoyt, *The Phoenix Riot, November 8, 1898* (Greenwood, S.C.: n.p., 1938).

6. On the Tolbert family, see Tom Henderson Wells, "The Phoenix Election Riot," *Phylon* 31 (1) (1970): 58–69.

7. Benjamin Mays, "My View: Mob Rule," *PC*, August 31, 1946.

8. Prather, "Origins of the Phoenix Racial Massacre of 1898," 68. For another read on the net effects of Jim Crow, see William H. Chafe, Raymond Gavins, and Robert Korstad, *Remembering Jim Crow: African Americans Tell about Life in the Segregated South* (New York: New Press, 2001).

9. For the level of political dissemblance in South Carolina, see Orville Vernon Burton, foreword to Mays, *Born to Rebel*, xvii–xix.

10. On the Lost Cause and religion, see W. Scott Poole, *Never Surrender: Confederate Memory and Conservatism in the South Carolina Upcountry* (Athens: University of Georgia Press, 2004); Charles Reagan Wilson, *Baptized in Blood: The Religion of the Lost Cause, 1865–1920* (Athens: University of Georgia Press, 1980); and Gaines M. Foster, *Ghosts of the Confederacy: Defeat, the Lost Cause and the Emergence of the New South* (New York: Oxford University Press, 1987). For a more contemporary take on the Lost Cause, see Tony Horowitz, *Confederate in the Attic: Dispatches from the Unfinished Civil War* (New York: Pantheon Books, 1998).

11. James Allen et al., *Without Sanctuary: Lynching Photography in America* (Santa Fe, N.M.: Twin Palms, 2000); Phillip Dray, *At the Hands of Persons Unknown: The Lynching of Black America* (New York: Random House, 2002). On lynching as religious ritual, see Orlando Patterson, *Rituals of Blood: Consequences of Slavery in Two American Centuries* (New York: Basic Civitas Books, 1999); and Donald G. Mathews, "Lynching Is Part of the Religion of Our People: Faith in the Christian South," in *Religion in the American South*, ed. Beth Barton Schweiger and Donald G. Mathews (Chapel Hill: University of North Carolina Press, 2004), 153–94.

12. David W. Blight, *Race and Reunion: The Civil War in American Memory* (Cambridge, Mass.: Harvard University Press, 2001).

13. Rayford Logan, *The Betrayal of the Negro: From Rutherford B. Hayes to Woodrow Wilson* (New York: Collier, 1965).

14. Mays, *Born to Rebel*, 10.

15. Albert Raboteau, *Slave Religion: The "Invisible Institution" in the Antebellum South* (New York: Oxford University Press, 1978), chap. 4.

16. Steven Hahn, *A Nation under Our Feet: Black Political Struggles in the Rural South from Slavery to the Great Migration* (Cambridge, Mass.: Harvard University Press, 2003), 230.

17. Ibid., 232.

18. Orville Vernon Burton, *In My Father's House Are Many Mansions: Family and Community in Edgefield, South Carolina* (Chapel Hill: University of North Carolina Press, 1985), 21–28, 230–50.

19. Benjamin Mays, "I Have Been a Baptist All My Life," in James S. Childers, *A Way Home: The Baptists Tell Their Story* (Atlanta: Tupper and Love, 1964), 165.

20. George Brown Tindall, *South Carolina Negroes, 1877–1900* (Baton Rouge: Louisiana State University Press, 1966), 187.

21. I. A. Newby, *Black South Carolinians: A History of Blacks in South Carolina from 1895 to 1968* (Columbia, S.C.: University of South Carolina Press, 1973).

22. Mays, *Born to Rebel*, 13.

23. Arthur F. Raper and Ira De A. Reid, *Sharecroppers All* (Chapel Hill: University of North Carolina Press, 1941), 22–25.

24. Raboteau, *Slave Religion*, 177–78.

25. Mays, "Why I Believe There Is a God," *Ebony*, December 1961, 3; Mays, *Born to Rebel*, 10.

26. The literature on South Carolina African American life, and especially in the South Carolina low country, is voluminous. See, for example, Daniel C. Littlefield, *Rice and Slaves: Ethnicity and the Slave Trade in Colonial South Carolina* (Baton Rouge: Louisiana State University Press, 1981); Charles Joyner, *Down by the Riverside: A South Carolina Slave Community* (Urbana: University of Illinois Press, 1984); and Peter H. Wood, *Black Majority: Negroes in Colonial South Carolina from 1670 through the Stono Rebellion* (New York: Knopf, 1974).

27. See, for example, Mechal Sobel, *The World They Made Together: Black and White in Eighteenth Century Virginia* (Princeton: Princeton University Press, 1988).

28. Sterling Stuckey, *Nationalist Theory and the Foundation of Black America* (New York: Oxford University Press, 1987).

29. Mechal Sobel, *Trabelin' On: The Slave Journey to an Afro-Baptist Faith* (Princeton, N.J.: Princeton University Press, 1979).

30. Ibid., 235–36.

31. Historian Wilson Jeremiah Moses cautions scholars about reading too much of the African past in North American black life and religion. He is absolutely correct. However, in certain areas of South Carolina, coastal Georgia, and the Gulf Coast, it has been sufficiently documented that the cultural retentions from West and West Central Africa were evident. Those patterns and affinities, as Moses and many others have shown, were employed to make life in the Americas more bearable. Mays's formative religious experience was replete with patterns from what the historian Eugene Genovese provocatively called "the world the slaves made." See Wilson Jeremiah Moses, *Black Messiahs and Uncle Toms: Social and Literary Manipulations of a Religious Myth* (University Park, Pa.: Pennsylvania State University Press, 1982), chap. 2.

32. Mays, "I Have Been a Baptist All My life," 165–66.

33. On being called "Bubba," see Mays's last interview, in Rex Barnett's video recording *Benjamin E. Mays* (New York: Carousel Film & Video, c 1992).

34. On black women's religiosity, see Cheryl Townsend Gilkes, "The Politics of 'Silence': Dual-Sex Political Systems and Women's Traditions of Conflict in African-American Religion," in *African American Christianity: Essays in History*, ed. Paul Johnson (Berkley: University of California Press, 1994); Cheryl Townsend Gilkes, *If It Wasn't for the Women: Black Women's Experience and Womanist Culture in Church and Community* (Maryknoll, N.Y.: Orbis Books, 2001); and Marla F. Frederick, *Between Sundays: Black Women and Everyday Struggles of Faith* (Berkeley: University of California Press, 2003).

35. Gilkes, *If It Wasn't for the Women*, 35.

36. On black preaching, see Gerald L. Davis, *I Got the World in Me and I Can Sing It, You Know: A Study of the Performed African-American Sermon* (Philadelphia: University of Pennsylvania Press, 1985); Henry L. Mitchell, *Black Preaching: The Recovery of a Powerful Art* (Nashville, Tenn.: Abingdon Press, 1990); William H. Pipes, *Say Amen, Brother! Old-Time Negro Preaching: A Study in Frustration* (Westport, Conn.: Negro Universities Press, 1951); and Albert Raboteau, "The Chanted Sermon," chap. 7 in *A Fire in the Bones: Reflections on African Religious History* (Boston: Beacon Press, 1995).

37. Mays, *Born to Rebel*, 14–16; Lawrence Levine, *Black Culture and Black Conscious-ness: Afro-American Folk Thought from Slavery to Freedom* (New York: Oxford Univer-sity Press, 1977), 166–72; Gayraud S. Wilmore, *Black Religion and Black Radicalism: An Interpretation of the Religious History of Afro-American People*, 2nd ed. (Maryknoll, N.Y.: Orbis Books, 1983), 143–45.

38. Reginald F. Hildebrand, *Times Were Strange and Stirring: Methodist Preachers and the Crisis of Emancipation* (Durham, N.C.: Duke University Press, 1995); Hahn, *Nation under Our Feet*, 232–34.

39. "Mays Writing Project Interview with Susie Glenn November 24, 1967," BEMP.

40. Mays, *Born to Rebel*, 16.

41. Ibid.

42. Paul Harvey, *Freedom's Coming: Religious Culture and the Shaping of the South from the Civil War through the Civil Rights Era* (Chapel Hill: University of North Carolina Press, 2005), 62.

43. Hahn, *Nation under Our Feet*, 451–52.

44. Raboteau, *Slave Religion*, 238.

45. Mays, "I Have Been a Baptist All My Life," 167.

46. Mays, *Born to Rebel*, 2.

47. Ibid., 14.

48. Raboteau, "Chanted Sermon," 146.

49. Mays, *Born to Rebel*, 15.

50. Mays, First draft autobiography, installment 2, Box 42, p. 258, BEMP.

51. Mays, *Born to Rebel*, 14.

52. Ibid., 16–17.

53. Ibid., 20.

54. Sally G. McMillen, *To Raise Up the South: Sunday Schools in Black and White Churches*, 1865–1915 (Baton Rouge: Louisiana State University Press, 2001), 169–71.

55. Eugene Genovese, *Roll, Jordan, Roll: The World the Slaves Made* (New York: Pantheon Books, 1974), 283.

56. Mays, *Born to Rebel*, 20.

57. Ibid., 20.

58. Ibid., 5.

59. Ibid., 13.

60. Ibid., 5.

61. Lacy K. Ford, "Rednecks and Merchants: Economic Development and Social Ten-sions in the South Carolina Upcountry, 1865–1900," *Journal of American History* 71 (2): 294–318; Ronald L. F. Davis, *Good and Faithful Labor: From Slavery to Sharecropping in the Natchez District*, 1860–1890 (Westport, Conn.: Greenwood Press, 1982), 12–16.

62. Tindall, *South Carolina Negroes*, 115–19.

63. See, for example, Orville Vernon Burton "The Rise and Fall of Afro-American Town Life," in *Toward a New South?*, ed. Orville Vernon Burton and Robert McMath Jr. (Westport, Conn.: Greenwood Press, 1982).

64. Mays, *Born to Rebel*, 9–10.

65. "Outline for Autobiography, Trial Run No. 2 Born to Rebel," Benjamin Mays to John Hope Franklin, January 18, 1968, Installation 1, Box 39, F. John Hope Franklin, BEMP.

66. On men's alcohol abuse, see Burton, *In My Father's House*, 115, 244; W. Scott Poole, *Never Surrender: Confederate Memory and Conservatism in the South Carolina Upcountry* (Athens: University of Georgia Press, 2004), 42; and Ted Ownby, *Subduing Satan: Religion, Recreation, and Manhood in the Rural South,* 1865–1920 (Chapel Hill: University of North Carolina Press, 1990), 11.

67. Mays, *Born to Rebel*, 20.

68. For another example of a difficult father-son relationship in the cotton fields note the quarrelsome relationship Neb Cobb, aka Nate Shaw, had with his father in Theodore Rosengarten's *All God's Dangers: The Life of Nate Shaw* (New York: Knopf, 1974).

69. On patriarchy, see Burton, *In My Father's House*.

70. Ibid.

71. Mays, *Born to Rebel*, 3–4; Carrie M. Dumas, *Benjamin Elijah Mays: A Pictorial Life and Times* (Macon, Ga.: Mercer University Press, 2006), 102; U.S. Census Bureau, *Fourteenth Census of the United States:* 1920, Population Schedule, Greenwood County Enumeration District 67, 6.

72. Mays, *Born to Rebel*, 3; Dumas, *Benjamin Elijah Mays*, 103.

73. Leon Litwack, *Been in the Storm So Long: The Aftermath of Slavery* (New York: Knopf, 1979), chap. 8.

74. Regarding these kinds of gendered cultural issues in the white South, see Ted Ownby's splendid study, *Subduing Satan*; and Edward Ayers, *Vengeance and Justice: Crime and Punishment in the Nineteenth-Century American South* (New York: Oxford University Press, 1984). Studies looking at the cultural life of African American men in the rural South have yet to be written. However, two books in particular explore some of the cultural issues around ethnic identity and masculinity in the rural black South. See Adam Gussow, *Seems Like Murder Here: Southern Violence and the Blues Tradition* (Chicago: University of Chicago Press, 2002); and William Van Deburg, *Hoodlums: Black Villains and Social Bandits in American Life* (Chicago: University of Chicago Press, 2004).

75. Mays, *Born to Rebel*, 12.

76. Ibid., 12.

77. Ibid., 26–27.

78. Ibid., 9.

79. Ibid., 21.

80. On the complex ideology surrounding sexuality and white women's role, see Jane E. Dailey, *Before Jim Crow: The Politics of Race in Postemancipation Virginia* (Chapel Hill: University of North Carolina Press, 2000); and Glenda Gilmore, *Gender and Jim Crow: Women and the Politics of White Supremacy in North Carolina,* 1896–1920 (Chapel Hill: University of North Carolina Press, 1996).

81. Gail Bederman, *Maniliness and Civilization: A Cultural History of Gender and Race in the United States,* 1880–1917 (Chicago: University of Chicago Press, 1995).

82. Ownby, *Subduing Satan*, 16–17.

83. Mays, *Born to Rebel*, 45.

84. Ann Douglas, *The Feminization of American Culture* (New York: Knopf, 1977).

85. Barbara Dianne Savage, *Your Spirit Walk Beside Us: The Politics of Black Religion* (Cambridge, Mass.: Harvard University Press, 2008), 228. On changing notions of black masculinity, see Martin Summers, *Manliness and Its Discontents: The Black Middle Class and the Transformation of Masculinity, 1900–1930* (Chapel Hill: University of North Carolina Press, 2005). What is interesting in Mays's *Born to Rebel* is the absence of his sisters' realities as black southern women. He largely constructs black woman-hood in terms of an urban social respectability but never describes his sisters' frustration with being socially immobilized or their fears of being harmed by the power unleashed by southern white supremacy. On this topic, see Farah Jasmine Griffin, *"Who Set You Flowin'?": The African-American Migration Narrative* (New York: Oxford University Press, 1995), 36–42.

86. Ibid., 49.

87. Ibid., 32–33.

88. Ibid., 33–34.

89. Levine, *Black Culture and Black Consciousness*,154–55.

90. Mays, *Born to Rebel*, 20.

91. Ibid., 34.

CHAPTER TWO

1. Benjamin Elijah Mays, *Lord, the People Have Driven Me On* (New York: Vantage, 1981), 1.

2. Janet Duitsman Cornelius, *When I Can Read My Title Clear: Literacy, Slavery, and Religion in the Antebellum South* (Columbia: University of South Carolina Press, 1991), 3.

3. Steven Mailloux, "Misreading as a Historical Act: Cultural Rhetoric, Bible Politics, and Fuller's 1845 Review of Narrative," in *Readers in History: Nineteenth–Century American Literature and the Contexts of Response*, ed. James L. Machor (Baltimore: Johns Hopkins University Press, 1983), 20. For how the Bible was used materially in the late nineteenth century and through the twentieth, see Colleen McDannell's *Material Christianity: Religion and Popular Culture in America* (New Haven, Conn.: Yale University Press, 1995), chap. 3.

4. Carter G. Woodson, *The History of the Negro Church* (Washington, D.C.: The Associated Publishers, Inc., 1921), 269.

5. For great insights into this subject, see James D. Anderson, *The Education of Blacks in the South, 1860–1935* (Chapel Hill: University of North Carolina Press, 1988); and Heather Andrea Williams, *Self-Taught: African American Education in Slavery and Free-dom* (Chapel Hill: University of North Carolina Press, 2005).

6. Benjamin Elijah Mays, *Born to Rebel: An Autobiography* (New York: Scribner, [1971]; reprint, with a revised foreword by Orville Vernon Burton. Athens: University of Georgia Press, 2003), 11.

7. Ibid., 11–12.

8. Williams, *Self-Taught*, 5.

9. On universal education in the South, see James D. Anderson's invaluable work *Education of Blacks in the South*, chap. 1; and Williams, *Self-Taught*, chap. 9. On the gendered politics surrounding the Common School, see Jane Dailey, *Before Jim Crow: The Politics of Race in Postemancipation Virginia* (Chapel Hill: University of North Carolina Press, 2000), chap. 3.

10. Williams, *Self-Taught*, 96.

11. Mays, *Born to Rebel*, 36.

12. Ibid.

13. Lewis McMillan, *Negro Higher Education in the State of South Carolina* (Orangeburg: S.C.: n.p., 1953).

14. For a comparable view on the strains of fathers and sons, see Theodore Rosengarten, *All God's Danger: The Life of Nate Shaw* (New York: Knopf, 1974).

15. "Outline for Autobiography: Trial Run No. 2 Born to Rebel," Benjamin Mays to John Hope Franklin, January 18, 1968, Installation 1, Box 39, F. John Hope Franklin, BEMP.

16. Mays, *Born to Rebel*, 36.

17. See, for example, James M. Washington, ed., *Conversations with God: Two Centuries of Prayers by African Americans* (New York: HarperCollins, 1994); and Marla F. Frederick, *Between Sundays: Black Women and Everyday Struggles of Faith* (Berkeley: University of California Press, 2003).

18. "Outline for Autobiography: Trial Run No. 2 Born to Rebel," Benjamin Mays to John Hope Franklin, January 18, 1968, Installation 1, Box 39, F. John Hope Franklin, BEMP.

19. Mays, *Born to Rebel*, 37.

20. For the statistical data on black education in Greenwood County and the surrounding area see Orville Vernon Burton, foreword to Mays, *Born to Rebel*, xxiii.

21. On personal and civic freedoms, see Orlando Patterson's *Freedom in the Making of Western Culture* (New York: Basic Books, 1991).

22. Mays, *Born to Rebel*, 33.

23. George Brown Tindall, *South Carolina Negroes, 1877–1900* (Baton Rouge: Louisiana State University Press, 1966), 230.

24. Mays, *Born to Rebel*, 42–44.

25. Ibid., 41.

26. Benjamin Mays, "Southern View: I Apologize," *PC*, November 12, 1955, A10.

27. Mays, *Born to Rebel*, 38.

28. Benjamin Mays, "Dr. Mays: Lincoln U. (PA) Has Had A Great Influence Upon Dr. Mays' Life," *PC*, May 15, 1954, 22.

29. Beth Tompkins Bates, *Pullman Porters and the Rise of Protest Politics in Black America, 1925–1945* (Chapel Hill, N.C.: University of North Carolina Press, 2001), 20–23.

30. Quoted in Burton, foreword, x.

31. Mays, *Born to Rebel*, 40–41.

32. Ibid., 42.

33. Benjamin Mays, "Rebel Draft," BEMP.

34. Mays, *Born to Rebel*, 42.

35. Ibid., 48–49.

36. On the early days of Virginia Union, see A. H. Grundman, "Northern Baptists and the Founding of Virginia Union University: The Perils of Paternalism," *Journal of Negro History* 63 (1) (1978): 26–41.

37. On Hovey, see Anderson, *Education of Blacks in the South*, 252; and Jackson Davis Collection, Albert and Shirley Small Special Collections Library, University of Virginia Library, http://www.lib.virginia.edu/small/collections/jdavis/name.html. On the attack on classics at black colleges, see Kenneth Goings and Eugene O'Connor, "Creating a 'Culture of Dissemblance': African American Resistance to the Suppression of the Classics at Historically Black Colleges," in the authors possession.

38. Mays, *Born to Rebel*, 52–53.

39. Ibid., 53 (Mays refers to Wakefield as Wingfield, but Bates College records indicate that Wakefield is correct); Mays, *Lord*, 18; Benjamin E. Mays, "Why I Went to Bates," Bates College Bulletin, Alumnus Issue, January 1966, Edmund Muskie Archives and Special Collections Library, Bates College, Lewiston, Me.

40. Hadley and Wakefield went on to have long distinguished careers in higher education. On Wakefield, see *Bates Alumnus*, Summer 1945; and on Hadley, see *Bates Alumnus*, July 1975, 28.

41. Mays, "Why I Went to Bates"; Mays, *Lord*, 18-19; Benjamin E. Mays, "Recollections: At Bates College He Learned His Color Did Not Make Him an Inferior," *PC*, July 12, 1947, 7.

42. William Anthony, *Bates College and Its Background: A Review of Origins and Causes* (Philadelphia: Judson Press, 1936).

43. Laurence Veysey, *The Emergence of the American University* (Chicago: University of Chicago Press, 1965), 203–12.

44. Faculty Minutes (March 16, 1920), 277, Edmund Muskie Archives and Special Collections Library Bates College, Lewiston, Me.; Mays, *Born to Rebel*, 59; Mays, *Lord*, 23–24.

45. Bates College Bulletin Annual Catalogue, 1919–20, 112–15, Edmund Muskie Archives and Special Collections Library, Bates College, Lewiston, Me.

46. Mays, *Lord*, 34.

47. Wayde Larson, *Faith by Their Works: The Progressive Tradition at Bates,* 1855–1877 (Lewiston, Me.: Bates College, n.d.), http://www.bates.edu/x65002.xml.

48. Mays, "Recollections," 7.

49. Mays, *Born to Rebel*, 56.

50. "The Supposed Speech of John Adams," in *McGuffey's Fifth Eclectic Reader*, lesson 64, The 19th Century School Book Collection, University of Pittsburgh Digital Collection, http://digital.library.pitt.edu/cgi-bin/t/text/pageviewer-idx?c=nietz;cc=nietz;g=text-all;xc=1;xg=1;q1=McGuffey%20s%20Fifth%20Eclectic%20Reader;idno=00acg9659m;rgn=full%20text;didno=00acg9659m;view=image;seq=0200;node=00acg9659m%3A1.8.63.

51. On the importance of the *McGuffey Readers*, see Richard D. Mosier, *Making the American Mind: Social and Moral Ideas in the McGuffey Readers* (New York: King's Crown Press, 1947); and John H. Westerhoff III, *McGuffey and His Readers: Piety, Morality, and*

Education in Nineteenth-Century America (Nashville: Abingdon, 1978). John Westerhoff notes that by the mid- to late nineteenth century, the content of the *McGuffey Readers*, originally rooted in Calvinist theology, shifted to concerns for "the need of national unity and the dream of a melting pot for the world's oppressed masses. Their lessons were especially appropriate for a small-town, rural population that experienced stable, semi-extended family life, minimal mobility, and a simple life style." I think that Westerhoff overstates the case here because aspects of Calvinist theology lend themselves to what Robert Bellah calls "Civil Religion," though a case can be made that Mays adapted this speech to highlight his own personal aspirations as an African American. See Bellah's *The Broken Covenant: American Civil Religion in Time of Trial* (Chicago: University of Chicago Press, 1992).

52. Lawrence Levine, *Black Culture and Black Consciousness: Afro-American Folk Thought from Slavery to Freedom* (New York: Oxford University Press, 1977), 142–44.

53. *McGuffey's Fifth Eclectic Reader*.

54. Ibid.

55. Samuel DuBois Cook, introduction to Benjamin Mays, *Quotable Quotes of Benjamin E. Mays* (New York: Vantage Press, 1983), xviii.

56. Much of this material comes from Robert James Branham's "Emancipating Myself: Mays the Debater," in *Walking Integrity: Benjamin Elijah Mays: Mentor to Generations*, ed. Lawrence E. Carter (Atlanta: Scholars Press, 1996).

57. Mays, *Born to Rebel*, 50.

58. Branham, "Emancipating Myself," 78–80.

59. Mays, *Born to Rebel*, 14.

60. Edward Blum, *Reforging the White Republic: Race, Religion, and American Nationalism, 1865–1898* (Baton Rouge: Louisiana State University Press, 2005), 9.

61. Colin Kidd, *Forging of Races: Race and Scripture in the Protestant Atlantic World, 1600–2000* (New York: Cambridge University Press, 2006); David Goldenberg, *The Curse of Ham: Race and Slavery in Early Judaism, Christianity and Islam* (Princeton, N.J.: Princeton University Press, 2003).

62. Bates College Bulletin Annual Catalogue, Edmund Muskie Archives and Special Collections Library Bates College, Lewiston, Me; James Stalker, *The Life of Jesus Christ*, new and rev. ed. (New York: Fleming H. Revell, 1909).

63. Stalker, *Life of Jesus Christ*, 69.

64. Ibid., 68–77.

65. Ibid., 113.

66. Ibid., 143.

67. Ibid., 145–47.

68. Ibid., 61. Biographical sketches of Purinton are found in the *General Catalogue of Bates College and Cobb Divinity School, 1864-1930* (Lewiston, Me.: Bates College, 1931), 486.

69. "Beloved Bates Professor Dies at Lewiston Home," *The Bates Student*, November 7, 1934, 1; Fred A. Knapp, "In Memoriam: A Neighbor's Tribute," *Bates Alumnus*, November 1934, 9.

70. Bates College Bulletin Annual Catalogue, 1919-20, 39–41; and Bates College Bulletin Annual Catalogue, 1916-17, 46–47, Edmund Muskie Archives and Special Collections Library, Bates College, Lewiston, Me.

71. Herbert Purinton, "Some Recent Books on Religion," *Bates Alumnus*, May 1928, 11.

72. Kenneth Cauthen, *The Impact of American Religious Liberalism* (New York: Harper & Row), 27–30.

73. Ibid.

74. Ralph Luker, *The Social Gospel in Black and White: American Racial Reform, 1885–1912*. Chapel Hill: University of North Carolina Press, 1992.

75. William Hutchinson, *The Modernist Impulse in American Protestantism* (Cambridge, Mass.: Harvard University Press, 1976), chap. 3; Cauthen, *Impact of American Religious Liberalism*, 35.

76. See the works by Rauschenbusch listed in the Bibliography. For a biography of Rauschenbusch, see Paul M. Minus, *Walter Rauschenbusch: American Reformer* (New York: Macmillan, 1988). For an excellent interpretation of Rauschenbusch's thought, see Gary Scott Smith, "To Reconstruct the World: Walter Rauschenbusch and Social Change," *Fides et Historia: Journal of the Conference on Faith and History* 23 (1991): 40–63.

77. Peter Paris, *The Social Teachings of the Black Churches* (Philadelphia: Fortress Press, 1985), 10–11; Mays, *Born to Rebel*, 11.

78. Susan Curtis, "The Son of Man and God the Father," in *Meanings for Manhood: Constructions of Masculinity in Victorian America*, ed. Mark C. Carnes and Clyde Griffen (Chicago: University of Chicago Press, 1990), 74.

79. Burton, foreword, x.

80. George M. Marsden, *Fundamentalism and American Culture: The Shaping of Twentieth-Century Evangelicalism, 1870–1925* (New York: Oxford University Press, 1980).

81. Benjamin E. Mays, *A Gospel for the Social Awakening: Selections, Edited and Compiled from the Writings of Walter Rauschenbusch* (New York: Association Press, 1950); Luker, *Social Gospel*, 321.

82. On the abolitionist legacy, see James McPherson, *The Abolitionist Legacy: From Reconstruction to the NAACP* (Princeton, N.J.: Princeton University Press, 1975); on the abolitionist legacy in a communal context, see Randal Jelks, *African Americans in the Furniture City: The Struggle for Civil Rights in Grand Rapids* (Urbana: University of Illinois Press, 2006), chap. 3.

83. Mays, *Born to Rebel*, 60.

84. Kevin Gaines, *Uplifting the Race: Black Leadership, Politics, and Culture in the Twentieth Century* (Chapel Hill: University of North Carolina Press, 1996); for a religious history on the subject of uplift, see Edward Wheeler's *Uplifting the Race: The Black Minister in the New South, 1865–1902* (Lanham, Md.: University Press of America, 1986).

85. Stalker, *Life of Christ*, 64–65.

86. Mays, *Lord*, 34.

87. Mays, *Born to Rebel*, 65.

88. Benjamin E. Mays, oral history interview by J. Oscar McCloud, January 1982, Atlanta, Ga. Used with permission of J. Oscar McCloud, executive director of the Fund for Theological Education, New York, New York.

89. Q. A. Newby, *Jim Crow's Defense: Anti-Negro Thought in America, 1900–1930* (Baton Rouge : Louisiana State University Press, 1965), 90.

CHAPTER THREE

1. John Britton, oral history interview with Benjamin E. Mays, 9, Ralph J. Bunche Oral History Collection, Moorland-Spingarn Research Center, Manuscript Department, Howard University, Washington, D.C.

2. On black Baptist polity, see Floyd Massey and Samuel B. McKinney's *Church Administration in the Black Perspective*, rev. ed. (Valley Forge, Pa.: Judson Press, 2003).

3. "Employment Card of Ben Elijah Mays," Pullman Company Papers, RG 06, Newberry Library, Chicago, Ill.

4. Scholarship on the Pullman Porters, and the activism of A. Philip Randolph in particular, has grown considerably. See, for example, Brailsford R. Brazeal, *The Brotherhood of Sleeping Car Porters: Its Origin and Development* (New York: Harper & Brothers, 1946); William H. Harris, *Keeping the Faith: A. Philip Randolph, Milton P. Webster and the Brotherhood of Sleeping Car Porters, 1925–1937* (Urbana, Ill.: University of Illinois Press, 1977); Jack Santino, *Miles of Smiles, Years of Struggle: The Untold History of the Black Pullman Porter* (Urbana, Ill.: University of Illinois Press, 1991); Beth Tompkins Bates, *Pullman Porters and the Rise of Protest Politics in Black America, 1925–1945* (Chapel Hill, N.C.: University of North Carolina Press, 2001); Eric Arnesen, *Brotherhoods of Color: Black Railroad Workers and the Struggle for Equality* (Cambridge, Mass.: Harvard University Press, 2002); Larry Tye, *Rising from the Rails: The Pullman Porters and the Making of the Black Middle Class* (New York: Holt, 2005); and Cynthia Taylor, *A. Philip Randolph: The Religious Journey of African American Labor Leader* (New York: New York University Press, 2006).

5. Mays, *Born to Rebel*, 61.

6. Ibid., 62.

7. Ibid., 63.

8. "Employment Card of Ben Elijah Mays," Pullman Company Papers, RG 06, Newberry Library, Chicago, Ill.

9. Mays, *Born to Rebel*, 62–65.

10. Ibid., 42, 68; William Tuttle's *Race Riot: Chicago in the Red Summer of* 1919 (Urbana, Ill.: University of Illinois Press, 1996) still remains the classic on the subject.

11. Mays, *Born to Rebel*, 42.

12. Ibid., 65.

13. "Divinity School Students 1921/Summer 21, 3 & 7," Correspondence, Box 31, Folder 6, CDS. Ellen Harvin Mays is listed as an unclassified student.

14. For the history of Morris College see Mary Vereen-Gorden and Janet Smith Clayton, *Morris College: A Noble Journey* (Gloucester Point, Va.: Hallmark Publishing Company, Inc., 1998).

15. Ridgely Torrence, *The Story of John Hope* (New York: Macmillan Co., 1948), 237.

16. Leroy Davis, *A Clashing of the Soul: John Hope and the Dilemma of African American Leadership and Black Higher Education in the Early Twentieth* (Athens: University of Georgia Press, 1998), 259.

17. Benjamin E. Mays, *Born to Rebel: An Autobiography* (New York: Scribner, [1971]; reprint, with a revised foreword by Orville Vernon Burton. Athens: University of Georgia Press, 2003), 66.

18. Ibid., 67.

19. John Dittmer, *Black Georgia in the Progressive Era, 1900–1920* (Urbana: University of Illinois Press, 1977), chap. 1.

20. On late-nineteenth- and early-twentieth-century black Atlanta, see Allison Dorsey, *To Build Our Lives Together: Community Formation in Black Atlanta, 1875–1906* (Athens: University of Georgia Press, 2004).

21. Ronald H. Bayor, *Race and the Shaping of Twentieth Century Atlanta* (Chapel Hill: University of North Carolina Press, 1996), 56–57.

22. On black working-class life in Atlanta, see Tera Hunter, *To 'Joy My Freedom: Southern Black Women's Lives and Labor After the Civil War* (Cambridge, Mass.: Harvard University Press, 1997). For a wonderfully rich photographic history of this era, see Herman "Skip" Mason, *Black Atlanta in the Roaring Twenties* (Mount Pleasant, S.C.: Arcadia Publishing, 1997). For another take on Atlanta's Vaudeville shows and clubs, see Ethel Waters, *His Eyes Is on the Sparrow: An Autobiography* (Garden City, N.J.: Doubleday, 1951).

23. Bayor, *Race and the Shaping of Twentieth Century Atlanta*, 54–55.

24. Mays, *Born to Rebel*, 68.

25. Ibid., 75.

26. Ann Wells Ellis, "A Crusade against 'Wretched Attitudes': The Commission on Interracial Cooperation's Activities in Atlanta," *Atlanta Historical Journal* 23 (Spring 1979): 21–44.

27. On the troublesome use of the term "race relations," see Barbara J. Fields, "Origins of the New South and the Negro Question," *Journal of Southern History* 67 (4) (November 2001): 811–26.

28. Karen Ferguson, *Black Politics in New Deal Atlanta* (Chapel Hill: University of North Carolina Press, 2002), 43.

29. Mays, *Born to Rebel*, 88.

30. On Samuel Graves, see Randal Jelks, *African Americans in the Furniture City: The Struggle for Civil Rights in Grand Rapids* (Urbana: University of Illinois Press, 2006), 45.

31. James D. Anderson, *The Education of Blacks in the South, 1860–1935* (Chapel Hill: University of North Carolina Press, 1988), chap. 7.

32. Edward J. Blum, *Reforging the White Republic: Race, Religion and American Nationalism, 1865–1898* (Baton Rouge: Louisiana State University Press, 2005).

33. Dorsey, *To Build Our Lives Together*, 151.

34. Unless otherwise noted, the material in this paragraph comes from Leroy Davis's rich biography of John Hope, *Clashing of the Soul*, chaps. 7 and 8.

35. Nina Mjagkij, "True Manhood: The YMCA and Racial Advancement, 1890–1930," in *Men and Women Adrift: the YMCA and the YWCA in the City*, ed. Nina Mjagkij and Margaret Spratt (New York: New York University Press, 1997), 138–59.

36. Howard Thurman, in *With Head and Heart: The Autobiography of Howard Thurman* (New York: Harcourt Brace Jovanovich, 1979), 36, writes movingly of his years at Morehouse in the early 1920s:

> Our manhood, and that [of] our fathers, was denied on all levels by white society, a fact insidiously expressed in the way black men were addressed. No matter what his age, whether he was in [his] burgeoning twenties or full of years, the black man was never referred to [as] "mister," nor even by his surname. No. To the end of his days, he had to absorb the indignity of being called "boy," or "nigger," or "uncle." No wonder then that every time Dr. Hope addressed us as "young gentlemen," the seeds of self-worth and confidence, long dormant, began to germinate and sprout. The attitudes we developed toward ourselves, as a result of this influence, set Morehouse men apart. It was not unusual, for example, to be identified as a Morehouse man by complete strangers, because of this subtle but dramatic sense of self.

37. Mays, *Born to Rebel*, 89.

38. Davis, *A Clashing of the Soul*, 236.

39. On the term "New Negro," see Henry Louis Gates, "The Trope of the New Negro and the Reconstruction of the Image of the Black," *Representations* 24 (Autumn 1988): 129–55; and Wilson Jeremiah Moses, "The Lost World of the New Negro, 1895–1919," *Black American Literature Forum* 21 (1/2) (Spring–Summer 1987): 61–84.

40. Wallace Best, *Passionately Human, No Less Divine: Religion and Culture in Black Chicago, 1915–1952* (Princeton, N.J.: Princeton University Press, 2005).

41. Mays, *Born to Rebel*, 91.

42. Ibid., 92.

43. Ibid.

44. Ibid., 93.

45. Thurman, *With Head and Heart*, 42–43. Thurman notes,

> At that time, Morehouse offered a course in logic and a course in ethics, neither of which was strictly in the field, and no courses whatever in formal philosophy. I do not think that this was accidental. In the missionary colleges of the South, few (if any) courses were offered in the formal study of philosophy. I believe that the shapers of our minds, with clear but limited insight into the nature of our struggle for survival and development in Americans life, particularly in the South recognized the real possibility that to be disciplined in the origins and development of ideas would ultimately bring under critical judgment the society and the predicament in it. This, in turn, would contribute to our unease and restlessness, which would be disastrous, they felt, for us and for our people.

46. Benjamin E. Mays to Mary Jennes, February 12, 1936, in Walter Earl Fluker, ed., *The Papers of Howard Washington Thurman*, vol. 1 (Columbia, S.C.: University of South Carolina Press, 2009), 324–25.

47. Kimetris N. Baltrip, "Samuel Narbit, 98, Scientist and Pioneer in Education Dies," *New York Times*, January 6, 2004.

48. Mays, *Born to Rebel*, 97.

49. In her interesting but deeply flawed book, *Black Politics in New Deal Atlanta* (Chapel Hill: University of North Carolina Press, 2002), Karen Ferguson discusses black reform efforts without actually reading source material from black religious life. It is quite incredible, since churches are where African Americans in Atlanta can freely meet. Dr. Ferguson follows the lead of Kevin Gaines, the author of *Uplifting the Race*, and so many other scholars who discuss the problematic ideas of racial uplift without addressing what was at the heart of uplift, the theological concept about aid to the poor and the defenseless. Uplift was later made a civil religious doctrine by reform-minded African American ministers. Their respective congregations reinforced the idea that they had a religious duty to serve those in need. But those in need, as any black Baptist will attest, were not passive. Uplift was always in creative tension with what economic poor or disfranchised actually wanted. It is unfortunate that Gaines's perspective on racial uplift has not been challenged and examined more fully.

50. For a discussion of middle-class sensibilities of the National Baptist Convention, see Evelyn Brooks Higginbotham, *Righteous Discontent: The Women's Movement in the Black Baptist Church, 1880–1920* (Cambridge, Mass.: Harvard University Press, 1994).

51. Mays, *Born to Rebel*, 98.

52. Ibid., 93.

53. Benjamin Mays, "Southern View: I Apologize," *PC*, November 12, 1955, A10.

54. Mays, *Born to Rebel*, 99.

55. Allan H. Spear, *Black Chicago: The Making of a Negro Ghetto, 1890–1920* (Chicago: University of Chicago Press, 1967), 129–46.

56. Ibid.

57. Ibid., 100.

58. On Ames, see Jacquelyn Dowd Hall, *Revolt against Chivalry: Jessie Daniel Ames and the Women's Campaign against Lynching* (New York: Columbia University Press, 1993).

59. Mays, *Born to Rebel*, 103.

60. Nina Mjagkij, *Light in the Darkness: African Americans and the YMCA, 1852–1946* (Lexington: University of Kentucky Press, 1994).

61. Mays, *Born to Rebel*, 103.

62. Benjamin Mays, "New Negro Challenges the Old Order," in *Sketches of Negro Life and History in South Carolina*, ed. As a H. Gordon (1929; reprint, New York: Columbia University Press, 1971), 193–94.

63. Ibid., 202.

64. Ibid., 203.

65. John F. Potts, *A History of South Carolina State College, 1896–1978* (Orangeburg: South Carolina State College, 1978), chap. 3.

66. Mays, "Southern View."

67. On Sadie Mays's vita, see Benjamin Mays to Jesse O. Thomas, August 21, 1926, NULP.

68. On the formation of the Colored Methodist Episcopal Church, see Charles Henry Phillips, *The History of the Colored Methodist Episcopal Church in America* (1898; New York: Arno Press, 1972); Katherine Dvorak, *An African American Exodus: The Segregation of the Southern Churches* (Brooklyn, N.Y.: Carlson Publishing, 1991), 160–63; and Will Gravely, "The Social, Political, and Religious Significance of the Formation of the Colored Methodist Church (1870)," *Methodist History* 18 (October 1979): 3–25. On black women in the Colored Methodist Church, see Bertha Payne Newell, "Social Work of Women's Organizations in the Church: I. Methodist Episcopal Church South," *Journal of Social Forces* 1 (3) (1923): 310–14. See also Stephanie Shaw, *What a Woman Ought to Be and to Do: Black Professional Women Workers during the Jim Crow Era* (Chicago: University of Chicago Press, 1996), for a discussion of professional women in Sadie Mays's generation.

69. Mays, *Born to Rebel*, 103.

70. Jesse O. Thomas to Benjamin Mays, August 11, 1926, NULP.

71. Benjamin Mays to Jesse O. Thomas, August 21, 1926, NULP.

72. Mays, *Born to Rebel*, 106.

73. Robert Ingalls, "Lynching and Establishment Violence in Tampa, 1858–1935," *Journal of Southern History* 53 (1987): 615.

74. Ibid., 620.

75. Michael Perman, *Struggle for Mastery: Disfranchisement in the South, 1888–1908* (Chapel Hill: University of North Carolina Press, 2001), 258–59.

76. On Afro-Cubans of Tampa, see Susan Greenbaum, *More Than Black: Afro-Cubans in Tampa* (Gainsville: University Press of Florida, 2002); and Nancy Raquel Mirabal, "The Afro-Cuban Community in Ybor City and Tampa, 1886–1910." *OAH Magazine* 7 (4) (Summer 1983): 19–22.

77. Jonathan Holloway, *Confronting the Veil: Abram Harris Jr., E. Franklin Frazier, and Ralph Bunche, 1919–1941* (Chapel Hill: University of North Carolina Press, 2002), 86–87.

78. Justin George, "Tampa Urban League to Disband," *St. Petersburg Times*, July 18, 2006.

79. Keith Halderman, "Blanche Armwood of Tampa and the Strategy of Interracial Cooperation," *Florida Historical Quarterly* 74 (3) (1996): 288.

80. Nancy Hewitt, *Southern Discomfort: Women's Activism in Tampa, Florida, 1880s–1920s,* Women in American History Series (Urbana: University of Illinois Press, 2001), 259.

81. Jesse O. Thomas, *My Story in Black and White: The Autobiography of Jesse O. Thomas* (New York: Exposition Press, 1967), 103–4.

82. Halderman, "Blanche Armwood of Tampa," 297.

83. B. E. Mays to Jessie O. Thomas, October 8, 1926; Thomas to Mays, October 8, 1926; and Mays to Thomas, October 14, 1926, NULP.

84. Jesse O. Thomas to B. E. Mays, October 20, 1926, NULP.

85. Mays, *Born to Rebel*, 107.

86. B. E. Mays to Jesse O. Thomas, October 27, 1926, NULP; Wilma Dykeman and James Stokely, *Seeds of Southern Change: The Life of Will Alexander* (Chicago: University of Chicago Press, 1962), 114–15.

87. B. E. Mays to Jesse O. Thomas, January 13, 1927, NULP.

88. Ibid.

89. The complete study (Benjamin Mays, Arthur Raper, and J. H. McGrew, *Negro Life in Tampa*) can be found in the Arthur F. Raper Papers, Part I, F. 2A3, University of North Carolina, Southern Historical Collection, Wilson Library, Chapel Hill, N.C.; and Southern Regional Files, Box G1, Printed Matter, 1923–35, NULP.

90. Nancy Weiss, *The National Urban League, 1910–1940* (New York: Oxford University Press, 1974), 217–19.

91. Ibid., 219.

92. Mays, Raper, and McGrew, *Negro Life in Tampa*, introduction.

93. Ibid.; also see Greenbaum, *More Than Black*.

94. "Negro Population," in Mays, Raper, and McGrew, *Negro Life in Tampa*.

95. "Professionals," in ibid.

96. "Churches," in ibid.

97. Ibid.

98. Ibid.

99. Mays, *Born to Rebel*, 107–8.

100. Ibid.; Hewitt, *Southern Discomfit*, 263.

101. B. E. Mays to Jesse O. Thomas, January 13, 1927, NULP.

102. For a different take on Armwood Beatty, see Michele Alsihahi, "'For Peace and Civic Righteousness': Blanche Armwood and the Struggle for Freedom and Racial Equality in Tampa, Florida" (master's thesis, University of South Florida, Tampa, 2003).

103. Mays, *Born to Rebel*, 111–12.

104. B. E. Mays to Jesse O. Thomas, June 30, 1927, NULP.

105. Ibid.

106. Hewitt, *Southern Discomfit*, 265–66.

107. Walter T. Howard and Virginia M. Howard, "Family, Religion, and Education: A Profile of African-American Life in Tampa, Florida, 1900–1930," *Journal of Negro History* 79 (1) (1994): 1–17.

108. B. E. Mays to Jesse O. Thomas, July 27, 1927, NULP. For a northern perspective on black leaders' impotence, see Jelks, *African Americans in the Furniture City*.

109. B. E. Mays to T. Arnold Hill, September 19, 1927, NULP.

110. Mays, *Born to Rebel*, 114–17.

111. Ibid., 113.

112. Ibid., 116.

113. Thomas, *My Story in Black and White*, 105.

114. Mays, *Born to Rebel*, 117–18.

115. See Grace Hale's *Making Whiteness: The Culture of Segregation in the South, 1890–1940* (New York: Pantheon Books, 1998).

116. Thomas, *My Story in Black and White*, 106.

117. Ibid.

118. B. E. Mays, "Executive Secretary's Report Tampa Urban League," 1–2, General Office, Southern Regional Files, NULP.

119. Ibid.

120. Ibid., 10.

121. Ibid., 11.

122. Mays, *Born to Rebel*, 123.

123. Ibid., 125.

124. Channing H. Tobias (1882–1961), http://www.blackpast.org/?q=aah/tobias-channing-h-1882-1961; Benjamin Mays Eulogy of Channing Tobias, Riverside Church, New York City, November 8, 1961, Tobias, Channing H., Biographical, 1911–95, Box 205, YMCA Biographical Files, YMCA Papers, YMCAA.

125. Mjagkij, *Light in the Darkness*, 8–10.

126. Ibid., 18–21.

127. On the concerns of black men and boys in the context of the Baptist Church, see Angela Hornsby-Gutting, *Black Manhood and Community Building in North Carolina, 1900–1930* (Gainesville: University Press of Florida, 2009).

128. "Letter to Dr. R. R. Morton, Chairman, Colored Work Department from the Committee of Eleven April 28, 1928," YMCA Papers, YMCAA.

129. "Problems Facing Negro Student Y.M.C.A. Work Nationally" (Letter No. 1), May 3, 1928; "Problems Facing Negro Student Y.M.C.A. Work Nationally" (Letter No. 2), May 9, 1928; "Problems Facing Negro Student Y.M.C.A. Work Nationally" (Letter No. 3), May 17, 1928; "Problems Facing Negro Student Y.M.C.A. Work Nationally" (Letter No. 1); "Problems Facing Negro Student Y.M.C.A. Work Nationally" (Letter No. 4), May 19, 1928; Channing H. Tobias to Leaders of Colored Student Associations, May 9, 1928, all in YMCA Papers, Colored Division Records, YMCAA.

130. Quoted in "Report of the Commission Appointed by the Home Division to Study Future of the Colored Work Especially Its Relation to the New Student Division," May 24, 1928, YMCAA.

131. "Minutes of Meeting of Special Committee to Consider the Organizational Status of Negro Students . . . ," Chicago, Ill., October 29, 1929, YMCAA.

132. Mays, *Born to Rebel,* 125–26.

133. B. E. Mays, "The Kings Mountain Student Conference," *Intercollegian* 1 (4) (March–April 1929): 1–2, YMCAA.

134. Aldon Morris, *The Origins of the Civil Rights Movement: Black Communities Organizing for Change* (New York: Free Press, 1984), 139.

135. Ibid.

136. Sudarshan Kapur, *Raising Up a Prophet: The African-American Encounter with Gandhi* (Boston, Mass.: Beacon Press, 1992), 81; Frank T. Wilson, "The Mysore Meeting," *Intercollegian* 1 (2) (March–April 1929): 2–3, YMCAA. On Juliette Derricotte, see David Anthony, *Max Yergan: Race Man, Internationalist, Cold Warrior* (New York: New York University Press, 2006), 128–31.

137. Mays, *Born to Rebel*, 128; Robert Martin, "A Prophet's Pilgrimage: The Religious Radicalism of Howard Anderson Kester, 1921–1941," *Journal of Southern History* 48 (4) (1982): 513–14.

138. "What White Students Think of Kings Mountain," *Intercollegian* 1 (1) (November–December 1928): 2, YMCAA.

139. Morris, *Origins of the Civil Rights Movement*, 140.

140. B. E. Mays, "College Students and Religion," 2–3, YMCAA.

141. Ibid.

142. Ibid.

143. Britton, oral history interview with Mays, 9.

CHAPTER FOUR

1. Barbara Dianne Savage, *Your Spirits Walk Beside Us: The Politics of Black Religion* (Cambridge, Mass.: Harvard University Press, 2008), 39–40.

2. *The Rockefellers: John D. Rockefeller, Junior,* 1874–1960, RFAC, http://archive.rockefeller.edu/bio/jdrjr.php.

3. Pero Dagbovie, *The Early Black History Movement, Carter G. Woodson, and Lorenzo Johnston Greene* (Urbana: University of Illinois Press, 2007), 141–42.

4. Jacqueline Goggins, *Carter G. Woodson: A Life in Black History* (Baton Rouge: Louisiana State University Press, 1993), 69–70; Savage, *Your Spirits Walk Beside Us*, 50–51.

5. Benjamin Mays Eulogy of Channing Tobias, Riverside Church, New York City, November 8, 1961. Tobias, Channing H., Biographical, 1911–95, Box 205, YMCA Biographical Files, YMCA Papers, YMCAA.

6. Religious Interests (Institute for Social and Religious Research), RG2, Box 41, F. 331, RFAC.

7. Benjamin E. Mays to Jesse O. Thomas, September 30, 1930, Southern Regional File, NULP.

8. Mays, *Born to Rebel*, 131.

9. Jesse O. Thomas to Benjamin E. Mays, October 2, 1930, Southern Regional File, NULP.

10. Benjamin E. Mays to John C. Dancy, Detroit Urban League, October 14, 1930; and Jesse O. Thomas to Mays, October 16, 1930, NULP.

11. Published proceedings of "Whither the Negro Church?" seminar, foreword and editor's note by Jerome Davis, YDS.

12. A. Philip Randolph, "The Negro Church and Economic Relations—I," in published proceedings of "Whither the Negro Church?" seminar, 5, YDS.

13. Benjamin E. Mays responds to A. Philip Randolph, re. "Negro Church and Economic Relations," in published proceedings of "Whither the Negro Church?" seminar, 9, YDS.

14. Benjamin E. Mays, "Future Leadership of the Negro Church," in published proceedings of "Whither the Negro Church?" seminar, 39, YDS.

15. Ibid., 40.

16. Benjamin Elijah Mays and Joseph W. Nicholson, *The Negro's Church* (New York: Institute of Social and Religious Research, 1933), 1–3.

17. Ibid., 291–92.

18. Benjamin Mays to Jesse O. Thomas, January 28, 1933, NULP.

19. Ibid., March 18, 1933.

20. Walter White, review of *The Negro's Church*, by Benjamin E. Mays and Joseph W. Nicholson, *New York Herald Tribune Book Review*, 1933.

21. Howard Thurman, review of Mays and Nicholson, *The Negro's Church*, June 1933, in Walter Earl Fluker, ed., *The Papers of Howard Washington Thurman*, vol. 1 (Columbia, S.C.: University of South Carolina Press, 2009), 173.

22. Robert L. Sutherland, review of *The Negro's Church*, by Benjamin E. Mays and Joseph W. Nicholson, *Journal of Religion* 13 (3): 363–64.

23. Savage, *Your Spirits Walk Beside Us*, 21–22. For one of the best denominational histories of black Pentecostalism see Anthea Butler's *Women in the Church of God in Christ: Making a Sanctified World* (Chapel Hill: University of North Carolina Press, 2007).

24. Gary Dorrien, *The Making of American Liberal Theology: Idealism, Realism, and Modernity, 1900–1950* (Louisville, Ky.: Westminster John Knox Press, 2003), 10–11.

25. For a discussion of the Chicago School, see Charles Harvey Arnold, *Near the Edge of Battle: A Short History of the Divinity School and "Chicago School Theology," 1866–1966* (Indianapolis, Ind.: Bobbs-Merrill Co., 1966); William J. Hynes, *Shirley Jackson Case and the Chicago School: The Socio-historical Method* (Chico, Calif.: Scholars Press, 1981); Creighton Peden, *The Chicago School: Voices in Religious Liberal Thought* (Bristol, Ind.: Wyndham Hall Press, 1987); and Dorrien, *Making of American Liberal Theology*.

26. Arnold, *Near the Edge of Battle*, 38–40; Dorrien, *Making of American Liberal Theology*, 181–91.

27. Richard R. Wright Jr., *Eighty-seven Years behind the Black Curtain: An Autobiography* (Philadelphia: Rare Book Company, 1965), 37–43.

28. Terrell Goddard, "The Black Social Gospel in Chicago, 1896–1906: The Ministries of Reverdy C. Ransom and Richard R. Wright, Jr.," *Journal of Negro History* 84 (3) (Summer 1999): 240.

29. Dorrien, *Making of American Liberal Theology*, 134.

30. Benjamin Elijah Mays, *Lord, the People Have Driven Me On* (New York: Vantage, 1981), 35; author's correspondence with Maxine Hunsinger Sullivan, University of Chicago, Registrar and Transcript Office, June 14, 1991, and August 1991. Mays attended the university during the summers of 1925, 1926, and 1930. His transcripts show that he took courses with J. N. Wilt, H. N. Weiman, Theodore G. Soares, E. E. Aubrey, Shailer Mathews, S. C. Kincheloe, Edward Schaub, Herbert L. Willet, Albert E. Haydon, and A. E. Holt. Much of his work from 1932 to 1935 was done with E. E. Aubrey and H. N. Weiman.

31. Arnold, *Near the Edge of Battle*, 27.

32. Hynes, *Shirley Jackson Case*, 35–86.

33. Mays, *Lord*, 45.

34. Benjamin E. Mays, "Pagan Survival in Christianity," M.A. Thesis, University of Chicago Divinity School, 1925, 5.

35. Ibid., 29.

36. Ibid., 56.

37. Dorothy Ross, *The Origins of American Social Science* (New York: Cambridge University Press, 1991), 357–61.

38. Ibid., 438–40; Ralph Ellison, "An American Dilemma: A Review," *Shadow and the Act* (New York: Random House, 1964), 305–8; Booker T. Washington and Robert E. Park,

The Man Farthest Down: A Record of Observation and Study in Europe (Garden City, N.Y.: Doubleday, 1912); see St. Clair Drake's introduction.

39. Robert E. Park and Ernest W. Burgess, *Introduction to the Science of Sociology* (Chicago: University of Chicago Press, 1924), 872–952. For a critique of Park's theory, see Aldon D. Morris, *Origins of the Civil Rights Movement: Black Communities Organizing for Change* (New York: Free Press, 1984), esp. chap. 11.

40. Mays, First draft autobiography, installment 1, Box 42, p. 358, BEMP.

41. Mays, *Lord*, 47.

42. George M. Marsden, *Fundamentalism in America: The Shaping of Twentieth-Century Evangelicalism, 1870–1925* (New York: Oxford University Press, 1980).

43. Jeffrey Moran, "The Scopes Trial and Southern Fundamentalism in Black and White: Race, Region, and Religion," *Journal of Southern History* 70 (1) (February 2004): 104.

44. This same question that Moran poses is central to Colin Kidd, *The Forging of Races: Race and Scripture in the Protestant Atlantic World, 1600–2000* (New York: Cambridge University Press, 2006). It had vexed Christian thinkers since the eighteenth-century Enlightenment in Scotland and England.

45. Moran, "Reading Race into the Scopes Trial," 906.

46. Mathews quoted in Dorrien, *Making of American Liberal Theology*, 186–87.

47. Ibid., 193.

48. Walter Rauschenbusch, *A Theology for the Social Gospel* (1917; Louisville, Ky.: Westminster John Knox Press, 1997), 119.

49. Ibid., 129–30.

50. Carter G. Woodson, *The History of the Negro Church* (Washington, D.C.: The Associated Publishers, Inc., 1921); on the importance and limitations of Woodson's work, see Albert Raboteau et al., "Retelling Carter Woodson's Story: Archival Sources for Afro-American Church History," *Journal of American History* 77 (1) (June 1990): 183–99.

51. Mays and Nicholson, *Negro's Church*, 86.

52. Peden, *Chicago School*, 87; Mays, *Lord*, 44.

53. Mays, *Lord*, 44.

54. Arnold, *Near the Edge of Battle*, 66.

55. Ibid., 88–89.

56. While I have no documentation to prove it, I believe King wrote his dissertation on Wieman and Tillich (parts of which are now known to have been plagiarized) because of Mays's influence. King himself noted that Mays was his spiritual mentor, and no doubt King's study of Wieman was intended to be complementary to Mays's scholarship, and perhaps Mays suggested the subject to King. See *Journal of American History* (Spring 1991) for information on King's alleged plagiarism while a student.

57. Channing Tobias to Howard Thurman, November 1, 1934, in Fluker, *Papers of Howard Washington Thurman*, 214.

58. Howard Thurman to Benjamin Mays, April 15, 1935, in Fluker, *Papers of Howard Washington Thurman*, 255.

59. Interestingly, E. A. Aubrey served as president of Crozer Theological Seminary, where King began his seminary training upon Mays's recommendation.

60. Mays, *Lord*, 45–46.

61. Benjamin Mays to Howard Thurman, December 29, 1935, in Fluker, *Papers of Howard Washington Thurman*, 318–19.

62. Thomas J. Mikelson, "The Negro's God in the Theology of Martin Luther King, Jr." (Ph.D. diss. Harvard University Divinity School, 1988), 51–92. Mikelson offers an excellent theological analysis of Mays's *The Negro's God* as it influenced the work of Martin Luther King Jr., but its historical content leaves a lot to be desired.

63. Benjamin E. Mays, *The Negro's God, as Reflected in His Literature* (New York: Russell and Russell, [1968]), 18.

64. Ibid., 14.

65. Ibid., 17.

66. "'Ethiopia Shall Soon Stretch for Her Hands': Black Destiny in Nineteenth-Century America," chap. 2 in Albert Raboteau, *A Fire in the Bones: Reflections on Black Religious History* (Boston: Beacon Press, 1995).

67. Henry May, *The End of American Innocence: A Study of the First Years of Our Own Time, 1912–1917* (New York: Knopf, 1959).

68. Barbara Dianne Savage, "W. E. B. DuBois and 'The Negro Church,'" *Annals of the American Academy of Political and Social Science* 568 (March 2000): 235–49.

69. Cynthia Taylor, *A. Philip Randolph: The Religious Journey of an African American Labor Leader* (New York: New York University Press, 2006), 39–84.

70. Glenda Gilmore, *Defying Dixie: The Radical Roots of Civil Rights, 1919–1950* (New York: W. W. Norton, 2008).

71. James O. Young, *Black Writers of the Thirties* (Baton Rouge: Louisiana State University Press, 1973; William J. Maxwell, *New Negro, Old Left: African-American Writing and Communism Between the Wars* (New York: Columbia University Press, 1999); James E. Smethurst, *The New Red Negro: The Literary Left and African American Poetry, 1930–1946* (New York: Oxford University Press, 1999).

72. On the "New Negro," see August Meier, *Negro Thought in America, 1880–1915: Racial Ideologies in the Age of Booker T. Washington* (Ann Arbor: University of Michigan Press, 1963), chap. 14; David Levering Lewis, *When Harlem Was In Vogue* (New York: Knopf, 1981), chap. 4; Raymond Wolters, *The New Negro on Campus: Black College Rebellions of the 1920s* (Princeton, N.J.: Princeton University Press, [1975]).

73. Mays, *Negro's God*, preface.

74. Marcus Cook Connelly, *The Green Pastures*, ed. Thomas Cripps (Madison: University of Wisconsin Press, 1979), 20–21, 35–36.

75. Judith Weisenfeld, *Hollywood Be Thy Name: African American Religion in American Film, 1929–1949* (Berkeley: University of California Press, 2007), 6.

76. Mays, *Negro's God*, preface; Weisenfeld, *Hollywood Be Thy Name*, 81.

77. Mays, *Negro's God*, 126.

78. Ibid., 15–16.

79. Ibid., 17–18.

80. Ibid., 184–87.

81. Ibid., 224.

82. Savage, *Your Spirits Walk Beside Us*, 62.

83. Dorrien, *Making of American Liberal Theology*, 424.

84. Carter G. Woodson, review of *The Negro's God*, by Benjamin E. Mays, *Journal of Negro History* 24 (1) (1939): 119.

85. Edwin Aubrey, review of *The Negro's God*, by Benjamin E. Mays, *Journal of Negro Education* 8 (2) (April 1939): 226–27.

86. Benjamin E. Mays, "Why I Believe There Is a God," *Ebony*, December 1961, 4.

87. Ibid., 5–6.

88. Eugene McCarraher, *Christian Critics: Religion and the Impasse in Modern American Social Thought* (Ithaca, N.Y.: Cornell University Press, 2000), chap. 1; David L. Chappell, A *Stone of Hope: Prophetic Religion and the Death of Jim Crow* (Chapel Hill: University of North Carolina Press, 2004), chap. 1.

89. Benjamin Mays, "Why I Believe There Is a God," *Why I Believe There Is a God*, ed. Howard Thurman (Chicago: Johnson Publishing Company, 1965), 6.

90. Ibid., 7.

91. Benjamin Mays, "The Inescapable Christ," in *Representative American Speeches: 1944–1945* (New York: H. W. Wilson, 1945), 128.

92. Ibid.

93. Benjamin E. Mays, "The Faith of the Church," *Intercollegian* 72 (4) (1954): 10.

94. John Lee Eighmy, "Religious Liberalism in the South during the Progressive Era," *Church History* 38 (September 1969): 359–72.

95. Paul Harvey, *Redeeming the South: Religious Cultures and Racial Identities among Southern Baptists, 1865–1925* (Chapel Hill: University of North Carolina Press, 1992).

96. Abram Harris Jr., quoted in Jonathan Holloway, *Confronting the Veil: Abram Harris, Jr., E. Franklin Frazier, and Ralph Bunche, 1919–1941* (Chapel Hill: University of North Carolina Press, 2002), 107.

97. Benjamin Mays, "Nature, Grace and Community," March 1940, Theological Discussion Group Papers, Box 2, Folder 23, YDS.

98. Ibid.

99. Ibid.

100. Dwight G. Billings, "Religion as Opposition: A Gramscian Analysis," *American Journal of Sociology* 96 (1) (1990): 1, 4.

101. Cornell West, *Prophesy Deliverance!: An Afro-American Revolutionary Christianity* (Philadelphia: Westminster Press, 1982), 103. For more information on black theology, see Gayraud S. Wilmore and James H. Cone, *Black Theology: A Documentary History, 1966–1979* (Maryknoll, N.Y.: Orbis Books, 1979).

102. Mays, "Faith of the Church," 12.

CHAPTER FIVE

1. Benjamin E. Mays, "Education of Negro Ministers," *Journal of Negro Education: A Survey of Negro Higher Education* 2 (3) (1933): 342–43.

2. Ibid., 350–51.

3. Walter Dyson, *Howard University, The Capstone of Negro Education, a History: 1867–1940* (Washington, D.C.: The Graduate School, Howard University, 1941).

4. John Edgerton, *Speak Now Against the Day: The Generation Before the Civil Rights Movement* (New York: Knopf, 1994), 237.

5. For biographical sketches of these figures see, for example, Genna Rae McNeil, *Groundwork: Charles Hamilton Houston and the Struggle for Civil Rights* (Philadelphia: University of Pennsylvania Press, 1983); Kenneth Robert Janken, *Rayford W. Logan and the Dilemma of the African American Intellectual* (Amherst, Mass.: University of Massachusetts Press, 1993); Anthony Platt, *E. Franklin Frazier Reconsidered* (New Brunswick, N.J.: Rutgers University Press, 1991); Kenneth R. Manning, *Black Apollo of Science: The Life of Ernest Everett Just* (New York: Oxford University Press, 1983); Brian Urquhart, *Ralph Bunche: An American Life* (New York: W. W. Norton, 1993); and Joanne V. Gabbin, *Sterling A. Brown: Building the Black Aesthetic Tradition* (Westport, Conn.: Greenwood Press, 1985).

6. On the rise of the professionalism of theological education from a sociological perspective, see Magali Sarfattu Larson, *The Rise of Professionalism* (Berkeley: University of California Press, 1977).

7. Dyson, *Howard University*, 211.

8. Joe M. Richardson, *Christian Reconstruction: The American Missionary Association and Southern Blacks, 1861–1890* (Athens: University of Georgia Press, 1986), 151.

9. Dyson, *Howard University*, 213.

10. On Judge Stanton J. Peelle, see Biographical Directory of the United States Congress, http://bioguide.congress.gov/scripts/biodisplay.pl?index=P000185.

11. Dyson, *Howard University*, 202–5, 206–9.

12. Rayford Logan, *Howard University: The First Hundred Years, 1867–1967* (New York: New York University Press, 1969).

13. Benjamin E. Mays, *Born to Rebel: An Autobiography* (New York: Scribner, [1971]; reprint, with a revised foreword by Orville Vernon Burton. Athens: University of Georgia Press, 2003), 139.

14. Raymond Wolters, *The New Negro on Campus: Black College Rebellions of the 1920s.*

15. Mays, *Born to Rebel*, 140.

16. Mordecai Johnson, "Chosen for a Purpose," in Richard McKinney, *Mordecai, The Man and His Message: The Story of Mordecai Wyatt Johnson* (Washington, D.C.: Howard University Press, 1997), app. A, 237.

17. "Inaugural Presidential Address of Mordecai Wyatt Johnson," in ibid., app. B, 257–58.

18. David Butler Pratt to Howard Thurman, August 30, 1932, in Walter Earl Fluker, ed., *The Papers of Howard Washington Thurman*, vol. 1 (Columbia, S.C.: University of South Carolina Press, 2009), 166–69.

19. Thurman, *With Head and Heart: The Autobiography of Howard Thurman* (New York: Harcourt Brace Jovanovich, 1979), 87; also see Thurman's earliest letter to Mordecai Johnson, June 18, 1918, in Fluker, *Papers of Howard Washington Thurman*, 1–3.

20. D. Butler Pratt, "Howard University Was Born in a Prayer Meeting," *News.*

21. "Memorial Service in Honor of D. Butler Pratt," *News* 16 (3) (March 1940): 1–8.

22. Benjamin Mays Eulogy of Channing Tobias, 1961 Tobias, Channing H., Biographical, 1911–95, Box 205, YMCA Biographical Files, YMCA Papers, YMCAA.

23. Mays, *Born to Rebel*, 139.

24. Jonathan Holloway, *Confronting the Veil: Abram Harris, Jr., E. Franklin Frazier, and Ralph Bunche, 1919–1941* (Chapel Hill: University of North Carolina Press, 2002), 48.

25. Mays, *Born to Rebel*, 144.

26. Ibid., 145.

27. "Dean Mays Defines Objectives," *News* 10 (1) (January 1935): 6–8.

28. Conrad Cherry, *Hurrying toward Zion: Universities, Divinity Schools, and American Protestantism* (Bloomington: Indiana University Press, 1995), 135–36.

29. William Adams Brown, *Ministerial Education in America*, vol. 1 of *The Education of American Ministers* (New York: Institute of Social and Religious Research, [1934]); Mark May, *The Profession of Ministry*, vol. 2 of *The Education of American Ministers*; Mark May, *The Institutions That Train Ministers*, vol. 3 of *The Education of American Ministers*.

30. Brown, *Ministerial Education in America*, 4.

31. May, *The Profession of Ministry*, 11; for a description of white Southern Baptist ministry and the professionalization of the clergy, see Paul Harvey's "The Ideal of Professionalism and the White Southern Baptist Ministry, 1870–1920," *Religion and American Culture* 5 (1) (1995): 99–123.

32. In his analysis of divinity schools, Cherry (*Hurrying toward Zion*) glosses over the regional dimension of theological education. In his compelling examination of black Protestants in the white Protestant establishment, David Wells misses the southern region as a whole as it related to mainline denominations. See David W. Wills, "An Enduring Distance: Black Americans and the Establishment," in *Between the Times: The Travail of the Protestant Establishment in America, 1900–1960*, ed. W. R. Hutchinson (New York: Cambridge University Press, 1989), 168–92.

33. Benjamin Elijah Mays, "Dean Mays Defines Objectives," *News* 10 (1) (September 1935): 6–8.

34. "The School of Religion," *Howard University Bulletin*, 1937–38, 10–11, Moorland-Spingarn Research Center, Manuscript Department, Howard University, Washington, D.C.

35. Ibid.

36. Ibid.

37. The definitive histories in the area of black Christianity and the Great Migration are Milton Sernett, *Bound for the Promised Land: African American Religion and the Great Migration* (Durham, N.C.: Duke University Press, 1997); Wallace Best, *Passionately Human, No Less Divine: Religion and Culture in Black Chicago, 1915–1952* (Princeton, N.J.: Princeton University Press, 2005); and, most recently, Judith Wiesenfeld, *Hollywood Be Thy Name: African American Religion in American Film, 1929–1949* (Berkeley: University of California Press, 2007).

38. "Dean's Opening Message," *News* 14 (1) (November 1937): 11–12.

39. Sernett, *Bound for the Promised Land*.

40. "The Feminine Side of The News," *News* 13 (3) (March 1937): 10.

41. Best, *Passionately Human, No Less Divine*, 149.

42. Hazel V. Carby, *Race Men* (Cambridge, Mass.: Harvard University Press, 1998), 5.

43. "The New Faculty Members," *News* 15 (1) (November 1938): 2–3.

44. Farmer, *Lay Bare the Heart: An Autobiography of the Civil Rights Movement* (New York: Arbor House, 1985), 135.

45. Ibid., 136.

46. Daniel Immerwahr, "Caste or Colony? Indianizing Race in the United States," *Modern Intellectual History* 4 (2) (2007): 283.

47. Clifford L. Muse Jr., "Howard University and U.S. Foreign Affairs during the Franklin D. Roosevelt Administration, 1933–1945," *Journal of African American History* 87 (Autumn 2002): 403–15.

48. Leroy Davis, *Clashing of the Soul: John Hope and the Dilemma of African American Leadership and Black Higher Education in the Early Twentieth Century* (Athens: University of Georgia Press, 1998), 185–87; McKinney, *Mordecai*, 35–36, 57.

49. See, for example, Lamin O. Sanneh, *Abolitionist Abroad: American Blacks and the Making of Modern West Africa* (Cambridge, Mass.: Harvard University Press, 1999); and James Campbell, *Song of Zion* (New York: Oxford University Press, 1995).

50. On this issue, see Penny Von Eschen, *Race against Empire: Black Americans and Anticolonialism, 1937–1957* (Ithaca, N.Y.: Cornell University Press, 1997).

51. Glenda Gilmore, *Defying Dixie: The Radical Roots of Civil Rights, 1919–1950* (New York: W. W. Norton, 2008).

52. *News* 10 (1) (January 1935): 3.

53. Thurman, *With Head and Heart*, 106.

54. David Anthony III, "Max Yergan in South Africa: From Evangelical Pan-Africanist to Revolutionary Socialist," *African Studies Review* 34, no. 2 (September 1991): 27–55.

55. Thurman, *With Head and Heart*, 85; *Intercollegian News-Letter* 1 (4) (March–April 1929): cover page.

56. Fluker, *Papers of Howard Washington Thurman*, 181. Also see William R. Hutchinson, *Errand to the World: American Protestant Thought and Foreign Missions* (Chicago: University of Chicago Press, 1987).

57. Fluker, *Papers of Howard Washington Thurman*, 180–92.

58. Thurman, *With Head and Heart*, 105–8; *News* 13 (3) (March 1937): 6; Muriel Lester, *It Occurred to Me* (New York: Harper & Brothers, 1937), chap. 17.

59. Thurman, *With Head and Heart*, 108–36; Sudarshan Kapur, *Raising a Prophet: The African-American Encounter with Gandhi* (Boston, Mass.: Beacon Press, 1992), 85–93.

60. "With Our Negro Guests," March 14, 1936, in Fluker, *Papers of Howard Washington Thurman*, 332–37.

61. Mays, *Born to Rebel*, 155–56.

62. M. K. Alexander, "Six Systems of Indian Philosophy," *News* 14 (1) (November 1937): 7.

63. "Interview to Prof. Mays," in *Mahatma Gandhi, The Collected Works of Mahatma Gandhi*, vol. 64 (New Delhi: Publications Division Ministry of Information and Broadcasting Government of India, Patiala House, 2000), 221–23.

64. Ibid.

65. For a fuller explanation of the internal dispute on the caste question in India and American race relations, see Immerwahr, "Caste or Colony?," 275–301.

66. Charles Howard Hopkins, *John R. Mott: A Biography* (Grand Rapids, Mich.: William B. Eerdmans, 1979), 684.

67. Mays, *Born to Rebel*, 157.

68. Ibid., 158. Also see Harry Emerson Fosdick's *A Great Time to Be Alive* (New York: Harper & Brothers, 1944), 148–49. I am grateful to Daniel Immerwahr for bringing Fosdick's sermon to my attention.

69. Leroy Davis, *Clashing of the Soul*, 338.

70. "Dean Mays Returns," *News* 13 (3) (March 1937): 1, 12.

71. Benjamin E. Mays, "The Color Line Around the World," *Journal of Negro Education: A Survey of Negro Higher Education* 6 (2) (1937): 134.

72. Ibid., 141.

73. Ibid., 143.

74. Benjamin E. Mays, "Gandhi's Contribution to India," *News* 13 (4) (May 1937): 7–8; Mays's *Journal and Guide* articles: "Background of Present Political Crisis in India over New Constitution Is Cited by Dean B. E. Mays," May 8, 1937, 9; "British Continue Divide and Rule Policy in New Constitution, India's Leaders Say," May 15, 1937, 9; "Gandhi and Non-Violence," May 22, 1937, 8; "Gandhi Rekindled Spirit of Race Pride in India, Dr. Mays Finds," May 29, 1937, 9; "What Are the Differences between Gandhi and Nehru; Dr. Mays Asks, Gives Answer," June 5, 1937, 9; "Jewish-Arab Situation in Palestine Puzzling," June 12, 1937, 9; "Dr. Mays Relates: How Americans Are Blamed for Color Discrimination Abroad," June 19, 1937, 9.

75. Benjamin E. Mays, "Christianity in a Changing World," *National Educational Outlook among Negroes* 1 (4) (1937): 18.

76. Ibid., 19.

77. Ibid., 20.

78. Benjamin E. Mays, "Hitler Would Be 'God' to Germans, Asserts Dr. Mays," *Journal and Guide*, November 13, 1937, 9.

79. Benjamin E. Mays, "The Church Surveys World Problems," *Crisis* 44 (October 1937): 299, 316–17.

80. Mays, "Christianity in a Changing World," 18–20.

81. Benjamin E. Mays, "Christian Youth and Race," *Crisis* 46 (December 1939): 364–65, 370.

82. Robin D. G. Kelley, "'But a Local Phase of a World Problem': Black History's Global Vision, 1883–1950," *Journal of American History* 86 (3) (December 1999).

83. Leonard E. Terrell, "Faculty Activities," and S. L. Gandy, "And Time Marches On," *News* 13 (2) (January 1937): 5 and 11.

84. S. L. Gandy, "And Time Marches On," *News* 14 (4) (May 1938): 8.

85. *News* 14 (2) (January 1938): 1–8. One student, Henry Yergan Sideboard, reported on the Second Meeting of the National Negro Congress in Philadelphia, and another, Henry Butler Jr., reported on the Interseminary Movement, to which he was a delegate.

86. Benjamin E. Mays, "The Dean's Opening Message," and Amos R. Ryce, "Assembly Report," *News* 14 (1) (November 1937): 4, 12.

87. *News* 14, no. 4, May 1938, 1–5.

88. *News* 15, no. 4, May 1939, 1–5.

89. Benjamin E. Mays, "Most Neglected Area in Negro Education," *Crisis* 12 (1938): 268.

90. *News* 15 (1) (November 1938): 1.

91. Mays, "Most Neglected Area in Negro Education," 269.

92. Benjamin E. Mays, "A Mother Passes," *News* 14 (4) (May 1938): 6. Mays never mentions his mother's physical toil in the pages of *Born to Rebel.*

93. Stephen Preskill, "Combative Spirituality and the Life of Benjamin E. Mays," *Biography* 19 (4) (1996): 404–16.

94. Ibid.

95. "Dean Mays's Father Interred in S.C.," *Baltimore Afro-American*, June 18, 1938, 9.

96. Benjamin E. Mays, "Accredited," *News* 16 (2) (January 1940): 1–3.

97. "About Our Library," *News* 16 (4) (May 1940): 5.

98. "New Dean of School of Religion Given Hearty Welcome," *News* 17 (1) (November 1940): 1.

99. "Dean Mays Goes to Morehouse," *News* 16 (4) (May 1940): 1–2.

CHAPTER SIX

1. "Dr. Mays Elected President of Morehouse," *ADW*, May 11, 1940, 1.

2. Biographical information on John Hervey Wheeler can be found in Robert Penn Warren, *Who Speaks for the Negro?* (New York: Random House, 1965), 300.

3. "Morehouse Has a New President," *The Georgia Baptist*, May 15, 1940, 2; Benjamin E. Mays, *Born to Rebel: An Autobiography* (New York: Scribner, [1971]; reprint, with a revised foreword by Orville Vernon Burton. Athens: University of Georgia Press, 2003), 174.

4. Clarence Bacote, *The Story of Atlanta University: A Century of Service, 1865–1965* (Atlanta, Ga.: Atlanta University, 1969), 394.

5. Hugh M. Gloster quoted in Dereck Rovaris, "Developer of an Institution: Dr. Benjamin E. Mays, Morehouse College President, 1940–1967" (Ph.D. diss., University of Illinois, Urbana-Champaign, 1990), 96.

6. Mays, *Born to Rebel*, 172.

7. Tracy Strong to Benjamin E. Mays, October 11, 1939; and Mays to Strong, November 6, 1939, JRMP.

8. Benjamin E. Mays to John R. Mott, March 7, 1940, JRMP.

9. Benjamin E. Mays to John R. Mott, June 4, 1940, JRMP.

10. "Memorandum Accompanying the Letter Accepting the Presidency of Morehouse, May 31, 1940," YDS.

11. Benjamin E. Mays to John R. Mott, October 1, 1946, JRMP.

12. David Anthony, *Max Yergan: Race Man, Internationalist, Cold Warrior* (New York: New York University Press, 2006), 166.

13. On Yergan's transformation, see Glenda Gilmore's *Defying Dixie: The Radical Roots of Civil Rights, 1919–1950* (New York: W. W. Norton, 2008), 236–46.

14. On Atlanta, see Ronald Bayor, *Race and the Shaping of Twentieth-Century Atlanta* (Chapel Hill: University of North Carolina Press, 1996).

15. For a wonderful description of Atlanta in the years surrounding the Herndon case, see Gilmore, *Defying Dixie*, 163–85.

16. Clifford Kuhn, Harlon Joye, and E. Bernard West, *Living Atlanta: An Oral History of the City, 1914–1948* (Athens: University of Georgia Press, 1990), 12.

17. Benjamin E. Mays, "Opening Chapel Service, September 18, 1940," *Morehouse Alumnus*, 6–7.

18. Ibid.

19. Dr. B. E. Mays, "College Stundents [*sic*] Urged to Complete Their Education," *ADW*, September 1, 1940, 5.

20. Ibid., 7.

21. Ibid., 8.

22. Ibid.

23. Barbara Lewinson, "Three Conceptions of Black Education: A Study of the Educational Ideas of Benjamin Elijah Mays, Booker T. Washington, and Nathan Wright, Jr." (Ed.M. thesis, Rutgers University, New Brunswick, N.J., 1973), chap. 2.

24. "Misc Sermons and Speeches," BEMP.

25. Lewinson, "Three Conceptions of Black Education," 29.

26. Benjamin E. Mays, "Religious Life and Needs of Negro Students," *Journal of Negro Education: A Survey of Negro Higher Education* 9 (3) (1940): 332.

27. Ibid., 333.

28. Ibid., 336.

29. Ibid., 337.

30. Ibid., 343.

31. "What We Seek to Achieve at Morehouse College," General Education Board S.1.1, B. 62, F. 543, RFAC.

32. Ibid.

33. Ibid.

34. Rovaris, "Developer of an Institution," 151.

35. Mays, *Born to Rebel*, 177.

36. Ibid.

37. Rovaris, "Developer of an Institution," 79.

38. Benjamin E. Mays, "The Role of the Negro Liberal Arts College in Post-War Reconstruction," *Journal of Negro Education: A Survey of Negro Higher Education* 11 (3) (1942): 406.

39. See Willard B. Gatewood, *Aristocrats of Color: The Black Elite, 1880–1920* (Fayetteville: University of Arkansas Press, 2000).

40. On black reformist politics in Atlanta, see Gary Pomerantz, *Where Peachtree Meets Sweet Auburn: The Saga of Two Families in the Making of Atlanta* (New York: Scribner, 1996); Bayor, *Race and the Shaping of Twentieth-Century Atlanta*.

41. Karen Ferguson, *Black Politics in New Deal Atlanta* (Chapel Hill: University of North Carolina Press, 2002).

42. Winston A. Grady-Willis, *Challenging U.S. Apartheid: Atlanta and Black Struggles for Human Rights, 1960 1977* (Durham, N.C.: Duke University Press, 2006).

43. Martin Luther King Sr. with Clayton Riley, *Daddy King: An Autobiography* (New York: William Morrow, 1980), 110–11.

44. Ibid., 303–4.

45. Ira Joe Johnson and William G. Pickens, *Benjamin E. Mays and Margaret Mitchell: A Unique Legacy in Medicine* (Winter Park, Fla · Four-G Publishers, 1996); "Margaret Mitchell and Black Atlanta," http://www.gwtw.org/margaretmitchell-blackatlanta.html. For a rich depiction of the film debut in Atlanta, see Pomerantz's *Where Peachtree Meets Sweet Auburn*, chap. 8.

46. Oral history interview with Hylan Lewis, January 31, 1991, Documenting the American South, 43, http://docsouth.unc.edu/sohp/A-0361/A-0361.html.

47. All Russell Adams quotations in this section are from Jonathan Reider's *The Word of the Lord Is Upon Me: The Righteous Performance of Martin Luther King, Jr.* (Cambridge, Mass.: Belknap Press of Harvard University Press, 2008), 100–101.

48. Martin Summers, *Manliness and Its Discontent: The Black Middle Class and the Transformation of Masculinity, 1900–1930* (Chapel Hill: University of North Carolina Press, 2005), 8, suggests that there was a shift from the Victorian notion of manliness, which valued character, thrift, respectability, etc., to a masculinity driven by consumerism. Summers may be correct in his assessment, but Mays seems to be a counterpoint to his theory.

49. On black men's sexuality, see George Chauncey, *Gay New York: Gender, Urban Culture, and the Makings of the Gay Male World, 1890–1940* (New York: Basic Books, 1994); John D' Emilio, *The Lost Prophet: The Life and Times of Bayard Rustin* (Chicago: University of Chicago Press, 2003); Thaddeus Russell, "The Color of Discipline: Civil Rights and Black Sexuality," *American Quarterly* 1 (60) (March 2008): 101–28; and Allen Drexel, "Before Paris Burned: Race, Class, and Male Homosexuality on the Chicago South Side, 1935–1960," in *Creating a Place for Ourselves: Lesbian, Gay, and Bisexual Community Histories*, ed. Brett Beemyn (New York: Routledge, 1997), 119–44.

50. Mays, *Born to Rebel*, 168–69. Mays reveals in his manuscript drafts of *Born to Rebel* that Sadie required emergency surgery because of racial discrimination in the Cuban medical services.

51. Benjamin E. Mays, "World Aspects of Race and Culture," *Missions: American Baptist International Magazine* 147 (2) (1949): 85.

52. Gunnar Myrdal, *An American Dilemma: The Negro Problem and Modern Democracy* (New York: Harper, 1944). For a historical analysis of Myrdal, see Walter Jackson, *Gunnar Myrdal and America's Conscience: Social Engineering and Racial Liberalism, 1938–1987* (Chapel Hill: University of North Carolina Press, 1990); and David Southern, *Gunnar Myrdal and Black-White Relations: The Use and Abuse of An American Dilemma, 1944–1969* (Baton Rouge: Louisiana State University Press, 1987).

53. On civil religion see Robert Bellah, *The Broken Covenant: American Civil Religion in Time of Trial* (New York: Seabury Press, 1975).

54. Mays, *Born to Rebel*, 168–69. See, for example, Max Yergan's pamphlet published by the National Negro Congress, *Democracy and the Negro People Today* (Washington, D.C.: National Negro Congress, 1940).

55. Benjamin E. Mays, "Interracial Leadership in This Time of Crisis," *Georgia Observer* 3 (3–4) (1942): 2–4.

56. Benjamin E. Mays, "Democratizing and Christianizing America in This Generation," *Journal of Negro Education: A Survey of Negro Higher Education* 14 (4) (1945): 528, 532–33. For Roosevelt's, "four freedoms," see http://www.americanrhetoric.com/speeches/fdrthefourfreedoms.htm.

57. Mays, "Democratizing and Christianizing America."

58. Mays, *Born to Rebel*, 265.

59. "Anti–Poll Tax Law: Dr. Mays," *CD*, December 23, 1944, 11.

60. Mays, *Born to Rebel*, 213–20; see also Gavin, *Perils and Prospects of Black Southern Leadership: Gordon Blaine Hancock, 1884–1970* (Durham, N.C.: Duke University Press, 1977).

61. Mays, *Born to Rebel*, 198–99; see also "Segregation and Discrimination: Complaints and Responses, 1940–1955," Part 15, Benjamin Mays File, NAACPP.

62. For a great description of the "Journey of Reconciliation," see Raymond Arsenault, *Freedom Riders: 1961 and the Struggle for Racial Justice* (New York: Oxford University Press, 2006), 22–57.

63. Mays, *Born to Rebel*, 310.

64. Benjamin E. Mays, "Advice to Graduates," *PC*, June 7, 1947, 7.

65. United Negro College Fund Oral History Interview with Benjamin Mays, Columbia University Archive, New York, N.Y.

66. Oscar R. Williams, *George S. Schuyler: Portrait of a Black Conservative* (Knoxville: University of Tennessee Press, 2007).

67. "Distinguished Alumni Testimonial," October 19, 1949; and Mays to Bernard Loomer, November 1, 1949, Accession 1083–044, Box 10, CDS.

68. William M. Banks, *Black Intellectuals: Race and Responsibility in American Life* (New York: W. W. Norton, 1996), 121.

69. Benjamin E. Mays, "How to Kill Prejudice," *PC*, April 19, 1947, 7.

70. Lerone Bennett Jr., "Last of the Great Schoolmasters," *Ebony* 32 (December 1977): 74–79.

CHAPTER SEVEN

1. On Methodist women's publishing, see Alice Knotts, *Fellowship of Love: Methodist Women Changing American Racial Attitudes, 1920–1968* (Nashville, Tenn.: Kingswood Books, 1996).

2. Benjamin E. Mays, "Seeking to Be Christians in Race Relations," *Methodist Woman* 7 (6) (1947): 8–9, 13. It should be noted that these booklets were distributed without fanfare in many northern, and some southern, mainline churches.

3. Benjamin E. Mays, "NAACP and Women of Methodist Church Did Much to End Uncivilized Era," *PC*, January 23, 1954, 8. The United Methodist women also funded Pauli

Murray's book, an important contribution to the civil right movement, called *States' Laws on Race and Color* (Cincinnati, Ohio: Women's Division of Christian Service, Board of Missions and Church Extension, Methodist Church, 1951).

4. Benjamin E. Mays, review of *The Protestant Church and the Negro*, by Frank Loescher, *Journal of Religion* 28 (4) (October 1948): 299.

5. George McKenna, *The Puritan Origins of American Patriotism* (New Haven, Conn.: Yale University Press, 2007), 260–80; David Chappell, *A Stone of Hope: Prophetic Religion and the Death of Jim Crow* (Chapel Hill: University of North Carolina Press, 2004), chap. 2.

6. On Race Relations Sunday, see "Martin Luther King Jr. and the Global Freedom Struggle," http://mlk-kpp01.stanford.edu/index.php/encyclopedia/encyclopedia/enc_ national_ council_of_the_churches_of_christ_in_america_ncc.

7. On Mays's role at the FCC, see David W. Wills, "An Enduring Distance: Black Americans and the Establishment," in *Between the Times: The Travail of the Protestant Establishment in America, 1900–1960*, ed. W. R. Hutchinson (New York: Cambridge University Press, 1989), 168–92.

8. "Protestants at Pittsburgh," *Time*, December 11, 1944, http://www.time.com/time/ magazine/article/0,9171,883914,00.html.

9. Barbara Dianne Savage, "Benjamin Mays, Global Ecumenism, and Local Religious Segregation," *American Quarterly* 59 (3) (September 2007): 790–91.

10. See, for example, John D'Emilio, *Lost Prophet: The Life and Times of Bayard Rustin* (Chicago: University of Chicago Press, 2003); and Marian Mollin, "The Limits of Egalitarianism: Radical Pacifism, Civil Rights, and the Journey of Reconciliation," *Radical History Review*, no. 88 (Winter 2004): 113–38.

11. Darlene Clark Hine, *Black Victory: The Rise and Fall of the White Primary in Texas* (Columbia: University of Missouri Press, 2003). On the effect of *Smith v. Allright* in Atlanta, see Gary Pomerantz, *Where Peachtree Meets Sweet Auburn: The Saga of Two Families in the Making of Atlanta* (New York: Scribner, 1996), 194.

12. Benjamin E. Mays, "World Aspects of Race and Culture," *Missions: American Baptist International Magazine* 147 (2) (1949): 85.

13. Benjamin E. Mays, *Seeking to Be Christian in Race Relations* (New York: Friendship Press, 1946).

14. Benjamin E. Mays, "The South's Racial Policy," *Presbyterian Outlook* 132 (45) (1950): 5.

15. On the function of revivals in the civil rights movement, see Chappell, *Stone of Hope*, 97; also see Charles Marsh, *God's Long Summer: Stories of Faith and Civil Rights* (Princeton, N.J.: Princeton University Press, 1997). Mays revised *Seeking to Be Christian in Race Relations* in 1964.

16. Benjamin E. Mays, "The American Negro and the Christian Religion," *Journal of Negro Education: A Survey of Negro Higher Education* 8 (3) (1939): 530–38.

17. Ibid., 533–34.

18. Ibid., 534.

19. Ibid., 535.

20. Ibid., 537.

21. Ibid., 538.

22. Mays, *Seeking to Be Christian in Race Relations*, 5.

23. See Waldo E. Martin, *The Mind of Frederick Douglass* (Chapel Hill: University of North Carolina Press, 1984), on the long-standing debate on the oneness of humanity.

24. Mays, *Seeking to Be Christian in Race Relations*, 24.

25. Ibid.

26. Ibid., 27–28.

27. Ibid., 40.

28. Ibid., 43.

29. Ibid., 46.

30. Edwin E. Aubrey to Benjamin E. Mays, September 20, 1945, BEMP.

31. Albert Outler to Benjamin E. Mays, September 1, 1945, BEMP.

32. Mays, *Seeking to Be Christian in Race Relations*, 47.

33. Ibid.

34. Ibid., 48.

35. Benjamin E. Mays, "Segregation," *PC*, March 22, 1947, 7.

36. The literature on Niebuhr is extensive. The best biography remains Robin Wright Fox, *Reinhold Niebuhr: A Biography* (New York: Harper & Row, 1987); for a more recent and critical interpretation of Niebuhr, see Eugene McCarraher, *Christian Critics: Religion and the Impasse in Modern American Social Thought* (Ithaca, NY: Cornell University Press, 2000).

37. Benjamin E. Mays, "Obligations of Negro Christians in Relation to an Interracial Program," *Journal of Religious Thought* 31 (1945): 48–49.

38. See Memorandum on Plans for "The Commission of the American Churches on Democracy in Racial and Cultural Relations," August 24, 1942, RG 18, Box 17, F. 23, NCC.

39. On the ambivalence of the intellectual establishment, see Chappell, *Stone of Hope*, chap. 1; and Carol Polsgrove, *Divided Minds: Intellectuals and the Civil Rights Movement* (New York: W. W. Norton, 2001).

40. Benjamin E. Mays, "What's Wrong with Negro Leaders," *Negro Digest* 50 (1951): 45–49.

41. Benjamin E. Mays, "The Obligations of the Individual Christian," in *The Christian Way in Race Relations*, ed. W. S. Nelson (New York: Harper & Brothers, 1948), 209.

42. Benjamin E. Mays, "Democracy in the U.S.A. and in India," *Presbyterian Survey* 55 (1953): 28–29.

43. Benjamin E. Mays, "Power of Spirit," *PC*, December 21, 1946, 7.

44. Benjamin E. Mays, "Non-violence," *PC*, February 28, 1948, 6.

45. Mays, "World Aspects of Race and Culture," 85.

46. Benjamin E. Mays, "If Man Is Neither Good Enough Nor Wise Enough to Avoid War, Perhaps He Should Die," *PC*, July 22, 1950, 19.

47. Benjamin E. Mays, "Mays: We Must Spell Out D-e-m-o-c-r-a-c-y at Home as Well as Abroad for Victory Over Reds," *PC*, February 3, 1951, 19.

48. James L. Roark, "American Black Leaders: The Response to Colonialism and the Cold War, 1943–1953," *African Historical Studies* 4 (2) (1971): 253–70; Carol Anderson,

Eyes off the Prize: The United Nations and the African American Struggle for Human Rights, 1944–1955 (New York: Cambridge University Press, 2003); Mary Dudziak, *Cold War Civil Rights: Race and the Image of American Democracy* (Princeton, N.J.: Princeton University Press, 2001); James Meriwether, *Proudly We Can Be Africans: Black Americans and Africa, 1935–1961* (Chapel Hill: University of North Carolina Press, 2002).

49. Benjamin E. Mays, "Mays: No Man Who Believes in American Democracy Can Doubt the Validity of NAACP's Objectives," *PC*, July 21, 1951, 21.

50. On the relationship between the Truman administration and black American leaders, see Roark, "American Black Leaders," 266–69.

51. Mays, *Born to Rebel*, 223–27; "Negro Denied Seat as Georgia Delegate," *Atlanta Constitution*, September 19, 1950, 1; "Negroes Play Big Roles at Mid-Century Confab," *CD*, December 16, 1950, 13; "White House Confab Smacks Jim Crow, Oks Civil Rights Plan," *CD*, December 16, 1950.

52. Benjamin E. Mays, "Mays: Whether Robeson Should or Should Not Speak Is Irrelevant, U.S. Should Wake Up," *PC*, October 15, 1949, 15.

53. Benjamin E. Mays, "Dr. Mays: Are We Destroying the Freedom and Democracy We Fight to Defend?" *PC*, March 20, 1954, 8.

54. George S. Schuyler, "Views and Reviews," *PC*, September 13, 1947, 7.

55. Benjamin E. Mays, "Mays: Negroes Should Only Accept the Insults That They Are Forced to Accept," *PC*, July 23, 1949, 15.

56. Mark L. Chapman, *Christianity on Trial: African-American Religious Thought Before and After Black Power* (Maryknoll, N.Y.: Orbis Books, 1996), 37–38.

57. Benjamin E. Mays, "MAYS: To Accept Anything Less Than Integration Is Not the Mark of Free Men's Minds," *PC*, April 30, 1949, 15.

58. Benjamin E. Mays, "Communism: In Greece, Turkey and U.S., the Best Way to Kill Communism Is to Make Democracy Work," *PC*, April 26, 1947, 7.

59. Benjamin E. Mays, "Foreign Affairs: If U.S. Has Right to Arm and Train Small Nations, Russia Has the Same Right," *PC*, July 5, 1947, 7.

60. Mays was one of 300 signatories of a public letter published in the *Washington Post* asking President Harry Truman to hold talks with the Soviet Union instead of forming NATO; see Associated Press, "300 Ask President to Talk with Reds," *Washington Post*, April 11, 1949, 2; Benjamin E. Mays, "Peace and Bombs," *PC*, August 9, 1947, 7.

61. Benjamin E. Mays, "MAYS: Why Spend Millions To Defend Ideologies So Far Removed from Our Democratic Beliefs?" *PC*, September 16, 1950, 21.

62. Benjamin E. Mays, "White Baptists Retreat: Dr. Mays Asks 'Can Christians Stand Up and Be Counted?,'" *PC*, January 18, 1947, 7. For another perspective on the social ethics of white Southern Baptists, see George Kelsey's *Social Ethics among Southern Baptists, 1917–1969* (Metuchen, N.J.: Scarecrow Press, 1973).

63. Patricia Sullivan, *Days of Hope: Race and Democracy in the New Deal Era* (Chapel Hill: University of North Carolina Press, 1996), 213–14; Patricia Sullivan, *Lift Every Voice: The NAACP and the Making of the Civil Rights Movement* (New York: New Press, 2009), 319.

64. Benjamin E. Mays, "A Religious Problem: Inability of Authorities to Apprehend Monroe Lynchers Unconvincing to Dr. Mays," *PC*, January 25, 1947, 7; Sullivan, *Lift Every Voice*, 331.

65. Southern Baptist Convention statement from Glenda Gilmore, *Defying Dixie: The Radical Roots of Civil Rights, 1919–1950* (New York: W. W. Norton, 2008), 415–16.

66. See *Journal of Bible and Religion* 20 (2) (April 1952): 141.

67. George McKenna, *The Puritan Origins of American Patriotism* (New Haven, Conn.: Yale University Press, 2007), 251–58.

68. Benjamin E. Mays, "Billy Graham Speaks," *PC*, April 2, 1955.

69. Steven P. Miller, *Billie Graham and the Rise of the Republican South* (Philadelphia, Pa.: University of Pennsylvania Press, 2009).

70. Gilmore, *Defying Dixie*, 183.

71. Benjamin E. Mays, "Paradox of Jews," *PC*, September 13, 1947, 7.

72. Benjamin E. Mays, "Mays: He Would Add One More Item Pledge Sponsored by Congress of Racial Equality," *PC*, February 17, 1951, 21.

73. Benjamin E. Mays, "Jews and Arabs," *PC*, April 12, 1947, 7.

74. "Ending Religious and Racial Bars Urged at the Conference of Christians and Jews," *New York Times*, November 10, 1954, 18.

75. Benjamin E. Mays, "Mays: Mrs. Bethune's Successor Must Be a Woman Who Has Prestige and Has Built up a Noble Record," *PC*, November 12, 1949, 15.

76. David Levering Lewis, *W. E. B. DuBois: The Fight for Equality and the American Century, 1919–1963* (New York: Henry Holt, 2000), 558–59.

CHAPTER EIGHT

1. Benjamin Mays, *Quotable Quotes of Benjamin E. Mays* (New York: Vantage, 1983), 16.

2. Peter R. Sigmund, "Mays Gives Views on School Case," *CD*, March 28, 1953, 1.

3. Benjamin E. Mays, "We Are Unnecessarily Excited," *New South* 9 (2) (February 1954): 1–3.

4. Benjamin E. Mays, "Dr. Mays: Negroes Will Win Even If High Court Oks Separate but Equal," *PC*, March 13, 1954, 8.

5. Benjamin E. Mays, "Our Colleges and the Supreme Court," BEMP.

6. Benjamin E. Mays, "The Supreme Court Decision and Our Responsibility," *YWCA Magazine* 48 (7) (1954): 8–9, 35.

7. George Breathett, "Black Educators and the United States Supreme Court Decision of May 17, 1954," *Journal of Negro History* 68 (2) (Spring 1983): 202.

8. On the role of Black Baptists in the World Council of Churches, see Pearl L. McNeil, "Baptist Black Americans and the Ecumenical Movement," *Journal of Ecumenical Studies* 17 (2) (1980): 103–17.

9. "Church Most Segregated Agency in America Declares Dr. Mays," *Atlanta Daily World*, March 15, 1950, 4.

10. Benjamin E. Mays, *Born to Rebel: An Autobiography* (New York: Scribner, [1971]; reprint, with a revised foreword by Orville Vernon Burton. Athens: University of Georgia Press, 2003), 256–57.

11. Quoted in Mays, *Born to Rebel*, 257.

12. See Arnold Ohrn, ed., *Eighth Baptist World Congress, Cleveland, Ohio U. S. A., July 22–27, 1950* (Valley Forge: Judson Press, 1950).

13. Mays, *Born to Rebel*, 259; B. H. Logan, "Wipe Out Segregation, Baptist Told," *PC*, August 5, 1950, 13; Benjamin E. Mays, "Baptist World Alliance Takes Definite Steps on Problems of Bias in Connection's Churches," *PC*, August 5, 1950, 19; Benjamin E. Mays, "Baptists in Cleveland Behaved as Human Should Always Do under Christian Fellowship," *PC*, August 12, 1950, 13.

14. Mays, *Born to Rebel*, 260–61.

15. "Great Preachers: Ten Most Popular Ministers Lead Rigorous Public Lives," *Ebony*, July 1954, 26–27.

16. "Our Opinions," *CD*, August 28, 1954, 9; "Camera Spotlights Church Meeting," *CD*, September 4, 1954, 4; George Daniels, "WCC Approves May's Plan for Brotherhood," *CD*, September 11, 1954, 1.

17. Mays, *Born to Rebel*, app. B, "The Church Amidst Ethnic and Racial Tensions," 349–56.

18. Barbara Diane Savage, "Benjamin Mays, Global Ecumenism, and Local Religious Segregation," *American Quarterly* 59 (3) (September 2007): 793.

19. See William Faulkner, Benjamin E. Mays, and Cecil Sims, *The Segregation Decisions: Papers Read at a Session of the Twenty-first Annual Meeting of the Southern Historical Association, Memphis, Tennessee, November 10, 1955* (Atlanta: Southern Regional Council, 1956).

20. Carol Polsgrove, *Divided Minds: Intellectuals and the Civil Rights Movement* (New York: W. W. Norton, 2001), 9–11; see also John Edgerton, *Speak Now Against the Day: The Generation Before the Civil Rights Movement* (New York: Knopf, 1994), 619.

21. Benjamin E. Mays, "My View: Negroes Should Protest More," *PC*, March 19, 1955, 15.

22. Benjamin E. Mays, "My View: The Dark and Bright Side," *PC*, October 22, 1955, 24.

23. Benjamin Mays to Charles Batten, February 28, 1948, in Clayborne Carson, *The Papers of Martin Luther King, Jr.* vol. 1 (Stanford, Calif.: Martin Luther King, Jr., Papers Project, 1992).

24. Lewis V. Baldwin, *There Is a Balm in Gilead: The Cultural Roots of Martin Luther King, Jr.* (Minneapolis: Fortress Press, 1991), 125.

25. In his book *The Preacher King: Martin Luther King Jr. and the Word That Moved America* (New York: Oxford University Press, 1995), Richard Lischer argues that King wanted big words to move people by. Unfortunately, like so many King scholars, he gives the influence of Mays and Howard Thurman short shrift.

26. Martin Luther King Jr., *Stride Toward Freedom* (New York: Harper & Row, 1958), 145–46.

27. Benjamin E. Mays, "My View," *PC*, February 18, 1956, A4. For a constitutional and legal analysis of the Montgomery bus boycott, see Randall Kennedy, "Martin Luther King's Constitution: A Legal History of the Montgomery Bus Boycott," *Yale Law Journal* 98 (6) (April 1989): 999–1067.

28. Martin Luther King Jr. to Benjamin Mays, June 17, 1957, in Carson, *Papers of Martin Luther King, Jr.*, vol. 4.

29. Quotation from Freddie Colson Jr., "Dr. Benjamin E. Mays: His Impact as Spiritual and Intellectual Mentor of Martin Luther King Jr.," in *Walking Integrity: Benjamin Elijah Mays, Mentor to Generations*, ed. Lawrence E. Carter (Atlanta: Scholars Press, 1996), 226–27.

30. See Benjamin E. Mays, comp., *A Gospel for the Social Awakening: Selections, Edited and Compiled from the Writings of Walter Rauschenbusch* (New York: Association Press, 1950). It is interesting that none of the major King scholars has given Mays credit for the motto.

31. Adam Fairclough, *To Redeem the Soul of America: The Southern Christian Leadership Conference and Martin Luther King, Jr.* (Athens: University of Georgia Press, 1987), 68; also see Aldon Morris, *The Origins of the Civil Rights Movement: Black Communities Organizing for Change* (New York: Free Press, 1984), chaps. 4, 5, and 6; and David J. Garrow, *Bearing the Cross: Martin Luther King, Jr., and the Southern Christian Leadership Conference, 1955–1968* (New York: Morrow, 1986).

32. Morris, *Origin of the Civil Rights Movement*, 36–37.

33. Benjamin E. Mays, "My View: Compliment to Martin Luther King, Jr.," *PC*, August 13, 1960; and "My View: Mr. Kilpatrick and the Law," *PC*, December 17, 1960.

34. Benjamin E. Mays, "My View: This I Believe," *PC*, March 5, 1960; and "My View: Persecution or Prosecution or Both?," *PC*, November 12, 1960.

35. Benjamin E. Mays, "My View: A Book Review of MLK, Jr.'s *Strive Toward Freedom*, *PC*, October 25, 1958, A7.

36. Harold L. Keith, "Courier Forum Analyst: Our Ministers Ignoring Fight for Civil Rights," *PC*, March 1, 1952, 30.

37. Benjamin E. Mays to George Kelsey, October 30, 1958, and Mays to Kelsey, November 17, 1958, GKP.

38. George Kelsey to Benjamin Mays, n.d., GKP.

39. For more information on the Interdenominational Theological Center, see Harry V. Richardson, *Walk Together, Children: The Story of the Birth and Growth of the Interdenominational Theological Center* (Atlanta, Ga.: Interdenominational Theological Center Press, 1981); and the Harry V. Richardson Papers, Robert Woodruff Library Archives, Atlanta University Center.

40. Benjamin E. Mays, "A Dream Come True," *PC*, June 28, 1958.

41. "Defender Camera Highlights Baptist Meet in Miami (2)" *CD*, September 19, 1953, 12; Ethel L. Payne, "One Year after Miami, Baptists Are Progressing with Joe Jackson," *CD*, September 11, 1954, 12.

42. Joseph H. Jackson, *A Story of Christian Activism: The History of the National Baptist Convention, U.S.A., Inc.* (Nashville, Tenn.: Townsend Press, 1980), 190–91.

43. One of the better histories of the National Baptist Convention is James M. Washington's *Frustrated Fellowship: the Black Baptist Quest for Social Power* (Macon, Ga.: Mercer, 1986). Washington covers the NBC from its inception in the 1890s until 1960s.

44. Roi Ottley, "The Brotherhood of Man Shown in Negro Preacher's Deeds," *CD*, March 7, 1954, 7.

45. Quotation from Wallace Best, "The Right Achieved and the Wrong Way Conquered: J. H. Jackson, Martin Luther King, Jr., and the Conflict over Civil Rights," *Religion and American Culture* 16 (2) (2006): 199.

46. For Jackson's interpretation of the events at the NBC's 1953 convention, see his *Story of Christian Activism*, chap. 5.

47. Most of the information on Joseph H. Jackson comes from Best, "Right Achieved and the Wrong Way Conquered," 195–226. See also Ralph David Abernathy, *And the Walls Came Tumbling Down: An Autobiography* (New York: Harper & Row, 1989), 171–74.

48. Benjamin E. Mays, "My View: Reflections on Baptist," *PC*, October 5, 1957, A5; and "My View: Further Reflections," *PC*, October 19, 1957, A7.

49. James Melvin Washington, "Jesse Jackson and the Symbolic Politics of Black Christendom," *ANNALS of the American Academy of Political and Social Science* 480 (1) (July 1985): 99.

50. See Nick Salvatore's *Singing in a Strange Land: C. L. Franklin, the Black Church, and the Transformation of America* (New York: Little, Brown, 2005). C. L. Franklin, the father of R&B artist Aretha Franklin, was a supporter of Jackson and King.

51. Benjamin E. Mays, "My View: Negro Baptists," *PC*, August 5, 1961.

52. Jackson, *Story of Christian Activism*, 249–50, 255–66.

53. Benjamin E. Mays, "My View: Baptists," *PC*, August 12, 1961.

54. Benjamin E. Mays, "My View: Baptists," *PC*, August, 19, 1961; and "2nd Baptist Head Calls for Neutral Leader," *CD*, March 18, 1961, 22.

55. Jackson, *Story of Christian Activism*, 473, 479.

56. Benjamin E. Mays "My View: MLK, Baptist Convention," *PC*, September 30, 1961; and "2nd Baptist Head Calls for Neutral Leader," *CD*, March 18, 1961, 22.

57. Taylor Branch, *Parting the Waters: America in the King Years: 1954–1963* (New York: Simon and Schuster, 1988, 335–39, 500–503).

58. Benjamin E. Mays to Lyndon Johnson, Presidential Papers of Lyndon Johnson, Lyndon B. Johnson Library, Austin, Tex.

59. Barbara Ransby, *Ella Baker and the Black Freedom Movement: A Radical Democratic Vision* (Chapel Hill: University of North Carolina Press, 2005), chap. 6.

60. Barbara Dianne Savage, *Your Spirits Walk Beside Us: The Politics of Black Religion* (Cambridge, Mass.: Harvard University Press, 2008), 230–31.

61. On SNCC, see Howard Zinn, *SNCC, the New Abolitionists* (Boston: Beacon Press, 1964); Clayborne Carson, *In Struggle: SNCC and the Black Awakening of the 1960s* (Cambridge, Mass.: Harvard University Press, 1981).

CHAPTER NINE

1. In popular parlance it is often forgotten that the civil rights movement was a national movement with both southern and northern phases. See Martha Biondi, *To Stand and Fight: The Struggle for Civil Rights in Postwar New York City* (Cambridge, Mass.: Harvard University Press, 2006); Davison M. Douglas, *Jim Crow Moves North: The Battle over Northern School Segregation, 1865–1954* (New York: Cambridge University Press, 2005); Randal Maurice Jelks, *African Americans in the Furniture City: The Struggle for Civil Rights in Grand Rapids* (Urbana: University of Illinois Press, 2006); and Sidney Fine, *Expanding the Frontiers of Civil Rights: Michigan, 1948–1968* (Detroit: Wayne State University Press, 2000).

2. Marian Wright Edelman, "Spelman College: A Safe Haven for a Young Black Woman," *Journal of Blacks in Higher Education* 27 (Spring 2000): 118-23.

3. Civil Rights Movement Veterans, "An Appeal for Human Rights," Civil Rights Movement Veterans Website, http://www.crmvet.org/docs/aa4hr.htm.

4. Vincent Fort, "Atlanta Sit-In Movement, 1960–1961: An Oral Study," in *Atlanta, Georgia, 1960–1961: Sit-Ins and Student Activism*, ed. David J. Garrow (Brooklyn: Carlson, 1989), 134.

5. Winston A. Grady-Willis, *Challenging U.S. Apartheid: Atlanta and Black Struggles for Human Rights, 1960–1977* (Durham, N.C.: Duke University Press, 2006), 11–12. On Lonnie King, see Benjamin E. Mays, *Born to Rebel: An Autobiography* (New York: Scribner, [1971]; reprint, with a revised foreword by Orville Vernon Burton. Athens: University of Georgia Press, 2003), 287–88.

6. Mays, *Born to Rebel*, 295–96.

7. Benjamin E. Mays to Roy Wilkins, March 19, 1960, NAACP 1940–55, General Office File, Board of Directors, NAACPP, Reel 16.

8. Vernon E. Jordan, *Vernon Can Read!: A Memoir* (New York: PublicAffairs, 2001), 126–43.

9. Benjamin E. Mays to Roy Wilkins, June 9, 1960, NAACP 1940–55, General Office File, Board of Directors, NAACPP, Reel 16.

10. Edelman, "Spelman College," 119–20.

11. Benjamin E. Mays, "My View: The Meaning of Sit Down Protest," *PC*, March 26, 1960.

12. Benjamin E. Mays, "My View: Adult Responsibility," *PC*, March 11, 1961.

13. Barbara Dianne Savage, "Benjamin Mays, Global Ecumenism, and Local Religious Segregation," *American Quarterly* 59 (3) (September 2007): 797.

14. "Benjamin Mays's Introduction," in Mathew Ahmann, ed., *Race: Challenge to Religion, Original Essays and an Appeal to the Conscience* (Chicago: H. Regnery Co., 1963), 5.

15. Anna Arnold Hedgeman, *The Trumpet Sounds: A Memoir of Negro Leadership* (New York: Holt, Rinehart and Winston, 1964), 175–76.

16. Mark Chapman, *Christianity on Trial: African-American Religious Thought Before and After Black Power* (Maryknoll, N.Y.: Orbis Books, 1996), 142–43.

17. Benjamin E. Mays, "My View: The Freedom Riders Did It," *PC*, March 17, 1960; "Less Fear and More Respect," *PC*, April 2, 1960; and "My View: They Show the Way," *PC*, July 28, 1962.

18. Benjamin E. Mays, "My View: Dr. DuBois at 93," *PC*, January 6, 1962.

19. Benjamin E. Mays, "After College, What Next for the Negro," *Crisis* 37 (12) (1930): 408–10.

20. Benjamin E. Mays, "My View: W. E. B. DuBois Is Dead," *PC*, September 12, 1963, 7; and "Plan Memorial Tribute to the Late W. E. B. DuBois," *CD*, December 31, 1963, 15.

21. Benjamin E. Mays, "My View: I Marched in Washington," *PC*, September 14, 1963.

22. Taylor Branch, *Pillar of Fire: America in the King Years, 1963–1965* (New York: Simon & Schuster, 1998), 305.

23. Benjamin E. Mays, "My View, The King-Hoover Episode," *PC*, December 5, 1964.

24. Branch, *Pillar of Fire*, 516.

25. Ralph David Abernathy, *And the Wall Came Tumbling Down: An Autobiography* (New York: Harper & Row, 1989), 480; also see Clayborne Carson, Tenisha Armstrong, Susan Carson, Adrienne Clay, and Kieran Taylor, eds., *Threshold of a New Decade, January 1959–December 1960*, vol. 5 of *The Papers of Martin Luther King, Jr.* (Berkeley: University of California Press, 2005), nn. 288, 338, 506, 573, and 575, which explains how much King borrowed from Mays's rhetoric and writings.

26. Benjamin E. Mays, "Desegregate and Integrate to What End?," in *The Negro Speaks: The Rhetoric of Contemporary Black Leaders*, edited by Jamey Coleman Williams and McDonald Williams (New York: Noble and Noble Publishers, Inc., 1970), 89–98.

27. Ibid.

28. Benjamin E. Mays, "I Find This Bias Hard to Believe," *PC*, August 14, 1965, 7.

29. Arnold Hirsch, "Urban Renewal," http://www.encyclopedia.chicagohistory.org/pages/1295.html.

30. In a letter to Randolph and Dorothy Compton in 1969, Mays poignantly admitted that the black colleges had not done as much for young people in the ghetto as he would have liked. See Mays to Randolph and Dorothy Compton, January 29, 1969, Installation 2, B. 38, F. C-1968–69, BEMP.

31. Benjamin E. Mays, "Who's to Blame for a Malcolm X?," *PC*, March 2, 1965, 7.

32. See Mays on the Watts riot in Los Angeles: "There Are Many Gulfs to Cross," *PC*, August 28, 1965; and "We Cannot Say One Factor Caused Riot," *PC*, September 4, 1965.

33. Robert Williams, the former NAACP chapter president in Monroe, North Carolina, who had been forced to live in exile in Cuba and later in China after fleeing the state of North Carolina, had used the term "black power." Willie Ricks, one of Carmichael's compatriots in SNCC, had also used the term. Rick changed his name to Mukassa Dada.

34. Winston A. Grady-Willis, *Challenging U.S. Apartheid: Atlanta and Black Struggles for Human Rights, 1960–1977* (Durham, N.C.: Duke University Press, 2006), 171. On Samuel Williams, see Benjamin E. Mays, "A Special Tribute to Samuel Williams," *CD*, November 7, 1970.

35. Benjamin E. Mays, "Black Power Is Capable of Many Interpretations," *PC*, August 6, 1966.

36. Benjamin E. Mays, "The Black Power Convention," *PC*, July 22, 1966, 6.

37. Benjamin E. Mays, "Basic Need for Excellence," *PC*, October 14, 1967, 14.

38. Benjamin E. Mays, "Definition of Black Power," *PC*, November 4, 1967, 14.

39. For discussions on black intellectuals, see William M. Banks, *Black Intellectuals: Race and Responsibility in American Life* (New York: W. W. Norton, 1996); and Ross Posnock, *Color and Culture: Black Writers and the Making of the Modern Intellectual* (Cambridge, Mass.: Harvard University Press, 1998). These two volumes, however, assiduously avoid any discussion of African American religious intellectuals. On an African American religious intellectuals, see Clarence Taylor's introduction to *Black Religious Intellectuals: The Fight for Equality from Jim Crow to the Twenty-First Century* (New York: Routledge, 2002).

40. Recent important works about the theological origins of the civil rights movement are Charles Marsh, *God's Long Summer: Stories of Faith and Civil Rights* (Princeton, N.J.:

Princeton University Press, 1997), and David L. Chappell, *Stone of Hope: Prophetic Religion and the Death of Jim Crow* (Chapel Hill: University of North Carolina Press, 2004). Also see James Melvin Washington, "Jesse Jackson and the Symbolic Politics of Black Christendom," *ANNALS of the American Academy of Political and Social Science* 480 (1) (July 1985): 89–105.

41. For the Black Power critique of black clergymen in this period, see Nick Salvatore's *Singing in a Strange Land: C. L. Franklin, the Black Church, and the Transformation of America* (New York: Little, Brown, 2005), chaps. 9–10.

42. "Mays Defines Black Power as Ability to Achieve," *CD*, May 18, 1968, 6.

43. "Mays tells His Morehouse Grads He Kept His Vow to Give His All," *ADW*, May 31, 1967, 1.

44. "Dr. King's Tragic Doctrine" and "Jackie Robinson Says: Want to Hear from Dr. King," *PC*, April 15, 1967.

45. Benjamin E. Mays, "South Vietnam," *PC*, March 13, 1965, 7.

46. Benjamin E. Mays, "My View: Dr. King Is Sincere," *PC*, May 20, 1967.

47. See David C. Carter, *The Music Has Gone Out of the Movement: Civil Rights and the Johnson Administration, 1965–1968* (Chapel Hill: University of North Carolina Press, 2009).

48. Benjamin E. Mays, "Rioting Is Not Civil Rights," *PC*, August 19, 1967.

49. Julius Lester, "The Angry Children of Malcolm X," *Sing Out*, October–November 1966, 20–25.

50. Benjamin E. Mays, "Not on a White Campus," *CD*, March 16, 1968; see also Jack Bass and Jack Nelson, *Orangeburg Massacre* (Macon, Ga.: Mercer University Press, 1996).

51. Howell Raines, *My Soul Is Rested: Movement Days in the Deep South Remembered* (New York: Putnam, 1977), 459–60.

52. Benjamin E. Mays to Martin Luther King Jr., quoted in Colston, "Dr. Benjamin E. Mays: His Impact as Spiritual Mentor of Martin Luther King Jr.," in *Walking Integrity: Benjamin Elijah Mays, Mentor to Generations*, ed. Lawrence E. Carter (Atlanta: Scholars Press, 1996), 228.

53. Coretta Scott King, *My Life With Martin Luther King, Jr.* (New York: Holt, Rinehart and Winston, 1969), 306.

54. Tobias, Channing H., Biographical, 1911–95, Box 205, YMCA Biographical Files, YMCA Papers, YMCAA.

55. Abernathy, *And the Wall Came Tumbling Down*, 463–64.

56. Mays, *Born to Rebel*, app. C, 357–60.

57. Joel Smith eulogizing Dr. M. L. King Jr.; "Mays Says All Americans Should Search Their Hearts," *ADW*, April 10, 1968, 3.

58. Farah Jasmine Griffin, "*Who Set You Flowin'?*": The African-American Migration Narrative* (New York: Oxford University Press, 1995), 43.

59. "Black Power: Statement by the National Committee of Negro Churchmen," July 31, 1966, in *Black Theology: A Documentary History* (Maryknoll, N.Y.: Orbis Books, 1979), 26–27.

60. See James Cone, *Black Theology and Black Power* (Maryknoll, N.Y.: Orbis Book, 1999).

61. Vincent Harding, "Black Power and the American Christ," *Christian Century* 84 (1) (January 4, 1967): 10–13. On the IBW, see Grady-Willis, *Challenging U.S. Apartheid*, chap. 6.

62. Correspondence between Benjamin E. Mays and John Hope Franklin, Installation 1, B. 39, F. John Hope Franklin, BEMP.

63. Sylvia Cook to Benjamin Mays, December 3, 1968; Samuel DuBois Cook to Benjamin Mays, April 11, 1969; Sylvia Cook to Benjamin Mays, April 21, 1969; and Samuel DuBois Cook to Benjamin Mays, August 5, 1969, all BEMP.

64. Mays, *Born to Rebel*, 311–14; Grady-Willis, *Challenging U.S. Apartheid*, 145–46.

65. History of Sadie G. Mays Rehabilitation Center, http://www.sgmays.org/about/history.htm.

66. Oral History Interview with Hylan Lewis, January 13, 1991, Documenting the American South, 43, http://docsouth.unc.edu/sohp/A-0361/A-0361.html.

67. Benjamin Mays to Dr. Leland DeVinney, Atlanta, Georgia, May 13, 1967; Leland DeVinney, interview with Benjamin E. Mays, May 14, 1968; and Mays's Foundation Grant Report, New York, June 20, 1968, all RFAC.

68. V. P. Franklin, *Living Our Stories, Telling Our Truths: Autobiography and the Making of the African-American Intellectual Tradition* (New York: Scribner, 1995), 12.

69. Drafts of *Born to Rebel*, BEMP.

70. Benjamin Mays to Robert Allen, May 27, 1969, BEMP; Robert L. Allen, *Black Awakening in Capitalist America: An Analytic History* (Garden City, N.Y.: Doubleday, 1969).

71. Benjamin E. Mays, "Mays Raps Black Studies Separatism," *CD*, November 14, 1970.

EPILOGUE

1. George Kelsey, "Theological Analysis and Criticism in the Thought of Benjamin E. Mays," 23, GKP.

2. See James Cone's excellent theological analysis *Martin & Malcolm & America: A Dream or a Nightmare?* (Maryknoll, N.Y.: Orbis Books, 1991).

3. Randal Maurice Jelks, "Religious Dimensions of the American Civil Rights Movement," *Church History* 73 (4) (December 2004): 828–33.

4. Ishmael Reed, "Born to Rebel," review of *Born to Rebel: An Autobiography*, by Benjamin E. Mays, *New York Times Book Review*, April 25, 1971, 47–48.

5. See, for example, Van Deburg, *New Day in Babylon: The Black Power Movement and American Culture, 1965–1975* (Chicago: University of Chicago Press, 1992).

6. Reed, "Born to Rebel." 48.

7. Mays's views on respectability serve as a reminder that not all black leaders used the discourse of uplift as a way of advancing their own interests above the concerns of the black working class and poor, as described in Kevin Gaines's much quoted *Uplifting the Race*. Religious altruism combined with notions of respectability also inspired many black leaders to seek social change that included addressing the black poor's concerns. At the heart of the SCLC's Poor People's Movement is this mixture of respectability and solidarity with the black working classes and poor.

8. "Elect Benjamin E. Mays Board of Education 7th Ward October 7, 1969," (brochure), courtesy of the Atlanta Historical Society; "Dr. Mays Elected to Head Atlanta's School Board," *CD*, January 5, 1970, 9; "A Black Thorn in White Conscience," *Atlanta Constitution*, January 18, 1970, 9-M. For a more thorough historical background on Mays's election, see Alton Hornsby Jr., "Black Public Education in Atlanta, Georgia, 1954–1973: From Segregation to Segregation," *Journal of Negro History* 76 (1/4) (Winter–Autumn 1991): 21–47; and Susan McGrath, "From Tokenism to Community Control: Political Symbolism in the Desegregation of Atlanta," *Georgia Historical Quarterly* 79 (4) (Winter 1995): 842–72.

9. Kevin Cruse, *White Flight: Atlanta and the Making of Modern Conservatism* (Princeton, N.J.: Princeton University Press, 2005).

10. Benjamin E. Mays, "Atlanta—Living with *Brown* Twenty Years Later," *Black Law Journal* 3 (2–3) (1974): 184–92.

11. Benjamin E. Mays, "Nixon's Busing Stand a Threat to Education," *CD*, August 21, 1971, 8.

12. Benjamin E. Mays, "White Private Schools in Dixie Mushrooming," *CD*, November 28, 1970, 8.

13. See James Cone, *Black Theology and Black Power* (Maryknoll, N.Y.: Orbis Books, 1997) and *The God of the Oppressed* (Maryknoll, N.Y.: Orbis Books, 1997).

14. See Randall Kennedy, "Martin Luther King's Constitution: A Legal History of the Montgomery Bus Boycott," *Yale Law Journal* 98 (6) (April 1989): 999–1067. In this interesting piece, however, Kennedy neglects to comment on how Mays's public theology shaped King's understanding of the Constitution.

15. For one aspect of this larger story, see Joseph Crespino's *In Search of Another Country: Mississippi and the Conservative Counterrevolution* (Princeton, N.J.: Princeton University Press, 2007); and Paul Harvey, *Freedom's Coming: Religious Culture and the Shaping of the South from the Civil War through the Civil Rights Era* (Chapel Hill: University of North Carolina Press, 2005), chap. 5.

16. For the best discussion on this subject, see Robert Wuthnow, *The Restructuring of American Religion: Society and Faith since World War II* (Princeton, N.J.: Princeton University Press, 1988).

17. In 1971, Whitney Young drowned while in Lagos, Nigeria. Mays and Howard Thurman gave eulogies at Riverside Church in New York City. On Young's death, see Vernon Jordan's, *Vernon Can Read!: A Memoir* (New York: PublicAffairs, 2001), 220–21, and Dennis Dickerson's *Militant Mediator: Whitney M. Young Jr.* (Lexington: University of Kentucky Press, 1996).

18. Benjamin E. Mays, "Meeting Tomorrow's Challenges Today with Academic, Moral and Spiritual Preparation," *Am-African Journal of Research and Education* 1 (1) (1981): 1–6.

19. Lynn Darling, "Honors for an Elder," *Washington Post*, October 23, 1980, D3; "Educator and Poet Join the State Hall of Fame," *Greenville News & Greenville Piedmont*, January 7, 1984; "Mays, Rutledge Inducted into the SC Hall of Fame," *Columbia Record*, January 6, 1984.

20. Benjamin E. Mays, "Response by Dr. Benjamin E. Mays," *Journal of Religious Thought* 32 (1) (1975): 130–31.

21. Richard N. Ostling, "Moving into the Mainstream," *Time*, May 19, 1983, http://www.time.com/time/magazine/article/0,9171,954053,00.html.

22. Frank Prial, "Benjamin Mays, Educator, Dies; Served as Inspiration to Dr. King," *New York Times*, March 29, 1984, D23; "Benjamin Mays Remembered as Great Educator," *Atlanta Constitution*, March 30, 1984; "Benjamin Mays, Renowned Black Educator, Dies," *Washington Post*, March 29, 1984, C6.

23. Last Will and Testament of Benjamin E. Mays, June 13, 1983, Probate Court of Fulton County, Atlanta, Ga.

24. Joseph R. Washington Jr., *Black Religion: The Negro and Christianity in the United States* (Boston, Mass.: Beacon Press, 1964), 54, 104–5.

25. On the transformation of theological education, see Charles Shelby Rooks, *Revolution in Zion: Reshaping African American Ministry, 1960–1974: A Biography in the First Person* (New York: Pilgrim Press, 1990).

26. Oral history interview with Hylan Lewis, January 13, 1991, Documenting the American South, 43, http://docsouth.unc.edu/sohp/A-0361/A-0361.html. A biographical portrait of Lewis can be found at The Black Past: Remembered and Proclaimed website, http://www.blackpast.org/?q=aah/lewis-hylan-garnet-1911-2000.

27. Samuel DuBois Cook, "Eulogy of Benjamin Elijah Mays, 1894–1898," *Southern Changes: The Journal of the Southern Regional Council* 6 (3) (1984): 22.

28. "Educator of the Spirit," *New York Times*, April 1, 1984.

Selected Bibliography

Benjamin E. Mays's papers are rich and vital for any scholar studying religion, education, and the civil rights movement in the United States. Housed at various locations, they are especially strong from 1940, the year Mays became president of Morehouse College, until his death in 1989. The collection at Howard University's Moorland-Spingarn Research Center, a valuable body of letters, articles, and correspondence, is the place to begin for any study on Mays. The only drawback to the Mays papers is that, although they are organized, they have never been fully processed and cataloged as an archival collection. The other important collection of Mays's papers is housed at the archives of the Rockefeller Foundation, which funded so much of the activity of historic black colleges. The archives are treasure trove of material on Mays's earliest years at Morehouse. The other great collection of materials on Mays is the YMCA collection housed at the University of Minnesota. Mays, a lifelong member and participant in YMCA activities, is thoroughly chronicled in its materials on African Americans in the YMCA, especially in the 1920s. The collection of letters between John R. Mott and Mays in the Mott Papers at the Yale University Divinity School library was quite illuminating regarding the ecumenical movement and Mays's connection to leaders in the Protestant establishment. Also in this regard, this study was significantly enhanced by the Presbyterian Historical Society's collection of the papers of the Federal Council of Churches and the National Council of Churches, in which Mays and numerous other black religious intellectuals and activists were heavily involved. The George Kelsey Papers housed at Drew University in Madison, New Jersey were particularly helpful, as were the fabulous papers of the NAACP and the National Urban League Papers housed at the Library of Congress and available on microfilm.

Unfortunately, the materials of the Morehouse College Board of Trustees were not available for this study. When they do become available, they are likely to shed new light on Mays's activities altogether. There is a paucity of material on Mays at the Regenstein Library Special Collection of the University of Chicago. Chicago produced the most African American Ph.Ds before World War II. Professor Danielle Allen, formerly a University of Chicago faculty member and currently a faculty member at the Institute for Advance Study in Princeton, did an outstanding job of recovering aspects of this little-known black history in her web exhibit, "Integrating the Life of the Mind: African Americans at the University of Chicago, 1870–1940," http://www.lib.uchicago.edu/e/webexhibits/Integrating TheLifeOfTheMind/.

PRIMARY SOURCES

Archival and Manuscript Collections

Atlanta University Center, Robert Woodruff Library Archives, Atlanta, Georgia
  Harry V. Richardson Papers
Columbia University Archive, New York, New York
  United Negro College Fund Oral History Collection
Drew University Archives, Madison, New Jersey
  George Kelsey Papers
Kautz Family YMCA Archives, University of Minnesota Libraries, Minneapolis,
    Minnesota
  Channing Tobias Papers
  Young Men Christian Association Papers
Library of Congress, Washington, D.C.
  Nannie Helen Boroughs Papers
  National Association for the Advancement of Colored People Papers
  National Urban League Papers
Lyndon B. Johnson Library, Austin, Texas
  Presidential Papers of Lyndon Johnson
Moorland-Spingarn Research Center, Manuscript Department, Howard University,
    Washington, D.C.
  Ralph J. Bunche Oral History Collection
    John Britton, Oral History Interview with Benjamin Mays
  Benjamin E. Mays Papers
Newberry Library, Chicago, Illinois
  Pullman Company Papers
Presbyterian Historical Society, Philadelphia, Pennsylvania
  Federal Council of the Churches of Christ in America Records, 1894–1952
  National Council of the Churches of Christ in the United States of America–
    Division of Home Missions Records, 1950–1964
Rockefeller Foundation Archive Center, Sleepy Hollow, New York
University of Chicago Divinity School, Department of Special Collections, Chicago, Ill.
University of North Carolina, Southern Historical Collection, Wilson Library, Chapel Hill,
    North Carolina
  Oral History Interview with Hylan Lewis
  Arthur Raper Papers
Yale University Divinity School Library, Special Collections, New Haven, Connecticut
  John R. Mott Papers
  Theological Discussion Group Papers

Newspapers and Periodicals

Atlanta Constitution
Atlanta Daily World
Atlanta Inquirer
Atlantic Monthly
Baltimore Afro-American
Chicago Defender

Ebony
New York Times
Norfolk's Journal and Guide
Pittsburgh Courier
Washington Post

Selected Writings of Benjamin Mays

Mays, Benjamin Elijah. "After College, What Next for the Negro?" *Crisis* 37 (12) (1930): 408–10.

———. "Realities in Race Relations." *Christian Century* 48 (12) 1931: 404–6.

———. "The Education of Negro Ministers." *Journal of Negro Education: A Survey of Negro Higher Education* 2 (3) (1933): 342–51.

Mays, Benjamin Elijah, and Joseph W. Nicholson. *The Negro's Church.* New York: Institute of Social and Religious Research, 1933.

Mays, Benjamin Elijah. "Dean Mays Defines Objectives." *The News* (Howard University School of Religion) 10 (1) (1935): 6–8.

———. "Christianity in a Changing World." *National Educational Outlook among Negroes* 1 (4) (1937): 18–20.

———. "The Church Surveys World Problems." *Crisis* 6 (1937): 299, 316.

———. "The Color Line Around the World." *Journal of Negro Education: A Survey of Negro Higher Education* 6 (2) (1937): 134–43.

———. "The Most Neglected Area in Negro Education." *Crisis* 12 (1938): 268–69.

———. "The American Negro and the Christian Religion." *Journal of Negro Education: A Survey of Negro Higher Education* 8 (3) (1939): 530–38.

———. "Benjamin Griffith Brawley." *National Educational Outlook among Negroes,* February 1939, 31.

———. "Christian Youth and Race." *Crisis* 10 (1939): 364–65, 370.

———. "The Training of Negro Ministers." *National Educational Outlook Among Negroes,* 1939.

———. "Amsterdam on the Church and Race Relations." *Religion in Life* 9 (1) (1940): 95–104.

———. "The Negro Church in American Life." *Christendom* 16 (1940): 387–98.

———. "The Religious Life and Needs of Negro Students." *Journal of Negro Education: A Survey of Negro Higher Education* 9 (3) (1940): 332–43.

———. "Interracial Leadership in This Time of Crisis." *Georgia Observer* 3 (3–4) (1942): 2–4.

———. "The Negro and the Present War." *Crisis* 18 (1942): 160, 162.

———. "Negroes and the Will to Justice." *Christian Century* 22 (1942): 1316–18.

———. "The Role of the Negro Liberal Arts College in Post-War Reconstruction." *Journal of Negro Education: A Survey of Negro Higher Education* 11 (3) (1942): 400–411.

———. "Yesterday and Tomorrow in Negro Leadership." *Missions: American Baptist International Magazine* (1942): 74–79.

———. "The Eyes of the World Are upon America." *Missions: American Baptist International Magazine* 35 (2) (1944): 74–79.

———. "When Do I Believe in Man?" *International Journal of Religious Education* 21 (1) (1944): 3.

———. "Democratizing and Christianizing America in This Generation." *Journal of Negro Education: A Survey of Negro Higher Education* 14 (4) (1945): 527–34.

———. "Obligations of Negro Christians in Relation to an Interracial Program." *Journal of Religious Thought* 31 (1945): 42–52.

———. "Veterans: It Need Not Happen Again." *Phylon* 6 (3) (1945): 205–11.

———. "Financing of Private Negro Colleges." *Journal of Negro Sociology* 19 (8) (1946): 466–70.

———. "The Hazen Conference and Warren Wilson College." *Women and Missions* 22 (11) (1946): 264–66.

———. "Editorial." *Prophetic Religion: Journal of Christian Faith and Action* 8 (1) (1946): 1–3.

———. *Seeking to Be Christian in Race Relations*. New York: Friendship Press, 1946.

———. "Seeking to Be Christians in Race Relations." *Methodist Woman* 7 (6) (1947): 8–9, 13.

———. "The Negro Rural Church." *Christendom* 41 (1948): 108–9.

———. "The Obligations of the Individual Christian." In *The Christian Way in Race Relations*, edited by W. S. Nelson. New York: Harper & Brothers, 1948.

———. "Conflict in Czechoslovakia." *Christian Century* 44 (1949): 1324–25.

———. "How America Exports Race Hate." *Negro Digest* 42 (1949): 65–70.

———. "Segregation in Higher Education." *Phylon* 45 (1949): 401–6.

———. "World Aspects of Race and Culture." *Missions: American Baptist International Magazine* 147 (2) (1949): 83–87.

———, ed. *A Gospel for Social Awakening: Selections, Edited and Compiled from the Writings of Walter Rauschenbusch*. New York: Association Press, 1950.

———. "How Christian Can I Afford to Be?" *Southern Baptist Home Missions* 20 (1950).

———. "Improving the Morale of Negro Children and Youth." *Journal of Negro Education: A Survey of Negro Higher Education* 19 (3) (1950): 420–25.

———. "The South's Racial Policy." *Presbyterian Outlook* 132 (45) (1950): 2–6.

———. "What's Wrong with Negro Leaders." *Negro Digest* 50 (1951): 45–49.

———. "Have You Forgotten God?" *Our World*, November 1952, 40–41.

———. "The Present Status and Future Outlook for Racial Integration in the Church-Related White Colleges in the South." *Journal of Negro Education: A Survey of Negro Higher Education* 21 (3) (1952): 350–52.

———. "Democracy in the U. S. A. and in India." *Presbyterian Survey* 55 (1953): 28–29.

———. "Religious Roots of Western Culture." *Child Study* 30 (4) (1953): 27–31.

———. "The Second Assembly of the World Council of Churches." *Journal of Religious Thought* 53 (1953): 144–48.

———. "Christianity and Race." *Christianity and Crisis* 62 (1954): 11-13.

———. *The Church amidst Ethnic and Racial Tensions.* Evanston, Ill.: World Council of Churches, Second Assembly, 1954.

———. "The Church Will Be Challenged at Evanston." *Christianity and Crisis* 63 (1954): 106-8.

———. "The Faith of the Church." *Intercollegian* 72 (4) (1954): 9-12.

———. "I Report Progress." *Lutheran Woman's Work* 47 (2) (1954): 1-3.

———. "I Was Glad to Report Progress in Race Relations." *Presbyterian Life* 58 (1954): 8-9.

———. "The Supreme Court Decision and Our Responsibility." *YWCA Magazine* 48 (7) (1954): 8-9, 35.

———. "We Are Unnecessarily Excited." *New South* 9 (2) (February 1954): 1-3.

———. "America's Ten Most Powerful Negroes." *Our World*, April 1955, 48-55.

———. "The Gulf Between Our Gospel and Our Practice." *Presbyterian Survey*, April 1955.

———. "The Moral Aspects of Segregation." Paper read at the Southern Historical Association, November 10, 1955, Memphis, Tennessee.

———. "Of One Blood." *Presbyterian Life* 67 (1955): 7-8, 29.

———. "A Recent Supreme Court Decision: How Decisive?" *Chicago Review* 9 (3) (1955): 21-26.

———. "In Behalf of All." *Wesley Quarterly* 15 (1) (1956): 10-12.

———. "The Moral Aspects of Segregation Decisions." *Journal of Negro Sociology* 29 (9) (1956): 361-66.

———. "The Challenge of a College Education." *Intercollegian* 75 (1) (1957): 7.

———. *Christian in Race Relations.* Henry Wright Lectures, The Yale University Divinity School. West Haven, Conn.: Promoting Enduring Peace, 1957.

———. "Full Implementation of Democracy." *New South* 12 (3) (1957): 10-12.

———. "A Negro Educator Gives His Views." *Christian Science Monitor* 49 (46) (1957).

———. "The Road to Blessed Immortality." *Pulpit* 74 (1957): 30-31.

———. "Creative Living for Youth in a Time of Crisis." In *The Bennett College Social Justice Lecture Series*, edited by Millicent E. Brown and Lea E. Williams Greensboro. North Carolina: Bennett College, [1958].

———. "Race in America: The Negro Perspective." In *The Search for America*, edited by H. Smith. Englewood Cliffs, N.J.: Prentice-Hall, 1959.

———. "Obligations of Negroes in Relation to an Interracial Society." *Sepia* 16 (1960).

———. "The Only Way to Make the Youth 'Sit Down Protests' Effective." *The Worker* 23 (105) (1960): 113-16.

———. A Plea for Straight Talk Between the Races. *Atlantic Monthly* 206 (6) (1960): 85-86.

———. "The Significance of the Negro Private and Church-Related College." *Journal of Negro Education: A Survey of Negro Higher Education* 29 (3) (1960): 245-51.

———. "What Is the Future of Negro Colleges?" *Southern School News* 17 (10) (1961): 11-13.

———. "Why I Believe There Is a God." *Ebony*, December 1961, 3.

———. "Does Integration Doom Negro Colleges?" *Negro Digest*, May 1962.

———. "What's Ahead for Our Negro Schools?" *Together*, 1962, 32–34.

———. "The New Social Order When Integrated." *Religious Education*, March–April 1963, 155–60.

———. "The President's Charge to the Class of 1963: Three Things in Three Minutes." *Morehouse College Bulletin* 31 (97).

———. "The Churches Will Follow." *Christian Century* 93 (1964): 513–14.

———. "The Role of Schools in a Social Revolution." *Teachers College Record* 95 (1964): 684–88.

———. "The President's Charge to the Class of 1965." *Morehouse College Bulletin* 33 (105).

———. "Role and Future of the Negro College." *Crisis*, August-September 1965, 419–22.

———. "The Achievements of Negro Colleges." *Atlantic Monthly* 97 (1966): 90–92.

———. "Why I Went to Bates." *Bates College Bulletin, Alumnus Issue*, January 1966.

———. "A Centennial Commencement Address." *Journal of Religious Thought* 24 (1967): 4–12.

———. "Mays Defines Black Power as Ability to Achieve." *Chicago Daily Defender (Big Weekend Edition) (1966–1973)*, May 18, 1968, 6.

———. *The Negro's God, as Reflected in His Literature*. New York: Russell and Russell, [1968].

———. "Desegregate and Integrate to What End?" In *The Negro Speaks: The Rhetoric of Contemporary Black Leaders*, edited by Jamey Coleman Williams and McDonald Williams. New York: Noble and Noble Publishers, Inc., 1970.

———. "The Diamond Jubilee of the National Medical Association." *Journal of the National Medical Association* 62 (6) (1970): 407–10.

———. *Born to Rebel: An Autobiography*. New York: Scribner, [1971]. Reprint, with a revised foreword by Orville Vernon Burton. Athens: University of Georgia Press, 2003.

———. "What Man Lives By." In *Best Black Sermons*, edited by W. M. Philpot. Valley Forge: Judson Press, 1972.

———. "Atlanta—Living with *Brown* Twenty Years Later." *Black Law Journal* 3 (2–3) (1974): 184–92.

———. "Black Colleges: Past, Present and Future." *Black Scholar* 6 (1) (1974): 32–37.

———. "Response by Dr. Benjamin E. Mays." *Journal of Religious Thought* 32 (1) (1975): 131–32.

———. "Education Is . . . ." *Going to College Handbook* 30 (1976): 3.

———. "William Stuart Nelson, as I Knew Him." *Journal of Religious Thought* 35 (1978): 57.

———. "Progress and Prospects in American Race Relations." *Journal of Ecumenical Studies* 16 (1979): 28–32.

———. Introduction to *Daddy King*, edited by M. L. King Sr., with Clayton Riley. New York: William Morrow, 1980.

———. "Meeting Tomorrow's Challenges Today with Academic, Moral and Spiritual Preparation." *Am-African Journal of Research and Education* 1 (1) (1981): 1–6.

———. *Lord, the People Have Driven Me On.* New York: Vantage, 1981.

Other Published Primary Sources

Arnold, Reverend Tashereau. "On the Reel: Growing Disrespect for Ministers." *Atlanta Daily World*, February 10, 1940, 2.

Arthur, George Robert. *Life on the Negro Frontier.* New York: Association Press, 1934.

Aubrey, Edwin E., Review of *The Negro's God*, by Benjamin E. Mays. *Journal of Negro Education* 8 (2) (April 1939): 226–27.

Baltrip, Kimetris N. "Samuel Nabrit, 98, Scientist and Pioneer in Education Dies." *New York Times*, January 6, 2004.

Barbour, J Pius "The Pastorate." *Home Mission College Review* 2 (1) (1928): 20–23.

"A Black Thorn in White Conscience." *Atlanta Constitution*, January 18, 1970, 9-M.

Boulware, Marcus H. *The Oratory of Negro Leaders, 1900–1968.* Westport, Conn.: Negro Universities Press, 1969.

Brawley, Benjamin E., *History of Morehouse College.* 1917. College Park, Md.: McGrath Publishing Company, 1970.

Carson, Clayborne, ed. *The Papers of Martin Luther King, Jr.* Vols. 1–6. Stanford, Calif.: Martin Luther King, Jr., Papers Project, 1992–2007.

Crawford, D. D., "Morehouse Has a New President." *The Georgia Baptist*, May 15, 1940, 2.

Daniels, W. A. *The Education of Negro Ministers.* New York: Doran Company, 1925.

Davis, Allison. *The Negro Church and Associations in Chicago: A Research Memorandum Prepared by J. G. St. Clair Drake.* Vol. 2, Carnegie-Myrdal Study: Negro in America. New York: Carnegie Corporation, 1940.

"Elaborate Plans Made for Morehouse Founder's Day." *Atlanta Daily World*, February 11, 1940, 5.

Fisher, Miles Mark. "The Negro as Christian Minister." *Journal of Negro Education* 4 (1) (1935): 53–59.

———. "Young Men and the Ministry." *Home Mission College Review* 2 (1) (1928): 25–28.

"Five College Heads Deny Pro-Communist Charges." *Chicago Defender*, November 19, 1955, 1.

Fluker, Walter Earl, ed. *The Papers of Howard Washington Thurman.* Vol. 1. Columbia, S.C.: University of South Carolina Press, 2009.

Fosdick, Harry Emerson, *A Great Time to Be Alive: Sermons on Christianity in Wartime.* New York: Harper & Brothers, 1944.

Houser, S. "Olivet—A Community-Serving Church in Chicago." *Messenger* 6 (1924): 282–87.

"Gandhi Declares India Will Not Help to Exploit Africa." *Atlanta Daily World*, February 17, 1940, 6.

Hancock, Gordon B. "The Challenge to Christianity To-Day." *Home Mission College Review* 2 (1) (1928): 25–29.

Hedgeman, Anna Arnold. *The Trumpet Sounds: A Memoir of Negro Leadership.* New York: Holt, Rinehart and Winston, 1964.

"Hint Mays to Hampton Post." *Chicago Defender*, August 14, 1948, 7.

Jackson, Joseph H. *A Story of Christian Activism: The History of the National Baptist Convention, U.S.A., Inc.* Nashville, Tenn.: Townsend Press, 1980.

Jones, Edward. *A Candle in the Dark: A History of Morehouse College*. Valley Forge, Pa.: Judson Press, 1967.

———. "Morehouse College in Business Ninety Years—Building Men." *Phylon* 18 (3) (1957): 231–45.

King, Coretta. *My Life with Martin Luther King Jr.* New York: Holt, Rinehart and Winston, 1969.

King, Martin Luther, Jr. *Stride Toward Freedom*. New York: Harper & Row, 1958.

King, Martin Luther, Sr., with Clayton Riley. *Daddy King: An Autobiography*. New York: William Morrow, 1980.

Miller, Kelly. *Out of the House of Bondage*. 1914. New York: Schocken Books, 1971.

Murray, Pauli, ed. *States' Laws on Race and Color*. Cincinnati, Ohio: Women's Division of Christian Service, Board of Missions and Church Extension, Methodist Church, 1951.

"Omega Psi Phi Plan 36th Grand Conclave (2)." *Chicago Defender*, December 17, 1949, 5.

"Omegas Slate Mays(2)." *Chicago Defender*, December 26, 1953, 12.

Raper, Arthur F., and Ira De A. Reid. *Sharecroppers All*. Chapel Hill: University of North Carolina Press, 1941.

"Raps Bigots Who Would Block Mays." *Chicago Defender*, March 11, 1961, 1.

Rauschenbusch, Walter. *Christianity and the Social Crisis*. New York: Macmillan Company, 1907.

———. *Christianizing the Social Order*. New York: Macmillan Company, 1913.

———. *For God and People: Prayers of the Social Awakening*. Boston, Mass.: Pilgrim Press, 1910.

———. *The Social Principles of Jesus*. New York: Association Press, 1916.

———. *A Theology for the Social Gospel*. 1917. Louisville, Ky.: Westminster John Knox Press, 1997.

Read, Florence M. *The Story of Spelman College*. Princeton, N.J.: Princeton University Press, 1961.

Reid, Ira De A. "Let Us Prey!" *Opportunity*, September 1926, 274–78.

Reid, Ira De A., and the Joint Survey of the Baptist Inter-Convention Committee, ed. *The Negro Ministry*. Philadelphia: H & L Advertising Company, 1951.

Religion's Role in Racial Crisis: A Report on the National Conference on Religion and Race. New York: National Conference on Religion and Race, 1963.

Richardson, Harry V. *Walk Together, Children: The Story of the Birth and Growth of the Interdenominational Theological Center*. Atlanta, Ga.: Interdenominational Theological Center Press, 1981.

Rooks, Charles Shelby. *Revolution in Zion: Reshaping African American Ministry, 1960–1974: A Biography in the First Person*. New York: Pilgrim Press, 1990.

Shaffer, Helen B. *Segregation in Churches*. Washington, D.C.: Editorial Research Reports, 1954.

Shedd, Clarence P. *The History of World's Alliances of the Y.M.C.A.s.* London: World's Committee of YMCAs, 1955.

Stalker, James. *The Life of Christ.* New and revised ed. New York: Fleming H. Revell, 1909.

Thomas, Jesse O. *My Story in Black and White: The Autobiography of Jesse O. Thomas.* New York: Exposition Press, 1967.

Thurman, Howard. *With Head and Heart: The Autobiography of Howard Thurman.* New York: Harcourt Brace Jovanovich, 1979.

White, Walter. *A Man Called White.* New York: Viking Press, 1948.

———. Review of *The Negro's Church,* by Benjamin E. Mays and Joseph W. Nicholson. *New York Herald Tribune Book Review,* 1933.

Wilmore, Gayraud S., and James H. Cone, ed. *Black Theology: A Documentary History, 1966–1979.* Maryknoll, N.Y.: Orbis Books, 1979.

Woodson, Carter G., ed. *Addresses Mainly Personal and Racial.* Vol. 1 of *The Works of Francis Grimke.* Washington, D.C.: The Associated Publishers, Inc., 1942.

———. *The History of the Negro Church.* Washington, D.C.: The Associated Publishers, Inc., 1921.

———. Review of *The Negro's God,* by Benjamin E. Mays. *Journal of Negro History* 24 (1) (1938): 118–19.

Wright, Richard R., Jr., *Eighty-seven Years Behind the Black Curtin: An Autobiography.* Philadelphia: Rare Book Company, 1965.

Secondary Sources

Anderson, Carol E. *Eyes off the Prize: The United Nations and the African American Struggle for Human Rights, 1944–1955.* New York: Cambridge University Press, 2003.

Anderson, James D. *The Education of Blacks in the South, 1860–1935.* Chapel Hill: University of North Carolina Press, 1988.

Ansboro, John J. *Martin Luther King, Jr.: The Making of a Mind.* Maryknoll, N.Y.: Orbis Books, 1982.

Anthony, William. *Bates College and Its Background: A Review of Origins and Causes.* Philadelphia: Judson Press, 1936.

Arnold, Charles Harvey. *Near the Edge of Battle: A Short History of the Divinity School and "Chicago School Theology," 1866–1966.* Indianapolis, Ind.: Bobbs-Merrill Co., 1966.

Arsenault, Raymond. *Freedom Riders: 1961 and the Struggle for Racial Justice.* New York: Oxford University Press, 2006.

Ayers, Edward L. *Promise of the New South: Life After Reconstruction.* New York: Oxford University Press, 1992.

———. *Vengeance and Justice: Crime and Punishment in the Nineteenth Century American South.* New York: Oxford University Press, 1984.

Baldwin, Lewis V. *There Is a Balm in Gilead: The Cultural Roots of Martin Luther King, Jr.* Minneapolis: Fortress Press, 1991.

Barnes, Catherine. *A Journey from Jim Crow: The Desegregation of Southern Transit.* New York: Columbia University Press, 1983.

Bauerlein, Mark. *Negrophobia: A Race Riot in Atlanta, 1906.* San Francisco, Calif.: Encounter Books, 2001.

Bayor, Ronald H. *Race and the Shaping of Twentieth-Century Atlanta.* Chapel Hill: University of North Carolina Press, 1996.

Bellah, Robert N. *The Broken Covenant: American Civil Religion in Time of Trial.* New York: Seabury Press, 1975.

Bennett, Lerone, Jr. *What Manner of Man: A Biography of Martin Luther King, Jr.* Chicago, Ill.: Johnson Publishing Co., 1968.

Berderman, Gail. *Manliness and Civilization: A Cultural History of Gender and Race in the United States, 1880–1917.* Chicago: University of Chicago Press, 1996.

Best, Wallace D. *Passionately Human, No Less Divine: Religion and Culture in Black Chicago, 1915–1952.* Princeton, N.J.: Princeton University Press, 2005.

———. "The Right Achieved and the Wrong Way Conquered: J. H. Jackson, Martin Luther King, Jr., and the Conflict over Civil Rights." *Religion and American Culture* 16 (2) (2006): 195–226.

Billings, Dwight G. "Religion as Opposition: A Gramscian Analysis." *American Journal of Sociology* 96 (1) (1990): 1–31.

Blight, David W. *Race and Reunion: The Civil War in American Memory.* Cambridge, Mass.: Harvard University Press, 2001.

Blum, Edward J. *Reforging the White Republic: Race, Religion, and American Nationalism, 1865–1898.* Baton Rouge: Louisiana State University Press, 2005.

Branch, Taylor. *Parting the Waters: America in the King Years: 1954–1963.* New York: Simon and Schuster, 1988.

———. *Pillar of Fire: America in the King Years, 1963–1965.* New York: Simon & Schuster, 1998.

Brundage, W. Fitzhugh. *Lynchings in the New South: Georgia and Virginia, 1880–1930.* Urbana: University of Illinois, 1993.

———, ed. *Under Sentence of Death: Lynching in the South.* Chapel Hill: University of North Carolina Press, 1997.

Bullock, Henry Allen. *A History of Negro Education in the South: From 1619 to the Present.* Cambridge, Mass.: Harvard University Press, 1967.

Burkett, Randall, and Richard Newman, ed. *Black Apostles: Afro-American Clergy Confront the Twentieth Century.* Boston, Mass.: Hall Publisher, 1978.

Burton, Orville Vernon. Foreword to *Born to Rebel: An Autobiography*, by Benjamin E. Mays. Athens: University of Georgia Press, 1987.

———. *In My Father's House Are Many Mansions: Family and Community in Edgefield, South Carolina.* Chapel Hill: University of North Carolina Press, 1985.

———. "Race and Reconstruction: Edgefield, South Carolina." *Journal of Social History* 12 (Fall 1978): 31–56.

Chapman, Mark, *Christianity on Trial: African-American Religious Thought before and after Black Power.* Maryknoll, N.Y.: Orbis Books, 1996.

Chauncey, George. *Gay New York: Gender, Urban Culture, and the Makings of the Gay Male World, 1890–1940.* New York: Basic Books, 1994.

Cherry, Conrad. *Hurrying toward Zion: Universities, Divinity Schools, and American Protestantism.* Bloomington: Indiana University Press, 1995.

Cohen, William. *At Freedom's Edge: Black Mobility and the Southern White Quest for Racial Control, 1861–1895.* Baton Rouge: Louisiana State University Press, 1991.

Connelly, Marcus Cook. *The Green Pastures.* Edited by Thomas Cripps. Madison: University of Wisconsin Press, 1979.

Crawford, Evans E., Jr. "Benjamin E. Mays: Resonant Rebel." *Journal of Religious Thought* 32 (1) (1975): 123–29.

Curtis, Susan. "The Son of Man and God the Father: The Social Gospel and Victorian Masculinity." In *Meanings for Manhood: Constructions of Masculinity in Victorian America,* edited by Mark C. Carnes and Clyde Griffen, 67–77. Chicago: University of Chicago Press, 1990.

Davis, Gerald L. *I Got the Word in Me and I Can Sing It, You Know: A Study of the Performed African-American Sermon.* Philadelphia: University of Pennsylvania Press, 1985.

Davis, Leroy. *Clashing of the Soul: John Hope and the Dilemma of African American Leadership and Black Higher Education in the Early Twentieth Century.* Athens: University of Georgia Press, 1998.

D'Emilio, John. *The Lost Prophet: The Life and Times of Bayard Rustin.* Chicago: University of Chicago Press, 2003.

Dickerson, Dennis. "African American Religious Intellectuals and the Foundation of the Civil Rights Movement, 1930–55." *Church History* 2 (74) (June 2005): 217–35.

——. *Militant Mediator: Whitney M. Young Jr.* Lexington: University of Kentucky Press, 1996.

Donahue, Don. "Prophets of a New Social Order: Presbyterians and the Fellowship of Southern Churchmen, 1934–1963." *American Presbyterian* 74 (Fall 1996): 209–21.

Dorrien, Gary. *The Making of American Liberal Theology: Idealism, Realism and Modernity.* Louisville, Ky.: Westminster John Knox Press, 2003.

Doyle, Don H. *New Men, New Cities, New South: Atlanta, Nashville, Charleston, Mobile, 1860–1910.* Chapel Hill: University of North Carolina Press, 1990.

Drake, St. Clair. "The International Implications of Race and Race Relations." *Journal of Negro Education* 20 (3) (1951).

——. "The Tuskegee Connection: Booker T. Washington and Robert E. Park." *Society* 20 (4) (1983): 82–92.

Drexel, Allen. "Before Paris Burned: Race, Class, and Male Homosexuality on the Chicago South Side, 1935–1960." In *Creating a Place for Ourselves: Lesbian, Gay, and Bisexual Community Histories,* edited by Brett Beemyn, 119–44. New York: Routledge, 1997.

Dudziak, Mary. *Cold War Civil Rights: Race and the Image of American Democracy.* Princeton, N.J.: Princeton University Press, 2001.

Dvorak, Katharine L. *An African-American Exodus: The Segregation of the Southern Churches.* Brooklyn, N.Y.: Carlson Publishing, 1991.

Dykeman, Wilma, and James Stokely. *Seeds of Southern Change: The Life of Will Alexander.* Chicago: University of Chicago Press, 1962.

Edgerton, John. *Speak Now against the Day: The Generation Before the Civil Rights Movement*. New York: Knopf, 1994.

Eighmy, John Lee. *Churches in Cultural Captivity: A History of Social Attitudes of Southern Baptists*. Knoxville: University of Tennessee Press, 1972.

Ellis, Ann Wells. "A Crusade against 'Wretched Attitudes': The Commission on Interracial Cooperation's Activities in Atlanta." *Atlanta Historical Journal* 23 (Spring 1979): 21–44.

———. "'Uncle Sam Is My Shepherd': The Commission on Interracial Cooperation and the New Deal in Georgia." *Atlanta Historical Journal* 30 (Spring 1986): 47–64.

Evans, Christopher H. *The Kingdom Is Always but Coming: A Life of Walter Rauschenbusch*. Grand Rapids, Mich.: William B. Eerdmans, 2004.

Evans, Curtis. *The Burden of Black Religion*. New York: Oxford University Press, 2008.

Fairclough, Adam. *To Redeem the Soul of America: The Southern Christian Leadership Conference and Martin Luther King, Jr.* Athens: University of Georgia Press, 1987.

———. "Tuskegee's Robert R. Moton and the Travails of the Early Black College President." *Journal of Blacks in Higher Education* 31 (Spring 2001): 94–105.

Ferguson, Karen. *Black Politics in New Deal Atlanta*. Chapel Hill: University of North Carolina Press, 2002.

Ford, Lacy K. "Rednecks and Merchants: Economic Development and Social Tensions in the South Carolina Upcountry, 1865–1900." *Journal of American History* 71 (2): 294–318.

Fox, Richard Wightman. *Reinhold Niebuhr: A Biography*. New York: Harper & Row, 1987.

Fredrickson, George M. *Black Liberation: A Comparative History of Black Ideologies in the United States and South Africa*. New York: Oxford University Press, 1995.

———. "Reform and Revolution in American and South African Freedom Struggles." In *Crossing Boundaries: Comparative History of Black People in Diaspora*, edited by Darlene Clark Hine and Jacqueline McLeod, 71–85. Bloomington: University of Indiana Press, 2000.

———. *White Supremacy: A Comparative Study in American and South African History*. New York: Oxford University Press, 1982.

Fultz, Michael. "'The Morning Cometh': African-American Periodicals, Education, and the Black Middle Class, 1900–1930." *Journal of Negro History* 80 (3) (1989): 97–112.

Garrow, David J., ed. *Atlanta, Georgia, 1960–1961*. Brooklyn, N.Y.: Carlson Publishing, 1989.

———. *Bearing the Cross: Martin Luther King, Jr., and the Southern Christian Leadership Conference*. New York: William Morrow, 1987.

Grady-Willis, Winston A. *Challenging U.S. Apartheid: Atlanta and Black Struggles for Human Rights, 1960–1977*. Durham, N.C.: Duke University Press, 2006.

Greenbaum, Susan D. *More Than Black: Afro-Cubans in Tampa*. Gainesville: University Press of Florida, 2002.

Griffin, Farah Jasmine. *"Who Set You Flowin'?": The African-American Migration Narrative*. New York: Oxford University Press, 1995.

Grundman, Adolph H. "Northern Baptists and the Founding of Virginia Union University: The Perils of Paternalism." *Journal of Negro History* 63 (1) (1978): 26–41.

Halberstam, David. *The Children*. New York: Random House, 1998.

Halderman, Keith. "Blanche Armwood of Tampa and the Strategy of Interracial Cooperation." *Florida Historical Quarterly* 74 (3) (1996): 288–304.

Hamilton, Charles V. *The Black Preacher in America*. New York: William Morrow, 1972.

Harlan, Louis R. *Separate and Unequal*. Chapel Hill: University of North Carolina Press, 1958.

Harvey, Paul. *Freedom's Coming: Religious Culture and the Shaping of the South from the Civil War through the Civil Rights Era*. Chapel Hill: University of North Carolina Press, 2005.

———. "The Ideal of Professionalism and the White Southern Baptist Ministry, 1870–1920." *Religion and American Culture* 5 (1) (1995): 99–123.

———. *Redeeming the South: Religious Cultures and Racial Identities among Southern Baptists, 1865–1925*. Chapel Hill: University of North Carolina Press, 1992.

Hatch, Robert D. "Racism and Religion: The Contrasting Views of Benjamin Mays, Malcolm X, and Martin Luther King, Jr." *Journal of Religious Thought* 36 (2): 26–36.

Heffron, John. "To Form a More Perfect Union: The Moral Example of Southern Baptist Thought and Education, 1890–1920." *Religion and American Culture* 8 (2) (1998): 179–204.

Hewitt, Nancy A. *Southern Discomfort: Women's Activism in Tampa, Florida, 1880s–1920s*. Women in American History Series. Urbana: University of Illinois Press, 2001.

Holloway, Jonathan Scott. *Confronting the Veil: Abram Harris, Jr., E. Franklin Frazier, and Ralph Bunche, 1919–1941*. Chapel Hill: University of North Carolina Press, 2002.

Hopkins, Charles Howard. *John R. Mott, 1865–1955: A Biography*. Grand Rapids, Mich.: William B. Eerdmans, 1979.

———. *The Rise of the Social Gospel in American Protestantism, 1865–1915*. New Haven, Conn.: Yale University Press, 1940.

Howard, Walter T., and Virginia M. Howard. "Family, Religion, and Education: A Profile of African-American Life in Tampa, Florida, 1900–1930." *Journal of Negro History* 79 (1) (1994): 1–17.

Hoyt, James A. *The Phoenix Riot, November 8, 1898*. Greenwood, S.C.: n.p., 1938.

Hunter, Tera W. *To 'Joy My Freedom: Southern Black Women's Lives and Labor After the Civil War*. Cambridge, Mass.: Harvard University Press, 1997.

Hutchison, William. *Errand to the World: American Protestant Thought and Foreign Missions*. Chicago: University of Chicago Press, 1987.

———. *The Modernist Impulse in American Protestantism*. Cambridge, Mass.: Harvard University Press, 1976.

Immerwahr, Daniel. "Caste or Colony? Indianizing Race in the United States." *Modern Intellectual History* 4 (2) (2007): 275–301.

Ingalls, Robert P. "Lynching and Establishment Violence in Tampa, 1858–1935." *Journal of Southern History* 53 (1987): 613–44.

Jackson, Roswell F., and Rosalyn M. Patterson. "A Brief History of Selected Black Churches in Atlanta, Georgia." *Journal of Negro History* 74 (1/4) (1989): 31–52.

Jackson, Walter A. *Gunnar Myrdal and America's Conscience: Social Engineering and Racial Liberalism, 1938-1987*. Chapel Hill: University of North Carolina Press, 1990.

Janken, Kenneth Robert. *Rayford W. Logan and the Dilemma of the African American Intellectual*. Amherst, Mass.: University of Massachusetts Press, 1993.

Jelks, Randal Maurice. "The Academic Formation of Benjamin E. Mays, 1917–1936." In *Walking Integrity: Benjamin Elijah Mays, Mentor to Generations*, edited by Lawrence E. Carter. Atlanta: Scholars Press, 1996.

———. *African Americans in the Furniture City: The Struggle for Civil Rights in Grand Rapids*. Urbana: University of Illinois Press, 2006.

———. "The Religious Dimensions of the American Civil Rights Movement." *Church History* 73 (4) (December 2004): 828–33.

Johnson, Paul E., ed. *African-American Christianity: Essays in History*. Berkeley: University of California Press, 1994.

Jones, Jacqueline. *Soldiers of Light and Love: Northern Teachers and Georgia Blacks*. Chapel Hill: University of North Carolina Press, 1980.

Joyner, Charles. *Down by the Riverside: A South Carolina Slave Community*. Urbana: University of Illinois Press, 1984.

Kantrowitz, Stephen. *Ben Tillman and the Reconstruction of White Supremacy*. Chapel Hill: University of North Carolina Press, 2000.

Kapur, Sudarshan, *Raising Up a Prophet: The African-American Encounter with Gandhi*. Boston, Mass.: Beacon Press, 1992.

Keating, Larry. *Atlanta: Race, Class, and Urban Expansion*. Philadelphia: Temple University Press, 2001.

Kelsey, George D. *Racism and the Christian Understanding of Man*. New York: Charles Scribner's Sons, 1965.

———. *Social Ethics among Southern Baptists, 1917–1969*. Metuchen, N.J.: Scarecrow Press, 1973.

Lal, Barbara Ballis. "Black and Blue in Chicago: Robert E. Park's Perspective on Race Relations in Urban America, 1914–44." *British Journal of Sociology* 38 (4) (1987): 546–66.

Larson, Magali Sarfattu. *The Rise of Professionalism*. Berkley: University of California Press, 1977.

Lewis, David Levering. *W. E. B. DuBois: The Fight for Equality and the American Century, 1919–1963*. New York: Henry Holt, 2000.

Littlefied, Daniel C. *Rice and Slaves: Ethnicity and the Slave Trade in Colonial South Carolina*. Baton Rouge: Louisiana State University Press, 1981.

Litwack, Leon F. *Trouble in Mind: Black Southerners in the Age of Jim Crow*. New York: Knopf, 1998.

Loescher, Frank. *The Protestant Church and the Negro*. New York: Association Press, 1948.

Love, Edgar. "The Role of the Church in Maintaining the Morale of the Negro in World Wars I and II." *Journal of Negro Education* 12 (3) (1943): 502–10.

Luker, Ralph E. "Murder and Biblical Memory: The Legend of Vernon Johns." *Virginia Magazine of History and Biography* 112 (Spring 2005): 372–418.

——. *The Social Gospel in Black and White: American Racial Reform, 1885–1912.* Chapel Hill: University of North Carolina Press, 1992.

Mailloux, Steven. "Misreading as a Historical Act: Cultural Rhetoric, Bible Politics, and Fuller's 1845 Review of Narrative." In *Readers in History: Nineteenth-Century American Literature and the Contexts of Response*, edited by James L. Machor. Baltimore: Johns Hopkins University Press, 1983.

Manis, Andrew Michael. *Southern Civil Religions in Conflict: Black and White Baptists and Civil Rights, 1947–1957.* Athens: University of Georgia Press, 1987.

Martin, Robert F. "Critique of Southern Society and Vision of a New Order: The Fellowship of Southern Churchmen, 1934–1957." *Church History* 52 (1983): 66–80.

——. "A Prophet's Pilgrimage: The Religious Radicalism of Howard Anderson Kester, 1921–1941." *Journal of Southern History* 48 (4) (1982): 511–30.

Martin, Sandy Dwayne. "American Baptist Home Mission Society and Black Higher Education, 1865–1920." *Foundations* 24 (4) (1981): 310–27.

McDannell, Colleen. *Material Christianity: Religion and Popular Culture in America.* New Haven, Conn.: Yale University Press, 1995.

McKenna, George. *The Puritan Origins of Patriotism.* New Haven, Conn.: Yale University Press, 2007.

McNeil, Pearl L. "Baptist Black Americans and the Ecumenical Movement." *Journal of Ecumenical Studies* 17 (2) (1980): 103–17.

Meijer, August, and David Lewis. "History of the Negro Upper Class in Atlanta, Georgia, 1890–1958." *Journal of Negro Education* 28 (2) (1959): 128–39.

Miller, Patrick B. "'To Bring the Race along Rapidly': Sport, Student Culture, and Educational Mission at Historically Black Colleges during the Interwar Years." *History of Education Quarterly* 35 (2) (1995): 111–33.

Minus, Paul M. *Walter Rauschenbusch: American Reformer.* New York: Macmillan Co., 1988.

Mjagkij, Nina. *Light in the Darkness: African Americans and the YMCA, 1852–1946.* Lexington: University of Kentucky Press, 1994.

Mjagkij, Nina, and Margaret Spratt, eds. *Men and Women Adrift: the YMCA and the YWCA in the City.* New York: New York University Press, 1997.

Mollin, Marian. "The Limits of Egalitarianism: Radical Pacifism, Civil Rights, and the Journey of Reconciliation." *Radical History Review* (88) (2004): 113–38.

Moore, Moses Nathaniel. "Orishatukeh Faduma and the New Theology." *Church History* 63 (1) (1994): 60–80.

Moore, Winfred B., Jr., Joseph F. Tripp, and Lyon Tyler Jr., eds. *Developing Dixie: Modernization in a Traditional Society.* Westport, Conn.: Greenwood Press, 1988.

Morris, Aldon D. *The Origins of the Civil Rights Movement: Black Communities Organizing for Change.* New York: Free Press, 1984.

Moses, Wilson Jeremiah. *Black Messiahs and Uncle Toms: Social and Literary Manipulations of a Religious Myth.* University Park, Pa.: Pennsylvania State University Press, 1982.

————. *The Wings of Ethiopia: Studies in African-American Life and Letters*. Ames: Iowa
  State University Press, 1990.

Myrdal, Gunnar. *American Dilemma: The Negro Problem and Modern Democracy*. New
  York: Harper, 1944.

Newell, Bertha Payne. "Social Work of Women's Organizations in the Churches: I. Methodist Episcopal Church South." *Journal of Social Forces* 1 (3) (1923): 310–14.

Paris, Peter J. *The Social Teachings of the Black Churches*. Philadelphia: Fortress Press,
  1985.

Perlman, David. "Stirring the White Conscience: The Life of George Edmund Haynes."
  Ph.D. diss., New York University, New York, 1972.

Phillips, Charles Henry. *The History of the Colored Methodist Episcopal Church in America*.
  1898. New York: Arno Press, 1972.

Piper, John F. Jr. *The American Churches in World War I*. Athens: Ohio University Press,
  1985.

Pipes, William H. *Say Amen, Brother! Old-Time Negro Preaching: A Study in American
  Frustration*. Westport, Conn.: Negro Universities Press, 1951.

Plank, David N., and Marcia Turner. "Changing Patterns in Black School Politics: Atlanta,
  1872–1973." *American Journal of Education* 95 (4) (1987): 584–608.

Polsgrove, Carol. *Divided Minds: Intellectuals and the Civil Rights Movement*. New York:
  W. W. Norton, 2001.

Pomerantz, Gary. *Where Peachtree Meets Sweet Auburn: The Saga of Two Families and the
  Making of Atlanta*. New York: Scribner, 1996.

Ponock, Ross. *Color and Culture: Black Writers and the Making of the Modern Intellectual*.
  Cambridge, Mass.: Harvard University Press, 1998.

Poole, W. Scott. *Never Surrender: Confederate Memory and Conservatism in the South
  Carolina Upcountry*. Athens: University of Georgia Press, 2004.

Potts, John F., Sr. *A History of South Carolina State College, 1896–1978*. Orangeburg: South
  Carolina State College, 1978.

Prather, H. Leon, Sr. "The Origins of the Phoenix Racial Massacre of 1898." In *Developing
  Dixie: Modernization in a Traditional Society*, edited by Winfred B. Moore Jr., Joseph
  F. Tripp, and Lyon Tyler Jr. Westport, Conn.: Greenwood Press, 1988.

Preskill, Stephen. "Combative Spirituality and the Life of Benjamin E. Mays." *Biography* 19
  (4) (1996): 403–10.

Puckett, Newbell N. "The Negro Church in the United States." *Social Forces* 4 (3) (1926):
  581–87.

Rabinowitz, Howard N. "Half a Loaf: The Shift from White to Black Teachers in the Negro
  Schools of the Urban South, 1865–1890." *Journal of Southern History* 40 (1974): 565–94.

Raboteau, Albert. *Slave Religion: The "Invisible Institution" in the Antebellum South*. New
  York: Oxford University Press, 1978.

Raper, Arthur F., and Ira De A. Reid. *Sharecroppers All*. Chapel Hill: University of North
  Carolina Press, 1941.

Record, Wilson. "Negro Intellectuals and Negro Movements in Historical Perspective."
  American Quarterly 8 (1) (1956).

Reimers, David. *White Protestantism and the Negro*. New York: Oxford University Press, 1965.

Rieder, Jonathan. *The Word of the Lord Is Upon Me: The Righteous Performance of Martin Luther King, Jr.* Cambridge, Mass.: Harvard University Press, 2008.

Roark, James L. "American Black Leaders: The Response to Colonialism and the Cold War, 1943–1953." *African Historical Studies* 4 (2) (1971): 253–70.

Roberts, J. Deotis. "Ecumenical Concerns among National Baptists." *Journal of Ecumenical Studies* 17 (2) (1980): 38–48.

Ross, Dorothy. *The Origins of American Social Science*. New York: Cambridge University Press, 1991.

Rouse, Jacqueline Anne. *Lugenia Burns Hope: Black Southern Reformer*. Athens: University of Georgia Press, 1989.

Russell, James Michael. *Atlanta, 1847–1890: City Building in the Old South and the New*. Baton Rouge: Louisiana State University Press, 1988.

Russell, Thaddeus. "The Color of Discipline: Civil Rights and Black Sexuality." *American Quarterly* 1 (60) (March 2008): 101–28.

Savage, Barbara Dianne. "Benjamin Mays, Global Ecumenism, and Local Religious Segregation." *American Quarterly* 59 (3) (September 2007): 785–806.

———. *Broadcasting Freedom: Radio, War, and the Politics of Race, 1938–1948*. Chapel Hill: University of North Carolina Press, 1998.

———. *Your Spirits Walk Beside Us: The Politics of Black Religion*. Cambridge, Mass.: Harvard University Press, 2008.

Sernett, Milton. *Bound for the Promised Land: African American Religion and the Great Migration*. Durham, N.C.: Duke University Press, 1997.

Shaw, Stephanie J. *What a Woman Ought to Be and to Do: Black Professional Women Workers during the Jim Crow Era*. Chicago: University of Chicago Press, 1996.

Simkins, Francis Butler. *Pitchfork Ben Tillman*. Baton Rouge: Louisiana State University Press, 1944.

———. *The Tillman Movement in South Carolina*. Durham, N.C.: Duke University Press, 1926.

Smith, Gary Scott. "To Reconstruct the World: Walter Rauschenbusch and Social Change." *Fides et Historia: Journal of the Conference on Faith and History* 23 (1991): 40–63.

Sobel, Mechal. *Trabelin' On: The Slave Journey to an Afro-Baptist Faith*. Princeton, N.J.: Princeton University Press, 1979.

Southern, David W. *Gunnar Myrdal and Black-White Relations: The Use and Abuse of an American Dilemma, 1944–1969*. Baton Rouge: Louisiana State University Press, 1987.

Spear, Allan H. *Black Chicago: The Making of a Negro Ghetto, 1890-1920*. Chicago: University of Chicago Press, 1967.

Sullivan, Patricia. *Days of Hope: Race and Democracy in the New Deal Era*. Chapel Hill: University of North Carolina Press, 1996.

Summers, Martin. *Manliness and Its Discontents: The Black Middle Class and the Transformation of Masculinity, 1900–1930*. Chapel Hill: University of North Carolina Press, 2005.

Taylor, Clarence. *Black Religious Intellectuals: The Fight for Equality from Jim Crow to the Twenty-First Century*. New York: Routledge, 2002.

Teel, Leonard Ray. "Benjamin Mays: Teaching by Example, Leading Through Will." *Change* 14 (7) (1982).

Tindall, George Brown. *South Carolina Negroes, 1877–1900*. Baton Rouge: Louisiana State University Press, 1966.

Van Deburg, William. *New Day in Babylon: The Black Power Movement and American Culture, 1965–1975*. Chicago: University of Chicago Press, 1992.

Vereen-Gordon, Mary, and Janet Smith. *Morris College: A Noble Journey*. Gloucester Point, Va.: Hallmark Publishing Company, Inc., 1998.

Veysey, Laurence. *The Emergence of the American University*. Chicago: University of Chicago Press, 1965.

Washington, Joseph R., Jr. *Black Religion, the Negro and Christianity in the United States*. Boston, Mass.: Beacon Press, 1964.

Weis, Nancy J. *The National Urban League, 1910–1940*. New York: Oxford University Press, 1974.

Weisbrot, Robert. *Father Divine and the Struggle for Racial Equality*. Urbana: University of Illinois Press, 1983.

Werner, Randolph D. "'New South' Carolina: Ben Tillman and the Rise of Bourgeois Politics, 1880–1893." In *Developing Dixie: Modernization in a Traditional Society*, edited by Winfred B. Moore Jr., Joseph F. Tripp, and Lyon Tyler Jr. Westport, Conn.: Greenwood Press, 1988.

West, Cornel. *Prophesy Deliverance!: An Afro-American Revolutionary Christianity*. Philadelphia: Westminster Press, 1982.

Williamson, Joel. *The Crucible of Race: Black-White Relations in the American South since Emancipation*. New York: Oxford University Press, 1984.

Williams, Juan. *Thurgood Marshall: An American Revolutionary*. New York: Crown Publishing, 1998.

Williams, Zachery. "Prophets of Progress: Benjamin E. Mays and Howard W. Thurman, Pioneering Black Religious Intellectuals." *Journal of African American Men* 5 (4) (Spring 2001): 23–36.

Willie, Charles V. "The Education of Benjamin Elijah Mays: An Example in Effective Teaching." *Teachers College Record* 84 (4) (1983).

Wills, David W. "An Enduring Distance: Black Americans and the Establishment." In *Between the Times: The Travail of the Protestant Establishment in America, 1900–1960*, edited by W. R. Hutchinson, 168–92. New York: Cambridge University Press, 1989.

Wood, Peter H. *Black Majority: Negroes in Colonial South Carolina from 1670 through the Stono Rebellion*. New York: Knopf, 1974.

Unpublished Theses and Papers

Alishahi, Michele. "'For Peace and Civic Righteousness': Blanche Armwood and the Struggle for Freedom and Racial Equality in Tampa, Florida." Master's thesis, University of South Florida, Tampa, 2003.

Farrell, Sean Anthony. "Trumpet of Prophecy: The Fellowship of Southern Churchmen and Neo-Orthodoxy, 1934–1957." Master's thesis, University of Southern Mississippi, 1985.

Fluker, Walter. "Howard Thurman as Opener of the Way." Paper read at American Church History Association, January 7, 2006, Philadelphia.

Gavins, Doris Levy. "The Ceremonial Speaking of Benjamin Elijah Mays." Ph.D. diss., Louisiana State University, Baton Rouge, 1978.

Lewinson, Barbara. "Three Conceptions of Black Education: A Study of the Educational Ideas of Benjamin Elijah Mays, Booker T. Washington, and Nathan Wright, Jr." Ed.M. thesis, Rutgers University, New Brunswick, N.J., 1973.

Mikelson, Thomas J. "The Negro's God in the Theology of Martin Luther King, Jr." Ph.D. diss. Harvard University Divinity School, 1988.

Nicholson, Joseph W. "An Occupational Study of the Christian Ministry Among Negroes." Ph.D. diss., Northwestern University, Evanston, Ill., 1932.

Rovaris, Dereck Joseph. "Developer of an Institution: Dr. Benjamin E. Mays, Morehouse College President, 1940–1967." Ph.D. diss., University of Illinois, Urbana-Champaign, 1990.

Smith, John Douglass. "Managing White Supremacy: Politics and Culture in Virginia, 1919–1939." Ph.D., University of Virginia, Charlottesville, 1998.

Index

Dunbar, Paul Laurence, 17
Durham Conference, 161

Eastern Orthodox Church, 169
Ebony magazine, 3, 197
The Education of Negro Ministers (Daniels), 80
Ellison, Ralph, 72, 242
England, 16, 38, 40, 46, 74, 111, 130, 195
Epworth, South Carolina, 2, 19, 33, 46, 247
Eschatology, 18, 83, 85, 176
"The Ethics of Living Jim Crow" (Wright), 23
Evangelicalism, 14, 27, 43, 49, 86–87, 92, 118, 123, 183–84
Evanston, Illinois, 196
Evolutionary theory, 85–86, 91–92
The Evolution of Christianity: A Genetic Study of First-Century Christianity in Relation to Its Religious Environment (Case), 88

Fanon, Frantz, 227
Farmer, James, Sr., 3, 121
Farmer, James, Jr., 3, 121–22
Farmers' alliances, 19
Father Divine's Peace Mission, 107
Faulkner, William, 198–99
Federal Bureau of Investigation (FBI), 182, 221
Federal Council of Churches (FCC), 4, 82, 165
Fellowship of Reconciliation (FOR), 162, 165
First Baptist Church (Charleston, West Virginia), 111
Fisk University, 109, 114
Florida Memorial College, 76
Florida State Conference of Social Work, 74
Fosdick, Harry Emerson, 41, 171
Foster, Trufant, 41
Franco, Francisco, 182
Franklin, John Hope, 237
Frazier, E. Franklin, 4, 80, 91, 110
Freedmen's Bureau, 109
Freedom of conscience, 7, 16
"From Darkness to Light" pageant, 72
Fundamentalism, 2

Gandhi, Mohandas, 77, 122–26
Gandhian nonviolent resistance, 3, 125–26, 127, 136
Gandy, Samuel, 134

Garvey, Marcus, 100, 242
Gentlemen's Quarterly, 153
Georgia, 54–56, 68, 74, 135, 158, 178, 182, 204, 213–14, 236–37, 246
The Georgia Baptist, 139
Germans, 129, 131
Germany, 128–32, 158, 185
Glenn, Susie Mays, 28
Gloster, Hugh M., 139, 229
Gloster, Yvonne King, 229
"God's Minute" (poem) 189
Gone with the Wind, 153
Graham, Billy, 184
Gramsci, Antonio, 6
Grandfather Blount, 25
Grant, Ulysses S., 9
Graves, Reverend Samuel, xi, 55
Gray, Sadie. *See* Mays, Sadie (Gray)
Greek, 38, 46, 89, 184, 242
Greene, Lorenzo, 80
Green Pastures (Broadway musical), 98–99, 153
Greenwood County (South Carolina), 9–10, 16, 22–23, 26, 31, 226, 240
Grier, William, 234

Hadley, Charles E., 38
Hahn, Steven, 11
Hamburg, South Carolina, 20
Hamlet, 40
Hampton Institute, 31
Hampton, General Wade, 20, 33
Happy Haven Nursing Home, 238
Harding, Vincent, 235
Harper, William Rainey, 86, 116
Harper's Magazine, 199
Harris, Abram, Jr., 104, 110
Har Sinai Congregation, 123
Harvey, Paul, 253 (n. 12)
Harvin, Ellen. *See* Mays, Ellen (Harvin)
Hecker, Julius, 123
Hedgeman, Anna, 217
Herndon, Angelo, 142
Hillsboro County (Florida), 70
The History of the Negro Church (Woodson), 85, 93
Hitler, Adolf, 102, 123, 131, 247. *See also* Nazis
Hollowell, Donald, 215